Torts

BLACK LETTER OUTLINES

Torts

SIXTH EDITION

Edward J. Kionka
Professor of Law Emeritus
Southern Illinois University at Carbondale

Jamie R. Abrams
Professor of Law
American University Washington College of Law

Angi Porter
Associate Professor of Law
American University Washington College of Law

BLACK LETTER SERIES®

WEST ACADEMIC

860 Blue Gentian Road, Suite 350
Eagan, MN 55121
1-877-888-1330

Published in the United States of America

ISBN: 978-1-68561-765-3

Acknowledgments

The authors extend their sincerest thanks to Ruth Shultz for their editorial support with this manuscript.

The authors are deeply grateful for the enthusiasm and dedication of Research Assistants Sarah Register, Abigail Rubin, Miriam Sopin-Vilme, and Jamelia Watson, who provided excellent research assistance and editing for this edition. Thank you for sharing your insights, feedback, and skills with future generations of Torts students.

The authors also thank a robust team of enthusiastic and committed student editors, including Angelica Afanador, Samantha Boccia, Isabel Capecci, Collin Cheng, Dhanya Chittaranjan, Sarah Elliott, Grace Hall, Courtney Haley, Corinne Karabulut, Katie Krawcheck, Carrington Lowe, Samuel B. Mercer, Reagan Powers, Sophie L. Putrim, and Delisha Thompson. Thank you all for investing your time and energy into this manuscript.

Finally, the authors, respectively, would like to thank our wonderful families for encouraging and supporting our work.

How to Navigate and Use This Book Successfully

I. The Study of Torts

Welcome to the study of tort law. Tort law is a first-year law school course in which students study the civil remedies that exist to compensate injured parties for the wrongs that others have committed. It stands in contrast to how parties might resolve a contract claim or how the state might impose criminal liability for harms or wrongdoing.

Torts is a "core" law school course, meaning it is typically required for all students nationwide. Your school might invest five or six hours in the course allowing you to examine topics like defamation and products liability with depth. It might also be a shorter three or four credits with a more abbreviated treatment to other topics beyond intentional torts and negligence.

Regardless of the credits devoted to your study of torts, you likely have sensed its immense practical importance to lawyers and to the law. Torts is an engaging field because it shapes so many aspects of how we interact together in society. For example, it might shape your reluctance to text and drive or your decision to restrain your hyper dog on a leash or the lid warnings on your hot coffee. It can also differ from community to community. For example, one community might find it unreasonable to not build a locked fence around a pool while another would not.

The field is also often quite accessible to students and quite dynamic to study in a classroom environment. It is a great chance to interrogate how standards might differ from rural to urban environments or what damage recoveries are appropriate. All students can draw upon their experiences to engage.

Torts is about wrongdoing and injury. Necessarily, this content may intersect with your experiences in a way that can make this material difficult to read. While we sought to avoid unnecessary references to trauma, we also selected content and practice questions that align with the bar exam and major coursebooks in the field. Accordingly, you will encounter some topics, such as gun violence, sexual misconduct, suicidality, pregnancy loss, and other sensitive content.

Torts is also an enduring bar exam subject. Even in the NextGen Bar era, tort law remains a central subject for testing.

This book is addressed to students striving for a high-level overview of the field. This might be to succeed on your course exam, on the bar exam, or to launch a career in this area.

II. Organization of the Torts Course and This Book

Law students—like lawyers, judges, and legislators—must start with, and build upon, the existing framework of rules. Therefore, whatever else a torts course may do, it must fundamentally teach the student much about where tort law is, where it has come from, and what the justifications are for its rules. Books such as this are intended to help with that basic task.

There are various ways to subdivide this vast subject. For example, we could divide it according to the type of fault involved—torts that are based on intentional conduct, negligence, or strict liability. One of the most common divisions is between physical harm (injuries to persons and property) and non-physical harm (injuries to relations). Examples of the latter include defamation, misrepresentation, business torts, and injuries to family relations.

This book reflects the coverage of the typical first-year torts course, which emphasizes the torts involving injuries to persons and property. It also includes topics in the non-physical harm category that are ordinarily covered in the first-year torts course, such as defamation and misrepresentation. Other topics within the non-physical harm category are not covered here because they are almost never taught in the first-year torts course: misuse of legal procedure; interference with family relations; and injuries to economic relations, sometimes called "business torts."

There are many other possible ways to organize this material, as is reflected in the various casebooks. This outline may not track your casebook's organization. However, each chapter should be self-sufficient and should more or less correspond to some identifiable part of your casebook. Remember—this book is only one tool. The final product in your studies must be a synthesis of several sources. Only when that synthesis is your own will you be able to truly learn and understand the subject.

III. Reverse Design as Study Strategy

To use these materials, it is important to think about reverse design. What brought you to this book? What exam are you studying for? What case are you studying for? The answers to these questions will help you access these materials the most successfully.

A few success strategies can carry you far. Remember that a book like this is not a replacement for class preparation. Do, however, interrogate the vital shift that occurs between preparing for class and preparing for an exam. The organizational structure is very different. When you are preparing to be on call in class, you must go deep on each case, extracting the facts, holdings, rules, rationales, and procedural standing of each case to unpack all its lessons. This is a case-driven organizational structure.

From there, students must perform on a course exam or bar exam. Here, you will be asked to apply rules to new facts that you have not seen before. To do this, you have to shift into a rule-based organizational structure. Rules are transferrable nuggets of information that you can apply to a new set of facts that you have not considered before. Often, the cases fade away in this format as the author focuses on stating crisp, clear rules and reasoning through the facts. The process of moving from a case-based structure to a rule-based structure involves a major shift.

This shift resembles the work of a miner for precious stones. The miner has to sift through lots of silt and debris before locating the precious stone just like a student has to sift through a lot of case holdings and case facts before they extract a rule with elements. This book can be very helpful to you as you polish and shine your precious gems—the legal rules that build the torts field. In that sense, this book could never substitute for your own personal notes and rules. Rather, it should be used as an aid to the preparation of your own outline.

Your outline, at bottom, should be preparing you to perform on *your* exam or in *your* case. Just like a sports team will study custom film of each unique opponent before a match, similarly, law students have to understand how their professor tests and assesses their work product. We have provided sample questions and answers here. Compare and contrast to any old exam questions or model answers that your professor provides.

While each professor will have their unique idiosyncrasies that they assess, at bottom, reviewers are generally looking for you to spot the torts causes of action. For each cause of action, you should state the rule in full. What elements comprise it? You will then apply the rule that you have stated to the facts that your professor has provided. This can be visualized as threading a rule through the facts to predict an outcome. This might include consideration of counter arguments, alternate theories, and defenses.

You will then have to engage in careful time management and space management to give each issue. You might outline all of the causes of action that you spot to help you prepare for this time management. This will allow you to better triage the claims. You might think of each claim as a waiting room of potential clients. Sure, that is a bit fictitious because your clients might be plaintiffs and defendants in the same case. It is, however, a useful visual to underscore the importance of addressing all issues.

Most professors now also include objective questions (e.g., multiple choice) in certain courses. There are resources that give advice on how to approach objective exam questions, but in our view, there is only one sure-fire winner—know the material.

This book is structured to provide several tools to aid your study. The first section, "Capsule Summary of Tort Law," is an outline of the outline. It models the type of outline you might build and finalize for an open book examination or for intensive final review just before the examination.

Within each chapter are some questions to test your knowledge. Appendix A contains the answers. Appendix B offers more comprehensive practice exams, much like the final examination itself. Appendix C provides assessment tools for the practice exams. Appendix D is a glossary of terms. Two of the major mistakes we see on students' examination papers are (1) the misuse of important legal terms basic to the course, and (2) a total failure to use these terms. Either of these errors is very prejudicial. Conversely, students who know and use the subject's terms correctly create a strong favorable impression. Learn and use the correct vocabulary. Help explain these concepts to your audience while using them precisely.

IV. Relationship to Other Fields of Study

Torts is also interconnected to many other expansive areas of study. Tort law cannot properly be understood except in the context in which it operates. Tort rules are born of litigation in the context of the American version of the adversary system. This may seem obvious, but its consequences are not.

The law student (not to mention the lawyer and judge) must appreciate the manner in which the lawsuit reached the point at which we examine it. Was the complaint dismissed at the pleading stage? Did a party win summary judgment? If there was a trial, did the case go to the jury or was there a directed verdict? If there was a jury verdict, what errors does appellant claim? How are tort law issues raised in appeals from jury verdicts?

What are the general differences between the roles of judges and juries in civil cases? It is vital in tort law to learn the distinction between issues which are issues for the court and those which are for the jury. On our examinations—just as in real life—it is not always necessary to conclude that "plaintiff wins" or "defendant wins." It is sometimes sufficient to say, there is enough evidence of, e.g., negligence, to permit submission of the case to the jury. We do not require you to predict what the jury will in fact do.

Therefore, the beginning law student would be wise to learn some civil procedure as quickly as possible. In addition, be sure that your case briefs include a section, "procedural history."

In addition to civil procedure, other subjects have an important relationship to tort law. Be alert to these relationships. For example, the institution of insurance, and especially liability insurance, has had a major impact on tort law. The law of agency is often used in determining rules of vicarious tort liability—sometimes when it doesn't fit. And the law of evidence can have a significant bearing on certain fact issues which may be critical to the resolution of tort law issues. Obviously, you should not attempt to study these topics in any depth but pay attention when they come up in your torts course and try to understand as much as is necessary to see the relationship.

V. Other Sources

A. Reference Tools for Additional Subject Matter Depth and Coverage

This book provides a high-level overview of the field. If you would like to go deeper in studying the field or a subpart of it, we offer a couple of references to well-regarded reference tools that you may find helpful:

1. Dan B. Dobbs; Paul Hayden; Ellen Bublick, HORNBOOK ON TORTS (2d ed. 2016).
2. John L. Diamond, Lawrence C. Levine, and Anita Bernstein, UNDERSTANDING TORTS (7th ed. 2023).
3. Flower V. Harper and Fleming James, HARPER, JAMES AND GRAY ON TORTS (2006).
4. RESTATEMENT (SECOND) OF TORTS; RESTATEMENT (THIRD) OF TORTS. One of the most significant projects of the American Law Institute—a national organization made up of distinguished judges, lawyers, and law professors—is to promulgate the various "Restatements" of the law. The Restatements are drafted by knowledgeable committees and are intended to represent the best thinking as to the state of the law in each of the areas covered. They consist of "black letter" statements of the rules, followed by explanatory comments and illustrations.
5. A CONCISE RESTATEMENT OF TORTS (3d ed. 2013). A handy reference guide published by the American Law Institute. A single softbound volume, it includes some of the important provisions of both the second and third restatements.

B. Critical Perspectives on Torts

Studying tort law through the lens of precedent alone can immunize the field from critiques regarding the origins of rules. Many of the cases that you might read in your casebook were likely decided when women, indigenous peoples, enslaved Africans, and many immigrant groups were legally subjugated. The question of which lived experiences fostered the development of the legal rules we study today is an important part of a well-rounded study of the field. Here are a couple of sources to think more critically and center diverse voices in the field.

1. FEMINIST JUDGMENTS—TORTS (Martha Chamallas and Lucinda Findley eds. 2020) (rewriting iconic torts decisions to "broaden and expand to tort law the insights of the series about how feminist reasoning can influence judicial opinions to make the law more equitable, inclusive, and responsive to the interests, needs, and perspectives of women and other marginalized groups").

2. Dorothy A. Brown, Critical Race Theory and Torts, *in* CRITICAL RACE THEORY: CASES, MATERIALS AND PROBLEMS (3d ed. West Academic, 2014).

In addition to these, here are other good one-volume references and study aids dealing with tort law generally and specific torts topics.

1. EDWARD J. KIONKA, TORTS IN A NUTSHELL (7th ed. 2020).
2. VINCENT R. JOHNSON, LEGAL MALPRACTICE LAW IN A NUTSHELL (3d ed. 2021).
3. DAVID G. OWEN, PRODUCTS LIABILITY IN A NUTSHELL (10th ed. 2022).
4. JEAN EGGEN, TOXIC TORTS IN A NUTSHELL (6th ed. 2018).
5. JACK HOOD, BENJAMIN HARDY & LAUREN SIMPSON, WORKERS' COMPENSATION AND EMPLOYEE PROTECTION LAWS IN A NUTSHELL (7th ed. 2022).

Summary of Contents

Table of Contents

Capsule Summary of Tort Law

PART ONE. INTENTIONAL TORTS

I. LIABILITY RULES FOR INTENTIONAL TORTS

A. Intent

1. What Is Intentional Conduct?

Conduct is intentional if the actor (a) desires to cause the consequences of their act ("purpose" intent), or (b) engages in conduct knowing that a result is substantially certain to result from their act.

2. Proof of Intent

Ordinarily, the plaintiff proves defendant's intent circumstantially—that is, inferred from the defendant's conduct.

3. Intent Distinguished from Motive

Intent is the desire to cause certain immediate consequences. Motive is the actor's reason for having that desire—revenge, protest, punishment, self-defense, defense of another, or even to be of help. The actor's motive is irrelevant on the issue of intent.

4. Intentional Conduct Distinguished from Negligent Conduct

What distinguishes intentional conduct is the level of certainty of harmful consequences. If the harmful result is intended or certain to occur, the tort is intentional. If a defendant's conduct merely creates a foreseeable risk of harm, which may or may not be realized, their conduct is negligent.

5. Children

Very young children may be held liable for intentional torts, even though they are so young that they are incapable of negligence, if the child is found capable of forming the required intent.

6. People with Mental Health Conditions

In most jurisdictions, people with mental health conditions that impact their conduct are liable for their intentional torts, even when incapable of forming a purpose or understanding the consequences of their conduct.

7. Transferred Intent

Transferred intent is a rule applied to the five intentional torts which are the progeny of the parent "trespass" action—assault, battery, false imprisonment, trespass to land, and trespass to chattels. A defendant's intent to commit any one of these torts automatically "transfers" and supplies the intent necessary to any of the other torts in this group. It also transfers from targeting Person A (Defendant's intended victim) to affecting Person B (Defendant's actual but unintended victim).

B. Battery

1. Rule

Battery is an intentional harmful or offensive contact (direct or indirect) with the person of the other.

2. Intent Required

The defendant must have acted intending (i.e., with purpose or knowledge) to cause a harmful or offensive contact with the plaintiff.

3. Plaintiff's Person

Plaintiff's "person" includes their body and those things in contact with it or closely connected to it and identified with it, such as clothing, an object held in the plaintiff's hand, or an object closely associated with the plaintiff.

4. Plaintiff's Awareness

The tort is the contact itself, and therefore the plaintiff need not have been aware of it at the time.

5. Jurisdictional Split When No Harm Intended

Courts are split on whether it is only required that a defendant intend to cause the contact, which ultimately turns out to be, in fact, harmful or offensive ("single intent"); or whether a defendant must intend to cause both the contact and also harm or offense ("dual intent").

6. Harmful Contact

A harmful contact is actionable only if it produces some bodily harm. Bodily harm includes any physical impairment or damage, however slight, to any part of Plaintiff's body; illness; and physical (but not emotional) pain.

7. Offensive Contact

Offensive contact is that which offends a reasonable sense of personal dignity, such as by being hostile, insulting, loathsome, or unduly personal.

8. Consent

If a plaintiff consents to the contact, the defendant is privileged to make it and there is no tort.

C. Assault

1. Rule

Assault occurs when a person intends to put—and does, in fact, put—another person in imminent apprehension of a harmful or offensive contact.

2. Intent Required

Defendant's conduct need not have been motivated by hostility. An assault can emanate from a practical joke, or even an attempt to be helpful.

3. Apprehension

"Apprehension" does not mean fear. It means awareness.

a. Threat Against Another

It is not necessary that defendant direct their act against plaintiff; it is sufficient that plaintiff reasonably perceives the threat of a battery to themself.

b. Defendant Apparently Intends Only Assault

Defendant's conduct may be an assault even if it is apparent to plaintiff that defendant intended only an assault and not a battery, provided plaintiff apprehends that the battery may occur.

c. Reasonableness of Apprehension

The apprehension of the imminent contact must be reasonable.

4. Imminent

There must be an apparent intent and ability to carry out the threat immediately.

a. Words

Mere words, unaccompanied by a physical act, are not an assault. But words may give a sufficiently threatening character to an otherwise innocuous movement.

b. Apprehension of Future Battery

If defendant's words or other circumstances are understood by plaintiff as only threatening a battery at some time other than the present, there is no assault.

c. Apparent Ability to Consummate

Defendant must have an apparent present ability to carry out the battery.

5. Conditional Threat

If defendant intentionally puts another in apprehension of an imminent harmful or offensive contact, there is still an assault, even if defendant gives plaintiff an option to escape the contact by obeying defendant's command.

D. False Imprisonment

1. Rule

False imprisonment occurs when a person intentionally confines another within fixed boundaries and the confined person is either aware of the confinement or harmed by it.

2. Intent

The requisite intent is merely the intent to confine another. A mistake of identity is no excuse. And no personal malice, hostility, or desire to harm is necessary. A good faith belief that the confinement is justified is no excuse

3. Confinement

a. Defined

It is enough if plaintiff is prevented from leaving a given area, such as a room, an automobile, a building, or perhaps even a larger area. Within that area, however, the confinement must be complete, and plaintiff must have no known reasonable or safe avenue of exit or escape.

b. Indirectly Caused

So long as the defendant has the requisite intent, it is immaterial whether Defendant's act directly or indirectly causes the confinement.

c. Means

The confinement may be by means of actual or apparent physical barriers; physical force, or credible threats of physical force, to which plaintiff submits; duress sufficient to vitiate plaintiff's consent.

4. Plaintiff's Knowledge

Ordinarily, plaintiff must be aware of the confinement. However, if plaintiff suffers some physical harm from the confinement, it is immaterial that, due to some mental or sensory defect or other circumstance, plaintiff did not know that they were confined.

5. Shoplifters

When defendant in good faith detains a suspected shoplifter, courts tend to deny liability. Most states have enacted statutes which give the shopkeeper a limited privilege to detain persons in a reasonable manner for a reasonable time based on reasonable suspicion.

E. Intentional Infliction of Emotional Distress (IIED)

1. Rule

When a person, by extreme and outrageous conduct, intentionally or recklessly causes severe emotional harm to another, that person is subject to liability for that emotional harm and—if the emotional harm causes bodily harm—also for the resulting bodily harm.

2. Defendant's Conduct

a. General Rule

Defendant's conduct must be extreme, outrageous, intolerable—not merely insulting, profane, abusive, annoying, or even threatening—"so extreme in degree as to go beyond all possible bounds of decency, and to be regarded as atrocious, and utterly intolerable in civilized society."

Unless the defendant knows of some special sensitivity or vulnerability of the plaintiff, mere verbal abuse, name-calling, rudeness, insolence, and threats to do that which Defendant has a legal right to do are generally not actionable, absent circumstances of aggravation.

A single instance of abusive or otherwise obnoxious conduct that falls short of the required standard may not be enough, but the same conduct can become actionable if repeated or carried out over a period of time.

3. Plaintiff's Response

Plaintiff's emotional distress must be severe.

4. Transferred Intent

The doctrine of transferred intent does not apply to IIED, at least insofar as defendant's intent was only to commit some other intentional tort. However, there can be transferred intent from defendant's intent to commit IIED against a third person, which actually results in IIED to plaintiff.

F. Trespass to Land

1. Rule

Defendant is subject to liability for trespass to land in the possession of plaintiff if defendant intentionally (a) enters the land or causes a thing or third person to do so, (b) remains on the land after their privilege to be there has expired, or (c) fails to remove from the land a thing which they are under a duty to remove.

2. Possession

Plaintiff is in "possession" (a) when they occupy the land with the intent to control it, or (b) if no one else is in possession, they were the last occupier or they have the right to immediate occupancy.

3. Intent

The intent required is merely to enter upon the land, cause the entry, or remain. Defendant's good faith (but erroneous) belief that they have a right to be on the land, or their reasonable mistake is no defense.

4. Manner

The trespass may be directly or indirectly caused.

a. Vertical Boundaries

The trespass may be by an intrusion at, above, or beneath the surface.

b. Exception: Airplanes

Plane flights over private property present a special problem. Several theories are used to balance the possessor's rights against the needs of aviation (e.g., actual use theory, nuisance theory).

c. Causing Trespass by Things

It is no less a trespass if Defendant does not personally enter the land but merely causes something to do so.

5. Damages

If the trespass is intentional, the tort is complete without proof of any actual harm.

6. Reckless or Negligent Intrusions

An intrusion upon plaintiff's land may result from defendant's negligent conduct or abnormally dangerous activity.

G. Intentional Interferences with Tangible Personal Property

1. Trespass to Chattels and Conversion Distinguished

A conversion is merely a trespass to a chattel that is so serious that defendant can be forced to pay the full value of the chattel.

2. Trespass to Chattels

a. Rule

Defendant commits a trespass to plaintiff's chattel when defendant intentionally interferes with it, either by physical contact or by dispossession.

b. Possession

Both the person in possession and one entitled to future possession may bring a trespass action.

c. Intent

No wrongful motive is necessary. The intent required is merely to act upon the chattel.

d. Interference by Physical Contact

One form of trespass is interference by physical contact, which may be direct or indirect, and consists of any impairment of the chattel's condition, quality or value.

e. Dispossession

A dispossession consists of taking a chattel from plaintiff's possession without plaintiff's consent, or by fraud or duress, or into custody of the law; blocking plaintiff's access to the chattel; or destroying it while it is in plaintiff's possession. Dispossession even for a short time is still a trespass.

f. Damages

In the case of physical contact, plaintiff must prove actual damages.

3. Conversion

a. Rule

Conversion is an intentional exercise of dominion or control over a chattel which so seriously interferes with a plaintiff's right to control it that a defendant may justly be required to pay plaintiff its full value.

b. Degree of Interference

There is no simple test for determining when the interference is so aggravated as to constitute a conversion. The important factors are set out in R.2d § 222A of the Second Restatement. The central focus here is on the degree, nature, extent, and duration of the defendant's actual interference.

c. Intent to Exercise Dominion or Control

The only intent required for the tort is an intent to exercise dominion or control over the chattel.

d. Types of Conversion

A conversion may occur when the defendant acquires possession, moves the chattel, makes an unauthorized transfer, delivery, or disposal, withholds possession, destroys or materially alters the chattel, or under certain circumstances, merely uses the chattel.

e. Possession

Either the person in possession or the person entitled to immediate possession may maintain the action.

f. "Chattel" Broadly Defined

Most courts have extended the definition of chattel to include intangible personal property represented by, or merged into, a document.

g. Damages as Full Value of the Chattel at the Time of Conversion

Damages include the full value of the chattel at the time of conversion, plus interest.

II. INTERFERENCE WITH FEDERAL CONSTITUTIONAL RIGHTS

A. Persons Acting Under Color of State Law

42 U.S.C. § 1983 creates a tort cause of action against one who "under color of" state law interferes with a federal constitutional right of another.

B. Federal Officers and Employees

One whose federal constitutional rights have been violated by a federal officer or employee may have an action against him for damages.

III. DEFENSES TO LIABILITY FOR INTENTIONAL TORTS: PRIVILEGES

A. Privilege

1. Introduction

"Privilege" is the general term applied to various defenses in which special circumstances justify conduct which would otherwise be tortious.

2. Privileges Compared to Other Defenses

Privileges differ from other legal defenses that the defendant might assert, which operate to reduce or bar a plaintiff's recovery entirely or partially but do not negate the tortious character of defendant's underlying conduct. Privileges justify the defendant's conduct.

3. Defendant Generally Bears the Burden of Proof

Privileges are affirmative defenses which the defendant must plead and prove.

B. Consent

1. In General

Consent is a defense to virtually any tort, but it is applied most frequently to the intentional torts.

2. Actual Consent

There is actual consent when one is, in fact, explicitly willing for conduct to occur. It is a matter of the plaintiff's subjective state of mind. Consent is valid whether or not communicated to the defendant because otherwise the plaintiff has suffered no harm.

3. Apparent Consent

Plaintiff's words or conduct manifesting consent are sufficient to create a privilege to defendant to act in light of the apparent consent, even if plaintiff's actual state of mind was to the contrary.

4. Conduct May Imply Consent

Conduct can manifest consent. Even silence and inaction may indicate consent.

5. Consent May Be Inferred from Custom or Usage

Consent may be inferred from custom and usage, from prior dealings between the parties, or from the existence between them of some relationship.

6. The Consenting Party Must Have Capacity

Lawful consent must be given by one having the capacity to do so, or one authorized to consent on behalf of another. Infancy, intoxication, or mental incapacity normally will vitiate effective consent. Generally, minors lack legal capacity. A sufficiently experienced and intelligent minor, however, may expressly or impliedly consent to everyday or necessary contacts in appropriate circumstances.

7. Apparent Consent

When an emergency actually or apparently threatens death or serious bodily harm and there is no time or opportunity to obtain the plaintiff's consent or substituted consent, consent will be implied.

8. Scope of Consent

The consent is to defendant's conduct, and once given, plaintiff cannot complain of the consequences of that conduct, however unforeseen.

9. Mistake, Ignorance, Misrepresentation

Plaintiff's consent is effective as manifested unless defendant knows of the mistake or induced it by their misrepresentation. Misrepresentation may include intentionally concealing material facts.

10. Informed Consent

If the defendant misrepresents or fails to disclose to the plaintiff the possible consequences or risks of defendant's proposed conduct (e.g., a medical procedure), plaintiff's consent is not an informed one and therefore is not valid.

11. Duress

Consent given under duress is not effective. Duress includes physical coercion or threats that overcome the plaintiff's free will.

12. Revocation of Consent

Plaintiff can revoke their consent at any time by communicating the revocation to defendant and giving the defendant a reasonable time to avoid or cease that conduct.

13. Consent to Crime

Consent is not effective if the conduct consented to is a crime.

C. Self-Defense and Defense of Others

1. Self-Defense

a. Rule

Defendant has a privilege to use so much force as reasonably appears to be immediately necessary to protect himself against imminent physical harm, offensive bodily contact, or confinement threatened by the intentional or negligent conduct of another.

b. Timing of Threat

Mere provocation is generally not enough to trigger the self-defense privilege. Insults and arguments ordinarily do not justify a physical attack in retaliation.

c. Only Reasonable Force Allowed

i. Privilege Limited to Defensive Force

Defendant may use only so much force as reasonably appears to be necessary for their defense.

ii. The Limits on Deadly Force

Defendant may use force likely to inflict death or serious bodily harm only when they reasonably believe that they are in danger of similar harm, or a sexual assault. Retreat is not required if the defendant, located in their dwelling, reasonably believes that they or another occupant is in imminent danger of death or serious bodily harm. The duty-to-retreat rule has been modified by statute in some states, and case law in a few others.

d. Form of Defensive Conduct

Defendant may threaten a harmful or offensive contact (assault) even though the contact itself would not be privileged, provided their act is intended and reasonably believed to be likely to do no more that create an apprehension of such contact.

e. Effect of Defendant's Mistake

The privilege exists even when defendant reasonably but mistakenly believes that self-defense is necessary, judged by the objective standard of the reasonable person of average courage.

2. Defense of Third Persons Is Also Permitted

a. Rule

Defendant is privileged to come to the defense of any other person under the same conditions and by the same means as they would be privileged to defend themself.

b. Effect of Mistake

Under one view, defendant's privilege exists only if and to the extent that the third person in fact had a right of self-defense. If defendant is wrong, their mistake, however reasonable, is irrelevant.

D. Defense and Recovery of Property

1. Defense of Property

a. Rule

A possessor is privileged to use reasonable force to expel another or a chattel from their land, or to prevent another's imminent intrusion upon or interference with their land or chattels, or to prevent their dispossession, even though such conduct would otherwise be an assault, battery, false imprisonment, or trespass to the chattel.

b. Request Desist First

A possessor of land must first request that the intruder desist, unless it appears that the request would be useless or cannot be made before substantial harm is done.

c. Amount of Force

Force likely to cause death or great bodily harm is not privileged, except in those jurisdictions where, by statute, a lawful occupant is entitled to use deadly force to defend his abode against any felony.

d. Watchdogs, Spring Guns

Spring guns, concealed traps, and other mechanical devices, and vicious animals, used to defend defendant's property are used at defendant's risk.

e. Effect of Mistake

If the intruder has a privilege to enter the land, then the defendant has no privilege to defend their property, even though the defendant through ignorance or mistake reasonably believes that the intruder has no privilege, unless the intruder was responsible for that mistake.

f. Property of Others

There is a similar privilege to defend the property of others, at least if the third person is a member of the defendant's immediate family or household or is one whose possession defendant has a duty to protect.

2. Forcible Retaking of Chattels

a. Rule

There is a limited self-help privilege to use force or threats of force to recapture defendant's chattel, wrongfully and forcibly taken from defendant's possession, even under claim of right, or obtained by fraud or duress. The defendant must first demand their chattel's return, unless such a demand would be futile, and begin the recapture efforts promptly.

E. Necessity

1. Rule

The privilege of necessity may be invoked when defendant, in the course of defending himself or his property (or others or their property) from some threat of imminent serious harm for which the plaintiff is not responsible, intentionally does some act reasonably necessary toward that end, which results in injury to the plaintiff's property and which would otherwise be a trespass or conversion.

2. Public Necessity

If the danger affects an entire community, or so many persons that the public interest is involved, the law treats this as a complete privilege. This means that the defendant's tort liability is entirely excused so long as the actor was reasonable in their belief that the action was necessary, and the action taken was reasonable. Compensation may be available as a constitutional "takings."

3. Private Necessity

If the danger threatens only harm to the defendant's property (or to a third person or their property), then the defendant is privileged to commit the act which causes the trespass or conversion, so long as the actor was reasonable in their belief that the action was necessary and the action taken was reasonable, but they are subject to liability for compensatory damages for any resulting actual physical harm.

F. Authority of Law

1. Rule

One acting under authority of law is privileged, under certain circumstances, to commit acts which would otherwise constitute an assault, battery, false imprisonment, trespass, or conversion. Ministerial acts are not privileged if done improperly, regardless of the defendant's good faith.

G. Discipline

1. Children

a. Parents

A parent is privileged to apply such reasonable force or to impose such reasonable confinement upon his child as they reasonably believe to be necessary for the child's proper control, training, or education.

b. Loco Parentis

The privilege extends to persons (e.g., school officials) having responsibility for the custody, control, training, or education of the child, except so far as the parent has restricted their authority to do so.

c. Reasonableness

The reasonableness of the force or confinement depends upon whether the defendant is a parent; the age and condition of the child; the nature of the offense and the child's apparent motive; the influence of the child's example to other children in the family; its necessity and appropriateness to compel obedience to a proper command; and whether disproportionate to the offense, unnecessarily degrading, or likely to cause serious or permanent harm.

PART TWO. NEGLIGENCE

I. THE NEGLIGENCE CAUSE OF ACTION

"Negligence" is both the name of a primary tort cause of action and the descriptive term given to conduct that falls below the standard required by law. In other words, negligent conduct is one element of the negligence cause of action when a defendant breaches a standard of care. The prima facie elements of a negligence cause of action are:

(1) A *duty* owed by defendant to act or refrain from acting;

(2) A *breach* of that duty by defendant's failure to conform their conduct to the required standard of care they owed (i.e., defendant's negligent conduct);

(3) A sufficient *causal connection* between the defendant's negligent conduct and plaintiff's injury (i.e., both a factual connection (known as actual cause or cause-in-fact) and a jury willing to impose liability without concluding that the harm suffered is too remote as to be recoverable (known as proximate cause)); and

(4) The plaintiff suffered *harm* resulting from the defendant's breach in the standard of care (i.e., monetary harm that the law recognizes as measurable and compensable).

SECTION 1. DUTY OF CARE

I. DUTY OF CARE OWED

A. Sweeping General Rule with Limitations

A putative defendant's duty of care to a plaintiff can best be analyzed as a general principle with exceptions and limitations, rather than as a collection of specific duties. Generally, a defendant's duty of care arises: (a) out of a pre-existing relationship between the plaintiff and the defendant (e.g., doctor-patient, business-patron), or (b) because the putative defendant could have foreseen that their conduct, if creating an unreasonable risk of harm, would endanger the plaintiff or plaintiff's property.

II. DUTY BASED ON SPECIAL RELATIONSHIP WITH ANOTHER

Certain pre-existing relationships will support a duty to aid or protect another when the risk arises within the scope of that relationship (e.g., parent-child, employer-employee).

III. LIMITATIONS ON DUTIES OWED

A. Duty to *This* Plaintiff

Negligence law has traditionally held that a putative defendant is not subject to liability to the plaintiff unless the defendant breached a duty owed to the plaintiff and not to someone else.

B. Nature and Scope of the Risk

Conduct may be negligent because it foreseeably threatens property damage, but it instead causes some unforeseen personal injury. Conduct may also be negligent because it foreseeably threatens one type of harm to the plaintiff, but it actually causes another type of harm, as to which the risk was not unreasonable. Conduct may also be negligent because it creates a risk of injury to A, but unexpectedly injures B.

C. Limits on Certain Interests

Certain types of interests are given less than full protection against negligent invasion. A few are noted conceptually here and expounded upon in later chapters.

1. Economic Loss

a. In General

Tort law has been reluctant to extend liability for negligent conduct that results solely in economic harm to the plaintiff. Courts reason that only a limited amount of *physical* damage will ordinarily ensue from a single act, whereas the number of economic interests a tortfeasor may destroy in a moment of carelessness is practically limitless.

b. Economic Loss Caused by Physical Harm to Another

In general, plaintiff cannot recover in negligence for economic loss resulting from physical harm to another or to property in which plaintiff has no proprietary interest.

2. Harm to the Unborn

a. Child Born Alive

Traditionally, one who tortiously causes fetal harm is subject to liability for fetal harms if the child is subsequently born alive. The prevailing view is that the fetus need not have been viable at the time of the injury. If the fetus is born alive but then dies from the injury (however briefly the child was alive, and whether or not viable when born), a wrongful death action can be maintained.

b. Child Not Born Alive

If a defendant negligently causes fetal harm and the fetus dies from the injuries prior to birth, the authorities are divided, but most courts now allow the wrongful death action provided the fetus was viable at the time of the injury.

After the Supreme Court's decision in *Dobbs v. Jackson Women's Health Org.*, 597 U.S. 215 (2022), states are no longer bound by the viability line, which is leading restrictive abortion states to upend these traditional tort lines. It is likely that restrictive abortion states will vastly expand their tort liability based on adopting a fetal personhood model.

c. Damages for Unintended Children

i. Wrongful Conception

When a defendant's negligent conduct fails to prevent conception (e.g., negligence with respect to failed fertility management methods such as tubectomy, vasectomy, etc.) and results in an unplanned birth, the prevailing view is that the parents may recover, but their damages are limited to the cost of prenatal care and delivery and the associated pain and other general and special damages.

ii. Wrongful Birth and Wrongful Life

(a) Description

Another category of claims arises when a defendant's negligence results in the unplanned birth of a child who is born with a physical or mental disability caused by a genetic (or other) disorder for which a defendant is not responsible.

(b) Wrongful Birth

After initially rejecting wrongful birth claims, most courts now allow recovery. Some courts limit damages to the parents' pecuniary losses, but others now award damages for their emotional distress as well. In some jurisdictions, statutes bar wrongful birth actions.

(c) Wrongful Life

So far, almost all jurisdictions have rejected wrongful life claims. Courts find it too problematic to measure the value of life with a disability as compared to no life at all and find it philosophically difficult to support the child's claim that they should never have been born.

3. Emotional Distress

a. Negligent Infliction of Emotional Distress (NIED)

If a defendant is subject to liability to plaintiff for negligence based on bodily injury (e.g., a broken leg), the plaintiff can recover not only for the physical injury but also their resulting pain, suffering, mental, and emotional harm. Plaintiff's mental damages are "parasitic" to their damages for physical harm.

b. The Impact Rule

Under this rule, if the defendant's negligent conduct resulted in any impact, however slight, with the plaintiff's body, that impact would support liability for plaintiff's emotional distress resulting from the same negligent conduct. No impact meant no cause of action.

c. The Zone-of-Danger Rule

The Zone-of-Danger rule allows recovery for emotional distress when the defendant's negligent conduct threatens (but does not result in) bodily harm (impact) to the plaintiff (a "near miss" situation). Most courts that have adopted this approach will allow plaintiff to recover for *bodily harm* resulting from the fear, shock or other emotional disturbance caused by his presence in the zone of danger.

d. The Bystander Rule: Emotional Harm Caused by Witnessing Injury to Another

i. Dillon Factors

If plaintiff was not in the zone of danger but merely witnessed a shocking event in which defendant's negligent conduct caused serious physical harm or death to a third person, courts traditionally declined to hold defendant liable for plaintiff's severe emotional distress resulting from the shock.

Following *Dillon v. Legg* (Cal. 1968), however, most jurisdictions expanded liability to allow plaintiffs to recover in such situations under certain conditions. Typically, the plaintiff made their case for liability using factors considering whether (a) the actual injury to the third person was a serious one; (b) the plaintiff was a member of the immediate family of, or closely related to, the person in peril; (c) the shock resulted in serious emotional distress to plaintiff; and (d) the plaintiff actually witnessed the traumatic event, or at least comes upon the scene almost immediately and witnesses its aftermath

ii. The Restatement (Third) of Torts

R.3d Liability for Physical & Emotional Harm § 48 reframed the requirements of the bystander rule with more precision in its predictability: An actor who negligently causes sudden serious bodily injury to a third person is subject to liability for serious emotional harm caused thereby to a person who (a) perceives the event contemporaneously and (b) is a close family member of the person suffering the bodily injury.

iii. Zone of Danger, Fear for Another's Safety

In jurisdictions that have adopted the zone-of-danger rule but not the *Dillon* rule, most courts will allow plaintiff to recover for bystander shock under the circumstances stated in the preceding paragraph if plaintiff was also within the zone of danger.

e. Proximate Cause Limitations

i. Physical Manifestation Requirement

Absent impact, in some jurisdictions, plaintiff may recover only if their emotional distress results in physical illness or comparable objective bodily consequences.

ii. "Eggshell Plaintiff" Rule

Unless defendant has actual knowledge of some special sensitivity of plaintiff, defendant will be liable only to the extent that plaintiff's physical response to the emotional trauma was within the normal range of ordinarily sensitive persons. Defendant is not liable for unforeseeable physical consequences.

IV. DUTIES ARISING FROM CONTRACT

One possible source of defendant's duty to plaintiff is a contract between them under which defendant agrees to perform certain services. If defendant breaches that contract and as a result plaintiff sustains physical or other harm, special rules apply to determine whether that breach may give rise to tort liability, as outlined in this subpart.

A. General Rule—Duty Owed in Tort for Misperformance Not Nonperformance

Where defendant's duty to act arises because of a contractual relation between the defendant and plaintiff, defendant is not liable in tort for harm caused by their breach of that contract where the breach consists merely of their failure to commence performance at all. But once defendant has begun to perform, they will be liable for their tortious misperformance, whether consisting of acts or omissions to act.

1. Misperformance and Nonperformance Distinguished

It is hard to distinguish the line between misperformance and nonperformance, and any distinction is often illusory. In general, the question is whether defendant's performance (as distinct from their promise or preparation) has gone so far that it has begun to affect the interests of plaintiff beyond the expected benefits of the contract itself and may be regarded as a positive act assuming the obligation beyond the mere promise to perform.

2. The Contract Shapes the Scope of Duty

Assuming defendant's duty arises from the contract with plaintiff, defendant usually has no duty to notify plaintiff of, or repair, a dangerous condition that is outside the scope of the contractual duty, in most cases even if defendant actually discovers the condition.

B. Contracts for Security Services

The Restatement (Third) of Torts provides that when a defendant contracts to provide security services intended to reduce the risk of physical harm, defendant is liable for failure to use reasonable care in doing so if the failure increases the risk of harm beyond that which otherwise would have existed, or the other person relies on the undertaking.

C. Fraud

A promise made without any intent to perform it may be fraud for which a tort action in deceit will lie.

D. Third Persons Not Parties to the Contract

1. Common Law Privity Rule

The general common law rule was that plaintiff, not a party to a contract between defendant and another, had no cause of action in tort for harm sustained as a result of defendant's misperformance or nonperformance.

2. Exceptions for Nonfeasance

In the case of nonfeasance, various exceptions to the privity rule have developed, thus creating a duty of care arising from nonperformance.

E. Dangerous Instrumentalities

Nonperformance of a contract to maintain, inspect, or repair an instrumentality which foreseeably creates a substantial risk of harm to third persons (e.g., elevator, scaffolding, boiler).

SECTION 2. BREACH—FAILURE TO CONFORM WITH STANDARDS OF CARE

I. GENERAL STANDARD OF REASONABLE CARE

A. Reasonable Care Defined

"Negligence" is conduct which falls below the standard of care established by law for the protection of others against unreasonable risks of harm. The standard is "reasonable care" under the circumstances.

B. An Objective Test

The test for negligence is objective.

C. When Is a Risk "Unreasonable"?

A risk is unreasonable when the foreseeable probability and gravity of the harm outweigh the burden to the defendant of alternative conduct that would have prevented the harm.

II. JURIES DECIDE STANDARDS OF CARE WITH JUDGES AS GATEKEEPERS

Whether conduct was negligent is a question of fact for the trier of fact. The judge, however, may enter summary judgment, direct a verdict, or otherwise take the case out of the jury's hands because the court decides whether the conduct in question was so clearly negligent that no reasonable person could reach any other conclusion.

III. ATTRIBUTES OF THE REASONABLE PERSON

A. Knowledge, Experience, and Perception

Defendants will be charged with what they actually knew and observed, and also with those things that a reasonable person would have known and perceived. If they have superior intelligence, memory perception, knowledge, or judgment, they will be held to that standard.

B. Knowledge Common to the Community

The reasonable person knows those things which at that time are common knowledge in the community.

C. Anticipating Conduct of Others

The reasonable person will regulate their conduct in light of what they can anticipate, expect or foresee others will do.

IV. SPECIAL STANDARDS OF CARE—MODIFICATIONS TO THE REASONABLY PRUDENT PERSON

A. Elevated Standard of Care Applied to Those with Specialized Skills and Knowledge

If one chooses to engage in an activity requiring specialized skills or knowledge, their conduct is measured against the hypothetical person who is reasonably skilled and knowledgeable in that activity. Beginners are held to the same standard.

B. Modified Objective Standard for Physical Characteristics

The "reasonable person" standard is modified to the extent that defendant has a physical deficiency or disability. Defendant's conduct is then measured against that of a reasonably prudent person with those same physical characteristics.

C. Minors Can Be Liable for Negligence and Modified Objective Standard Applies

If the defendant is a minor that the law recognizes as capable of negligence, the test examines what is reasonable conduct for a child of that defendant's age, intelligence, and experience under the circumstances. But this exception does not apply to minors engaging in "adult-like" or inherently dangerous activities requiring special skills and training. In those cases, the minor is held to the adult, objective standard of care.

D. Professionals and Specialists

The standard of care of medical professionals is *conclusively* established by the customary or usual practice of reasonably well-qualified practitioners in that field.

E. Physicians—Medical Malpractice

Negligent conduct by persons practicing a profession or, in some cases, a skilled trade (physician or other skilled health care provider, dentist, optometrist, lawyer, accountant, engineer, architect, veterinarian, etc.) is commonly termed "malpractice."

1. Locality Rule

When this rule was applied, the standard of care was the customary practice of reasonably well-qualified similar professionals in that particular geographic locality, or alternatively, in similar localities. Today, most jurisdictions have abandoned the locality rule.

2. Proving Medical Malpractice

a. Expert Testimony Required

In most cases involving a claim of professional negligence, the plaintiff must provide expert testimony establishing (1) the relevant standard of care, (2) that Defendant's conduct did not conform to that standard, and (3) that there was a causal relationship between Defendant's breach and Plaintiff's injury.

F. Informed Consent

The physician must disclose the risks and alternatives that a reasonable patient would want to know in order to make an intelligent choice, i.e., all risks material to the decision of the ordinary patient in the plaintiff's position. The plaintiff must prove that they would not have consented had they known this information.

G. Conduct in Emergencies

The fact that defendant is confronted with a sudden emergency that requires rapid decision is a factor that may be considered in determining the reasonableness of defendant's choice of action.

V. NO MODIFICATIONS TO THE REASONABLY PRUDENT PERSON STANDARD

A. No Modified Standard for Reduced Mental Capacity

The fact that the defendant is deficient in intelligence, judgment, memory, emotional stability, voluntarily intoxicated, or similar does not modify the standard of care.

VI. TYPES OF BREACHES IN THE STANDARD OF CARE

Negligence may consist of an act or a failure to act, lack of competence, or lack of preparation.

A. Failure to Warn or Instruct

One type of negligence is a failure to warn or instruct another so that they can take proper precautions for their own safety.

B. Negligent Entrustment

It may be negligent to entrust a chattel to a person defendant knows or should know is likely to use it in a dangerous way.

C. Negligent Hiring, Retention, or Supervision

Negligence may include failure to exercise reasonable care in the hiring, retention, or supervision of employees or independent contractors.

VII. SOURCES OF STANDARDS OF CARE

A. Statutes as Evidence of Standards of Care

Federal and state statutes can set out standards of conduct to protect others. For tort law purposes, two types may be distinguished: legislation which (a) expressly or (b) by necessary implication creates a civil remedy for damages for violation; and legislation which does not create a civil remedy.

B. Legislative Purpose to Protect This Class of Persons from This Harm

Legislation is relevant on the standard of care in a negligence case only if the statute was intended, at least in part, to protect a class of persons which includes plaintiff against the particular hazard and kind of harm which resulted.

C. Statutory Standards That Impose New Duties

If the statute creates a wholly new obligation (but not a new cause of action) and defendant had no corresponding common law duty to plaintiff, courts tend to give the statute no tort law effect at all.

D. Licensing Statutes

Most courts hold that violation of a statute requiring a license to engage in a particular trade, profession or activity (e.g., physician, physical therapist, car driver) is not negligence *per se* and therefore the fact that defendant did not have a valid license is not admissible to show that defendant was negligent on a particular occasion.

E. Effect of Statutory Violation

1. Majority Rule

The majority rule is that a relevant statute is prima facie proof of negligence or "negligence per se." If no evidence is introduced by defendant to excuse the violation, defendant's negligence is conclusively established.

2. Minority View

In some jurisdictions, violation of a statute is merely *evidence* of negligence, which the jury can consider along with all other evidence in determining whether defendant was negligent. The violation does not per se establish negligence.

3. Cause

A violation does not *per se* establish a sufficient causal relation between the violation and plaintiff's injury. Proximate cause rules still apply.

4. Children

A minor's violation of a statute does not constitute negligence *per se* but may be introduced as evidence of the minor's negligence.

5. Defenses

Contributory negligence and assumption of risk defenses apply (if and to the extent otherwise available).

F. Excused Violations

Courts will permit excuses for violations to be shown to rebut the per se or prima facie negligence. These include (a) physical circumstances beyond defendant's control; (b) innocent ignorance of facts which make the statute applicable; (c) sudden emergencies not of defendant's making; (d) situations in which it would be more dangerous to comply with the statute than to violate it; (e) violations that are reasonable in light of defendant's childhood, physical disability, or physical incapacity; and (f) defendant used reasonable care in attempting to comply with the statute.

G. Compliance with Statute

Defendant may also ordinarily show compliance with a statute as evidence of their reasonable care, but such compliance is not conclusive since a reasonable person might have taken precautions greater than the statutory minimum.

VIII. PROOF OF NEGLIGENCE

A. Burden of Proof

1. Elements

Whether a duty exists is usually determined by the court, but in making that determination the court may have to resolve disputed fact issues.

2. Defenses

Any applicable defenses, such as plaintiff's contributory negligence, are affirmative defenses for defendant to plead and prove by the same standard of proof.

3. Circumstantial Evidence

Parties may prove any fact by circumstantial evidence (facts that support an inference of the fact the party seeks to prove) as well as by direct evidence (e.g., eyewitness testimony).

4. Role of Judge and Jury

It is the jury's task to determine, based on the evidence, whether plaintiff has proved each element of their cause of action by a preponderance of the evidence. But if the evidence on any essential element is so weak that no reasonable person could find that element established, the judge will decide the case and enter judgment for defendant.

B. Presumptions

Each jurisdiction's tort law has its own set of legal presumptions, which are codified rules of circumstantial evidence.

C. Experts and Opinion Evidence

1. Expert Witnesses

In many tort cases, expert testimony is necessary or desirable to furnish the jury facts beyond its common knowledge. Expert testimony is usually required to establish the standard of care in professional negligence cases.

2. Opinions

Expert witnesses are permitted to testify to opinions or conclusions when they will be helpful to the jury.

D. Res Ipsa Loquitur

Like presumptions, *res ipsa loquitur* ("the thing speaks for itself") is basically a rule of circumstantial evidence.

1. Rule

If plaintiff can establish a prima facie res ipsa loquitur case, they need not prove by direct or other evidence the specific conduct of defendant which was negligent. If plaintiff makes a prima facie showing that:

a. their injury was caused by an instrumentality or condition which was under defendant's exclusive management or control at the relevant time(s);

b. in the ordinary course of events, plaintiff's harm would not have occurred unless defendant was negligent;

then the jury is instructed on res ipsa loquitur and may infer that defendant was negligent and that defendant's negligence was the cause of plaintiff's injury without any more specific proof of what really happened.

2. Control by Defendant

It is now regarded as sufficient if defendant had the right to control and the opportunity to exercise it at the relevant time.

3. Multiple Defendants

The control requirement ordinarily precludes use of res ipsa loquitor against multiple defendants, because if more than one defendant could have been the responsible cause of plaintiff's injury, the inference of negligence does not point to the culpable defendant.

4. Inference of Negligence

Plaintiff need not show that defendant's negligence is the only possible explanation for the injury-causing occurrence, but only that the inference that it was defendant's negligence outweighs the sum of the other possible causes.

5. Plaintiff's Conduct

At one time there was a third element. plaintiff was required to prove that their injury was not due to any "voluntary act" by plaintiff, or that plaintiff's own conduct was not a significant causative factor, or, most recently, that plaintiff was not contributorily negligent. However, with the adoption of comparative negligence, this requirement has been eliminated in most jurisdictions.

6. Procedural Effect

Once the court determines that plaintiff has established a prima facie res ipsa case, the issue becomes one for the jury to determine whether to draw the inference, taking into consideration defendant's contrary evidence (if any). The jury will be given a res ipsa instruction, but in most cases res ipsa is a permissible inference and not a presumption, so the jury is free to find against plaintiff even if it finds that plaintiff has proved the res ipsa elements.

C. Custom and Character

1. Custom and Usage

In determining whether conduct is negligent, the customary conduct of the community, industry, trade, business, or profession in similar circumstances is relevant but not conclusive.

2. Character

Evidence that defendant or plaintiff was or was not a careful person is generally not admissible to prove that they acted carefully or negligently on the occasion in question.

IX. DEGREES OF NEGLIGENCE

A. Degrees of Care

The duty of those who conduct certain dangerous activities is sometimes stated as greater than "ordinary" or "reasonable" care.

There is a trend away from such special degrees of care.

X. RECKLESS CONDUCT ("WILLFUL AND WANTON MISCONDUCT")

A. Definition

Conduct is in "reckless disregard of the safety of another" (also called "willful and wanton misconduct") when defendant knows or has reason to know that (1) it creates an unreasonable risk of harm and (2) the risk is relatively high, either in degree or in the probability that harm will occur.

B. Distinguished from Negligent Conduct

Negligent conduct merely creates an unreasonable risk; no awareness of that risk is required.

C. Distinguished from Intentional Torts

Conduct is intentional when defendant either intends to bring about the consequences or knows that they are substantially certain to occur.

D. When Required

Certain statutes (e.g., automobile and airplane guest statutes, governmental immunity acts, "Good Samaritan" laws) exempt defendant from liability for ordinary negligence, thereby requiring proof of reckless conduct for liability.

SECTION THREE. CAUSATION OF HARM

I. CAUSATION OF HARM

Plaintiffs must prove that the defendant's breach in the standard of care caused harm.

A. Overview of Causation Issues

Causation problems are common to many different torts (and to all torts involving physical harm). Causation problems are among the most difficult, conceptually, in tort law. They may be analyzed in two categories:

1. Cause in fact (Factual Cause) exists when the "cause-and-effect" chain of events leading to plaintiff's injury includes defendant's tortious conduct.

2. Proximate cause, also called "legal cause" or scope of liability. Some courts and writers use these terms to encompass all causal relation issues. Others distinguish between (a) proximate or legal cause and (b) cause in fact or factual cause. Many now categorize proximate cause issues under the term "scope of liability."

B. Cause in Fact

1. General Rule

Cause in fact is a question of fact, requiring proof that the injury would not have occurred "but for" defendant's conduct (the "sine qua non" rule).

2. Proof

Circumstantial evidence that links plaintiff's injury to defendant's tortious conduct is usually all that is required to prove cause-in-fact.

3. Multiple Causes

Defendant's conduct need only be "a" cause of Plaintiff's harm.

a. Concurrent Tortfeasors, Indivisible Injury

If the tortious conduct of multiple defendants coincides and both are causes in fact of plaintiff's injury, each or all are subject to liability for plaintiff's damages. It does not matter that the defendants did not act together "in concert," or that no defendant's conduct by itself would have caused the injury.

b. Concurrent Tortfeasors, Divisible Injury

i. General Rule

If multiple defendants each cause separate parts of plaintiff's harm, the defendants will each be liable only for the part an individual caused if it is possible to determine who caused which part.

ii. Exceptions

(a) Concert of Action

All defendants are liable for all of P's damages, even though divisible, if they were acting in concert or engaged in a joint enterprise.

(b) Risk of Further Injury

If defendant's tortious conduct injures plaintiff and foreseeably exposes plaintiff to the risk of further injury by another, defendant is liable both for the injury he caused and also for such further injury.

iii. Burden of Proof

A party alleging that damages are divisible has the burden to prove that they are divisible.

4. Concurrent Independent Tortfeasors, One Cause (Alternative Liability)

Suppose the tortious conduct of multiple defendants (acting independently) occurs so that each defendant (but not all) was the cause in fact of plaintiff's injury, but plaintiff cannot prove which one. Traditionally, plaintiff would lose. The modern and better view shifts the burden of proof to each defendant to prove that they were not the cause.

5. Enterprise and Market Share Liability

Some courts are willing to create new rules of causation when a plaintiff can prove that similar products were marketed during the relevant time by a group of manufacturers. The injury must have been caused by a common design feature of the similar products.

6. Liability for Reduced Chance

Suppose that defendant's tortious conduct does not cause plaintiff's harm in a "but for" sense but merely reduces plaintiff's chances of a favorable outcome. Some states deny all recovery unless the victim's chances were initially over 50% (the "traditional" rule). Other states allow damages if the jury finds that the defendant's negligence was a "substantial factor" in accelerating or triggering the adverse result. Finally, some states allow damages based on the percentage difference (in this case, 15%) attributable to the defendant's negligence times the plaintiff's total damages (the "value-of-the-chance" rule).

C. Scope of Liability (Proximate Cause)

1. General Principle

Proximate cause or scope of liability rules limit defendant's liability to (a) persons and (b) consequences that bear some reasonable relationship to defendant's tortious conduct. Whether and how scope of liability rules shall be applied is a question of law for the court.

(a) unforeseeable or remote or indirect consequences; and

(b) intervening causes.

2. Overview

Broadly defined, there are three typical approaches to the first category (unforeseeable or remote or indirect consequences): (a) the risk principle; (b) the direct consequences rule; and (c) the duty-risk rule. One of these approaches will be used, unless the case falls into a category of cases in which there is a fixed proximate cause or duty rule.

3. Unforeseeable or Remote or Indirect Consequences

a. The Risk Principle

Under the majority view, defendant's liability is limited (1) to those consequences, the foreseeability of which made defendant's conduct tortious in the first place, and (2) to persons within that foreseeable zone of danger. This is sometimes known as the "risk principle" or the "foreseeable-risk rule."

b. The Direct Consequences Rule

Under the direct consequences rule (a minority view), defendant is subject to liability for those consequences that are a direct result of defendant's tortious conduct, whether or not foreseeable. The result is direct if it follows in an unbroken natural sequence from the effect of defendant's act upon conditions existing and forces already in operation at the time, without the intervention of any external forces which were not then in active operation. Thus, the direct consequences rule embodies a hindsight test rewinding from the harm that resulted to the breach in the standard of care.

c. Rescuers

The intervention of would-be rescuers is usually deemed foreseeable as a matter of law, and therefore when defendant's tortious conduct endangers anyone (including themself), they are subject to liability to plaintiff who is injured in attempting a rescue, so long as the harm arises from a risk inherent in the effort to provide aid.

d. Physical Consequences (Eggshell Plaintiff)

Defendant is liable for the full consequences of plaintiff's injury even though, due to plaintiff's peculiar susceptibility to harm (of which defendant was unaware)—plaintiff's physical or mental condition or other characteristics—those consequences were more severe than they would have been in a normal person.

e. Intentional Torts; Strict Liability

Courts tend to expand the limits of foreseeability when Defendant's conduct amounts to an intentional tort and conversely confine liability to foreseeable consequences when liability is strict.

4. Intervening Cause

a. Definition

An intervening cause is conduct by some third person, or an event, which occurs after defendant's tortious conduct, and operates with or upon defendant's conduct to produce plaintiff's injury.

b. General Rule

If (1) an intervening cause was foreseeable, or (2) the intervening cause was not foreseeable but the consequences were of the type which defendant could foresee as resulting from his conduct, the intervening cause will not operate to relieve defendant of liability. But if both the intervening cause and the resulting consequences were not foreseeable, it is called a superseding cause and defendant's tortious conduct is not a proximate cause of plaintiff's injury.

c. Types of Intervening Causes

An intervening cause may consist of either human conduct or any other natural force or event (e.g., action of weather, animals).

d. Foreseeable Intervening Causes

Foreseeable intervening causes may include: 1) Weather; 2) Negligence; 3) Criminal conduct or intentional torts by third parties; 4) Self-inflicted harm; 5) Rescuers; 6) Further harm; 7) Foreseeable consequences.

PART THREE. DAMAGES

I. DAMAGES

A. Compensatory Damages

1. Categorizing General Damages Versus Special Damages (R.2d § 904)

a. General Damages or Noneconomic Loss

General damages are compensatory damages for a type of harm, like pain and suffering or loss of companionship, because they so frequently result from the tort involved that such damages are anticipated and hence need not be alleged with specificity in order for Plaintiff to prove and recover them. Today, such damages are more often categorized as noneconomic loss because they are losses not supported with itemized receipts.

b. Special Damages or Economic Loss

Special damages are those awarded for all other compensable harms (for example, medical expenses or lost wages).

2. Nominal Damages

Nominal damages are a trivial sum (e.g., one dollar) awarded to a litigant who has established a cause of action but has not established that they are entitled to compensatory damages. Some tort actions, such as negligence, do not support nominal damages.

3. Damages for Personal Injury

When a plaintiff proves a compensable personal injury, they may recover for all foreseeable adverse physical and mental consequences of that injury, past and future, in the following categories.

a. Past and future pecuniary or economic loss and out-of-pocket expenses

b. Noneconomic or nonpecuniary damages

c. Physical impairment

To the extent not recoverable under one of the foregoing, plaintiff may recover for physical impairment of some portion of the body. This is usually categorized under the "disability" element.

4. Defendant Responsible for Pre-Existing Conditions

Defendant is responsible in damages for all the consequences of plaintiff's injury, including those caused or aggravated by some pre-existing condition, predisposition, or vulnerability of the plaintiff that others would not have sustained, even if that condition was unknown to the defendant.

5. Awarding Future Losses at Present

a. Pecuniary Losses Awarded at Present Value

If a plaintiff is awarded damages for pecuniary losses which they will incur in the future, the amount of such damages must ordinarily be reduced to present cash value.

b. Some Jurisdictions Consider Inflation for Future Losses

Some jurisdictions still do not allow the jury to consider the effects of future inflation in calculating damages for future economic losses. A growing number do.

6. Collateral Source Rule

Under the general rule, payments made to, or benefits conferred on, a plaintiff from sources other than the defendant are not credited against the defendant, even though they cover all or part of the damages for which the defendant is liable.

Statutes in an increasing number of jurisdictions have either abolished or modified the collateral source rule.

7. Limitations on Damages or "Caps"

As a result of tort reform legislation, about half of the states place statutory caps (e.g., $250,000 maximum) or other limits on the amount of noneconomic damages recoverable, either in personal injury actions generally, or in medical malpractice cases only. Some statutes limit liability for certain types of defendants, such as alcohol providers. In some jurisdictions, these statutes have been held unconstitutional; in others, they have not.

8. Plaintiff's Duty to Mitigate Damages

Plaintiff must make reasonable efforts to mitigate the consequences of their injury and to take reasonable steps to prevent further harmful consequences from developing.

9. Damages Awards Not Generally Taxed

Damages for personal injuries involving physical harm are generally not subject to federal income taxation.

B. Punitive Damages

1. Rationale

In most jurisdictions, the trier of fact may award punitive damages when the defendant's misconduct is sufficiently serious, to punish defendant and to deter the defendant and others from similar conduct in the future.

2. Conduct Required

States that allow punitive damages have heightened requirements regarding the qualifying conduct. Defendants generally must have acted from a wrongful motive, or at least with gross or knowing indifference to the rights or safety of another.

3. Limitations on Punitive Damages

a. Constitutional Limitations

United States Supreme Court decisions have established due process limits on awards of punitive damages. Review of punitive damages by the trial and reviewing courts is constitutionally required, using three guideposts: (1) the degree of reprehensibility of the defendant's misconduct; (2) the disparity between plaintiff's actual or potential harm and the punitive damages award; and (3) the difference between the punitive damages awarded and any applicable civil penalties for similar misconduct. Defendant cannot be punished for conduct that bears no relation to plaintiff's harm, such as similar conduct that occurred elsewhere, or similar conduct that occurred in other cases, or harm to nonparties.

b. Statutory Limitations

There may be limits on how much can be awarded in punitive damages.

c. Discretionary Variations and Judicial Limitations

Whether to award punitive damages at all and the amount of the award is typically within the discretion of the trier of fact and may be subject to review for excessiveness.

d. Cause of Action Limitations

Punitive damages may not be available against an employer for any tort committed by their employee for which the employer is vicariously liable.

C. Derivative Claims for Spouse, Parent, and Child

Derivative actions can be brought by a spouse or parent that are independent of the injured spouse's or child's action. In these claims, the defendant may also invoke any defense (e.g., contributory negligence) that would have been available in a suit brought by the injured person directly, as well as defenses available against the plaintiff.

1. **Spouse (Loss of Consortium)**

In most jurisdictions, if defendant's tort has injured one spouse, the other spouse has a separate cause of action against the defendant for the damages resulting from their loss of the injured spouse's society, love, companionship, affection, and marital relations.

2. **Parent's Loss of Child's Services**

A parent can recover damages for reasonable loss of the services of their minor child resulting from an injury to the child caused by the tortious conduct of defendant.

3. **Child's Loss of Parent's Services**

Except in a few jurisdictions, a child has no action for loss of their parent's care, support, training, guidance, companionship, love, and affection resulting from a tortious injury to the parent.

PART FOUR. DEFENSES TO NEGLIGENCE

I. CONTRIBUTORY AND COMPARATIVE NEGLIGENCE

A. Defined

If the plaintiff creates an unreasonable risk of harm to themselves, their contributory fault can combine with the defendant's negligence to cause plaintiff's injury.

B. Causation

The defendant must prove that the plaintiff's harm resulted from the plaintiff's conduct.

C. Effect of Plaintiff's Contributing Fault

1. **Terminology**

"Contributory negligence" is when the legal rules adopted in a state yield a complete bar on the plaintiff's recovery. "Comparative negligence" or "comparative fault" is when the legal rules of the state merely reduce plaintiff's recovery by their own percentage of fault.

2. **Contributory Negligence**

Under the traditional common law rule, plaintiff's contributory negligence was a complete defense and totally barred any recovery against a negligent defendant. This is now the minority rule that remains in just five jurisdictions: Alabama, Maryland, North Carolina, Virginia, and the District of Columbia.

3. **Comparative Negligence**

Comparative negligence is the modern and majority rule. Plaintiff's contributing fault is not a complete bar to recovery; it merely reduces plaintiff's damages. Plaintiff's damages are calculated and then reduced by the relative percentage of plaintiff's own fault.

a. **Pure Comparative Negligence**

In a pure comparative negligence jurisdiction, adopted in 12 states, plaintiff may recover any portion of damages no matter how great their relative fault is.

b. **Modified Comparative Negligence**

The majority rule, adopted in 33 states, follows a modified comparative negligence approach, in which plaintiff recovers nothing if their negligence was "as great as" (50%) or "greater than" (51%) that of the defendant or defendants. Thus, if plaintiff was 51% at fault and the defendant was 49% at fault, plaintiff recovers nothing.

4. **Trier of Fact Assigns Relative Fault**

These rules reveal the importance of the trier of fact assigning the relative percentage of fault.

5. **Intentional or Reckless Conduct**

Traditionally, ordinary contributory negligence was not a defense to an intentional tort or to reckless conduct. In most comparative negligence jurisdictions, plaintiff's fault will reduce their recovery even though defendant's conduct was reckless, but not if defendant's conduct was intentional.

6. **Strict Liability**

Prior to the adoption of comparative negligence, contributory negligence was not a defense to a strict liability action, except when that conduct amounted to assumption of the risk. Today, some of the jurisdictions adopting comparative negligence permit plaintiff's ordinary contributory negligence to reduce plaintiff's damages. Others do not. The only damage-reducing defense is plaintiff's assumption of the risk.

7. **Serious Misconduct or Fault**

In some jurisdictions, if plaintiff's contributory fault was seriously unlawful conduct, they will be barred from recovery altogether. And in some cases, plaintiff's serious fault is considered a superseding cause of plaintiff's own harm. These latter cases are arguably inconsistent with comparative fault principles.

8. **Public Policy Exceptions**

Courts have sometimes refused to permit defendant to assert the defense of contributory negligence in cases where an overriding public policy prevails. For example, where a statute ensuring safe working conditions is intended to protect workers against economic pressure which might force them into unsafe employment, defendant employers cannot assert the defense that plaintiff employees consented to such unsafe conditions.

Some courts have refused to consider plaintiff contributorily negligent for engaging in some activity involving a right or entitlement, even though that conduct involves a risk of harm. For example, crossing a crosswalk without looking both ways when the walk sign is on, dining at a restaurant where outdoor seating abuts a busy road, or in person meetups to exchange items sold online.

D. Imputed Contributory Negligence

1. Negligence of Third Parties Not Generally Imputed to Plaintiff

With three exceptions, a third party's negligence will not be imputed to plaintiff to reduce or bar plaintiff's recovery for injuries caused by defendant's negligence, despite the existence of some relationship between plaintiff and the third party. For example, the negligence of a spouse is not imputed to the other spouse, nor a child to a parent.

a. Employee's Conduct Imputed to Employer

An employer's recovery against a negligent defendant is reduced or barred by the negligence of an employee acting within the scope of their employment.

b. Conduct Imputed to Members of a Joint Enterprise

Joint enterprises trigger an exception to the general rule. If plaintiff is a member of a joint enterprise and is injured by the concurrent negligence of defendant, a third party outside the enterprise, and a member of the enterprise, plaintiff's recovery against defendant is reduced by the member's negligence. Plaintiff in that scenario also has a cause of action against the member of the joint enterprise.

c. Conduct Will be Imputed for Relational Damage Claims

Where plaintiff has a cause of action based upon personal injuries to another, plaintiff's recovery is reduced by the other individual's contributory negligence.

2. Fault May Be Imputed for Driving an Automobile with Owner's Permission

Some state statutes make the owner of a vehicle vicariously liable for the negligence of a person they allow to drive it. The R.3d Apportionment of Liability § 5, Comment c, notes that the driver's negligence is not imputed to the owner when the owner is the plaintiff. Injured parties might also have a direct negligence claim against the owner for negligent entrustment.

E. Plaintiff's Fault May Arise from Negligent Failure to Exercise Control

1. General Rule

If plaintiff has a duty to control the conduct of A and negligently fails to do so, A's contributory negligence (combined with that of plaintiff bringing the suit) reduces or bars plaintiff's recovery (depending on whether in a comparative or contributory jurisdiction) against defendant whose negligence was also a cause of plaintiff's injury.

2. Parent

A parent's ability to recover for injuries to plaintiff's child caused by a third party's negligence is reduced by the parent's negligence in protecting or supervising their child, who was too young to be responsible for their own safety. Parents are barred from recovery if the child is too young to care for itself, the child contributed to their own harm, and the parent failed to exercise reasonable care to prevent the child from being in the dangerous situation.

II. LAST CLEAR CHANCE

A. Historical Rule Mitigating Harshness of Contributory Negligence

The "last clear chance" doctrine now only survives in a dwindling minority of jurisdictions. It was intended to ameliorate the harsh effects of the contributory negligence bar, and it was primarily an intermediate stop on the road to comparative fault. Most jurisdictions adopting comparative fault have also abolished this doctrine. However, it may still apply in jurisdictions that have not adopted comparative fault and might be relevant in assessing the parties' relative fault.

The "last clear chance" doctrine applies only when defendant's negligent act occurs later than plaintiff's contributorily negligent act.

B. Doctrine Limited to Subsequent Negligence, Not Antecedent Negligence

The "last clear chance" doctrine applies only when Defendant's negligence occurs after that point in time when they discover (or should have discovered) Plaintiff's peril.

C. Relevant Scenarios

Jurisdictions vary with respect to the fact situations in which they will permit application of the rule depending on (1) the nature of plaintiff's predicament and (2) the state of defendant's attentiveness to plaintiff's peril.

1. Helpless Plaintiff

The helpless plaintiff is one who has negligently placed themself in a position of peril from which they are now helpless to escape in time to avoid the harm.

2. Inattentive Plaintiff

The inattentive plaintiff has negligently placed themself in a position of peril and has failed to observe the danger.

3. Observant Defendant

The observant defendant sees plaintiff in time to act to avoid the harm (assuming that defendant has a duty to so act under the circumstances), and observes plaintiff's helpless or inattentive condition, but thereafter is negligent in failing to act to prevent plaintiff's harm. Defendant's conduct need not be the source of plaintiff's danger.

The better rule is that plaintiff need not prove that defendant actually perceived plaintiff's helplessness or inattentiveness; it is sufficient to show that defendant saw plaintiff and that any normal person in defendant's situation would have realized that plaintiff was helpless or inattentive.

4. Inattentive Defendant

The inattentive defendant is one under a duty to maintain a lookout such that they would have seen the plaintiff in time to avoid the harm, and (had they been looking) would have perceived their helpless or inattentive condition and exercised reasonable care to avoid the harm. But due to defendant's negligence in failing to maintain the necessary lookout, they fail to see plaintiff in time and the injury occurs.

D. Comparative Negligence Subsumes Last Clear Chance Doctrine

The doctrine does not survive the adoption of comparative negligence; it is subsumed.

III. ASSUMPTION OF RISK

A. Traditional Rule

Under the traditional common law rule, if Plaintiff voluntarily assumes a risk of harm arising from the negligent or reckless conduct of defendant, Plaintiff cannot recover for such harm.

B. Relevance in Comparative Negligence Jurisdictions

Prior to the widespread adoption of comparative negligence, most jurisdictions recognized this defense, some by a different name. A few have limited it to (1) employer-employee cases and (2) express assumption of risk cases. Some courts analyze plaintiff's assumption of risk as affecting defendant's duty, e.g., negating defendant's duty to exercise care for plaintiff's safety.

There is a strong trend to abolish the defense of implied assumption of risk as a separate defense in negligence cases because it overlaps completely with the doctrine of contributory negligence.

C. Express Assumption of Risk

1. Defined

If plaintiff, by contract or otherwise, expressly agrees to accept a risk of harm arising from Defendant's negligent or reckless conduct, Plaintiff cannot recover for such harm, unless the agreement is invalid as contrary to public policy.

2. Construction

Such agreements are strictly construed against defendant and are not enforceable if plaintiff reasonably was ignorant of that term. They are unenforceable as to intentional torts, and most courts will not enforce them as to reckless conduct.

3. Public Policy

Such agreements are unenforceable when contrary to public policy.

D. Implied Assumption of Risk

1. Defined

If plaintiff knows, appreciates, and understands the risk of harm created by defendant's negligent or reckless conduct, and nevertheless voluntarily subjects themself to the risk by conduct which impliedly manifests their consent to accept the risk, then they are subject to the assumption of risk defense.

2. Proving Manifestation of Consent

The essence of the defense is consent to accept the risk, and therefore plaintiff's conduct must impliedly manifest that consent. The defendant asserting the defense bears the burden of proof.

3. Proving Knowledge and Appreciation of Risk

The defendant must also prove knowledge and appreciation of the risk. The consent must be informed. Defendant must show that Plaintiff knew of the existence of the risk and understood and appreciated its unreasonable character.

4. Proving Voluntariness

Plaintiff's assumption of the risk must be voluntary.

a. Reluctance

Plaintiff's conduct in proceeding into the zone of danger, even reluctantly or under protest, may ordinarily be deemed voluntary. Even if Plaintiff has no reasonable alternative but to encounter the risk, Plaintiff's doing so is voluntary unless one of two exceptions applies. Plaintiff does not voluntarily encounter the risk if defendant's tortious conduct is responsible for plaintiff's predicament and plaintiff must encounter the risk to avert harm to themself or another. Plaintiff does not voluntarily encounter the risk if it requires plaintiff to exercise or protect a right or privilege of which Defendant has no right to deprive him.

b. Independent Circumstances

Defendants are not liable for independent circumstances that compel a plaintiff to assume risk, even if the plaintiff believes they have no other choice. The assumption of risk is still voluntary because the compulsion does not come from the defendant's tortious conduct.

c. Public Policy Limits

The same public policies which negate an express assumption of risk should similarly prevent the finding of an implied assumption.

5. Violation of Statute

Plaintiff's assumption of risk bars or reduces their recovery based on defendant's violation of a statute unless this result would defeat a policy of the statute to place the entire responsibility for such harm on defendant.

6. Distinguished from Contributory Negligence

Implied assumption of risk and contributory negligence can have some overlap as defenses. In theory, implied assumption of the risk is plaintiff's implied voluntary consent to encounter a known danger created by defendant's negligence. Contributory negligence is unreasonable conduct. The former is a subjective test; the latter is objective.

E. No Liability for Inherent Hazards Not Arising from Negligence

Plaintiff chooses to engage in an activity that has certain inherent and commonly accepted risks, even though the others involved exercise proper care—e.g., hazardous employment, spectators and participants in some sporting events. As to these risks, there is no negligence, and therefore no assumption of the risk of negligent conduct. Thus, the doctrine does not properly apply. Some courts call this "primary" assumption of the risk. These are "no duty" or "no negligence" cases.

PART FIVE. ADVANCED DUTY TOPICS

I. OWNERS AND OCCUPIERS OF LAND

American law inherited from England's common law an approach to premises liability that classified persons entering a defendant's land as trespassers, licensees, or invitees. The duty owed by a defendant to these categories of entrants varied greatly. These rules can best be understood by identifying the policy considerations underlying them.

A. Possessors of Land Can Be Liable for Conditions and Activities on the Premises

The possessor is a person in actual occupation and control of the land, or if there is no such person, a person entitled to immediate occupation and control. "Possessor" accordingly includes renters as well as owners.

B. Liability Arises from Conditions and Activities on the Premises

The following special duty rules apply to claims against possessors of land for injuries resulting from either a condition of the premises or an activity being conducted on the premises. The benefits and burdens of these special rules apply to (1) the possessor of the land, (2) activities carried on by members of the possessor's household, and (3) activities conducted by and conditions created by another who is acting for the possessor.

C. Traditional Liability Rules Governing Categories of Persons Entering the Premises

1. General Rule

A possessor must exercise reasonable care to see that activities (conduct) and artificial conditions on the land do not harm their neighbors or passers-by on adjacent ways.

2. Artificial Versus Natural Conditions

a. Traditional Rule

The traditional rule has been that a defendant's liability to persons off their premises was limited to dangers created by artificial conditions or activities on their land. If a defendant altered the natural condition of the land to create or aggravate the risk, the defendant was subject to liability for unreasonable risks thereby created. Defendants were not liable for physical harm to persons outside the premises or to adjoining land resulting from natural conditions.

D. Trespassing Adults

1. Trespasser Defined

A trespasser is one who enters or remains upon the defendant's land without the defendant's consent or other legal privilege.

2. Traditional Rule

Under the traditional common law rule, a possessor is under no duty to exercise reasonable care (1) to make the premises reasonably safe for a trespasser (or to warn trespasser of hidden dangers), or (2) to carry on activities on the premises so as not to endanger a trespasser. But a defendant's immunity from liability to trespasser does not extend to intentional torts or to harm caused by a defendant's reckless ("willful and wanton") misconduct.

3. Exceptions to General Rules

Under the traditional common-law rules, courts often hold that a defendant owes a duty of reasonable care to an adult trespasser in certain fact situations.

a. Frequent Trespassers on Limited Area

When a defendant knows (or from facts within their knowledge ought to be aware) that trespassers constantly intrude upon a limited area of their premises, the defendant is subject to liability to such trespasser if they fail to exercise reasonable care (1) in the conduct of active operations on the premises which create a risk of serious bodily harm to a trespasser (R.2d § 334) and (2) to warn a trespasser of a dangerous artificial condition on the land (created or maintained by the defendant) which the defendant has reason to believe a trespasser will not discover and which creates a risk of serious bodily harm.

b. Discovered Trespassers

i. Rule

Once a defendant discovers the presence of a trespasser on their land, the defendant must exercise reasonable care to (a) conduct their activities with regard to the trespasser's safety, (b) warn trespassers of an artificial condition which poses a risk of serious bodily harm, if a defendant knows or has reason to know that a trespasser is in dangerous proximity to it and that a trespasser will probably not discover the danger or realize the risk, and (c) control those forces within their control which threaten a trespasser's safety, or give a trespasser an adequate warning of them.

ii. Duty to Rescue

A defendant may have to exercise reasonable care to come to the aid of a discovered trespasser who is injured or in peril on the defendant's premises, even though the defendant is not responsible for the trespasser's situation.

4. Restatement (Third) Distinguishes Between Flagrant and Non-Flagrant Trespasser

The Restatement (Third) duty to a flagrant trespasser is the same as the traditional common law duty to all trespassers—not to injure them by intentional or "willful and wanton" conduct.

The Restatement provides no definition of the term "flagrant," but the comment discusses its meaning, summarized as "egregious or atrocious." According to R.3d, flagrant trespassers are the only entrants not owed a duty of reasonable care; but if the flagrant trespasser reasonably appears to be imperiled and (1) helpless or (2) unable to protect themselves, the possessor *does* owe the flagrant trespasser that duty.

E. Trespassing Children ("Attractive Nuisance" Doctrine)

1. Rule (Factors)

Most (but not all) jurisdictions have special rules applicable to child trespassers, sometimes called the "turntable" or "attractive nuisance" doctrine. A possessor of land is subject to liability for physical harm to trespassing children caused by an artificial condition upon the land if a defendant fails to exercise reasonable care to eliminate the danger to such children or otherwise protect them. Courts consider the following factors.

a. Knowledge of Child Trespassers

A defendant knows or has reason to know that the place where the condition exists is one where children are likely to trespass. It is not enough that child trespassers are merely foreseeable. A defendant need not inspect the premises to see if children trespass or if such dangerous conditions are present. A defendant is held to what they know about the premises and what they can reasonably anticipate based on that knowledge.

b. Shift from Child "Attracted" by Condition to the Foreseeability of Child Trespassers

It is enough that children who do foreseeably trespass can be expected to encounter the condition. It need not be an open and obvious condition, and the child need not even discover it prior to their injury.

c. Knowledge of Condition

A defendant must know or have reason to know of the condition and must realize or should realize that it involves an unreasonable risk of death or serious bodily harm to such children. A defendant need not have created the condition but merely maintained it or permitted it to exist.

d. Artificial Condition

The doctrine applies only to artificial conditions (not activities or natural conditions) upon the land.

e. Child's Lack of Knowledge of Risk

The child, because of their youth, does not (a) discover the condition or (b) realize the risk. While some courts have established arbitrary age limits (e.g., 14), the better (and Restatement) view does not. Nonetheless, the younger the child, the more dangers they will not understand or appreciate.

f. Utility to the Defendant

Courts weigh the risks of the condition against the utility of a condition when considering the burdens on the defendant. Courts consider whether the burden of eliminating the danger is outweighed by the risk to the children involved.

g. Defendant's Conduct Is Not Reasonable

The defendant fails to exercise reasonable care to eliminate the danger or otherwise protect the children.

2. General Duty of Reasonable Care as Alternate Rule

The duty created by R.2d § 339 approximates that which would be imposed by a general duty to exercise reasonable care toward children whose trespasses can be anticipated.

F. Licensees

1. Licensee Defined

A "licensee" is a person who has a privilege to enter or remain on a defendant's land but is not an invitee. Licensees include a person who enters a defendant's land with consent but solely for the entrant's own purpose, such as social guests attending a party. A defendant's consent may be express or implied from their conduct, or from custom, usages in the community, or prior dealings.

2. Duty to Licensees

A defendant's duty to a licensee is similar (but not identical) to that owed to a discovered trespasser.

a. Intentional and Reckless Conduct

A defendant is subject to liability to a licensee for intentional and reckless ("willful and wanton") misconduct.

b. Active Operations (Latent Dangers)

In conducting their activities on the premises, a defendant must exercise reasonable care for the safety of licensees, provided (i) licensors expect that licensees will not discover or realize the danger and (ii) licensees do not know or have reason to know of the defendant's activities and the risk involved.

c. Latent Conditions

A defendant is subject to liability for physical harm caused to a licensees by a condition of the land if (i) the defendant knows or has reason to know of the condition, and should realize that it involves unreasonable risk of harm, and that the licensees will not discover or realize the danger, (ii) the defendant fails to exercise reasonable care to make the condition safe, or to warn the licensee of the condition and the risk involved, (iii) the licensees do not know or have reason to know the condition and risk involved. A defendant must have actual knowledge of the condition (or of facts which are the equivalent of such knowledge). They have no duty to inspect or discover such conditions.

G. Invitee

1. Invitee Defined

An "invitee" is either a public invitee or a business visitor.

2. Duty to Invitees

a. Rule

As to invitees, there is no duty limitation. A defendant must exercise reasonable care for their safety with respect to the conduct of activities and the maintenance of the premises.

b. Open and Obvious Dangers

The emerging and better view is that the obviousness of the danger is merely one fact bearing on whether a defendant was negligent or on a plaintiff's contributory fault or assumption of risk and is not per se a duty limitation.

c. Acts of Third Persons

A defendant must exercise reasonable care to warn and protect their business invitees against foreseeable harm by third persons on the premises, and to discover that such acts by third persons are being done or are likely to occur.

H. Other Privileged Entrants

1. General Rule

One who enters a defendant's land by virtue of a privilege other than that created by the defendant's consent is ordinarily classified a licensee.

2. Public Employees Are Invitees

Public employees who are required by law regularly to enter a defendant's premises to make inspections, deliveries, or collections necessary to the defendant's operations.

3. Fire and Police Personnel Are Licensees

Firefighters, police, and other professional emergency responders have a privilege to enter premises in the course of their work but are typically classified as licensees.

4. Professional Emergency Responders

The possessor's duty to professional emergency responders may be limited by the so-called "firefighter's rule." Typically, the rule limits only a defendant's negligence liability, and in some jurisdictions operates only to bar a plaintiff with respect to injuries caused by the misconduct that created the risk which necessitated a plaintiff's presence on the premises.

5. Recreational Entrants

Most states now have statutes that negate any duty of reasonable care to persons permitted to come upon a defendant's land for recreational purposes (e.g., hunting, fishing, swimming), provided the defendant makes no charge to, or receives no consideration from, the visitor.

I. Modern Trend to Reject Categories in Favor of General Duty of Ordinary Care

About half the states have abolished the tedious classification of entrants upon land—either completely, by merging the licensee and invitee categories—substituting a general duty of ordinary care under the circumstances, one of the circumstances being the status of a plaintiff on the land.

J. Lessors

1. General Rule

Under the traditional rule, a lessor of real property is not liable to their lessee (or anyone else on the premises with the lessee's consent) for physical harm sustained by such persons during the term of the lease because of a condition of the leased premises, whether that condition arose or existed before or after the lessee took possession.

2. Exceptions

a. Latent Hazards

When the lessor knows or has reason to know of a condition, whether natural or artificial, involving unreasonable risk of harm at the time the lessee takes possession, and fails to make the lessee aware of the condition, is subject to liability for physical harm sustained as a result of that condition.

i. Lessor's Knowledge

The lessor need not inspect the premises to discover such conditions. They must know or have reason to know of the condition and realize or should realize the risk involved.

ii. Latency

The danger must be latent, in the sense that it may be expected that the lessee will not discover the condition or the extent of the risk. A defendant's duty is only to disclose the existence of the condition. There is no liability for open and obvious hazards, however dangerous.

iii. Persons Protected

A defendant's liability extends to the lessee and all persons on the premises with their consent or by their right.

b. Persons Outside the Premises

i. Pre-Existing Conditions

If there is a condition on the land existing at the time the lessee takes possession, which the lessor realizes or should realize may unreasonably endanger persons outside the premises, the lessor's liability to such persons survives the transfer of possession to the lessee.

ii. Conditions and Activities During Lease

The lessor is generally not liable for conditions on the premises that come into existence after the lessee takes possession or for the lessee's activities on the premises.

iii. Contract to Repair

In some jurisdictions, negligent failure to perform the lessor's contract to repair the premises subjects them to liability to persons off the premises.

c. Public Admission

When the lessor leases their premises for a purpose which involves the admission of the public, they must exercise reasonable care to inspect the premises and remedy unreasonably dangerous conditions which exist when possession is transferred, if they have reason to expect that the public will be admitted before the lessee has remedied the condition.

i. Lessee's Agreement

The lessee's agreement to make the repair does not exonerate the lessor unless the lessor could reasonably expect them to perform in time.

ii. Scope

A plaintiff need not be a business invitee of the lessee or lessor, nor need there be an admission charge. But a defendant's liability is limited to those parts of the premises open to the public under the lease, and to persons entering for the contemplated purpose.

d. Retained Control

i. Scope

The lessor is subject to liability for physical harm caused by a dangerous condition located on a part of the premises which the lessee is entitled to use and over which the lessor has retained control, provided the lessor by the exercise of reasonable care could have (1) discovered the condition and the unreasonable risk and (2) made it reasonably safe.

ii. Lease Exculpatory Clause

A clause in the lease exonerating the lessor from this liability may or may not be effective as to the tenant but is always ineffective as to third persons not party to the lease.

iii. Criminal Violence

The cases are divided on whether a landlord is subject to liability to their tenants for criminal violence by third persons occurring in common areas of the building, based on their failure to provide adequate security.

e. **Agreement to Repair**

i. **Scope**

The lessor's liability extends to the tenant and all others on the premises with the tenant's consent. The extent of their duty is defined by the contract.

ii. **Notice**

Unless otherwise provided by the lease, the lessor's duty is only to exercise reasonable care to make the repairs after they have notice of the need for them. They need not inspect the premises.

iii. **Consideration**

The contract to repair must be supported by consideration. As yet, there is no liability for failure to perform a gratuitous promise to repair.

iv. **Services**

The lessor may be liable for failure to provide a service required by the lease (e.g. heat, light) where the premises cannot be safely used without it.

f. **Negligent Repairs**

A lessor who undertakes (or purports to undertake) repair of the leased premises is subject to liability for physical harm resulting from the condition if (1) the lessee neither knows nor should know that (2) the repairs made the land more dangerous for use or gives the deceptive appearance of safety.

g. **Independent Contractors**

The lessor cannot escape their responsibilities by delegating the work to an independent contractor. They are liable for the contractor's negligence in performing the foregoing duties to the same extent as if the contractor were their employee.

h. **General Duty of Reasonable Care**

Several states have abolished the foregoing limited rules and substituted the rule that the lessor is under a general duty of reasonable care under the circumstances, either generally or only for residential leases.

i. **Statutes May Impose Further Duties**

Statutes and ordinances in many jurisdictions impose duties on lessors which have the effect of expanding their common law tort duties, particularly their duty to keep the premises in repair.

II. EMPLOYER'S LIABILITY TO EMPLOYEES

A. Common Law Duties of Employer to Employee

1. Safe Place to Work

The employer must provide their employee with reasonably safe working conditions and warn the employee of unsafe conditions which the employer should anticipate will not be discovered by the employee.

2. Defenses

The employer's defenses include assumption of risk, contributory negligence, and co-worker negligence.

B. Workers' Compensation

1. Workers' Compensation Acts

a. Introduction

Workers' compensation acts make the employer strictly liable to pay scheduled benefits for most employee injuries occurring "in the course of" and "arising out of" the employment. These scope-of-employment issues are often litigated.

b. Type of Occurrence

Ordinarily workers' compensation is available only for "accidental" injuries. If a plaintiff's injury was caused by environmental conditions over a period of time, their remedy arises under an occupational diseases act. Their remedy under the act is their exclusive remedy against the employer, even if for some reason the particular injury is not compensable. The employee has no common law tort action against their employer, except in rare instances.

PART SIX. STRICT LIABILITY

I. STRICT LIABILITY FOR ANIMALS

A. Intruding Animals

1. General Rule

Owners or possessors of all animals, including domesticated ones such as fowl, livestock, birds, and reptiles are strictly liable for physical harm resulting from the trespass of their animals on the property of another.

2. Exceptions

a. Cats and Dogs

Except where imposed by statute or ordinance, possessors of dogs and cats are not strictly liable for their intrusions under the general rule.

b. Livestock Straying on Highways v. Driven to Highway

Owners or possessors of livestock that stray onto a public highway are not strictly liable when the animals contribute to a highway accident. Rather, negligence rules apply in the majority of jurisdictions, thus allowing for consideration of the driver's conduct, the owner's conduct, and other factors. In contrast, when possessors of livestock *drive* the livestock on a highway, strict liability applies to resulting harms.

c. Liability for Livestock on Property ("Fencing Statutes")

The traditional English rule holds possessors of livestock strictly liable for their intrusions on the property of others. This is popularly known as a "fence in" requirement because of the functional incentives that strict liability creates toward fencing animals in. Many jurisdictions follow this approach as does the Third Restatement. Other jurisdictions follow a "fence out" rule allowing an affirmative defense asserting that the plaintiff should have protected their property by fencing out livestock intrusions.

B. Other Harm Caused by Animals

1. Domestic Animals

Owners or possessors of domestic animals are generally held to a negligence standard for harms caused, reflecting the rationale that these animals are not generally abnormally dangerous. Strict liability will only apply if (a) the owner or possessor knew or had reason to know that the animal had a harmful or dangerous propensity or trait, and (b) that particular trait or propensity was the cause of the harm.

2. Wild Animals

Wild animals are generally defined as those that are not generally domesticated in that geographic region and those that, if unrestrained, would likely cause physical harm. Both the owners and possessors of wild animals are strictly liable for all harm done by the animal as a result of a harmful or dangerous propensity or characteristic of such animals.

3. Scope of Strict Liability

According to the Restatement (Second) of Torts, plaintiffs cannot recover if they "knowingly and unreasonably" subjected themself to the risk.

4. Comparative Fault

If the plaintiff was negligent in failing to take reasonable precautions, then the plaintiff's recovery in a strict liability claim is reduced in proportion to their comparative fault.

II. STRICT LIABILITY FOR ABNORMALLY DANGEROUS ACTIVITIES

A. *Rylands v. Fletcher*: The Original Rule

Strict liability for abnormally dangerous activities originated in the 1868 English case of *Rylands v. Fletcher*, which held the defendant strictly liable for damage to the plaintiff's mine caused by water which escaped from defendant's reservoir. The court reasoned that because a reservoir was a "non-natural use" of land in that area and the plaintiff's harm was caused by the "escape" of the water from the defendant's land, strict liability governs.

B. *Rylands v. Fletcher*: The Modern Rule

1. General Rule

Defendants may be held liable for harm resulting from "abnormally dangerous activities" (formerly called "ultrahazardous" activities) on their property. It is no longer necessary that the activity was conducted on the defendant's land, or that the harm was caused by something which "escapes."

2. The Second Restatement Factors

a. Extent of Risk

Courts consider whether there is a high degree of risk or harm to others, and whether it is likely that the harm will be great.

b. Ability to Eliminate Risk

Courts consider whether the risk can be eliminated by the exercise of reasonable care.

c. Common Usage

Courts consider whether the activity is a matter of common usage. The more unusual the activity, the greater the justification for strict liability.

d. Location

Courts consider whether the activity is inappropriate to the place where it is being conducted.

e. Social Utility

Courts consider whether the activity's value to the community is outweighed by its dangerous attributes.

3. The Third Restatement Reduces the Analysis Down to Two Central Factors

The lengthier list of factors from the Second Restatement yields questions of predictability and consistency. The Third Restatement pares it down to two core inquiries: (1) whether the activity creates a foreseeable and highly significant risk of physical harm even when all actors exercise reasonable care; and (2) whether the activity is not one of common usage.

4. Activities Likely to Be Subject to Strict Liability

Blasting or the use of explosives are said to be typical examples of activities that likely rise to strict liability. Other activities that are good candidates for strict liability include crop dusting, pest control and fumigation, the escape of hazardous wastes, other high-energy activities (e.g., rocket testing, pile driving, oil well blowouts), and perhaps large fireworks displays.

5. Alternative Theories: Trespass or Nuisance

A dwindling minority of U.S. jurisdictions rejects the rule by name but usually reach the same result via trespass or nuisance theories.

C. Liability Limitations

1. Scope of Liability

The harm must result from the risk that gives rise to the abnormal danger. It is generally no defense that it was precipitated by an unforeseeable intervening cause. Thus, the defendant will not be held strictly liable if the plaintiff intentionally or negligently trespasses on the defendant's land where the activity is being conducted. And the defendant is not strictly liable to the extent that the plaintiff's harm results from the abnormally sensitive characteristics of the plaintiff.

2. Defenses and Apportionment of Liability

According to R.2d, assumption of the risk is a defense, but contributory negligence is not except when the plaintiff "knowingly and unreasonably subjects himself to the risk." According to R.3d, if the plaintiff has been contributorily negligent in failing to take reasonable precautions, the plaintiff's recovery in a strict liability claim for physical harm is reduced by the plaintiff's proportionate share of comparative fault.

3. Federal Tort Claims Act

There is no strict liability under the FTCA.

PART SEVEN. PRODUCTS LIABILITY

I. OVERVIEW OF PRODUCTS LIABILITY

Liability for physical harm caused by an unsafe product may be based on one or more of three legal theories: negligence, breach of warranty, or strict tort liability.

A. Injuries Arising from Products Can Be Pleaded as Negligence

Ordinary negligence principles apply to claims arising from product injuries that are pleaded under a negligence theory (as compared to claims pleaded under warranty or strict products liability).

1. Historic Privity Limitations

Prior to *MacPherson v. Buick Motor Co.* (N.Y. 1916), the general rule was that the manufacturer or other seller of an unsafe product was not liable in negligence to the user or consumer absent privity of contract between plaintiff and defendant (*Winterbottom v. Wright*)—that is, unless plaintiff had bought the product directly from defendant.

2. Modern Defendants Liable to Purchasers and Foreseeable Users or Consumers

Absent these historic privity limitations, modern product defendants are subject to liability not only to the ultimate purchaser or lessee of the product but also to all foreseeable users or consumers, and to all other persons foreseeably exposed to the risk it creates. Further, most jurisdictions allow recovery by "bystanders" (persons other than the above) whose exposure to the risk of injury was foreseeable.

3. Potential Product Defendants in Negligence

a. Product Manufacturers

Negligence in the manufacturing process includes negligent design; errors or omissions during production; failure to properly test or inspect; unsafe containers or packaging; inadequate warnings or directions for use; and misrepresentation. A subsequent seller's failure to inspect does not relieve the manufacturer of liability for its negligence.

b. Subsequent Product Sellers

Subsequent sellers (e.g., distributors, retailers) may also be negligent in failing to warn of the existence of an unsafe condition or otherwise protect the user. Under the majority view, such seller is liable only for dangers of which it knew or had reason to know; it has no duty to inspect or test the product to discover latent dangers.

c. Other Product Suppliers

Commercial lessors, and others who furnish chattels (tangible personal property) commercially, are liable for negligence in furnishing an unsafe chattel; their duty includes a duty to inspect. Other suppliers (e.g., donors, gratuitous bailors) are subject to liability if they knew or had reason to know that the product was unsafe. Supplying a chattel to one knowing or having reason to know they will incompetently use it also subjects the supplier to liability for resulting physical harm.

d. Independent Contractors

Contractors who make, rebuild, or repair a chattel are subject to similar rules.

B. Product Harms May Also Yield Breach of Warranty Claims

1. Types of Warranties

Warranty is not a tort concept. But breach of certain warranties gives rise to an action for resulting physical harm, which makes warranty claims part of the law of "products liability." The following warranties, codified by the Uniform Commercial Code, are involved.

a. Express Warranty

Express warranties are promissory assertions of fact or descriptions that are explicitly part of the basis of the bargain in purchasing the product.

b. Implied Warranty of Merchantability

The implied warranty of merchantability implies minimum standards of product quality including safety. Defendant must be a "merchant" with respect to goods of that kind.

c. Implied Warranty of Fitness for a Particular Purpose

This warranty arises when the buyer relies on the seller to furnish goods suitable for a particular specified use.

2. Strict Liability Applies to Breach of Express and Implied Warranties

Liability for breach of warranty is strict. The consumer need not prove negligence or other fault.

3. Limitations to Pursue Breach of Warranty Claims

The principal limitations on liability for breach of warranty are: (1) the seller must be given prompt notice of the breach, (2) the buyer must have relied upon the warranty, and (3) the seller in certain cases can limit or disclaim these warranties.

4. Historic Privity Limitations on Warranty Claims Lifted

As in the case of negligence, liability for breach of warranty was once limited to the parties to the contract of sale. The first exception was in cases involving products intended for human consumption, and then for intimate bodily use. Beginning in *Henningsen v. Bloomfield Motors, Inc.* (N.J. 1960), courts abolished the privity limitation as to the implied warranties.

C. Strict Tort Liability for Defective Products

Strict tort liability for defective products was first adopted in *Greenman v. Yuba Power Products, Inc.* (Cal. 1963). It is now the governing law in most jurisdictions.

1. Rule

Product defendants are strictly liable for any resulting physical or property harms to plaintiff caused by a defective condition of a product which renders it unreasonably dangerous, if (1) the product was in the same condition as when it left defendant's control, and (2) defendant is engaged in the business of furnishing such products.

2. Product Defendants in Strict Liability

Strict products liability extends to (1) the producer (manufacturer, processor, assembler, packager, or bottler) of the product and of the defective component part, and (2) all those in its distribution chain—wholesaler, distributor, retailer, and commercial lessors and bailors. Defendant must be "engaged in the business" of dealing in that product, but such product need not be their principal business.

3. Rationales for Strict Products Liability

Support for such strict products liability is based on some combination of rationales relating to consumer expectations, cost distribution, deterrence, proof considerations, litigation practicalities, manufacturer power, and fairness.

4. Product Defined

"Product" includes all forms of tangible personal property (chattels).

5. Elements of Plaintiff's Claim

In a strict products liability claim, plaintiff must prove that (1) the product was "defective" (and perhaps also that the defect made the product "unreasonably dangerous"); (2) the defect was a factual and proximate cause of plaintiff's harm; and (3) the product was defective when it left defendant's possession and control.

6. Proving a Product Is Defective

a. Types of Defects

In most jurisdictions, defendant is subject to liability to plaintiff only if the product contains a "defect" which renders it "unreasonably dangerous" to the user or consumer. The defect may be in the product itself, in its container or packaging, or in the documentation accompanying the product.

The types of defects include:

i. Design Defects

Design defects are those that are inherent in the product's design and thus are common to every unit of the product on the market. In design defect cases, the product is manufactured and sold exactly as the manufacturer intended it to be. The plaintiff's argument therefore is that the manufacturer's intended design was flawed and unsafe.

ii. Manufacturing Defects

A manufacturing defect is one that occurs in a particular product unit because of an error or omission in manufacturing, assembly, or processing. The product was *not* marketed or sold in the condition the manufacturer intended.

iii. Defects in Warnings or Instructions for Use (Informational Defects)

A product may be defective and unsafe because of inadequate directions for use or inadequate safety warnings (e.g., informational defects). Warnings and directions for use may be defective if they do not adequately and effectively communicate not just that there is a danger but its nature and extent, the possible consequences of encountering the risk, and, if applicable, alternatives that will minimize or negate the risk.

(a) No Duty to Warn of Open and Obvious Risks

A product that fails to warn of an open and obvious danger, or a danger that is common knowledge, may not be defective. But if defendant can anticipate harm despite the obviousness of the danger, the product could be defective if it could have been made safer, or if a warning could be found to have effectively prevented the harm.

(b) Plaintiff Must Also Prove Causation

Plaintiff must still prove causation—that is, that they would have read, understood, and heeded the warning or instructions that should have accompanied the product if the manufacturer had provided them. But courts often allow an inference that plaintiff would have read the proposed warning or instructions, and defendant will have the burden of rebutting that inference.

(c) Limited to Known or Knowable Risks

Almost all courts have held that a manufacturer has no duty to warn of risks that were not known or knowable when it sold the product.

(d) The Learned Intermediary Rule

When a physician buys prescription drugs or medical devices with physician-appropriate warnings, the manufacturer ordinarily can rely on the physician to protect the ultimate user. The manufacturer has no duty to provide a warning aimed at, or communicated to, the consumer. However, the rule may be otherwise if the manufacturer markets its drugs directly to consumers.

(e) Sophisticated Users

Similar rules apply to "sophisticated users"—those users who are already aware or should be aware of the product's dangers (e.g., members of a trade or profession who are presumed to have common knowledge of the risks).

b. Tests to Prove a Product Is "Unreasonably Dangerous"

Most jurisdictions follow the Restatement (Second) of Torts § 402A and require that the product be not only "defective" but also "unreasonably dangerous."

i. Risk-Benefit Balancing Test

The popular "risk-benefit" or "risk-utility" test requires the trier of fact to balance (1) the safety risks of the product as designed, and (2) the utility and other benefits of the product as designed, against (3) the safety risks and benefits of the product if it had been designed as plaintiff claims it should have been. In practice, this is the same kind of "Learned Hand Test" balancing that would occur if the cause of action were based on negligence. The difference is that the focus is on the *product* and not on the *conduct* of the manufacturer.

(a) Proving a Feasible Alternative Design

As part of plaintiff's risk-utility case, plaintiff will usually try to show that there was a feasible alternative design—that is, some practicable, cost-effective, and reasonable way to have designed the product that would likely have prevented plaintiff's harm.

(b) Consumer Expectation Test

Another popular test is known as the "consumer expectation" test, derived from the language of § 402A comment *i*, requiring the product to be dangerous "to an extent beyond that which would be contemplated by the ordinary consumer who purchases it, with the ordinary knowledge common to the community as to its characteristics."

(c) **Presumed Seller's Knowledge Test**

Another test implements the strict liability standard directly: would the seller have been negligent in marketing the product if the seller had known of its harmful or dangerous condition?

c. **Unavoidably Unsafe Products**

Some highly useful products (e.g., certain drugs and vaccines) may be "unavoidably unsafe" because of inherent dangerous side effects which "in the present state of human knowledge" cannot be eliminated. Such products, "properly prepared, and accompanied by proper directions and warnings," are not defective or unreasonably dangerous.

d. **Food Products**

In the case of food products that contain a harm-causing ingredient (e.g., a sharp one-inch chicken bone in a chicken enchilada, a piece of glass in a serving of slaw), most courts hold that the ingredient constitutes a defect if a reasonable consumer would not expect the food product to contain that ingredient, regardless of whether the ingredient is foreign (the glass) or natural (the chicken bone).

e. **Intrinsically Dangerous Products**

Certain intrinsically dangerous products (e.g., tobacco, firearms, and ammunition) are not per se defective even if they could be made safer or not sold at all. The risks arise from the intended use of the product, not from anything wrong with it.

7. **The Restatement (Third) of Torts: Products Liability**

a. **Revised Approaches to Proving a Defective Product**

The new products liability provisions in the Restatement (Third) of Torts: Products Liability now explicitly recognize the three categories of product defects: manufacturing defects, design defects, and informational defects (warnings and directions for use). Sellers remain strictly liable for manufacturing defects, but the Restatement's proposed liability for design defects is close to a negligence standard, imposing liability only for "foreseeable risks of harm" that could have been avoided by the adoption of a "reasonable alternative design" (§ 2(b)) or by "reasonable instructions or warnings" (§ 2(c)). As an alternative, plaintiff can recover if they can prove that the product as designed, or the warning, failed to comply with an applicable safety statute or administrative regulation (§ 4(a)).

Only a small number of jurisdictions have adopted the Restatement (Third) approach to products liability.

b. **Prescription Drug and Medical Device Liability**

The Restatement (Third) further restricts liability for defective prescription drugs and medical devices. Under § 6(c), a prescription drug or medical device is not defective in design unless the foreseeable risk of harm is so "great in relation to its foreseeable therapeutic benefits that reasonable health-care providers, knowing of such foreseeable risks and therapeutic benefits, would not prescribe the drug or medical device for any class of patients." Under § 6(d), manufacturers need only warn "health care providers" unless the manufacturer "knows or has reason to know that health-care providers will not be in a position to reduce the risks of harm in accordance with the instructions or warnings." Only in that case does the manufacturer owe an adequate warning to the patient.

Strict liability will still apply to drugs and medical products for manufacturing defects.

8. Type of Harms Recoverable

Strict products liability is almost always limited to damages for physical harm to persons or other property, and consequential damages resulting from physical harm, attributable to the defect. Pecuniary loss resulting from a defect in the product without an accidental injury to persons or other property or resulting from non-accidental physical damage confined to the product itself is recoverable only under a breach of warranty or contract theory. This is known as the "economic loss" rule.

9. Defenses

a. Contributory Negligence

Prior to the adoption of comparative fault, most jurisdictions held that plaintiff's "ordinary" contributory negligence was not a defense to strict products liability. Today, some jurisdictions adopting comparative negligence permit that type of contributory negligence to reduce plaintiff's damages; others continue to hold that such negligence is not a damage-reducing factor.

b. Implied Assumption of Risk

Prior to the adoption of comparative fault, in most jurisdictions implied assumption of the risk—that is, unreasonably proceeding to use the product after discovering the defect—was a complete bar to recovery under strict products liability. Today, in most comparative fault jurisdictions, implied assumption of the risk is only a damage-reducing factor, and in many, it is not even a separate concept, having been merged into contributory fault. It remains a complete bar in a few states.

c. Unforeseeable Misuse of the Product

Plaintiff's misuse of the product is not a defense at all but is relevant in plaintiff's prima facie case. If an unforeseeable misuse of the product causes plaintiff's injury, defendant is not liable, since either the product was not defective, or any defect was not a cause in fact of plaintiff's harm. But if plaintiff's use, even though not an intended use of the product, was a foreseeable misuse (e.g., standing on a chair, a child putting a toy in their mouth), the product may be found defective because it was not designed to be reasonably safe in light of the foreseeable misuse.

d. Statutes of Limitations and Repose

If plaintiff's claim is for personal injury and based on a tort theory, the statute of limitations does not begin to run until the product injures plaintiff. This can result in liability for some very old products.

Legislation in some jurisdictions imposes an additional limitation period, called a "statute of repose," which runs from the date of the product's manufacture or first sale. Although statutes of repose are typically long (e.g., 12 years), they can have the effect of barring a claim before it even arose.

e. Disclaimers Do Not Block Claims

A purported disclaimer of strict products liability is ineffective.

f. State of the Art Design

In some jurisdictions, defendants can defend a design defect case by showing that they designed the product in accordance with the "state of the art" practices at the time they manufactured and first sold it.

g. Preemption

Federal preemption is an increasingly important defense in products liability cases. Under the supremacy clause of the U.S. Constitution, federal law is supreme over state law. Thus, when federal legislation or regulations expressly or impliedly preempt a particular field (e.g., statutes governing cigarette warnings, certain medical products), state tort law either cannot regulate the field at all or cannot impose a lower standard than the applicable federal law. Preemption can apply in negligence and strict products liability cases.

h. Statutory Presumption of Non-Defectiveness

Some state statutes provide that when a product complies with a federal or state regulation concerning that product, there is a rebuttable presumption that the product is not defective with respect to its design or informational characteristics.

10. Nondelegable Duties

The manufacturer is usually not liable unless the product was defective when it left its control. An exception applies where the manufacturer places in the stream of commerce an unfinished or unassembled product that must be assembled or finished by its dealer, who in doing so creates the defect.

11. Post-Sale Duties

In some jurisdictions, when a defective condition arises post-sale, a manufacturer may be subject to liability for failure to "retrofit" a previously marketed product with safety devices (or to provide appropriate warnings). This obligation arises if locating current users and furnishing such devices or warnings is not an unreasonable burden compared to the risk of injury inherent in the product without them. This liability arises even though the product was arguably not unsafe when the manufacturer first marketed it.

PART EIGHT. SURVIVAL AND WRONGFUL DEATH

I. SURVIVAL AND WRONGFUL DEATH

A. Survival of Tort Actions

1. Common Law Rule

Historically, no cause of action for personal torts survived the death of either the tortfeasor or the person injured, regardless of the cause of death.

2. Statutory Modifications

All jurisdictions have altered the common law rule through statutory modifications. About one-third of the states provide that either (a) all tort actions or (b) all tort actions except defamation survive the death of either a plaintiff or a defendant. The rest have a wide variety of inclusions and exclusions.

3. Personal Injury Actions

A survival action is a legal cause of action that survives a person's death. Personal injury actions survive in almost all jurisdictions, but sometimes with limitations on the damages recoverable. In a few states, personal injury actions do not survive the injured person's death unless as part of an action for that death. In most states, wrongful death actions survive the death of the tortfeasor.

4. Damages

Damages are generally measured as if no one had died, except that the victim's death terminates the accumulation of certain kinds of future damages (pain and suffering, mental distress, medical expenses, loss of earnings, disability, etc.) that the victim otherwise could have recovered based on their life expectancy.

5. Punitive Damages

A plaintiff's right to seek punitive damages may cease if a defendant dies. In some states however, if the injured person's death may do the same, but in many jurisdictions, the estate of the decedent may seek punitive damages.

6. Medical, Funeral, and Burial Expenses

In some cases, funeral, burial expenses, and the decedent's last medical expenses may be elements of damages in the survival action, or, in the alternative, in the wrongful death action. In some jurisdictions, medical, funeral, and burial expenses are a separate claim altogether.

Decedent's estate would have no claim for medical, funeral, or burial expenses against a defendant to the extent that these expenses are causally unrelated to decedent's cause of action against defendant.

7. Defenses

A survival action is just a continuation of the decedent's tort case, so all the same defenses or liability limitations will apply. The fact that a beneficiary's negligence contributed to the death is not relevant and does not affect the damages recoverable. However, in a joint-and-several liability jurisdiction the defendant can seek contribution from the negligent beneficiary, thereby indirectly reducing or negating his share. In a several liability jurisdiction, fault will be apportioned, so defendant's proportional share may be lower due to the fault of a beneficiary, thereby reducing the estate's recovery.

B. Wrongful Death

1. Common Law Rule

Since *Baker v. Bolton* (Eng. 1808), the general common law rule has been that one whose tortious conduct results in the death of a person is not liable to that person's survivors (Hawaii alone to the contrary).

2. Statutory and Other Modifications

Beginning in 1846, statutes were passed in England and American jurisdictions creating a remedy for wrongful death, also known as "death statutes."

3. Basis

Any tort theory that would have supported a personal injury action will support an action for wrongful death.

4. Types of Statutes

There are two basic types of wrongful death acts.

a. Lord Campbell's Act

Most states have adopted a wrongful death act modeled after the 1846 English statute that creates a new cause of action for the benefit of specified near relatives of the decedent. This would be because the decedent would have had a cause of action had they been merely injured and not killed in the tortious act.

b. Survival

A few jurisdictions have a "survival"-type statute which preserves the cause of action that vested decedent's death and expands it to include the damages resulting from the death itself.

c. Statutory Torts

Most statutory tort actions (F.E.L.A., dram shop acts) have their own provisions for recovery in the event of death. If not, then an appropriate general death act will apply.

5. Concurrence of Remedies

If a plaintiff survived their injuries for a time before dying from them, in most jurisdictions either a survival action or a wrongful death action or both may be brought independently or in the same lawsuit. In some, the causes of action merge. In others, plaintiff's survivors must elect one or the other. In a few others, the survival action abates in whole or in part.

6. Beneficiaries

The beneficiaries are the relatives or classes of relatives designated in the wrongful death statute. Decedent's spouse and children, if any, receive the award to the exclusion of all other surviving relatives. If there is no surviving spouse or children, then typically certain other close relatives (parents, siblings, grandparents) may be able to claim pecuniary (monetary) loss but only if and to the extent they can show that they have been receiving, or probably would have received, support or services from the decedent. In some cases, parents or siblings may be able to recover nonpecuniary loss.

In most jurisdictions, stepchildren and unmarried cohabitants do not qualify as beneficiaries. However, some wrongful death statutes include domestic partners who have legal status, and a few include stepchildren.

Generally, a wrongful death claim survives the sole beneficiary who dies prior to judgment in the wrongful death case.

7. Damages

A wide variety of rules govern the elements of damages recoverable. The general types of statutes are:

a. Loss to the Survivors

Elements of damages include:

i. Pecuniary Loss

Many statutes include "pecuniary loss," which involves at the very least the present value of the loss of support, services, and contributions the beneficiaries would have received in the future but for the death. In some jurisdictions, this includes loss of a probable inheritance.

ii. Nonpecuniary Loss

Nonpecuniary loss—loss of plaintiff's society, companionship, love and affection—is recoverable in some jurisdictions, either by specific statutory language or by judicial construction of the term "pecuniary loss." A few allow recovery for the survivor's mental anguish (bereavement). In the case of decedents whose earnings were small or zero at the time of death (minor children, elderly parents), the entire claim may be based on nonpecuniary loss.

iii. Medical and Other Expenses

Medical and other expenses, such as funeral and burial costs, ordinarily may be recovered by the survivor paying them, either as part of the death action or separately.

b. Loss to the Estate

A minority of jurisdictions measure damages by the loss to the estate—decedent's future earnings minus their personal expenses, or their probable future accumulations or net savings. A few jurisdictions permit recovery of both the loss to survivors and the loss of to the estate (i.e., loss of inheritance).

c. Punitive Wrongful Death Acts

In two states damages are determined without reference to decedent's earnings or their family's needs but are based solely on defendant's fault.

d. Punitive Damages

Jurisdictions are split on whether punitive damages may be recovered in a wrongful death action. In a few states, they are expressly allowed by statute.

e. Limits

At one time, almost half the states had specific dollar limits on wrongful death awards. Today, most jurisdictions have removed such limits, but a few jurisdictions limit elements of damage, or limit damages as to certain beneficiaries.

8. Defenses

In wrongful death cases, the same defenses are available as if decedent had lived. In addition, a beneficiary's negligence that contributed to the death bars or reduces that beneficiary's recovery (but not that of other beneficiaries) consistent with the governing contributory and/comparative fault rules. Remarriage of decedent's spouse does not mitigate the spouse's damages. The intra-family immunities generally are not available as defenses in wrongful death actions.

Regarding the statute of limitations, courts are split as to whether beneficiaries are barred from bringing a wrongful death action which otherwise would have been viable if the statute of limitations applicable to decedent's cause of action had expired by the time the decedent died, or after they died before suit could be filed. Many, but not all, hold that the statute begins running at the time of death. Courts are also divided as to the application of the discovery rule in wrongful death cases.

C. Procedure

1. Survival Actions

The plaintiff is the executor or administrator of the decedent's estate, and the surviving cause of action is an asset of the estate. Any recovery in the survival action goes to the estate and is distributed based on the decedent's will, if any, or the applicable law governing intestacy. As such, it is subject to the claims of the estate's creditors.

2. Wrongful Death Actions

A wrongful death cause of action is an independent claim by the beneficiaries. It is not an asset of the decedent's estate and does not pass through the estate. In some jurisdictions, the plaintiff is the executor or administrator of the estate, but it is brought on behalf of the beneficiaries, and any recovery goes directly to them. It is not subject to claims of the estate's creditors. In some jurisdictions, the plaintiff is one of the beneficiaries or their representative who sues on behalf of all the beneficiaries. If there is more than one beneficiary for whom damages are awarded, the recovery is divided in accordance with applicable local procedure.

PART NINE. NUISANCE

I. INTRODUCTION

"Nuisances," public and private, are two distinct fields of tort liability. It is the extent of the invasion to plaintiff's interest, not the conduct of the defendant, which determines whether plaintiff has an action for nuisance. Liability can be based on intentional conduct, negligence, or strict liability.

II. PRIVATE NUISANCE

A. Definition

A private nuisance is a thing or activity which substantially and unreasonably interferes with the plaintiff's use and enjoyment of their land. Interferences can have a physical effect on the land itself, such as by vibration, objects thrown upon it, destruction of crops, flooding, or pollution of its water or soil. Interference can affect the comfort, convenience or health of the occupant, as by foul odors, smoke, dust, insects, noxious gases, excessive noise, excessive light, or high temperatures.

B. Relation to Trespass to Land

A trespass is an invasion of plaintiff's interest in the exclusive possession of land (e.g., by entry upon it). A nuisance is an interference with plaintiff's interest in the private use and enjoyment of the land, which does not require interference with their exclusive possession; but, unlike trespass, the interference must be unreasonable and cause substantial harm.

C. Basis of Liability

1. Fault

Liability is not absolute. Absent a statute, a defendant's interference with a plaintiff's protected interest must be intentional, reckless, negligent, or the result of an abnormally dangerous activity such that principles of strict liability will apply.

2. Substantial Interference

Nuisance liability requires substantial harm, of a type which would be suffered by an ordinary person in the community, or by property in normal condition and used for a normal purpose.

3. Continuing or Recurring Interference Not Required

At one time it was thought that a nuisance did not exist unless the interference was continuing or recurring. There is no such requirement now, although some interferences will not be sufficiently substantial unless they are.

4. Interference Must Be Unreasonable

The interference must be unreasonable, which generally means that either (a) the gravity of a plaintiff's harm outweighs the utility of the defendant's conduct, or (b) if intentional, the harm caused by a defendant's conduct is substantial and the financial burden of compensating for this and other harms does not render unfeasible the continuation of the conduct.

a. Weighing the Gravity of the Harm

Courts review the gravity of the harm by considering factors such as the (i) extent of the harm, (ii) character of the harm, (iii) the social value of plaintiff's use or enjoyment it affects, (iv) the suitability of that use or enjoyment to the locality, and (v) the burden for the plaintiff to avoid the harm.

b. Weighing the Utility of Defendant's Conduct

Courts review the utility of a defendant's conduct by considering factors such as the (i) social value of the defendant's conduct, (ii) its suitability to the locality, (iii) the feasibility of preventing or avoiding the interference, and (iv) the practicability of continuing the defendant's activity if it is required to bear the cost of compensating for the interference.

D. Remedies

1. Who Can Recover

Anyone whose use and enjoyment of any interest (possessory or non-possessory) in the land is affected can maintain the action.

2. Damages

If the nuisance is permanent, all damages must be recovered in one action. If the nuisance can be abated, plaintiff recovers all damages at the time of trial. If a defendant then fails to abate, future invasions give rise to a new cause of action.

3. Injunction

If the nuisance threatens to continue and the plaintiff has no adequate legal remedy, equitable relief may be sought. The court will then balance (i) the relative economic hardship to the parties from granting or denying the injunction, and (ii) the public interest in continuing the defendant's activity.

4. Self-Help

There is a limited privilege to enter another's land (or trespass upon their chattel) to abate a private nuisance.

E. Persons Liable

Liability includes one who carries on or participates in a nuisance-creating activity. In some cases, it can also include lessors and possessors who fail to prevent or abate a nuisance carried on by third persons on their land.

F. Defenses

1. Contributory Negligence and Assumption of Risk Are Viable Defenses

A plaintiff's contributory negligence or assumption of risk is a nuisance defense to the same extent as in other tort actions.

2. Coming to the Nuisance

The fact that a plaintiff has acquired or improved their land after a nuisance has come into existence is not itself sufficient to bar their action but is a factor to be considered in determining whether the nuisance is actionable.

3. Others Contributing to the Nuisance

Except as it may affect the character of the locality, the fact that others contribute to a nuisance is not a bar to a defendant's liability for their own contribution.

4. Legislation

Legislation authorizing a particular activity or use of land (e.g., zoning laws, licenses) may be used to establish that it is not a nuisance, but such authority is usually narrowly construed to include only reasonable conduct.

III. PUBLIC NUISANCE

A. Definition

A public nuisance is an unreasonable interference with a right common to the general public.

B. Public Right

The right interfered with must be common to the public as a class, and not merely that of one person or even a group of citizens.

C. Remedies

Available remedies include a criminal prosecution or suit to enjoin or abate the nuisance by public authorities or others on behalf of the public. A private citizen has no civil remedy for the harm they have sustained resulting from a public nuisance if that harm is of the same kind as that suffered by the general public, even though they have been harmed to a greater degree than others.

D. Concurrence of Remedies

If a public nuisance also interferes with a plaintiff's use and enjoyment of their land, the plaintiff may sue for their damages under either public or private nuisance theories.

PART TEN. MISREPRESENTATION, DEFAMATION, AND PRIVACY

I. MISREPRESENTATION

A. Introduction

1. Definition

Words or conduct asserting the existence of a fact constitute a misrepresentation if the fact does not exist, specifically where Defendant, in the course of some transaction (usually a bargaining situation) makes a false statement to Plaintiff (or another), Plaintiff acts in reasonable reliance on the statement, and Plaintiff therefore sustains pecuniary loss.

2. Basis

At common law, this action was called "deceit" and would exist only if Defendant's misrepresentation was fraudulent—i.e., made with "willful intent."

B. Deceit

1. Elements

The elements necessary to establish a prima facie case in an action for deceit are: (1) Defendant made a false representation, ordinarily of a fact. (2) Defendant must have known that the statement was false, or else they must have made it consciously or with reckless disregard for whether it was true or false. (3) Defendant must have intended that plaintiff act (or refrain from acting) in reliance upon the representation. (4) Plaintiff must have justifiably relied upon the representation in acting or failing to act. (5) Plaintiff must have sustained actual damage as a result of their reliance.

2. Fraudulent Misrepresentation

A misrepresentation is "fraudulent" if defendant

1) knows or believes that the character of the representation is not as they represent it to be,
2) does not have the confidence in the accuracy of their representation that they state or imply, or
3) knows that they do not have the basis for their representation that they state or imply.

3. Form of Representation

a. Misrepresentation of Fact, Not Opinion

In general, the representation must be of a fact. It may be by words or conduct. Statements that represent only defendant's opinion or prediction are not generally actionable. However, an opinion may be understood as an implied representation concerning its underlying facts.

b. Ambiguous Representations Can Be Actionable

A representation capable of two interpretations, one true and the other false, is actionable if made with the intent that it be understood in the false sense or with reckless indifference as to how it will be understood.

c. False Statements of Intent Are Actionable

A statement that the speaker or another person currently intends to do (or not do) something in the future is typically seen as a statement of fact which is actionable if untrue.

d. Incomplete Statements Are Actionable

A representation stating the truth that the maker knows or believes to be materially misleading because of the maker's failure to state additional or qualifying matter, is actionable.

e. **Fraudulent Concealment Is Actionable**

If defendant conceals or otherwise prevents plaintiff from acquiring material information, defendant is liable as though they had stated its nonexistence.

f. **Nondisclosure Not Generally Actionable**

At one time, mere silence could not amount to a misrepresentation. Parties to a transaction were free to knowingly take advantage of the other's ignorance of material facts. This rule is now subject to several significant exceptions:

i. **Fiduciary or Confidential Relations**

Fiduciary or confidential relations, such as principal-agent, guardian-ward, executory-beneficiary, bank-depositor, attorney-client, physician-patient, and parties to certain contracts (suretyship, insurance, partnership), carry with them the duty to make disclosure of all material facts.

ii. **Active Concealment**

The rule does not apply where defendant actively conceals material information or prevents investigation.

iii. **Subsequently Acquired Information**

Subsequently acquired information which makes the prior statement untrue or misleading must be disclosed if defendant knows or believes that plaintiff is still acting on the basis of the original statement.

iv. **Newly Discovered Reliance**

If defendant makes a statement without expecting that plaintiff will rely upon it, and defendant later discovers that plaintiff, in a transaction with them, is about to rely upon it, they have an affirmative duty to disclose its falsity.

v. **Material Facts Known to Defendant, Not Plaintiff**

There is a growing trend to find an affirmative duty to disclose material facts known to defendant, where those facts are peculiarly and exclusively within defendant's knowledge or when defendant has special access to those facts which plaintiff does not, and plaintiff is not in a position to discover the facts for themself.

vi. **Statutory Duty to Disclose**

Securities laws, consumer protection laws, and other statutes may impose an affirmative duty to disclose.

4. **Scope of Liability**

The scope of defendant's liability for a fraudulent misrepresentation is as follows.

a. Persons

Defendant is liable to the specifically identifiable person(s) or group of persons they (1) intend to act or (2) have reason to expect, will act (or refrain from acting) in reliance upon their representation.

b. Third Persons

If defendant intends or has reason to expect that their representation will be communicated to a specific third person, and that it will influence their conduct in the type of transaction involved, they are subject to liability to that third person.

c. Type of Transaction

Plaintiff's reliance must ordinarily be in the transaction or type of transaction in which defendant intends or has reason to expect that plaintiff's conduct will be influenced.

d. Actual and Proximate Cause

Defendant's representation must have been a substantial factor in influencing plaintiff's conduct, and plaintiff's loss from the reliance must have been reasonably foreseeable.

5. Justifiable Reliance

Plaintiff can recover only if they in fact relied on the representation, and their reliance was justifiable.

a. Materiality

Reliance is not justifiable unless the matter misrepresented is material.

b. Duty to Investigate

Plaintiff may justifiably rely on the other's statements without further investigation even when their falsity could have been easily and quickly discovered, unless something known to them or apparent in the situation at hand should have served as a warning to them that the statement should not to be accepted without further inquiry. Reliance may also be justified without investigation if defendant somehow prevents or deters further inquiry.

c. Opinion of Adverse Party

Plaintiff cannot justifiably rely on Defendant's statement in the form of an opinion, unless the fact to which the opinion relates is material and (1) Defendant claims to have special knowledge, (2) Defendant stands in a fiduciary or confidential relation to plaintiff, or (3) Defendant has some other special reason to expect that plaintiff will rely on defendant's opinion.

d. Opinion of Apparently Disinterested Person

Plaintiff can justifiably rely on the opinion of an apparently disinterested person if the fact that they hold the opinion is material.

6. Damages

Damages for fraudulent misrepresentations are measured by plaintiff's pecuniary loss, including the difference between the value of what they paid and the value of what they actually received, plus consequential damages.

7. Physical Harm

Defendant may also be liable for physical harm caused by reasonable reliance on an intentional, affirmative misrepresentation if defendant intends or knows it will induce reliance that involves a risk of physical harm to plaintiff, and if defendant knows that the statement is false or does not have the knowledge they profess.

C. Negligent Misrepresentation

1. Elements

Even though defendant honestly believed his mistaken statement to be true, they may have been negligent in (a) failing to exercise reasonable care to ascertain the true facts, or (b) failing to possess or apply the skill and competence required by their business or profession, or (c) expressing their assertion as they did.

2. Physical Harm

If Defendant's negligent misrepresentation proximately causes physical harm, ordinary negligence principles apply.

3. Pecuniary Loss

Most jurisdictions recognize a limited form of liability for such negligent misrepresentations as a separate tort action. Some courts have barred negligent misrepresentation actions under the economic loss rule, except in cases where defendant is in an information business or profession.

4. Scope of Liability

a. Interest in Transaction

Defendant is not liable for their negligent misrepresentation (causing only pecuniary loss) unless made in the course of their business, profession, or employment, or other transaction in which they had a pecuniary interest.

b. Actual Knowledge of Plaintiff

At first, defendant was liable only to the specific person or persons for whose benefit and guidance they intended to supply the information. Today, many courts have extended defendant's liability to include persons in a limited group, even though not specifically known to defendant, if defendant knows that one or more persons in that group will receive and rely upon that information, even though defendant had no knowledge of their specific identity or the particulars of the transaction in which it would be used.

c. Foreseeable Harm to One Remote User

Where defendant knows that the information they furnished will be used by a succession of persons whose specific identity is presently unknowable, but only one such person will suffer loss, some courts have extended defendant's liability to all who will foreseeably use and rely upon the information.

d. **Public Duty to Furnish Information**

Certain kinds of statutes (e.g., securities laws, recording acts) require defendant to furnish, file, or publish information for the protection of a class of persons. If such information is negligently erroneous, a member of that class who relies upon it to their detriment may recover.

e. **Transaction**

Liability is limited to the transaction for which the information was furnished or a substantially similar transaction.

5. Contributory Negligence

Plaintiff's contributory or comparative negligence in relying upon a negligent misrepresentation is a defense.

6. Damages

Damages for negligent misrepresentation include plaintiff's out-of-pocket loss and consequential damages, but not the benefit of the bargain.

D. Innocent Misrepresentation (Strict Liability)

1. Physical Harm: Products

If defendant is engaged in the business of selling a certain product, they are subject to strict liability for physical harm resulting from a misrepresentation made to the public concerning the character or quality of that product they sold.

2. Pecuniary Loss: Sale, Rental, or Exchange Transaction

The Restatement (Second) § 552C proposes strict liability for pecuniary loss sustained as the result of a misrepresentation made by defendant in a sale, rental or exchange transaction with plaintiff, upon which plaintiff justifiably relied.

II. DEFAMATION

A. General Rules

1. Elements of Cause of Action

The elements of a common-law defamation action are: (1) A false and defamatory statement concerning another. (2) An unprivileged publication to a third party, the publication being intentional or at least negligent on the part of defendant. (3) Depending on the status of the defendant, plaintiff may have to show some degree of fault on the part of defendant in knowing or failing to ascertain the falsity of the statement. (4) Some defamatory statements are actionable without proof of special damage (i.e., are actionable "per se"); others are not.

2. What Is Defamatory?

A communication is defamatory if it tends to harm plaintiff's reputation in the community, either by (1) lowering others' estimation of them, or (2) deterring others from associating or dealing with them.

A communication is defamatory if a substantial and respectable minority of plaintiff's community or associates would so regard it; it is not necessary that all or a majority would. However, it is not defamatory if the minority's views on that subject are so anti-social or extreme that it would not be proper for the courts to recognize them.

3. Truth

A defamatory statement is not actionable unless it is false. R.2d § 681A. Traditionally, truth has been regarded as an affirmative defense on which defendant has the burden of proof. In cases involving issues of public interest, however, the First Amendment now requires plaintiff to bear the burden of proving falsity. Additionally, the law now requires plaintiff to establish defendant's fault with respect to the falsity of the statement in at least some, if not all, defamation cases.

4. Who May Be Defamed

a. Deceased Persons

Unless a statute otherwise provides, no libel or slander action lies for the defamation of a deceased person. R.2d § 560. Whether the action survives plaintiff's death (where plaintiff was defamed while alive) depends on the local survival statute.

b. Entities

Corporations, partnerships, and unincorporated associations may be defamed. R.2d §§ 561.

5. Meaning of Communication

a. Understanding of Recipient

A communication is defamatory only if the recipient understands it in a defamatory sense and understands that it was so intended. R.2d § 563. If the recipient reasonably so understood it, it does not matter that they were mistaken. The context of the statement is considered.

b. Extrinsic Circumstances

Extrinsic facts and circumstances known to the recipient are considered.

6. Application to Plaintiff

The communication must have been understood by the recipient (correctly, or mistakenly but reasonably) as intended to refer to plaintiff. The applicability of the defamatory matter to plaintiff may depend upon extrinsic facts or circumstances known to the recipient.

7. Group Defamation

Generally, no action lies for the publication of defamatory words concerning a large group or class of persons, since they cannot reasonably be understood as applying to any one individual.

But a member of a small group may recover if the statement may reasonably be understood as applying to them specifically.

8. Types of Defamatory Communications

a. Fact

Typically, a defamatory communication consists of a statement of fact. R.2d § 565. It may be direct or indirect, as where words or pictures imply a defamatory meaning about plaintiff without so stating directly.

b. Opinion

At common law, a defamatory statement of opinion (if not privileged) was actionable the same as one of fact. This rule appears to have been modified by constitutional law interpretations. R.2d § 566.

If the defamatory opinion is based entirely on facts (a) known to those making and receiving the statement, or (b) stated as a predicate to the opinion, the First Amendment permits one to express one's opinion, however misguided or debatable, without defamation liability. "Under the First Amendment, there is no such thing as a false idea." *Gertz v. Robert Welch, Inc.*, 418 U.S. 323, 339 (1974).

On the other hand, if and to the extent that the opinion implies the allegation of undisclosed defamatory facts as the basis for the opinion, it may be actionable. *Milkovich v. Lorain Journal Co.*, 497 U.S. 1 (1990).

c. Ridicule

Humorous writings, verses, cartoons, or caricatures which may be understood as making a statement about plaintiff are similarly protected, at least to the extent that they represent merely negative opinions not implying false facts. *Hustler Magazine v. Falwell*, 485 U.S. 46 (1988).

d. Verbal Abuse

Profanity and similar statements, directed at plaintiff in anger and obviously intended as mere vituperation or abuse, ordinarily cannot be taken literally and therefore are not defamatory.

e. Fabricated Quotation

To attribute a fabricated quotation to plaintiff may be defamatory. *Masson v. New Yorker Magazine, Inc.*, 501 U.S. 496 (1991).

B. Libel and Slander Distinguished

1. Libel Defined

Libel is the publication of defamatory matter by (1) written or printed words, or (2) embodiment in physical form (e.g., photos, cartoons, sculpture, film, videotape, sound recordings), or (3) any other form of communication that has potentially harmful characteristics comparable to those of written or printed words.

2. Slander Defined

Slander is the publication of defamatory matter by spoken words, transitory gestures, or other form of communication not amounting to a libel.

3. Relevant Factors

The relevant factors to in distinguishing libel and slander are the area of dissemination, the deliberate and premeditated character of the publication, and the persistence or permanency of the publication.

C. Defamation Actionable Without Proof of Special Damage

1. Libel

In most jurisdictions, any libel is actionable per se, that is, without proof that plaintiff sustained any special harm or damage from the publication. Even if plaintiff cannot or does not prove actual damages, the trier of fact can infer harm sufficient to support an award of compensatory or nominal damages.

2. Libel Per Quod

In a minority of U.S. jurisdictions, a libel which is not defamatory on its face but requires reference to extrinsic facts to establish its defamatory meaning is not actionable without proof of special harm. This is sometimes called libel per quod.

3. Slander

Publication of a slander is not actionable without proof of special damages unless it defames plaintiff in one of four ways. If actionable without proof of special damages, it is called "slander per se"; if not, it is "slander per quod."

a. Criminal Conduct

It imputes to plaintiff conduct that constitutes a crime punishable by imprisonment or involving moral turpitude. R.2d § 571.

b. Communicable Disease

It imputes that plaintiff has a sexually transmitted disease or "other loathsome and communicable disease." R.2d § 572.

c. Business, Trade, Profession, or Office

It imputes to plaintiff conduct, characteristics or a condition that would adversely affect his fitness for the proper conduct of his business, trade, profession, or office. R.2d § 573.

d. Sexual Misconduct

It imputes serious sexual misconduct, regardless of gender. R.2d § 574.

4. Special Damage

In this context, special harm or damages refers to the loss of something having economic or pecuniary value resulting from the harm to plaintiff's reputation. It does not include plaintiff's emotional distress and resulting bodily harm, which may, however, be compensated if the defamation is otherwise actionable.

D. Publication

1. Definition

Publication is the communication of defamatory matter by defendant to someone other than plaintiff. R.2d § 577.

2. Fault

Even at common law (i.e., before *Gertz*), and today, defendant is not liable for unintended or accidental publication. The publication must have been intentional or the result of defendant's negligence.

3. Agent

In most jurisdictions, publication to defendant's agent is sufficient (but may be privileged). If dictated with the intent that it will be reduced to writing (a letter), it is libel. And defendant is liable for a publication by their agent where they directed or procured it.

4. Multiple Publications

Each of several communications to a third person by the same defendant is a separate publication.

5. Wills

Generally, an action will lie against defendant's estate for libelous matter published in their will after his death.

6. Liability of Republisher

One who repeats or otherwise republishes a defamation is subject to liability to the same extent as if he had originally published it. R.2d § 578.

One who only delivers or transmits defamatory matter published by a third person, such as those who deliver newspapers or mail, is subject to liability only if they know or have reason to know of its defamatory character. This exception does not apply to broadcasters. R.2d § 581.

By federal law, information published on the Internet is treated as published only by the content provider and not by the internet service provider or one who merely provides the web site. See 47 U.S.C.A. § 230(c)(1).

7. Causation: Liability of Original Publisher for Republication

Defendant is liable for the republication of his defamatory statement by another if (a) the third person was privileged to repeat it, or (b) defendant authorized or intended the repetition, or (c) the repetition was reasonably foreseeable. Cf. R.2d §§ 576, 662A. Ordinarily, defendant is not liable for a repetition by plaintiff.

E. Fault

1. Common Law

At common law, defamation liability was strict. Defendant did not have to be aware of the falsity or defamatory character of the statement or even be negligent in ascertaining these things; nor need they have intended or foreseen any harm, or that the statement could be understood as referring to plaintiff. The only fault required was with respect to its publication: Defendant had to intentionally or negligently publish the matter.

2. First Amendment

The Supreme Court has held that the First Amendment to the U.S. Constitution imposes fault requirements, at least in the case of defamatory matter concerning public officials, public figures, or matters of public concern when defendant is exercising the freedom of the press protected by that amendment. These decisions have led some states to impose fault requirements as common law rules, even where not strictly required by constitutional law.

3. Public Official, Public Figure

Under *New York Times Co. v. Sullivan*, 376 U.S. 254 (1964), one who publishes a false and defamatory communication concerning a public official or a public figure with regard to their conduct, fitness, or role in that capacity is subject to liability only if defendant (a) knows that the statement is false and that it defames plaintiff, or (b) acts in reckless disregard of these matters. R.2d § 580A.

a. Public Official

A public official is a governmental employee who has (or appears to have) responsibility for or control over the conduct of governmental affairs, and may include even relatively low-ranking personnel, such as police officers. To receive the benefit of this special First Amendment protection, the defamatory statement must concern the official's fitness for or performance in the office.

b. Public Figure

A public figure is one who has achieved a degree of fame or notoriety, either generally or as to a particular public issue or controversy (e.g., candidates for public office, professional athletes). The voluntary nature of plaintiff's participation is a relevant factor. The statement must affect plaintiff in their public capacity.

c. Public Concern

Whether a matter is one of public concern depends on its content, form, and context.

d. Fault

The requisite fault is "actual malice" (sometimes described as "constitutional malice"). Here, malice does not have its literal meaning. "Actual malice" means nothing more than knowledge of the statement's false and defamatory character or a reckless disregard of these matters, as when a statement is published despite a high degree of awareness of its probable falsity, or with serious doubts as to its truth. Actual ill will need not be proved. The availability of time and opportunity to check the truth of the statement may be relevant. Proof of defendant's fault must be clear and convincing.

e. Private Communications

The cases that impose the foregoing fault requirement so far have involved public statements in the press, media and books. It remains to be seen whether these fault requirements apply to other forms of communication, though most jurisdictions do not distinguish between media and non-media cases in applying these rules.

4. Private Persons

Under *Gertz v. Robert Welch, Inc.*, 418 U.S. 323 (1974), one who publishes a false and defamatory communication concerning a private person, or concerning a public official or public figure with regard to a purely private matter (i.e. not affecting his conduct, fitness or role in their public capacity) is subject to liability only if defendant (a) knows that the statement is false and that it defames plaintiff, or (b) acts in reckless disregard of these matters, or (c) acts negligently in failing to ascertain them. R.2d § 580B.

a. Effect of *Gertz*

After *Gertz*, strict liability for defamation published in the press, media, and possibly books is unconstitutional, regardless of the status of plaintiff. However, the states are free to determine the degree of fault required for defamation actions by persons described above, so long as at least negligence is required.

b. Majority Rule

Most states have followed the *Gertz* criteria, so that in those jurisdictions all those persons described above need only prove that defendant was negligent in ascertaining the falsity and defamatory character of the statement.

c. Minority Rule

In some jurisdictions, if the defamation concerns a matter of general or public interest, even those persons described above are required to prove that defendant either (1) knew that the statement was false and that it defames plaintiff, or (2) acted in reckless disregard of these matters (i.e., same as for public officials and public figures).

d. Burden of Proof

Those persons described above must prove falsity and the requisite fault by a preponderance of the evidence.

F. Defenses to Actions for Defamation

1. Consent

Plaintiff's consent to the publication of defamatory matter concerning them is a complete defense. R.2d § 583.

Defendant may be liable for a republication that results from plaintiff's honest inquiry or investigation to ascertain the existence, source, content, or meaning of the defamatory publication. R.2d § 584.

2. Absolute Privileges

a. Judicial Proceedings

While performing their functions in judicial proceedings, judges and judicial officers, attorneys, parties, witnesses, and jurors are absolutely privileged to publish defamatory matter that has some relation to the proceeding.

b. Legislative Proceedings

A member of Congress or a state or local legislative body is absolutely privileged to publish defamatory matter in the performance of his legislative functions. A witness is absolutely privileged to publish defamatory matter as part of a legislative proceeding in which he is testifying or in communications preliminary to the proceeding, if the matter has some relation to the proceeding.

c. Executive and Administrative Officers

An executive or administrative officer of the U.S., or a governor or other superior executive officer of a state, is absolutely privileged to publish defamatory matter in communications made in the performance of their official duties.

d. Spousal Privilege

Spouses are absolutely privileged to publish defamatory matter to the other.

e. Publication Required by Law

One who is required by law to publish defamatory matter is absolutely privileged to publish it, such as a newspaper required to publish an official notice.

3. Conditional or Qualified Privileges

a. In General

At common law, certain defamatory communications are *conditionally* or *qualifiedly* privileged, so that defendant is not liable provided defendant meets all the conditions or qualifications. As to these privileges, the chief limitation is that defendant must (1) believe their statement to be true, and (2) (a) in some jurisdictions, have reasonable grounds for believing it to be true, or (b) in other jurisdictions, not have acted recklessly in failing to ascertain its truth or falsity. But the *N.Y. Times* and *Gertz* cases, when applicable, require plaintiff to prove that defendant acted either recklessly or negligently in ascertaining the truth or falsity of the statement. Thus, if *N.Y. Times* and *Gertz* apply, the existence of a conditional privilege is partly or totally irrelevant. Therefore, the following privileges apply only when they are not superseded by the *N.Y. Times* or *Gertz* rules.

b. Protection of the Publisher's Interest

i. Rule

Defendant's defamatory communication is conditionally privileged when the circumstances cause defendant to correctly or reasonably believe that (1) the information affects a sufficiently important interest of defendant, and (2) the information will be of service to the recipient in the lawful protection of that interest.

ii. Value of Defendant's Interest

Interests of defendant worthy of protection include, for example (a) any lawful business or pecuniary interest, *other than* their interest in competition for prospective advantage (e.g., defamation to obtain customers), (b) their bodily security, (c) their present interest in land, chattels, or intangible property, (d) their family, and (e) their own reputation. In each case, the value of defendant's interest is to be balanced against the harm to plaintiff's reputation if the defamatory matter is false.

c. Protection of Interest of Recipient or Third Person

i. Rule

Defendant's defamatory communication is conditionally privileged when the circumstances cause defendant to correctly or reasonably believe that (1) the information affects a sufficiently important interest of the recipient or a third person, and (2) the recipient is one to whom (a) defendant is under a legal duty to publish it or (b) its publication is otherwise within generally accepted standards of decent conduct.

ii. Decent Conduct

Important factors in determining whether the publication is within generally accepted standards of decent conduct include whether (a) it is in response to a request, rather than volunteered by defendant, or (b) a family or other relationship exists between the parties.

iii. Examples

Fiduciaries discharging their duties; reports to proper authorities that defendant believes plaintiff is about to commit a crime against another; communications among members of a trade association; reports to an employer about the character or conduct of a present or prospective employee.

d. Protection of Common Interest

Defendant's defamatory communication is conditionally privileged when the circumstances cause defendant to correctly or reasonably believe that another who shares a common interest is entitled to know it.

e. Family Relationships

Defendant's defamatory communication is conditionally privileged when the circumstances cause defendant to correctly or reasonably believe that: (1) the recipient's knowledge will help protect the well-being of a member of defendant's immediate family; or (2) the recipient's knowledge will help protect the well-being of a member of the immediate family of the recipient or a third person, and the recipient has requested the information or is a person to whom its communication is otherwise within generally accepted standards of decent conduct.

f. Public Interest

Defendant's defamatory communication is conditionally privileged when the circumstances cause defendant to correctly or reasonably believe that a sufficiently important public interest requires its communication to a public officer or other person who is authorized or privileged to act if it is true.

g. Inferior State Officers

Lower-level state or local government employees who are not entitled to an absolute privilege have a conditional privilege for communications required or permitted in the performance of their duties.

h. "Abuse" (Loss) of the Privilege

i. Knowledge, Recklessness, or Negligence Concerning Falsity

Negligence

Prior to *Gertz*, in some jurisdictions a conditional privilege was lost if defendant did not honestly believe the truth of his statement, or if he did not have "reasonable grounds" to believe in its truth. It remains to be seen whether this rule has any purpose after *Gertz*.

Recklessness

Other jurisdictions have held that a conditional privilege is lost only if defendant knows that the statement is false or acts in "reckless disregard" as to its truth or falsity. Where *Gertz* or *N.Y. Times* applies, any conditional privilege will be irrelevant.

ii. Rumor

Defendant may be privileged to publish a defamatory rumor or suspicion, even though defendant believes or knows that it is untrue, provided: (a) they state the defamatory matter as a rumor or suspicion and not as a fact; and (b) the publication is reasonable, considering the relation of the parties, the importance of the interests affected, and the harm likely to be done.

iii. Purpose

There is no conditional privilege unless defendant publishes the defamatory matter for the purpose of protecting the interest which gives rise to the privilege and reasonably believes the publication to be necessary for that purpose.

iv. Excessive Publication

There is no conditional privilege to the extent that defendant knowingly publishes the defamatory matter to a person outside its scope, unless defendant reasonably believes that such publication is a proper means of communicating it to a proper person.

v. Unprivileged Matter

The privilege is lost to the extent that defendant adds unprivileged matter to the communication. If not severable, the entire privilege is lost.

i. Fair Comment on Matters of Public Concern

At common law, there was a qualified privilege for what was called "fair comment" (i.e., publicly expressing one's opinion) on matters of public concern. This former privilege appears to have been subsumed under the constitutional right to express such opinions without defamation liability.

4. **Special Types of Privilege**

a. **Report of Official Proceeding or Public Meeting**

Defendant is privileged to publish defamatory matter in a report of an official action or proceeding or of a meeting open to the public that deals with a matter of public concern, provided the report is accurate or a fair abridgment of the occurrence reported.

b. **Providing Means of Publication**

One who provides a means of publication of defamatory matter published by another is privileged to do so if the other is privileged to publish it. However, internet service providers are probably not liable for mere transmission of the matter regardless of the privilege.

G. Damages

1. **Types Recoverable**

Damages which may be recoverable in a defamation action include (a) nominal damages, (b) general (or "presumed") damages for harm to reputation, (c) damages for proved special harm caused by the harm to plaintiff's reputation, (d) damages for emotional distress and resulting bodily harm, and (e) punitive damages.

2. **Nominal Damages**

One who is liable for a libel or slander actionable per se is liable for at least nominal damages.

3. **General Damages**

a. **Rule**

At common law, once defendant's liability was established, the jury could award plaintiff general damages for harm to their reputation, whether plaintiff proved actual harm or not. In most jurisdictions these are known as "presumed" damages. In the absence of such proof, the jury could compensate plaintiff for the harm to their reputation that normally would be assumed to flow from a defamatory publication of the nature involved. However, *Gertz* holds that the First Amendment prohibits the states from permitting recovery for presumed damages unless plaintiff proves defendant's knowledge of the defamation's falsity or their reckless disregard for its truth; otherwise, proof of actual harm is required. "Actual harm" is not limited to pecuniary loss; it includes such intangibles as harm to plaintiff's reputation and emotional distress. No specific dollar value of such harm need be shown.

b. **Exception**

In *Dun & Bradstreet, Inc. v. Greenmoss Builders, Inc.*, 472 U.S. 749 (1985), the Supreme Court held that a state could award presumed damages when plaintiff was a private figure and the speech did not involve any issue of public interest or concern.

4. Special Damages

Special damages (i.e., economic or pecuniary loss) resulting from the defamation may always be recovered. In the case of slander per quod (and libel per quod in some jurisdictions), such damages are a prerequisite to liability.

5. Emotional Distress and Bodily Harm

Once defendant's liability is established, damages for emotional distress and resulting bodily harm are recoverable.

6. Punitive Damages

The common law generally allows punitive damages in a defamation action when defendant's conduct involves "actual malice," which usually means an intent to harm plaintiff or a reckless disregard of whether they will be harmed. In addition, the constitution prohibits punitive damages, at least against the press and media defendants, unless plaintiff proves defendant's knowledge of the statement's falsity or their reckless disregard for its truth.

7. Mitigation

By statute in some jurisdictions and common law in most others, a retraction by defendant is not a complete defense, but may be considered in mitigation of plaintiff's damages. Other mitigating circumstances may also be considered.

8. Right of Reply

Statutes requiring a newspaper to publish plaintiff's reply to a defamatory statement previously printed in it are unconstitutional.

III. PRIVACY

A. Introduction

The tort action for invasion of privacy encompasses four distinct wrongs:

1. Appropriation of one's name or likeness;
2. Intrusion upon another's privacy or private affairs;
3. Public disclosure of private facts about plaintiff; and
4. Placing plaintiff in a false light in the public eye.

Other forms may develop in the future; these categories are not limitations.

B. Appropriation

1. Rule

Defendant is subject to liability for appropriating the name or likeness of plaintiff for their own use or benefit. This is often called the "right of publicity," and primarily protects the right to control the commercial value of one's identity.

2. Commercial Use

The use need not be for business or commercial purposes. Many states, however, do impose a business or commercial purpose requirement. Commercial uses are mainly uses associated with sales. Plaintiff's identity may be used in noncommercial works, both because the right of publicity does not extend to such uses and because of constitutional free speech rights.

3. Appropriation

Plaintiff must prove that defendant used plaintiff's name or identity for the purpose of taking advantage of plaintiff's reputation, prestige, or other value associated with plaintiff's name or likeness. Merely adopting a name identical to that of another, or using another's name in a communication or publication, is not an invasion of privacy unless the purpose is to appropriate the benefit of its commercial value.

C. Intrusion

1. Rule

Defendant is subject to liability for intrusion (physical or other) upon the solitude, seclusion, or private life and affairs of another, provided the intrusion would be highly offensive to a reasonable person.

2. Form

The forms of intrusion are varied—unpermitted entry into plaintiff's home or hospital room; an illegal search of plaintiff's person or property; tapping plaintiff's telephone; using mechanical aids to observe plaintiff's private activities in his home; opening plaintiff's personal mail; hacking plaintiff's email account; and persistent and unwanted communications or close physical presence.

3. Publication

The tort is complete when the intrusion occurs. No publication or publicity of the information is required.

4. Private Matters

The intrusion must be into what is, and is entitled to remain, private. Photographing or watching plaintiff in a public place, or inspecting or copying nonprivate records, is not actionable.

5. Substantial Interference

The intrusion must be highly offensive to the ordinary person, resulting from conduct to which the reasonable person would strongly object.

6. Government Intrusion

The courts are beginning to recognize a constitutional right of privacy, to be free from excessive or unreasonable governmental intrusion.

D. Public Disclosure of Private Facts

1. Rule

Defendant is subject to liability for giving publicity to some private fact about plaintiff, provided the fact publicized would be highly offensive to a reasonable person and is not a matter of legitimate public concern.

2. Publicity

The information about plaintiff need not be "published." It is sufficient if it is disclosed so as to be likely to become public knowledge.

3. Private Facts

In this case, the facts disclosed are true. Thus, there is no liability for facts which are already known by, or available to, the public. The facts must be intimate or at least private details of plaintiff's private life, the disclosure of which would be embarrassing, humiliating or offensive.

4. Legitimate Public Concern or Interest

a. Constitutional Limitations

The First Amendment freedoms of the press and speech are a further limitation of this tort and permit publication of private facts which are matters of legitimate public concern or interest.

b. Public Figures

Persons who have voluntarily become public figures, and even those involuntarily in the public eye by being part of a newsworthy event, cannot complain of the publication of facts, otherwise private, which are of legitimate public concern or interest in connection with that person, activity, or event.

E. False Light in the Public Eye

1. Rule

Defendant is subject to liability for giving publicity to a matter which places plaintiff before the public in a false light, provided (a) the false light would be highly offensive to a reasonable person, and (b) Defendant had knowledge of the falsity of the matter and the false light it created, or acted in reckless disregard of these matters.

2. Relation to Defamation

In this case, the information communicated about plaintiff is false. Thus, if it is also defamatory, an action for libel or slander may be an alternative remedy. However, it is not necessary to this action that plaintiff be defamed. It is enough that they have given unreasonable and highly objectionable publicity that attributes to their characteristics, conduct, or beliefs that are false.

Because it largely overlaps defamation claims, some courts have rejected false light claims.

3. Highly Offensive

The matter must be highly offensive to a reasonable person.

4. Constitutional Limitations

The Supreme Court has extended the *N.Y. Times* rule to this type of invasion of privacy action, requiring plaintiff to prove by clear and convincing evidence that defendant knew of the statement's falsity or acted in reckless disregard of its truth or falsity.

F. Privileges

To the extent applicable, the absolute, conditional and special privileges to publish defamatory matter are also available in invasion of privacy cases.

G. Damages

In an action for invasion of privacy, plaintiff can recover damages for: (1) harm to the interest in privacy; (2) mental distress; and (3) special damages.

H. Persons Who May Sue

Unless otherwise provided by statute, and except for appropriation, an action for invasion of privacy can be maintained only by a living individual whose privacy is invaded.

PART ELEVEN. VICARIOUS LIABILITY

I. INTRODUCTION

A. General Rule

A person who, while acting on behalf of another, commits a tortious act and thus subjects themselves to tort liability may also thereby subject the person on whose behalf they are acting to tort liability. It is said that the latter person is vicariously liable to the plaintiff.

B. Relationships Giving Rise to Vicarious Liability

Three types of relationships give rise to vicarious liability: (1) employer-employee; (2) principal-agent; and (3) employer-independent contractor.

II. EMPLOYERS AND EMPLOYEES

A. Vicarious Liability

If, at the time of their negligent or reckless act, the employee-tortfeasor acted in the "scope" of their employment, then their employer is vicariously liable to the plaintiff for their employee's tort. This principle of vicarious liability in the context of employer-employee relationships is sometimes still referred to by the Latin phrase *respondeat superior*.

B. Defining an Employee

An employee is an agent whose principal controls or has the right to control the manner and means of the agent's work performance. Sometimes the employer-employee relationship is not clear, as this type of "work" can range from the formal to the informal. Typically, agency law is used to determine whether the actor is the employee of another. In determining whether one acting for another is an employee or an independent contractor, the following factors, among others, are considered:

1. the extent of control which the principal may exercise over the details of the work in their agreement;
2. whether the person doing the work is engaged in a distinct occupation or business;

3. whether that type of occupation, in the locality, usually done under the direction of an employer or by a specialist without supervision;
4. the skill required in the particular occupation;
5. whether the employer or the workman supplies the instrumentalities, tools, and workplace for the person doing the work;
6. the length of time for which the person is employed;
7. the method of payment, whether by the time or by the job;
8. whether the work is a part of the regular business of the employer;
9. whether the parties believe they are creating the relationship of employer and employee; and
10. whether the principal is or is not in business.

One can be an employee even without payment or the promise of payment for their services, provided the other incidents of the relationship are sufficient.

C. Scope of Employment

Whether the employee was acting in the scope of their employment is a question of fact, which depends upon (a) the employee's job description and assigned duties, (b) the time, place and purpose of the employee's act, (c) the similarity of their conduct to the things they were hired to do, or which are commonly done by such employees, and (4) the foreseeability of their act.

The fact that the employee disregarded the employer's instructions or work rules does not necessarily, in and of itself, remove the employee from the scope of his employment. The test is whether, at the relevant time, the employee was performing a service in furtherance of the employer's business, not whether it was done in exact observance of the detail prescribed by the employer.

D. Employees in Transit

Under the "going-and-coming" rule, an employee is normally outside the scope of their employment when in transit to and from work. However, where the trip involves some incidental benefit to the employer, not common to commuting trips by ordinary workers, or where the employee is traveling away from home on the employer's business, the employee may be found within the scope of their employment during the trip.

E. Frolic and Detour

An employee who is in transit during working hours on the employer's business, such as traveling from one job site to another, is still within the scope of employment if they make a minor or trivial deviation from the assigned travel for personal reasons (a "detour"). However, if the employee makes a substantial deviation, in time or space, from the expected route (a "frolic"), they may be found outside the scope of employment during that deviation.

F. Intentional Torts

Usually, an employer is not vicariously liable for the intentional torts of their employees. However, an employer may be vicariously liable for their employee's intentional torts committed in the scope of employment and in furtherance of the employer's business, at least if the employee's act was foreseeable. Statutory and other special relationships may also expand liability for acts that might otherwise be deemed outside the scope of employment.

G. Employer's Liability

An employer may be directly (not vicariously) liable for torts committed by their employee based upon the employer's own negligence or other conduct. Thus, the employer may have been negligent in selecting, hiring, instructing, or supervising the employee; or the employer may have commanded, authorized, or ratified the employee's tortious act.

H. Partnerships, Joint Ventures

Partners and joint venturers acting in the scope of the business subject the other partners and joint venturers to vicarious tort liability to third persons just as if they were employees. All members of a joint enterprise are jointly and severally liable to third persons injured by the tort of any member when engaged in the enterprise.

I. Employee's Liability

Even though the employer may be vicariously or otherwise liable for the tort of the employee, the employee (or contractor) is also subject to liability. If the employer is held vicariously liable, the employer may have a claim for indemnity from the employee.

J. Concert of Action

All who expressly or impliedly agree to jointly participate in tortious conduct are jointly and severally liable to third persons injured by any of the participants.

K. Independent Contractors

1. General Rule

An employer is not vicariously liable for physical harm caused by the tortious conduct of his independent contractor or their contractor's employees. An independent contractor is a person who contracts with another to do something for them but who is not controlled by the other nor subject to the other's right to control with respect to their physical conduct in the performance of the undertaking.

2. Exception: Employer's Own Negligence

a. Negligent Selection, Retention

An employer must exercise reasonable care to select a reasonably competent, experienced, careful, and properly equipped contractor, and is subject to liability for physical harm resulting from their failure to do so.

b. Negligent Instruction

An employer is subject to liability for the negligence of an independent contractor acting in accordance with the employer's instructions.

c. Failure to Inspect Completed Work

An employer has a duty to inspect their contractor's completed work, at least where they have a duty to third persons to maintain the land or chattels for their protection.

d. Failure to Require Precautions

If the work will create a foreseeable danger to third persons, the employer must require (in the contract or otherwise) that appropriate precautions be taken for their safety.

e. Retained Supervision and Control

To the extent that the employer retains or exercises supervision or control over the work of the contractor, they must do so with reasonable care.

f. Duty as Possessor of Land

A possessor of land held open to the public must exercise reasonable care to protect that public from unreasonably dangerous conditions or activities of an independent contractor on the land.

3. Exception: Nondelegable Duties

Where the safe performance of some duty is of sufficient importance to the community, an employer is vicariously liable for the negligence of their independent contractor in performing that duty which results in physical harm. In other words, these duties are personal to the defendant and are not "delegable" to an independent contractor so as to relieve the defendant of tort liability if they are negligently performed.

4. Exception: Inherently Dangerous Work

When the contracted work involves a special danger to others which the employer knows or has reason to know is inherent in, or normal to, the work, or which is contemplated at the time of the contract, the employer is vicariously liable for physical harm caused by the independent contractor's failure to take reasonable precautions against such danger.

L. Apparent Agency

If a principal creates the appearance that someone is their agent or employee, they are not permitted to deny the agency if a third party, who does not know otherwise, reasonably relies on the apparent agency.

PART TWELVE. JOINT TORTFEASORS

I. APPORTIONMENT AMONG JOINT TORTFEASORS

Many cases yield the division of liability among various actors. This broader inquiry can be a causal apportionment by which a factfinder concludes that one actor was responsible for a certain percentage of the harm and another actor for the remainder. Apportionment broadly can occur across the 'v.' between plaintiff and defendant(s) or on the same side of the 'v.' among multiple defendants.

II. JOINT AND SEVERAL LIABILITY

A. Joint and Several Liability Defined

There is a jurisdictional split between several liability, joint and several liability, and hybrid approaches. In joint and several liability jurisdictions, when two or more tortfeasors are responsible for the same harm to the plaintiff, all whose tortious conduct is found to be a legal and factual cause of that harm are jointly and severally liable for all of plaintiff's recoverable damages. The plaintiff may sue one, some, or all who are liable. The plaintiff may obtain judgements for the full amount of recoverable damages and may collect that judgement from one or any combination of those found liable.

As long as the judgment is not satisfied in full, plaintiff can continue to bring further suits or collection proceedings. Pure joint and several liability is the minority rule today. Joint and several liability has the effect of offering the plaintiff multiple sources of funds for recovery, but the plaintiff will never recover more than one satisfaction of the judgment.

B. Bases for Joint and Several Liability

There are three factual scenarios that trigger joint and several liability.

1. Acting in Concert

Persons acting in concert are liable for harm to a plaintiff if they (a) committed the tortious act pursuant to a common plan or design, (b) know the other's conduct constitutes a breach of duty and gives substantial aid or encouragement, or (c) give substantial aid to the other to accomplish the tortious result and their own conduct, when separately considered, constitutes a breach of duty to the plaintiff. When persons are liable because they acted in concert, all persons are jointly and severally liable to the plaintiff for the resulting harm.

2. Indivisible Injury

Joint and several liability can also apply when two negligent acts combine to create one indivisible injury. Here, each tortfeasor is liable for the entire judgment (not to exceed a single satisfaction).

3. Vicarious Liability

If Defendant 1's liability is entirely vicarious, or imputed, based on the tortious conduct of Defendant 2, Defendant 1 is jointly and severally liable for whatever share of the fault is assigned to Defendant 2. If Defendant 1 pays that share to plaintiff, Defendant 1 ordinarily has a right to obtain indemnity from Defendant 2. R.3d Apportionment of Liability § 13.

C. Joint and Several Liability Triggers a Right to Contribution

1. Common Law Rule—No Right to Contribution

When a plaintiff obtains a judgment against two or more tortfeasors in a joint and several liability jurisdiction, that plaintiff can collect that full judgment from any one, all, or any combination of defendants. The common law rule in most jurisdictions was that the defendant who paid the plaintiff more than their proportionate share of the judgment, was not entitled to obtain contribution from the other joint tortfeasors.

2. Modern Status—Contribution Applies to Joint and Several Liability

Contribution among joint tortfeasors is now the rule in joint and several liability jurisdictions. There is no right to contribution by or against a party who is only severally liable because the precondition of paying more than their proportionate share cannot occur.

3. Amount of Contribution

In most jurisdictions, the damages are allocated among the joint tortfeasors in proportion to their relative fault as determined by the trier of fact, and those shares determine contribution liability. A defendant (having made a successful contribution claim against other tortfeasors) who then pays a plaintiff more than the defendant's proportional share of the judgment has a right to recover the excess amount over their proportional share from the other contribution defendants.

4. Contribution Available Absent Judgment

Defendant can even seek contribution against other joint tortfeasors not sued by the plaintiff.

a. Immune Tortfeasors

There is a split of authority as to whether contribution can be obtained against a tortfeasor who is immune from suit by the plaintiff. Most require the defendant to prove that the tortfeasor was subject to liability to the plaintiff, so the defendant cannot seek contribution if Tortfeasor is immune with respect to the plaintiff.

b. Settlement

A tortfeasor who settles prior to trial can obtain contribution, provided they settle for all tortfeasors and they can prove the others' liability, the amount of the damages, and the reasonableness of their settlement.

5. Intentional Tortfeasors

In some jurisdictions, intentional tortfeasors cannot seek contribution.

III. SEVERAL LIABILITY

With the advent of comparative fault, some jurisdictions now make a joint tortfeasor only "severally liable" to the plaintiff—i.e., their liability is limited to their proportional share of the total liability. Several liability has the effect of placing the risk of an uncollectible judgment on the plaintiff. There is no right to contribution because the defendant cannot overpay beyond their apportioned harm.

IV. HYBRID ALLOCATION OF DAMAGES APPROACHES

Many U.S. jurisdictions have adopted a mixture of joint and several liability and several liability. Broadly defined, they can be described as:

A. Reallocation of Uncollectible Shares

This category begins with joint and several liability for independent tortfeasors who cause an indivisible injury to the plaintiff. It places the risk of a tortfeasor's uncollectible judgment on all parties who bear responsibility for the plaintiff's damages, including the plaintiff. An insolvent tortfeasor's comparative share of responsibility is reallocated to the other parties in proportion to their comparative responsibility.

B. Joint and Several Liability Threshold

All tortfeasors whose percentage of comparative responsibility exceeds a specified threshold are jointly and severally liable. Tortfeasors whose percentage falls below that threshold are only severally liable.

C. Type of Harm

In this category, the variable that determines joint and several liability or several liability is the type of harm suffered by the plaintiff. Independent tortfeasors are jointly and severally liable for damages for certain harms (e.g., "economic" or "pecuniary" harms, or pollution damage) but are severally liable for compensatory damages awarded for other types of harm.

D. Type of Defendant

In some jurisdictions, joint and several (or several) liability is restricted to certain categories of defendants.

E. Whether Plaintiff Was Free from Contributory Fault

In some cases, the plaintiff gets the benefit of joint and several liability only if they are free from contributory fault.

V. JOINT AND SEVERAL LIABILITY APPLIES TO INTENTIONAL TORTFEASORS

Intentional tortfeasors are jointly and severally liable for any indivisible injury caused by the tortious conduct, regardless of the jurisdiction's approach for nonintentional torts. Thus, if Defendant 1 and Defendant 2 are both intentional tortfeasors with respect to the plaintiff's indivisible injury, both are jointly and severally liable.

If Defendant 1 is negligent because of their failure to take precautions to protect Plaintiff against the specific risk created by Defendant 2 (the intentional tortfeasor) then Defendant 1 is jointly and severally liable for the share of comparative responsibility assigned to Defendant 2 as well the share assigned to Defendant 1.

Whether the negligence of Defendant 1 can be compared with the intentional or willful tort of Defendant 2 depends on interpretation of the comparative fault statute (if any), but if there is no such statute, the Restatement (Third) permits this comparison. Courts rarely permit Plaintiff's contributory negligence to reduce their recovery from an intentional tortfeasor.

VI. EFFECT OF SETTLEMENT OF PLAINTIFF'S CLAIM(S)

The existence of multiple tortfeasors dramatically changes the dynamics of the case strategy for the defendants. Some defendants might be motivated to get out of the case sooner and those resources might also be invaluable to plaintiffs facing a long litigation timeline. This section outlines some of these agreements that defendants can enter with plaintiffs, and their effects on the remaining tortfeasors.

A. Settlement Agreements Are Contracts

A plaintiff may enter into a settlement agreement with the defendant(s) by which the plaintiff settles their claim(s) against the defendant(s) for a fixed sum. The agreement may take the form of a release, covenant not to sue, or loan receipt agreement. Ordinary rules of contract interpretation apply. Settlement agreements may be set aside for fraud, duress, incapacity, or mutual mistake.

The prevailing view is that a settlement by the plaintiff during their lifetime (or a judgment during the plaintiff's lifetime for either party) will bar a wrongful death action by the plaintiff's survivors when the death results from the same injuries.

B. Release

A release is a form of settlement agreement whereby the plaintiff completely surrenders their claim against one or more potential defendants.

C. Covenant Not to Sue

A covenant not to sue (or not to execute) is a settlement device designed to avoid the former effects of a release. It is a contract by which the plaintiff does not release their claim against the defendant but merely promises to forego any further attempts to enforce it.

D. Effect of Partial Settlement on Remaining Defendants in Joint and Several Liability Jurisdictions

Partial settlements with one tortfeasor yield a credit to remaining joint defendants. If a plaintiff has a claim against more than one joint tortfeasor subject to joint and several liability, the plaintiff can settle with one tortfeasor prior to obtaining a judgment against the remaining joint tortfeasor(s), reserving the plaintiff's right to proceed against the others. If the plaintiff then succeeds in their remaining claim(s), the tortfeasor(s) against whom the plaintiff obtained a judgment receive a credit based on the plaintiff's prior settlement with the first tortfeasor. There are different approaches to handling that credit.

E. Effect of Partial Settlement on Remaining Defendants in Several Liability Jurisdictions

If a settling tortfeasor is only subject to several liability, any nonsettling tortfeasors simply pay their proportional share(s) as determined by applicable apportionment rules. The settling tortfeasor has settled their several liability, and it matters not whether the settlement is more or less than the amount of their proportional share as later determined.

VII. NON-PARTY TORTFEASORS

If a particular tortfeasor is not joined as a defendant or third-party defendant, the courts are split as to whether the factfinder can allocate that tortfeasor's proportional share of the total fault and included in the responsible fault calculation. Whether a tortfeasor is included or not may depend on the purpose of the calculation. A tortfeasor may be a nonparty because: (1) Tortfeasor cannot be identified by name, such as a hit-and-run driver; (2) Tortfeasor is immune from suit; (3) Tortfeasor has settled with the plaintiff before trial; (4) Tortfeasor cannot be served with process; (5) Tortfeasor is plaintiff's employer and plaintiff's injury occurred in the course and scope of plaintiff's employment; or (6) Plaintiff simply chose not to sue Tortfeasor for some other reason (e.g., Tortfeasor is uncollectible).

A. Joint and Several Liability

If all tortfeasors are subject to joint and several liability and there is no contribution claim, then there is no reason to allocate fault among multiple tortfeasors, whether joined or not. However, whether a tortfeasor is included could still make a difference in determining a plaintiff's share of the fault if the plaintiff is found contributorily at fault.

For purposes of calculating plaintiff's share, the total fault should include all tortfeasors, whether joined as a defendant or not. Not all states agree; in some jurisdictions, tortfeasors who are not parties to the suit are not included.

B. Several Liability

If some or all defendants are potentially subject only to several liability, then the factfinder must allocate fault proportionally, and it makes a difference whether a tortfeasor's fault is included in the fault calculation.

Jurisdictions are split. Some require a tortfeasor to be included if there is enough evidence from which the factfinder can assess fault against the tortfeasor. In others, only those who are party to the lawsuit can be included in the fault calculation.

C. Successive or Enhanced Injury Cases

These non-party rules differ for successive or enhanced injuries. Suppose Tortfeasor 1 drives negligently and crashes into a tree, injuring Plaintiff, their passenger. Plaintiff sues Defendant, the manufacturer of the car, on the theory that the design of the car enhanced their injuries or caused a fire that resulted in further injuries not sustained in the initial crash. Plaintiff's expert witness testifies and allocates the damages between Tortfeasor 1 and Defendant. In this case, Tortfeasor 1's share of the total fault is not considered with respect to the liability of Defendant. Defendant is liable for all of Plaintiff's recoverable separate or enhanced damages. Of course, Tortfeasor 1 is jointly and severally liable for all Plaintiff's damages, including those caused by the car's defective design.

Similarly, in a medical malpractice case, Defendant (the physician) is liable for any enhanced injury resulting from Defendant's negligent treatment, without reduction for any fault by Tortfeasor 1 that caused the initial injury for which Plaintiff is being treated.

However, if Plaintiff's injuries are indivisible, then fault will be apportioned between Defendant and Tortfeasor 1 in accordance with the applicable apportionment rules.

D. Contribution

Where contribution is available to some or all of the defendants (or in a separate action for contribution), it becomes necessary to allocate fault among tortfeasors. For this purpose, the calculation is restricted to the tortfeasors who are party to the action in which contribution is being sought. In most cases, contribution may not be sought from settling tortfeasors.

VIII. INDEMNITY

A. Distinguished from Contribution

Contribution is an equitable sharing of the loss among joint tortfeasors. Indemnification is a shifting of the entire loss from one tortfeasor to another. Indemnity can occur by law, based on equitable considerations, or through a prior agreement of the parties.

B. Indemnity by Agreement—Subject to Some Limitations

A contract in which Tortfeasor 2 agrees to indemnify Tortfeasor 1 if Tortfeasor 1 is held liable to Plaintiff is frequently enforceable, although in some instances agreements to indemnify for Tortfeasor 1's own negligence may be void by statute or as against public policy. Agreements to indemnify Tortfeasor 1 for Tortfeasor 1's liability for reckless or intentional misconduct are usually unenforceable.

C. Implied Indemnity (Indemnity by Operation of Law)

Implied indemnity is indemnity based on the concept of unjust enrichment. It is available when Tortfeasor 1 and Tortfeasor 2 are both liable for the same harm to Plaintiff, and (1) Tortfeasor 1's liability is based entirely on Tortfeasor 1's vicarious liability for the tort of Tortfeasor 2, or (2) Tortfeasor 1 is the seller of a product (e.g., a retailer), the product was supplied to Tortfeasor 1 by Tortfeasor 2 (e.g., the manufacturer), and Tortfeasor 1 is held liable to Plaintiff solely because they sold the product to Plaintiff (i.e., Tortfeasor 1 was not independently culpable). If Tortfeasor 1 satisfies Plaintiff's judgment, Tortfeasor 1 is entitled to indemnity from Tortfeasor 2 for the amount paid to Plaintiff plus reasonable legal expenses.

D. "Active-Passive" Implied Indemnity

Prior to the adoption of comparative contribution, implied indemnity was also available when there was a significant or qualitative difference between the blameworthiness of Tortfeasor 1 and Tortfeasor 2, both of whom are nevertheless legally liable to Plaintiff for their injury, such that the primary responsibility for the harm rests upon the defendant against whom indemnity is sought. This was often called "active-passive" indemnity, because the fault of the indemnitor was "active" or major and the fault of the indemnitee was "passive" or minor. In those jurisdictions adopting comparative contribution, contribution is usually deemed to supersede the "active-passive" form of implied indemnity.

PART THIRTEEN. DEFENSES TO LIABILITY—GENERAL

I. STATUTES OF LIMITATIONS AND REPOSE

A. Statutes of Limitations

1. In General

A statute of limitations is a statutory period within which the plaintiff must file their lawsuit. Statutes of limitations are designed to promote stability and avoid the uncertainties and burdens inherent in defending stale and possibly fraudulent claims.

2. Procedural Effect

A statute of limitations does not automatically extinguish the cause of action. It must be asserted by the parties as an affirmative defense.

3. Starting the Statute of Limitations Clock

a. Begins at Cause of Action Accrual

The statute of limitations begins to run on the date the cause of action "accrues."

b. Concealment or Nondisclosure Tolls the Statute of Limitations

If defendant fraudulently, actively conceals or misrepresents the existence of the cause of action from plaintiff, the statute of limitations is tolled.

c. Continuing Duty Can Extend the Statute of Limitations

In some contexts, the courts will extend the available time by finding a continuing duty to disclose or continuing negligence or other tort.

d. Discovery Rule Tolls the Statute of Limitations

Strict application of the statute of limitations can be especially harsh in certain cases where plaintiff justifiably failed to discover that they even had a cause of action until after the limitations period had expired. In response to this factual problem, courts have created a "discovery" rule whereby the statute is tolled and does not commence to run until plaintiff discovers (or by the exercise of reasonable care should have discovered) that (a) they are injured and (b) the injury is the result of someone's tortious conduct.

e. Latent Potential Harm

Plaintiff, because of defendant's negligence, may have been exposed to a toxic material resulting in no present symptoms or minor symptoms but a measurable risk that plaintiff may contract a serious or fatal illness at some uncertain time in the future.

4. Estoppel to Assert

If defendant actively induces plaintiff not to take timely legal action on a claim, and plaintiff reasonably relies on defendant's inducement, defendant may be estopped to assert the statute of limitations defense.

B. Statutes of Repose

Statutes of repose are special limitation periods which supplement and override statutes of limitations, the discovery rule, and other similar rules and exceptions.

C. Notice of Claim Statutes

In suits against state or local governments, statutes sometimes require plaintiff to give notice, in a specified form, to the potential defendant within a certain period after the date of the injury, or prior to filing suit, as a further condition on the right to sue.

II. IMMUNITIES

A. Liability of the Government and Its Employees

1. Immune at Common Law

At one time, all levels of government (federal, state, local, and their agencies) were entirely immune from tort liability.

2. United States Government

a. Federal Tort Claims Act

In the Federal Tort Claims Act (FTCA), the United States has waived its tort immunity for personal or property damage caused by the negligence of Government employees.

b. Exceptions to the Federal Tort Claims Act

i. Specified torts (assault, battery, false imprisonment, false arrest, malicious prosecution, abuse of process, libel, slander, misrepresentation, deceit, or interference with contract rights).

ii. Discretionary acts (acts done with due care in the execution of a statute or regulation).

iii. Strict tort liability.

iv. The Feres doctrine (no liability for injuries to members of the armed forces on active duty if the injury is "incident to service").

3. States

Most states have largely abolished state sovereign immunity. The rest provide some limited means of making a claim. Many states have comprehensive tort immunity legislation which limits the state's liability for certain governmental functions.

4. Local Governments

After a period during which the immunity of local governments was eroded, a strong trend has developed to abolish immunity entirely. Liability is now the rule in a majority of states, subject to various immunities for certain types of governmental functions.

5. Public Duty Rule

Under the public duty doctrine, public entities and officers are not liable for failure to perform a duty owed to the public at large, rather than to a particular individual or group. A special relationship can overcome the public duty limitation and give rise to liability.

6. Governmental Officers and Employees

Governmental officers and employees (state and federal) are immune from tort liability when exercising a judicial or legislative function. The highest executive officers of state and federal governments are absolutely immune, except where they have so far exceeded the scope of their official discretion. Lower-level executive and administrative employees have qualified immunity for the good faith exercise of a discretionary function but are liable for tortious ministerial acts.

B. Charities

Tort immunity for charitable, educational, religious, and benevolent organizations and enterprises has been generally abolished. Some vestiges of immunity remain, however, in the form of other liability limitations, such as caps on damages.

C. Immunity in Family Relationships

1. Spousal Immunity

At one time, the general common law rule was that spouses were each immune from tort liability to the other spouse. More than half the states have now abolished this immunity. Many of the remaining states recognize exceptions, as for suits brought after the marriage has been terminated, intentional torts, torts occurring in a business activity, and suits against persons vicariously liable for the spouse's tort.

2. Parental Immunity

The general common law rule was that a parent (or someone in loco parentis) and their unemancipated minor child were each immune from suit by the other for a personal tort. Today, a substantial minority of the states have abolished this immunity altogether. In the remainder, the number of exceptions is increasing.

3. No Immunity for Siblings and Other Kin

Brothers, sisters, and other kin are not, by reason of their relationship, immune from tort liability to one another.

D. Minors and Legal Incompetency

1. No *Per Se* Immunity for Minors

If plaintiff can establish the requisite mental state, an infant or minor is not immune from tort liability, unless the liability depends upon the enforceability of a contract the infant is privileged to disaffirm.

2. Legal Incompetency

One who has a mental disability is not, for that reason alone, immune from tort liability. Particularly in torts involving physical harm, a defendant with a mental disability is held to the same standard as others. However, defendant's mental health condition may be relevant in determining whether any tort has been committed.

III. PREEMPTION

When a federal statute or regulation expressly or impliedly preempts a particular field, state tort law either cannot regulate the field at all or cannot impose a higher standard than the applicable federal law.

Overview of Tort Law

■ ANALYSIS

I. Introduction

Torts are everywhere around us. From the moment you get into your car or become a passenger on the bus, train, or rideshare; to the moment you grab a coffee through the drive-through at a fast-food restaurant—you are stepping into the world of risks that may give rise to potential torts. We are all deciding how careful to be throughout our day, creating varying levels of risk in the decisions we make and experiencing levels of risk from the decisions made by those around us.

"Torts" is the general legal classification encompassing several civil causes of action providing a private remedy, almost always in the form of money damages, for an injury to a plaintiff caused by the tortious conduct of a defendant. Each tort is separately named and defined, and has its own rules of liability, defenses, and damages. The injured person must find a tort action or theory that fits the facts of their case to pursue this remedy.

II. Definitions

A. What Is a Tort?

A tort is a wrong that is usually redressed by the parties in a lawsuit for monetary compensation. For example, if A punches B, B may sue A to redress the harm. The process of seeking remedy for the punch is distinct from the criminal process, in which the government might prosecute A to punish A and deter others from punching people. In the tort lawsuit, providing B with a remedy is the main goal, and it is the private parties (A and B), not the government and public, who are left to negotiate that remedy.

B. Definition

The only common element of all torts is that someone has sustained a loss or harm as the result of some act or failure to act by another. In general, a tort is a civil wrong, wherein one person's conduct causes a compensable injury to the person, property, or recognized interest of another, in violation of a duty imposed by law. Sometimes the injury is slight, and the remedy awarded is $1.00 or less (in other words, it is a "nominal" award—an award in name only). Other times, the injury is so great (such as the loss of a loved one) that no amount of compensation can make the plaintiff whole again, and compensation represents the principle of responsibility and a chance to ease (rather than erase) the hardship caused by the loss.

C. Fault

Sometimes it is suggested that a common element of tort liability is fault—that tortious conduct is conduct that falls below accepted community standards of behavior. Some sort of fault is common to many torts, although it might more accurately be described as conduct that creates an unreasonable or unacceptable risk of harm. But even in this sense, fault is not a universal principle of liability. Various kinds of blameworthy conduct resulting in damage do not give rise to tort liability. Conversely, the law sometimes imposes tort liability simply because the defendant is doing a particular activity and the defendant can and should bear the cost of damage associated with it, although the conduct of the tortfeasor was morally blameless.

III. Bases, Purposes, and Functions of Tort Law

Tort law comes from case law and legislation. But where do judges and legislators get the values or principles that lead them to create a standard in the first place? This section summarizes the various bases, purposes, and functions that support the social and political value of tort law rules.

A. Morality or Corrective Justice

Morality or corrective justice attempts to hold the defendant liable and to compensate the plaintiff, only when it seems fair or right to do so. One criterion of justice is current community standards of fairness.

B. Social Utility or Policy

Social utility or policy can support a rule. If we impose liability for conduct we wish to discourage, tort law will deter people from engaging in that conduct. Conversely, if tort law immunizes certain conduct from liability, it encourages that conduct.

C. Compensation

The most important function of tort law is to restore the plaintiff, so far as money damages can, to their status prior to the injury caused by the defendant, and to compensate the plaintiff for harm or losses that cannot be restored.

D. Justice and the Promotion of Desired Policies

Tort law also seeks to impose the cost of compensating the plaintiff upon the defendant who caused the plaintiff's injury, or who, in justice or for policy reasons, should be financially responsible for it.

E. Deterrence

The threat of tort liability is intended to regulate human behavior by deterring tortious conduct, thereby preventing at least some injuries and making society safer. This is a function shared with criminal law.

F. Other Functions of Tort Law

Other secondary functions include vindicating the plaintiff, providing a substitute for private retaliation, and preventing resort to self-help remedies.

IV. Sources of Tort Law

The rules and principles of tort law have were historically created and developed almost entirely through judicial decisions—what we call "case law" or "common law." Modern tort law is increasingly affected by legislation. However, no jurisdiction has attempted a codification of tort law. The Civil Codes of California and Louisiana contain some general principles of tort liability.

V. Historical Development of Tort Law

A. Evolution of Tort Remedies

Tort law arises out of the specific governance tradition of English common law. The U.S., as a collection of former (mostly) British colonies, inherited this body of governance. English law in its earliest stages did not differentiate between tort and crime, as such terms were unknown. When one person harmed another, the remedy was a private war or "feud" in retaliation, the object being to cause an equivalent harm to the wrongdoer.

In their earliest form, English courts were local and applied local laws. After the Norman Conquest (1066 C.E.), the royal courts were created and gradually took limited jurisdiction over a specified list of wrongs—primarily felonies where there was a breach of the "king's peace," and disputes involving land.

At first, all prosecutions for wrongs in the king's courts were brought by the individual harmed. A plaintiff accused a defendant in open court and offered the appropriate form of trial (combat, ordeal, or oaths), but even if this plaintiff was successful, no compensation was awarded. This procedure was known as the "appeal of felony."

As time went on, royal writs became the grant of jurisdiction to a royal court to adjudicate a case. Gradually, a formal system of named writs evolved, and it became necessary for the plaintiff to purchase an appropriate writ from the king's chancellor to commence their action. The writs became crystallized into certain forms and contents, and if plaintiff could not fit their case into one of the prescribed writs, they had no action in the royal courts. By the fifteenth century, it became possible, and common, to commence an action by bill (complaint) instead of royal writ, but plaintiff's declaration still had to state a cause of action in the recognized form, corresponding to the writs they could have selected.

The most important personal civil action was trespass. Its great significance lay in the fact that the plaintiff could recover actual damages. For many years it also retained a quasi-criminal character in that a vanquished defendant was usually imprisoned or fined. It became immensely popular and largely supplanted the appeal in felony cases except for homicide. No civil action was permitted in the king's court for wrongful death until Lord Campbell's Act was passed in 1846.

The three common forms of the writ were (1) trespass *vi et armis* (with force and arms) for assault, battery, and false imprisonment; (2) trespass *de bonis asportatis* (taking of goods) for trespass to chattels; and (3) trespass *quare clausum fregit* (breach of the "close") for trespass to land.

Concurrent with the growth of trespass there developed a practice of issuing and honoring writs for wrongs which did not fit within the confines of the designated trespass actions. Such writs eventually became classified as an action of trespass on the case or, more correctly, "action on the case." Unlike the trespass writs, which had developed into inflexible forms, the "case" writs set forth the facts of a plaintiff's particular case. By the sixteenth century, "case" had become a distinct and generic form of action.

As time went on, certain recurring case actions crystallized and were separated into named actions having rules and writs of their own. Trespass, together with "case" and its progeny, account for almost all of the actions which we now refer to as the law of torts. The most important case-spawned action was negligence.

B. Evolution of Theories of Liability

In the final stages of their evolution, there were three basic differences between trespass and "case" so far as tort remedies were concerned:

1. Trespass was applicable when the defendant committed some affirmative act that caused a direct and immediate injury to the plaintiff; "case" was the remedy for indirect or consequential harm.

2. "Case" required proof of actual damages; trespass actions did not.

3. At one time, it was thought that trespass liability was "strict," or nearly so. It was said that the plaintiff did not have to prove the defendant's fault. More

recent analyses, however, suggest that the situation may have been more complicated, and to some extent may be beyond our knowledge because of the applicable rules of procedure and the limited reports available. It may be that if the defendant pleaded the general issue, under that defense they could prove their lack of fault. Whatever the true rule may have been, fault was not a part of the plaintiff's case. Absence of fault, if relevant at all, was a defense, but not an absolute defense because the jury could still decide for the plaintiff.

Negligence was, until relatively recently, merely one basis for liability in a number of different civil actions for which "case" was the appropriate writ. Gradually, during the nineteenth century, negligence emerged as a separate action.

In the United States, fault quickly became a necessary element of plaintiff's case in a trespass action. For example, in *Brown v. Kendall*, 60 Mass. 292 (1850), Defendant, attempting to beat two fighting dogs with a stick, accidentally struck the Plaintiff in the eye. In Plaintiff's suit against Defendant, even though trespass was the proper form of the action (direct injury), Plaintiff lost because he failed to prove fault (intentional or negligent misconduct).

VI. The Roles of Judges and Juries

In the United States, most tort cases are settled prior to trial, but they are settled largely based on counsel's predictions as to what a jury's verdict in the case is likely to be. This book briefly outlines the rules of tort law, but you should remember that for the most part, these rules do not decide actual cases. The pre-eminent power in resolving tort cases lies with the "trier of fact"—in most tort cases, a jury.

It is commonly said that questions of law are for the court and questions of fact are for the jury. This is not entirely true, and is a little misleading, since judges possess the ultimate power to decide which is which. But through well-established rules and customs, and using the general verdict, juries are given wide latitude to decide these controversies without court interference.

There are three kinds of questions of fact or jury questions. First, the jury must determine what in fact occurred. Then, in most cases, the jury is required to make one or more decisions as to the legal consequences of these facts—usually based on a general legal definition given by the court. Finally, the jury must determine whether the plaintiff was damaged by defendant's tortious act and the dollar value of plaintiff's compensable damages.

There are three types of questions of law for the court to decide. First, certain issues are invariably issues of law, such as (1) whether a defendant owed a plaintiff any recognized legal duty, or, conversely, whether the plaintiff has a legally protected right; (2) the elements of proof necessary to establish liability (or nonliability) and the measure of damages; and (3) whether, on the facts, some particular rule of law imposes or excuses liability as a matter of law—for example, the rule that violation of a certain safety statute is negligence per se, or that false statements of intent are not actionable misrepresentations. By embodying particular standards of conduct in rules of law, courts take from the jury the power to determine the legal consequences of certain facts and thereby transform questions of fact into questions of law and enable the court to decide the case instead of the jury.

Second, all issues which are ordinarily questions of fact for the jury become questions of law for the court if the judge decides that the evidence on that issue so overwhelmingly favors one conclusion that reasonable jurors could not reach the opposite conclusion.

Third, judges alone apply rules of procedure, which may have an important effect upon the outcome of the case—especially rules concerning the admission and exclusion of evidence, burden of proof, presumptions, etc. However, juries render the ultimate judgment in a substantial proportion of tort cases, particularly where the controlling issues involve disputes as to what occurred or mixed questions of law and fact.

Tort law is not merely a system of rules of actionable or nonactionable conduct, but also of rules that determine when the law will not decide cases and instead will leave the decision whether to impose liability to the discretion of the jury. In fact, one leading torts scholar suggested that "nearly all legal theory in negligence cases is designed to serve the ends of allocating the power of judgment respectively to judge and jury." (L. Green, Judge & Jury 261). In many—perhaps even most—tort cases, rules of law take one only so far, and the lawyer or judge cannot determine the ultimate liability question. In such cases, it is necessary and entirely appropriate to say that beyond a certain point, the remaining issues are jury questions, and therefore whether the defendant is liable to the plaintiff is merely an educated guess.

VII. Torts in Relation to Other Areas of Law

A. Torts and Contracts

When a defendant enters into a contract with a plaintiff, they voluntarily assume an obligation to take certain action (or, occasionally, to refrain from some action). Since this duty arises from the contract, its breach is actionable in contract and not in tort. However, some contractual undertakings are held to create, in addition to contractual duties, duties that may be actionable in tort if breached.

B. Torts and Criminal Law

In a very general sense, tort law is the private or civil counterpart of criminal law. Indeed, in the early stages of the common law, tort and crime were not separate concepts. There was one law of "wrongs." Today they are entirely distinct, but there are tort actions which roughly correspond to many crimes, and the same act may be both a tort and a crime—or one or the other but not both. The principles of liability of analogous torts and crimes are not necessarily the same and should not be confused.

VIII. Introductory Terms

To help you navigate this content, here are a few preliminary definitions of foundational tort law terms.

A. Tortious Conduct

"Tortious conduct" includes both acts and omissions. Almost any imaginable conduct may, in the right circumstances, be a source of injury to another and therefore is potentially tortious. But not every injury is actionable in tort. It is commonly said that conduct is tortious only if that conduct violates some duty imposed by law. But this test is meaningless, since it is tort law that determines which duties are actionable in tort. Therefore, no meaningful definition of "tort" or "tortious conduct" is possible, apart from the specific liability rules of the individual torts themselves.

B. Injury

An "injury" means the invasion of an interest protected by tort law. It is not limited to physical harm or even harm that is directly measurable in monetary terms.

C. Plaintiff

The party in a tort lawsuit that initiates a tort claim to redress the injury they experienced, which was caused by the tortious conduct of a defendant.

D. Defendant

The party in a tort lawsuit that the plaintiff alleges has acted tortiously and caused plaintiff harm.

Part One

Intentional Torts

■ ANALYSIS

- f. Property of Others
- 2. Forcible Retaking of Chattels
  - a. Rule
  - b. Chattel Rightfully Acquired
  - c. Entry upon Land
  - d. Privilege to Detain Suspected Shoplifters
- 3. Repossession of Land
  - a. Peaceful Repossession
  - b. Forcible Repossession

E. Necessity
- 1. Rule
- 2. Public Necessity
- 3. Private Necessity

F. Authority of Law
- 1. Rule
- 2. Types of Privileged Acts
- 3. Scope: Ministerial vs. Discretionary Acts
- 4. Use of Force

G. Discipline
- 1. Children
  - a. Parents
  - b. Loco Parentis
  - c. Reasonableness

H. Review Questions

I. Liability Rules for Intentional Torts

A. Intent

1. What Is Intentional Conduct?

Conduct is intentional if the actor (a) desires to cause the consequences of their act ("purpose" intent), or (b) engages in conduct knowing that a result is substantially certain to result from their act. R.2d § 8A; R.3d Liability for Physical & Emotional Harm § 1.

2. Proof of Intent

Ordinarily, the plaintiff proves defendant's intent circumstantially—that is, inferred from the defendant's conduct. We can infer that the defendant intended the natural and probable consequences of their acts in light of the surrounding circumstances of which they may be assumed to be aware.

3. Intent Distinguished from Motive

You may sometimes hear the word "motive" mentioned, particularly in the criminal law context. Intent is the desire to cause certain immediate consequences. Motive is the actor's reason for having that desire—revenge, protest, punishment, self-defense, defense of another, or even to be of help. So far as liability for intentional torts is concerned, the actor's motive is irrelevant on the issue of intent. However, motive may sometimes aggravate or mitigate the damage award, or be part of an affirmative defense (e.g., self-defense).

4. Intentional Conduct Distinguished from Negligent Conduct

It can be difficult to distinguish intentional conduct from other types of conduct (such as negligent or reckless conduct, which are central to other torts). What distinguishes intentional conduct is the level of certainty of harmful consequences. If the harmful result is intended or certain to occur, the tort is intentional. If a defendant's conduct merely creates a foreseeable risk of harm, which may or may not be realized, their conduct is negligent.

5. Children

Since intent is the desire to cause certain immediate consequences, very young children may be held liable for intentional torts, even though they are so young that they are incapable of negligence, if the child is found capable of forming the required intent. In some states, however, particularly young children (say, under age six or seven) are conclusively presumed incapable of harmful intent.

6. People with Mental Health Conditions

In most jurisdictions, people with mental health conditions that impact their conduct are liable for their intentional torts, even when incapable of forming a purpose or understanding the consequences of their conduct. *Accord* R.2d 895J. In effect, if they committed the act, any mental incapacity is ignored.

7. Transferred Intent

Transferred intent is a rule applied to the five intentional torts which are the progeny of the parent "trespass" action—assault, battery, false imprisonment, trespass to land, and trespass to chattels. A defendant's intent to commit any one of these torts automatically "transfers" and supplies the intent necessary to any of the other torts in this group. It also transfers from targeting Person A (Defendant's intended victim) to affecting Person B (Defendant's actual but unintended victim).

Example: Defendant intends to injure Person A, but at the same time (or instead) injures Person B. Defendant committed an intentional tort upon Person B, even though Defendant was unaware of Person B's existence or presence or of any risk of harm to Person B.

R.3d Liability for Physical & Emotional Harm § 33, comment *c.*; R.2d §§ 16(2), 21(1)(a), 35(1)(a).

8. Scope of Liability: The Extended Liability Principle

Broader scope-of-liability rules apply to intentional torts. A tortfeasor who intentionally causes physical harm is subject to liability for all the consequences of that harm even if those consequences were unintended, unlikely, or unforeseeable. R.3d Liability for Physical & Emotional Harm § 33.

B. Battery

(Dobbs §§ 28–32; R.2d §§ 13–20)

1. Rule

Battery is an intentional harmful or offensive contact (direct or indirect) with the person of the other. R.2d §§ 13, 18.

2. Intent Required

The defendant must have acted intending (i.e., with purpose or knowledge) to cause a harmful or offensive contact with the plaintiff. R.2d §§ 13, 14, 16, 18.

3. Plaintiff's Person

Plaintiff's "person" includes their body and those things in contact with it or closely connected to it and identified with it, such as clothing, an object held in the plaintiff's hand, or an object so closely associated or identified with the plaintiff that, considering the nature of the contact, a typical person would deem it an offense against their person.

Example: Defendant swings their arm at Plaintiff and forcefully knocks off Plaintiff's hat, or forcibly grabs a plate that Plaintiff is holding in Plaintiff's hand. Both are batteries.

4. Plaintiff's Awareness

The tort is the contact itself, and therefore the plaintiff need not have been aware of it at the time.

5. Jurisdictional Split When No Harm Intended

Courts are split on whether it is only required that a defendant intend to cause the contact, which ultimately turns out to be, in fact, harmful or offensive ("single intent"); or whether a defendant must intend to cause both the contact and also harm or offense ("dual intent").

For example, a harmful or offensive contact may occur where defendant intended only a practical joke. And surgery performed without a plaintiff's consent is a battery, even if the defendant had only the best of motives and the result was beneficial to the plaintiff because the surgical procedure meets the definition of physical harm.

6. Harmful Contact

A harmful contact is actionable only if it produces some bodily harm. Bodily harm includes any physical impairment or damage, however slight, to any part of Plaintiff's body (such as a cut, bruise, or burn), even if the "damage" is ultimately beneficial (e.g., a surgical procedure); illness; and physical (but not emotional) pain. R.2d § 15.

7. Offensive Contact

Offensive contact is that which offends a reasonable sense of personal dignity, such as by being hostile, insulting, loathsome, or unduly personal. R.2d § 19. A plaintiff can recover dignitary or mental distress damages for an offensive contact even if the plaintiff sustained no physical harm.

Contact can be offensive even if it would not offend a reasonable person, so long as the defendant was given notice that certain contact would be offensive to the plaintiff.

Example: Defendant flicks a glove in Plaintiff's face or angrily grabs Plaintiff's lapels. Defendant has made an offensive contact.

Example: Plaintiff is about to deliver a baby by cesarean section. Plaintiff informs the hospital personnel through her physician that her religious beliefs prohibit her from being seen unclothed by a male attendant. During the surgery, while the patient is unconscious, a male nurse observes and touches the patient. The touching is a battery.

8. Consent

If a plaintiff consents to the contact, the defendant is privileged to make it and there is no tort. (This is generally true of all intentional torts.) Consent may sometimes be assumed. In a crowded society, some unpermitted contact is inevitable and customary. And consent may be assumed because of some pre-existing relationship between plaintiff and defendant.

C. Assault

(Dobbs §§ 33–35; R.2d §§ 21–34)

1. Rule

Assault occurs when a person intends to put—and does, in fact, put—another person in imminent apprehension of a harmful or offensive contact. A defendant is also subject to liability for assault if they intend to cause a battery and the other person is put in imminent apprehension of that battery. R.2d § 21.

2. Intent Required

Defendant's conduct need not have been motivated by hostility. An assault emanating from a practical joke, or even an attempt to be helpful (e.g., medical treatment) is nonetheless an assault. R.2d § 34.

3. Apprehension

"Apprehension," as a legal term of art in this cause of action, does not mean fear. It means awareness. Thus, it is not necessary that plaintiff experience the emotion of fear. Plaintiff must merely be aware of an imminent contact. Plaintiff must have been aware of defendant's threatening act at the time before it is terminated. R.2d § 22.

a. Threat Against Another

It is not necessary that defendant direct their act against plaintiff. It is sufficient that plaintiff reasonably perceives the threat of a battery to themself. This is true by operation of transferred intent, as discussed previously. R.2d § 32. But plaintiff's apprehension of a battery only to a third person, and not to plaintiff, is not an assault against plaintiff, no matter how concerned plaintiff may be for the third person's safety. R.2d § 26.

b. Defendant Apparently Intends Only Assault

Defendant's conduct may be an assault even if it is apparent to plaintiff that defendant intended only an assault and not a battery, provided plaintiff apprehends that the battery may occur. R.2d § 28.

c. Reasonableness of Apprehension

Plaintiff's perception of the fact that a contact is imminent must be the same conclusion that a reasonable person would make.

Example: Bank Robber walked up to Bank Teller holding a bomb and threatened to blow up the bank. The bomb, which appeared to be real, was, in fact, fake; it was a harmless "bomb" full of colorful glitter. Bank Teller, seeing the "bomb," fully expected imminent bodily injury. Bank Robber may be liable for assault because Bank Teller's apprehension of an imminent (indirect) harmful contact was reasonable, due to the realistic appearance of the "bomb."

4. Imminent

Contact must be perceived as imminent, or, in other words, immediate (as opposed to contact sometime in the future). There must be an apparent intent and ability to carry out the threat immediately. R.2d §§ 24, 29.

a. Words

Mere words, unaccompanied by a physical act, are not an assault. But words may give a sufficiently threatening character to an otherwise innocuous or inoffensive movement. R.2d § 31.

b. Apprehension of Future Battery

If defendant's words or other circumstances are understood by plaintiff as only threatening a battery at some time other than the present, there is no assault.

c. Apparent Ability to Consummate

Defendant must have an apparent present ability to carry out the battery. If defendant is so located or confined or otherwise under some restriction or disability to be incapable of immediately carrying out the threat, and plaintiff is aware of this, there is no assault. On the other hand, if it appears to plaintiff that defendant has the present ability to commit the battery, it does not matter that, in fact, defendant does not have or believe they have that ability. R.2d § 33.

5. Conditional Threat

If defendant intentionally puts another in apprehension of an imminent harmful or offensive contact, there is still an assault, even if defendant gives plaintiff an option to escape the contact by obeying defendant's command. R.2d § 30.

Example: Batter, holding a baseball bat, approaches Baseball Fan menacingly, raising the bat and shouting, "Shut up now or I'll hit *you* out of the park!" Despite the words giving Baseball Fan an escape, this would still be considered an assault under the circumstances. The words here do not negate Batter's actions that created Baseball Fan's reasonable apprehension of an imminent harmful contact.

D. False Imprisonment

(Dobbs §§ 36–39; R.2d §§ 35–45A, 120A)

1. Rule

False imprisonment occurs when a person intentionally confines another within fixed boundaries and the confined person is either aware of the confinement or harmed by it. R.2d § 35.

2. Intent

The requisite intent is merely the intent to confine another. A mistake of identity is no excuse. And no personal malice, hostility, or desire to harm is necessary. A good faith belief that confinement is justified is no excuse. R.2d §§ 43, 44.

3. Confinement

a. Defined

Confinement may be broader than the term "imprisonment" implies. It is enough if plaintiff is prevented from leaving a given area, such as a room, an automobile, a building, or perhaps even a larger area. Within that area, however, the confinement must be complete, and plaintiff must have no known reasonable or safe avenue of exit or escape. Merely to block plaintiff's path in one direction is not sufficient. R.2d §§ 36, 38.

b. Indirectly Caused

So long as the defendant has the requisite intent, it is immaterial whether defendant's act directly or indirectly causes the confinement. R.2d § 37. One who instigates confinement, or uses another person to unlawfully detain another, may also be a tortfeasor.

c. Means

The confinement may be by means of:

1) Actual or apparent physical barriers. R.2d § 38.
2) Physical force, or credible threats of physical force, to which plaintiff submits. R.2d §§ 39, 40.
3) Duress sufficient to vitiate plaintiff's consent, as where defendant threatens to harm another or plaintiff's valuable property or restrains such property.
4) When confinement is achieved under color of legal authority, it is sometimes called false arrest. If defendant has or purports to have legal authority to take plaintiff into custody, exercises it, plaintiff believes that defendant has or may have such authority, and plaintiff submits against their will, there is confinement. False arrest is merely one form of false imprisonment, not a separate tort. False arrest may also give rise to a statutory civil rights claim.
5) Defendant's refusal to release plaintiff from a once-valid confinement, or to aid in such release by providing a means of escape, when defendant was under a duty so to act.

R.2d §§ 38, 39, 40. 40A, 41, 45.

4. Plaintiff's Knowledge

Ordinarily, plaintiff must be aware of the confinement. However, if plaintiff suffers some physical harm from the confinement, it is immaterial that, due to some mental or sensory defect or other circumstance, plaintiff did not know that they were confined. R.2d § 42.

5. Shoplifters

When defendant in good faith detains a suspected shoplifter, courts tend to deny liability, such as by finding that plaintiff voluntarily consented to remain or by creating a special privilege to detain them on the premises, without arrest. R.2d § 120A. And most states have enacted statutes that give the shopkeeper a limited privilege to detain such persons in a reasonable manner for a reasonable time to investigate, based on a reasonable suspicion.

E. Intentional Infliction of Emotional Distress (IIED)

(Dobbs §§ 303–07; R.2d §§ 46–48)

1. Rule

When a person, by extreme and outrageous conduct, intentionally or recklessly causes severe emotional harm to another, that person is subject to liability for that emotional harm and—if the emotional harm causes bodily harm—also for the resulting bodily harm. R.2d § 46; R.3d Liability for Physical & Emotional Harm § 46.

2. Defendant's Conduct

a. General Rule

Defendant's conduct must be extreme, outrageous, intolerable—not merely insulting, profane, abusive, annoying, or even threatening—"so extreme in degree as to go beyond all possible bounds of decency, and to be regarded as atrocious, and utterly intolerable in civilized society." R.2d § 46 cmt. *d*.

Unless the defendant knows of some special sensitivity or vulnerability of the plaintiff, mere verbal abuse, name-calling, rudeness, insolence, and threats to do that which defendant has a legal right to do are generally not actionable, absent circumstances of aggravation.

A single instance of abusive or otherwise obnoxious conduct that falls short of the required standard may not be enough, but the same conduct can become actionable if repeated or carried out over time.

b. Exception: Public Utility

Common carriers, innkeepers, and other public utilities may be liable to their patrons for profane, grossly insulting, or indecent language or conduct by their employees acting within the scope of their employment. R.2d § 48.

c. Intent

In most cases, the defendant had a purpose to cause plaintiff severe emotional distress. However, most jurisdictions also allow recovery where defendant knew or had reason to know that there was a high probability that emotional distress would follow from their conduct and defendant acted in conscious disregard of that risk.

d. Exercising One's Legal Rights

Exercising one's legal rights in a reasonable manner cannot be actionable, even if defendant knows that this will cause plaintiff severe emotional distress. But defendant is not immunized from liability if defendant's conduct goes so far beyond what is necessary to exercise the right that it is extreme and outrageous. R.3d § 46 cmt. *e*.

3. Plaintiff's Response

Plaintiff's emotional distress must be severe. If plaintiff merely becomes unhappy, humiliated, or despondent for a short time, plaintiff cannot recover. But if plaintiff's anguish is great, and especially if prolonged, most courts will allow the action even absent any physical manifestation of the mental suffering, or bodily harm (e.g., physical illness, heart condition, miscarriage) caused by it. A few jurisdictions apparently still require such bodily harm.

4. Abuse of Power

A common fact situation resulting in liability involves an abuse by Defendant of some relation or status which gives them actual or apparent power to damage Plaintiff's interests, e.g., threats by bill collectors, insurance adjusters, landlords, school officials, police, where such threats go beyond the ordinary means of persuasion or demands which they have a right to make and become flagrant abuses of power.

5. Conduct Directed at Third Persons

Even though defendant's distress-producing conduct is directed at a third person, if defendant's conduct intentionally or recklessly causes severe emotional distress in plaintiff, recovery may sometimes be allowed.

a. The Restatement (Second) rule limits recovery in such cases where either (i) Plaintiff is present and witnesses Defendant's conduct, Defendant knows of Plaintiff's presence, and Third Party is a member of Plaintiff's immediate family, or (ii) Plaintiff's severe emotional distress results in bodily harm. R.2d § 46(2).

b. As to this category, the Restatement (Third) removes the Restatement (Second) limitations and requires only that Plaintiff contemporaneously perceive the distress-producing event.

c. Some courts have relaxed the requirement of presence or contemporaneous perception in particularly compelling circumstances.

Example: Defendant kidnaps Plaintiff's child.

6. Extended Liability

In the case of most other torts, defendant must take plaintiff as they find plaintiff. Defendant is liable for all of plaintiff's physical consequences resulting from defendant's conduct, however unforeseeable those consequences are. With respect to IIED, however, defendant is not liable to the extent that plaintiff's emotional response is beyond the bounds of normal human reactions to that conduct. In other words, the distress must be such as a reasonable person of ordinary sensitivity would experience.

But if defendant knew that plaintiff had a special vulnerability, defendant may be liable for conduct which is extreme and outrageous in light of that special vulnerability, even though the same conduct would not be expected to produce a severe response in a normal, healthy adult. See R.3d Liability for Physical & Emotional Harm § 46 cmt. *j*. And if defendant's conduct satisfies the elements of IIED, defendant is liable not only for plaintiff's severe emotional distress but also for greater harm (e.g., illness or other bodily harm) even if that harm was unforeseeable. See R.3d §§ 31, 46 cmt. *j*.

7. Transferred Intent

The doctrine of transferred intent does not apply to IIED, at least insofar as defendant's intent was only to commit some other intentional tort. R.2d § 47. However, there can be transferred intent from defendant's intent to commit IIED against a third person, which actually results in IIED to plaintiff—even if defendant was unaware that plaintiff would be exposed to defendant's IIED conduct.

8. Mishandling of a Corpse

Intentional or reckless mishandling of a corpse may give rise to a cause of action in the next of kin who are thereby emotionally distressed. R.2d § 868.

F. Trespass to Land

(Dobbs §§ 50–58; R.2d §§ 157–166)

1. Rule

Defendant is subject to liability for trespass to land in the possession of plaintiff if defendant intentionally (a) enters the land or causes a thing or third person to do so, (b) remains on the land after their privilege to be there has expired, or (c) fails to remove from the land a thing which they are under a duty to remove. R.2d § 158.

2. Possession

Plaintiff is in "possession" (a) when they occupy the land with the intent to control it, or (b) if no one else is in possession, they were the last occupier or they have the right to immediate occupancy. R.2d § 157.

3. Intent

The intent required is merely to enter upon the land, cause the entry, or remain. Defendant's good faith (but erroneous) belief that they have a right to be on the land, or their reasonable mistake concerning title, right to possession, consent, or privilege, is no defense. R.2d § 164.

4. Manner

The trespass may be directly or indirectly caused.

a. Vertical Boundaries

The boundaries of land extend above and below the surface, and therefore the trespass may be by an intrusion at, above, or beneath the surface. R.2d § 159.

b. Exception: Airplanes

Plane flights over private property present a special problem. Several theories are used to balance the possessor's rights against the needs of aviation.

i. Zone Theory

Plaintiff owns only so much of the airspace as is in their "effective possession," i.e., the altitude up to which they might in the future make effective use of the airspace.

ii. Actual Use Theory

Plaintiff owns only so much of the airspace as they are actually using; there is no tort absent interference with plaintiff's present use and enjoyment.

iii. Privilege Theory

Plaintiff's ownership of the airspace is unlimited, but subject to a privilege of flight.

iv. Nuisance Theory

"Ownership" of the airspace is ignored. Plaintiff has an action in nuisance (or negligence) only if flights interfere with their use and enjoyment of the land.

v. Restatement

Compare R.2d § 159(2): Overflight is a trespass only if it (a) enters into the "immediate reaches" of the airspace next to the land, and (b) interferes substantially with plaintiff's use and enjoyment.

vi. Federal Aviation Laws

Under the Supremacy Clause, federal aviation laws and regulations may make privileged flights which would otherwise be a trespass.

c. Causing Trespass by Things

It is no less a trespass if defendant does not personally enter the land but merely causes something to do so.

Examples: A shot fired by Defendant from adjoining land across Plaintiff's property, though never touching the surface of Plaintiff's land; erecting a structure which overhangs Plaintiff's property line; utility wires.

5. Damages

If the trespass is intentional, the tort is complete without proof of any actual harm. Of course, plaintiff may recover for all harm resulting to their property, as well as resulting harm to persons and things upon it. R.2d §§ 162, 163.

6. Reckless or Negligent Intrusions

An intrusion upon plaintiff's land may result from defendant's negligent conduct or abnormally dangerous activity. In such cases liability is determined in the usual fashion by the rules of those other torts. R.2d § 165.

G. Intentional Interferences with Tangible Personal Property

(Dobbs §§ 59–67; R.2d §§ 21–244)

1. Trespass to Chattels and Conversion Distinguished

Trespass to chattels and conversion are the two principal intentional torts against plaintiff's personal property. A conversion is merely a trespass to a chattel (movable property) that is so serious that defendant can be forced to pay the full value of the chattel. In such cases, the plaintiff may choose either action, depending on whether or not they want the chattel back and perhaps also on the preferred measure of damages. Thus, virtually all conversions are also trespasses, but minor trespasses are not conversions.

2. Trespass to Chattels

a. Rule

Defendant commits a trespass to plaintiff's chattel when defendant intentionally interferes with it, either by physical contact or by dispossession. R.2d § 217.

b. Possession

At one time, only the person then in possession (or entitled to immediate possession on demand) could maintain an action for trespass to a chattel. The modern view is that both the person in possession and one entitled to future possession may bring a trespass action. R.2d §§ 216, 21–220.

c. Intent

No wrongful motive is necessary. The intent required is merely to act upon the chattel. Thus, defendant's good faith, reasonable (but mistaken) belief that defendant owns the chattel or for some other reason is privileged to deal with it is no defense. And defendant need not know that their conduct is a violation of the possessory rights of another. R.2d §§ 217, 244.

d. Interference by Physical Contact

One form of trespass is interference by physical contact, which may be direct or indirect, and consists of any impairment of the chattel's condition, quality or value. R.2d §§ 218, 219.

e. Dispossession

A dispossession consists of taking a chattel from plaintiff's possession without plaintiff's consent, or by fraud or duress, or into custody of the law; blocking plaintiff's access to the chattel; or destroying it while it is in plaintiff's possession. R.2d § 221. Dispossession even for a short time is still a trespass.

f. Damages

In the case of physical contact, plaintiff must prove actual damages. Thus, if defendant merely handles the chattel or moves it or perhaps even uses it, without harming or affecting it or impairing its usefulness, defendant has committed no tort. But any dispossession is a trespass for which at least nominal damages may be awarded. Given a trespass, the same broad damage rules apply as in the case of trespass to land, and defendant will be liable for all resulting damages to the chattel and to plaintiff, however innocently caused, including bodily harm.

3. Conversion

a. Rule

Conversion is an intentional exercise of dominion or control over a chattel which so seriously interferes with a plaintiff's right to control it that a defendant may justly be required to pay plaintiff its full value. R.2d § 222A.

b. Degree of Interference

There is no simple test for determining when the interference is so aggravated as to constitute a conversion. The important factors are set out in § 222A of the Second Restatement:

1) The extent and duration of the defendant's exercise of dominion or control;
2) Defendant's intent to assert a right inconsistent with plaintiff's ownership;
3) Defendant's good faith;
4) The extent and duration of the resulting interference with plaintiff's right of control;
5) The harm done to the property, if any; and
6) The inconvenience and expense caused to the plaintiff.

The central focus here is on the degree, nature, extent, and duration of the defendant's actual interference and whether defendant acted with the motives and intentions reflecting ownership of the property.

c. Intent to Exercise Dominion or Control

The defendant's intent inquiry is about the defendant's intent to interact with the property, not the defendant's intention to deprive the plaintiff of it. While the defendant's beliefs, motives and intentions may be relevant in assessing the seriousness of his interference, the only intent required for the tort is an intent to exercise dominion or control over the chattel. Thus, a defendant's good faith or honest mistake is no defense if the interference is sufficiently great (e.g., destruction or theft). R.2d §§ 224, 244. For example, when you accidentally walk out of your neighborhood coffee shop with another customer's drink, you have committed conversion, even though the mistake was inadvertent.

d. Types of Conversion

A conversion may occur when the defendant:

(1) acquires possession,

(2) moves the chattel,

(3) makes an unauthorized transfer, delivery, or disposal,

(4) withholds possession,

(5) destroys or materially alters the chattel, or

(6) under certain circumstances, merely uses the chattel. See R.2d § 223.

e. Possession

Either the person in possession or the person entitled to immediate possession may maintain the action. R.2d §§ 224A, 225. And to the extent not recovered by one of the former, a person entitled to future possession may recover his loss. R.2d § 243.

f. "Chattel" Broadly Defined

Originally, conversion was available only with respect to tangible chattels. Today, most courts have extended it to include intangible personal property represented by, or merged into, a document. R.2d § 242; U.C,C. § 3–419. It may even extend to intangibles represented by documents that do not embody the right but are merely important to its exercise (e.g., a bank deposit book).

g. Damages as Full Value of the Chattel at the Time of Conversion

Damages include the full value of the chattel at the time of conversion, plus interest. Under the prevailing view, plaintiff is never required to (but may) accept a tender of the chattel's return in mitigation of damages. Compare R.2d § 922.

II. Interference with Federal Constitutional Rights

A. Persons Acting Under Color of State Law

42 U.S.C. § 1983 creates a tort cause of action against one who "under color of" state law (i.e., state officers and employees and private citizens acting under the authority or protection of state law) interferes with a federal constitutional right of another. Municipalities are "persons" who may be liable under this section, but a municipality is liable only if the right is violated because of some municipal *policy* or *custom.*

Monell v. Dep't of Social Services, 436 U.S. 658 (1978). A failure to properly train certain municipal employees, such as police officers, can constitute "deliberate indifference" sufficient to be deemed a city policy, thereby satisfying *Monell*.

B. Federal Officers and Employees

One whose federal constitutional rights have been violated by a federal officer or employee may have an action against them for damages under the doctrine of *Bivens v. Six Unknown Named Agents of Federal Bureau of Narcotics*, 403 U.S. 388 (1971).

III. Review Questions

[Answers Provided in Appendix A]

1. Defendant locks Plaintiff in their second-floor dormitory room while Plaintiff is sound asleep. Defendant stands outside the only door with the intent to confine Plaintiff in the room until 6:00 p.m. At 5:50, Plaintiff wakes up and pushes on the door. Feeling the pushing, Defendant changes their mind and yanks open the door. Plaintiff falls forward breaking their wrist. Using the IRAC method of analysis, assess whether Defendant is liable for false imprisonment.

2. Same facts as above. Using the IRAC method of analysis, assess whether Defendant is liable for battery.

3. Use IRAC to reason through each of the conclusions below.

   (a) Defendant steals Plaintiff's hat from a hat rack. Five minutes later Defendant is apprehended, and they give the hat back to Plaintiff. Conversion or trespass to chattels? Explain your reasoning.

   (b) Defendant, justifiably mistaken, takes Plaintiff's hat from a hat rack, promptly discovers their error, and is about to replace it when the wind catches it and blows it down a sewer. Conversion or trespass to chattels? Explain your reasoning.

   (c) Defendant, justifiably mistaken, takes Plaintiff's hat from a hat rack, promptly discovers their error, and returns it unharmed five minutes later. Conversion or trespass to chattels? Explain your reasoning.

4. Multiple Choice: Defendant Homeowner builds a garage on what they and Plaintiff Neighbor both believe to be Defendant's land. Later a resurvey of the land establishes that the garage extends 2 inches into Plaintiff Neighbor's land.

   a. Defendant Homeowner is not liable to Plaintiff Neighbor for trespass because Homeowner does not live in the garage and thus is not occupying Plaintiff Neighbor's land.

   b. Defendant Homeowner is not liable to Plaintiff Neighbor for trespass because the invasion of Plaintiff Neighbor's land is minimal.

   c. Defendant Homeowner is not liable to Plaintiff Neighbor for trespass because Homeowner had no intent to enter onto Plaintiff Neighbor's land.

   d. Defendant Homeowner is liable to Plaintiff Neighbor for trespass because Homeowner built on Plaintiff Neighbor's property.

   e. Defendant Homeowner is liable to Plaintiff Neighbor for trespass because Homeowner was negligent in not searching the title and surveying the land before building.

IV. Defenses to Liability for Intentional Torts: Privileges

A. Privilege

(Dobbs §§ 68–69)

1. Introduction

"Privilege" is the general term applied to various defenses in which special circumstances justify conduct which would otherwise be tortious. In other words, even though a plaintiff has proven facts that establish the prima facie elements of a tort, the defendant can nonetheless prove other facts that establish a legal privilege rendering defendant's conduct non-tortious.

2. Privileges Compared to Other Defenses

Privileges differ from other legal defenses that the defendant might assert, such as contributory negligence and assumption of risk, which operate to reduce or bar a plaintiff's recovery entirely or partially but do not negate the tortious character of defendant's underlying conduct. Privileges justify the defendant's conduct. Privileges are created by law irrespective of consent.

3. Defendant Generally Bears the Burden of Proof

Generally, privileges are affirmative defenses which the defendant must plead and prove. In the case of the intentional torts against plaintiff's person (assault, battery, false imprisonment), absence of consent is an element of the prima facie case and therefore would not be a defense. However, it is doubtful that this distinction has much vitality any longer.

4. Mistake Is Generally Not a Defense

The defendant's mistaken belief that they have a privilege—however innocent or justified—is per se not a defense to an underlying intentional tort, nor does it negate the requisite intent. However, mistake may be relevant in determining the existence of a privilege; certain privileges are based on the defendant's reasonable belief concerning some fact(s), even though it later turns out that the belief was mistaken.

B. Consent

(Dobbs §§ 95–106; R.2d §§ 49–62, 167–175, 252–256, 892, 892D)

1. In General

Consent is a defense to virtually any tort, but it is applied most frequently to intentional torts.

2. Actual Consent

There is actual consent when one is, in fact, explicitly willing for conduct to occur. It is a matter of the plaintiff's subjective state of mind. Consent is valid whether or not communicated to the defendant because otherwise the plaintiff has suffered no harm. R.2d § 892.

3. Apparent Consent

Plaintiff's words or conduct manifesting consent are sufficient to create a privilege to defendant to act in light of the apparent consent, even if plaintiff's actual (but undisclosed) state of mind was to the contrary. R.2d §§ 50, 892(2). The critique of this rule is that appearances of consent may be misleading or interpreted differently across genders, ethnicities, and cultures.

4. Conduct May Imply Consent

Conduct (a nod, gesture, or movement) can manifest consent. Even silence and inaction may indicate consent, provided such conduct would ordinarily be so interpreted, as where a reasonable person would be expected to speak or move if they objected. For example, a person lining up to receive an immunization shot and leaving their arm exposed to the physician may have impliedly consented to the shot. R.2d § 892.

5. Consent May Be Inferred from Custom or Usage

Consent may be inferred from custom and usage, from prior dealings between the parties, or from the existence between them of some relationship. For example, the custom of a neighbor allowing a friend to hunt or fish on their property in prior years can infer consent.

6. The Consenting Party Must Have Capacity

Lawful consent must be given by one having the capacity to do so, or one authorized to consent on behalf of another. Infancy, intoxication, or mental incapacity normally will vitiate effective consent. R.2d § 892A. In addition, some case law and some statutes render any purported consent ineffective within certain relationships—for example, consent by a patient to sexual contact with his or her mental health professional.

As to minors, there is no blanket rule that covers every situation. Generally, minors lack legal capacity. A sufficiently experienced and intelligent minor, however, may expressly or impliedly consent to everyday or necessary contacts in appropriate circumstances—for example, playing sports. Teenagers or "mature minors" may consent to some medical procedures.

An adult family member or guardian may be empowered to give consent on behalf of a minor or an incapacitated adult if the child lacks capacity. In general, a competent patient may not be treated over their objection, even if the treatment is required to save their life. Further, when a patient is incompetent, family members, doctors, hospitals, or anyone else may not override the patient's wishes, even if those wishes would deny them life-saving treatment. When a patient is incompetent, the caregiver must first attempt to determine the patient's wishes with respect to medical procedures before the rules governing substituted consent will be applied.

7. Apparent Consent

When an emergency actually or apparently threatens death or serious bodily harm and there is no time or opportunity to obtain the plaintiff's consent or substituted consent, consent will be implied. R.2d § 892D. This could include exceeding the scope of a limited consent previously given. Some courts will construe surgical consents broadly to include closely related conditions discovered during surgery while the patient is anesthetized and no one with authority to consent for the patient is immediately available.

8. Scope of Consent

The consent is to defendant's conduct, and once given, plaintiff cannot complain of the consequences of that conduct, however unforeseen. But defendant's privilege is limited to the conduct consented to or acts substantially similar. The consent may be conditioned or limited as to time, place, duration, area, and extent. R.2d § 892A. For example, a homeowner may open their property to an overnight guest but restrict it to a limited duration and just the residential home. The homeowner might have a claim for trespass if the guest overstays the duration or accesses the adjacent detached garage.

9. Mistake, Ignorance, Misrepresentation

Even though given pursuant to plaintiff's material mistake, misunderstanding or ignorance as to the nature or character of defendant's proposed conduct or the extent of the harm to be expected from it, plaintiff's consent is effective as manifested unless defendant knows of the mistake or induced it by their misrepresentation. R.2d § 892B.

Misrepresentation may include intentionally concealing material facts. If the misrepresentation goes to the essential nature or character of the act, the consent is invalid. For example, plaintiff's consent to sexual contact based on the misrepresentation that it is medical treatment is invalid. And if defendant knows they have a sexually transmitted disease but neither warns plaintiff nor provides any protection, the plaintiff's consent is ineffective.

10. Informed Consent

Under the doctrine of informed consent, if the defendant (e.g., a physician) misrepresents or fails to disclose to the plaintiff the possible consequences or risks of defendant's proposed conduct (e.g., a medical procedure), plaintiff's consent is not an informed one and therefore is not valid. Under the prevailing view, such risks or possible consequences are deemed collateral, and therefore failing to properly disclose them is a matter of negligence only. The failure to disclose does not vitiate the consent and thus there is no battery.

11. Duress

Consent given under duress is not effective. Duress includes physical coercion or threats that overcome the plaintiff's free will. Duress includes threats of immediate harm directed against plaintiff, their family or valuable property, but usually not threats of future harm or of mere economic duress. R.2d § 892B.

12. Revocation of Consent

Plaintiff can revoke their consent at any time by communicating the revocation to defendant and giving the defendant a reasonable time to avoid or cease that conduct. For example, a homeowner can revoke consent to store a car on their property, but they must give the car's owner a reasonable chance to retrieve the car.

13. Consent to Crime

Under the majority view, consent is not effective if the conduct consented to is a crime, at least in battery cases. For example, two persons who consent to an illegal street race could each sue the other for resulting harms, no matter that the conduct was unlawful. The minority view (and R.2d §§ 60, 61, 892C) is that consent to criminal conduct is valid unless in violation of a statute making conduct criminal to protect a class of persons irrespective of their consent (e.g., statutory rape).

C. Self-Defense and Defense of Others

(Dobbs §§ 70–75; R.2d §§ 63–76, 156, 261)

1. Self-Defense

a. Rule

Defendant has a privilege to use so much force as reasonably appears to be immediately necessary to protect themselves against imminent physical harm, offensive bodily contact, or confinement threatened by the intentional or negligent conduct of another. R.2d §§ 63, 65–68, 70–75.

Self-defense is normally invoked against an assault. However, it may also be privileged as to false imprisonment (including false arrest), the threat of negligently-caused harm (R.2d §§ 66, 68), and trespass or conversion (R.2d § 261).

b. Timing of Threat

This defense is about responding to immediate threats. Mere provocation is generally not enough to trigger the self-defense privilege. Insults and arguments ordinarily do not justify a physical attack in retaliation. This defense does not extend to acts done in retaliation for a past aggression or attempt, or as a warning against the repetition of a past aggression. R.2d § 63.

c. Only Reasonable Force Allowed

i. Privilege Limited to Defensive Force

Defendant may use only so much force as reasonably appears to be necessary for their defense. If the defendant becomes the aggressor or continues to use force after the plaintiff has become subdued, disarmed, or helpless or has clearly withdrawn from the fray, then the defendant is subject to liability for harm to the extent that it results from the excessive force. R.2d §§ 70, 71.

ii. The Limits on Deadly Force

The general rule is that defendant may use force likely to inflict death or serious bodily harm only when they reasonably believe that they are in danger of similar harm, or a sexual assault. In some jurisdictions, the defendant must also show that there was no safe or expedient means of retreat or escape, at least when they are not at home. R.2d § 65.

Exception—The Castle Doctrine: Retreat is not required if the defendant, located in their dwelling, reasonably believes that they or another occupant is in imminent danger of death or serious bodily harm. And in some jurisdictions, a person may defend their abode with deadly force against an unlawful intruder, even without proving that they reasonably apprehended death or serious bodily harm to themself or another occupant. They need only reasonably believe that the intruder intended to commit a felony.

Exception—Stand-Your-Ground Laws: The duty-to-retreat rule has been modified by statute in some states, and case law in a few others, eliminating the requirement that, in locations outside their abode, defendant must attempt to retreat or escape if they can. In these jurisdictions, defendant may use deadly force in all lawfully occupied locations so long as they reasonably believe they are in imminent danger of death or serious bodily harm.

iii. Negligently-Created

The foregoing rules apply only if the threatened harm is battery or false imprisonment. If the threat arises from conduct which is merely negligent, defendant should reasonably avoid the harm, if possible. R.2d § 64.

d. Form of Defensive Conduct

Defendant's self-defensive conduct may take the form of an assault, battery, or false imprisonment, as appropriate to the situation. R.2d § 67. Defendant may threaten a harmful or offensive contact (assault) even though the contact itself would not be privileged, provided their act is intended and reasonably believed to be likely to do no more than create an apprehension of such contact. R.2d § 70.

e. Effect of Defendant's Mistake

The privilege exists even when defendant reasonably but mistakenly believes that self-defense is necessary. The reasonableness of defendant's belief is judged by the objective standard of the reasonable person of average courage. Relevant factors include the circumstances of the event and the past history of the relationship, if any, between the parties. R.2d §§ 63, 70.

f. Injuries to Third Persons

While defending oneself against the conduct of an attacker, the defendant might injure the plaintiff, yielding the following results:

1) If the defendant acted unintentionally, then ordinary negligence rules apply and whether the defendant is liable depends on the

reasonableness of defendant's conduct under the circumstances. R.2d § 75.

2) If the defendant acted intentionally, then defendant is subject to liability to plaintiff for compensatory damages, unless the harm to plaintiff was relatively minor and substantially less than that with which defendant was threatened. R.2d §§ 73, 74.

2. Defense of Third Persons Is Also Permitted

a. Rule

Defendant is privileged to come to the defense of any other person under the same conditions and by the same means as they would be privileged to defend themself. R.2d § 76.

b. Effect of Mistake

Under one view, defendant's privilege exists only if and to the extent that the third person in fact had a right of self-defense. If defendant is wrong, their mistake, however reasonable, is irrelevant. Other courts (and R.2d § 76) hold that defendant's reasonable mistake does not negate the privilege.

D. Defense and Recovery of Property

(Dobbs §§ 76–81; R.2d §§ 77–111, 260)

1. Defense of Property

a. Rule

A possessor is privileged to use reasonable force to expel another or a chattel from their land, or to prevent another's imminent intrusion upon or interference with their land or chattels, or to prevent their dispossession, even though such conduct would otherwise be an assault, battery, false imprisonment, or trespass to the chattel. R.2d §§ 77, 80, 87, 260.

Example: A bar may remove an unruly customer, even if it involves a touching that would otherwise constitute a battery.

b. Request Desist First

Before a possessor of land can use force, they must first request that the intruder desist, unless it appears that the request would be useless or cannot be made before substantial harm is done. R.2d § 77. In some states, however, the defendant may use deadly force to defend their abode against unlawful entrants who defendant reasonably believes have entered to commit a felony.

c. Amount of Force

Defendant may use force or the threat of force, but only such actual force as is minimally required to prevent or terminate the intrusion. Force likely to cause death or great bodily harm is not privileged, except in those jurisdictions where, by statute, a lawful occupant is entitled to use deadly force to defend his abode against any felony.

Of course, the intruder is not privileged to resist reasonable attempts to bar or evict them, and if the intruder does resist, the possessor's privilege of self-defense applies, under which deadly force could be justified. R.2d §§ 77, 79, 81, 82.

d. Watchdogs, Spring Guns

Spring guns, concealed traps, and other mechanical devices, and vicious animals, used to defend defendant's property are used at defendant's risk. Defendant is subject to liability for any harm caused to an intruder by these devices that they would not have been privileged to inflict themself if present. R.2d §§ 84, 85. This is because of a strong public policy preference for human life over property interests.

e. Effect of Mistake

There are some limited privileges that allow individuals to enter the land of another. If the intruder in fact has one of these privileges, then the defendant has no privilege to defend their property, even though the defendant through ignorance or mistake reasonably believes that the intruder has no privilege, unless the intruder was responsible for that mistake. Conversely, the intruder's mistake does not defeat defendant's privilege unless the mistake was caused by defendant's fault. R.2d §§ 77, 78.

f. Property of Others

There is a similar privilege to defend the property of others, at least if the third person is a member of the defendant's immediate family or household or is one whose possession defendant has a duty to protect. R.2d § 86.

2. Forcible Retaking of Chattels

a. Rule

There is a limited self-help privilege to use force or threats of force to recapture defendant's chattel, wrongfully and forcibly taken from defendant's possession, even under claim of right, or obtained by fraud or duress. R.2d § 100. To exercise this privilege, the defendant must first demand their chattel's return, unless such a demand would be futile. R.2d § 104. Defendant must begin the recapture efforts promptly after their dispossession, or immediately upon learning of it, and continue them without interruption. R.2d § 103. Only reasonable force (short of that likely to cause serious bodily harm) may be used. R.2d §§ 106, 107.

b. Chattel Rightfully Acquired

If the chattel was rightfully acquired but is merely being tortiously withheld from defendant, this privilege does not exist. R.2d § 108.

c. Entry upon Land

Under certain circumstances, there is a privilege to enter upon another's land in pursuit of the chattel. R.2d §§ 198, 200.

d. Privilege to Detain Suspected Shoplifters

There is a common law or statutory privilege to detain suspected shoplifters, subject to certain limitations. See II.D.5., supra.

3. Repossession of Land

a. Peaceful Repossession

Defendant, who is entitled to the immediate possession of land, may, if they can, peacefully enter and retake possession without liability for trespass, and thereafter defend their possession as outlined in part 1. above. R.2d §§ 97, 185.

b. Forcible Repossession

In most jurisdictions, the rules for forcibly reacquiring possession of land are codified in "forcible entry and detainer" statutes. In the absence of such a statute, see R.2d §§ 88–99.

E. Necessity

(Dobbs §§ 107–109; R.2d §§ 19–197, 262–263)

1. Rule

The privilege of necessity may be invoked when defendant, in the course of defending themselves or their property (or others or their property) from some threat of imminent serious harm for which the plaintiff is not responsible, intentionally does some act reasonably necessary toward that end, which results in injury to the plaintiff's property and which would otherwise be a trespass or conversion. The law differs depending on whether the threat of imminent serious harm affects the public or only a private individual.

2. Public Necessity

If the danger affects an entire community, or so many persons that the public interest is involved, the law treats this as a complete privilege. This means that the defendant's tort liability is entirely excused so long as the actor was reasonable in their belief that the action was necessary, and the action taken was reasonable. This is the case whether the defendant is a public official or a private citizen. R.2d §§ 196, 262.

Example: Defendant intentionally dynamites plaintiff's house to stop the spread of a fire that threatens a substantial part of the town. Plaintiff's house and all its contents are destroyed. Defendant is not subject to liability to plaintiff.

But where a state actor destroys private property for the public good in an emergency, some states extend their "takings" clause in the state constitution to allow "just compensation" to the owner. This is a constitutional argument, however, not a tort claim.

3. Private Necessity

If the danger threatens only harm to the defendant's property (or to a third person or their property), then the defendant is privileged to commit the act which causes the trespass or conversion, so long as the actor was reasonable in their belief that the action was necessary and the action taken was reasonable, but they are subject to liability for compensatory damages for any resulting actual physical harm. R.2d §§ 197, 263.

Example: Defendant intentionally keeps his boat moored to plaintiff's dock during a storm to save the boat. The dock is extensively damaged from the boat's presence. The defendant is privileged to moor the boat on the plaintiff's property (i.e., plaintiff may not resist or refuse), but the defendant is subject to liability to the plaintiff for the resulting damage.

F. Authority of Law

(Dobbs §§ 82–87; R.2d §§ 112–145, 20–215, 265–266, 273, 278)

1. Rule

One acting under authority of law is privileged, under certain circumstances, to commit acts which would otherwise constitute an assault, battery, false imprisonment, trespass, or conversion. The scope of the privilege varies according to the type of authority being exercised and other factors.

2. Types of Privileged Acts

The most common types of privileged acts are arrest and prevention of a crime (R.2d §§ 112–144, 200–207), execution of civil process, writs, or court orders (R.2d §§ 145, 208–210, 266), and acts required or authorized by legislation (R.2d §§ 211, 265, 273). In addition, the constitution and certain public accommodations laws require that persons cannot be denied access to certain designated areas open to the public based solely on race, gender, speech content, etc.

3. Scope: Ministerial vs. Discretionary Acts

If the defendant must exercise significant judgment or discretion in determining whether or how to act (e.g., to seek an indictment or close a public street), the act is privileged if done in good faith. Ministerial acts are not privileged if done improperly, regardless of the defendant's good faith.

4. Use of Force

Whether the defendant is privileged to break and enter an enclosure or building, or to use force against the plaintiff's person, and the amount of such force permitted, depends upon the source and nature of the privilege being exercised. See R.2d §§ 212, 213.

G. Discipline

(Dobbs § 104; R.2d §§ 147–155)

1. Children

a. Parents

A parent is privileged to apply such reasonable force or to impose such reasonable confinement upon his child as they reasonably believe to be necessary for the child's proper control, training, or education. R.2d § 147. It must be administered in good faith, for proper purpose, and without malice. R.2d § 151.

b. Loco Parentis

The privilege extends to persons (e.g., school officials) having responsibility for the custody, control, training, or education of the child, except so far as the parent has restricted their authority to do so. Public officials (including public schools) are not bound by the parent's restrictions so far as the child's education and training are concerned. R.2d §§ 147, 152–154.

c. Reasonableness

The reasonableness of the force or confinement depends upon:

1) whether the defendant is a parent;
2) the age and condition of the child;
3) the nature of the offense and the child's apparent motive;
4) the influence of the child's example to other children in the family;
5) its necessity and appropriateness to compel obedience to a proper command; and
6) whether disproportionate to the offense, unnecessarily degrading, or likely to cause serious or permanent harm. R.2d § 150.

H. Review Questions

[Answers Provided in Appendix A]

1. Traveler is en route to a business meeting when they come upon a detour that would take them miles out of the way. Traveler can see that the road construction necessitating the detour does not continue very far and decides to drive onto adjacent land to avoid the barricade. Owner sees Traveler drive upon their land. Advise Traveler on whether they have a valid defense to a Trespass claim. IRAC your answer.

2. Continuing the facts from Question 1. If Owner shouts to Traveler and tells them to leave the property and Traveler nonetheless continues to drive across Owner's land, what liability will Owner have to Traveler if they shoot at Traveler's vehicle to stop them from trespassing? Assume that Traveler is counter-suing Owner for Trespass to Chattel. Assume that Owner fired three times. One bullet hit a tire. One penetrated the car window. The third missed entirely. IRAC your answer.

3. Same facts as Question 1. While stopped for the construction and before trespassing on Owner's property, Traveler observes Owner spanking a small child and directing them not to play so close to the road. The child runs inside crying. Traveler is angry about what they observed. They drive onto Owner's land to confront Owner. Traveler slaps Owner. Can Owner successfully sue Traveler for battery. IRAC your answer.

4. Same facts as Question 1. Owner sees Traveler stopped at the detour sign. Owner gestures, intending to show Traveler the route they should take. Traveler instead reasonably believes that the Owner is gesturing their consent for Traveler to cross their property to reach the road beyond the construction. Traveler waves in thanks and enters Owner's property. Owner sues Traveler for trespass, and Traveler defends by arguing that Owner consented to their actions. What outcome will result for Traveler? IRAC your answer.

5. Same facts as Question 1. Owner gestures to allow Traveler to enter upon their land a short distance to reach the road beyond the construction. Traveler shifts into four-wheel drive and tears up Owner's hillside in route to the highway by driving aggressively and making unnecessarily sharp turns and accelerations. What result if Owner sues for trespass to land? IRAC your answer.

6. Same facts as Question 1. Owner sees Traveler about to enter their land and moves their tractor to block Traveler's progress. Traveler pulls a gun from their back seat and aims it at Owner. Owner moves the tractor out of Traveler's way, then sues for trespass to land. Will Traveler's defense that Owner consented to their conduct be successful? Explain why using an IRAC analysis.

7. Doctor tells Patient that they must undergo risky surgery or they will die. Patient consents to surgery, which results in their permanent disability. Patient then discovers that surgery was not actually necessary. What outcome occurs if Patient sues in battery? IRAC your answer.

8. In a suit for battery arising out of a punch to the chest delivered during a boxing match, Defendant asserts an affirmative defense against a battery claim that Plaintiff consented to the battery. Will Defendant prevail? IRAC your answer.

9. You have been hired to represent Buyer who purchased a car from a Seller. Buyer agrees to make timely payments. Shortly thereafter, Buyer discovers Seller in the process of hotwiring Buyer's newly purchased car. Buyer shoves Seller aside, punches Seller, and ties Seller to a bike rack, while Seller calls the police. Seller tells the police that Buyer had failed to make two payments, so Seller was entitled to retake the car. Advise Buyer on the liability they may face here. IRAC your answer.

Part Two

Negligence

■ ANALYSIS

- C. Anticipating Conduct of Others

IV. Special Standards of Care—Modifications to the Reasonably Prudent Person

- A. Elevated Standard Applied to Those with Specialized Skills and Knowledge
- B. Modified Objective Standard for Physical Characteristics
- C. Minors Can Be Liable for Negligence and Modified Objective Standard Applies
- D. Professionals and Specialists
- E. Physicians—Medical Malpractice
  - 1. Locality Rule
  - 2. Proving Medical Malpractice
    - a. Expert Testimony Required
    - b. Qualifications of Expert Witnesses
    - c. Substitutes for Expert Testimony
    - d. Res Ipsa Loquitur to Prove Malpractice
  - 3. Statutory Remedies
  - 4. The "Medical Malpractice Crisis" and Tort Reform
- F. Informed Consent
- G. Conduct in Emergencies
- H. Limited Modification for Sudden Incapacity

V. No Modifications to the Reasonably Prudent Person Standard

- A. No Modified Standard for Reduced Mental Capacity
- B. No Modified Standard for Elders

VI. Types of Breaches in the Standard of Care

- A. Failure to Warn or Instruct
- B. Negligent Entrustment
- C. Negligent Hiring, Retention, or Supervision

VII. Sources of Standards of Care

- A. Statutes as Evidence of Standards of Care
- B. Legislative Purpose to Protect This Class of Persons from This Harm
- C. Statutory Standards That Impose New Duties
- D. Licensing Statutes
- E. Effect of Statutory Violation
  - 1. Majority Rule
  - 2. Minority View
  - 3. Cause
  - 4. Children
  - 5. Defenses
- F. Excused Violations
  - 1. Certain Safety Statutes
  - 2. Other Statutes
- G. Compliance with Statute

VIII. Proof of Negligence

- A. Burden of Proof
  - 1. Elements
  - 2. Defenses
  - 3. Circumstantial Evidence
  - 4. Role of Judge and Jury
- B. Presumptions

5. Enterprise and Market Share Liability
    a. Enterprise Liability
    b. Market Share Liability
6. Liability for Reduced Chance

C. Scope of Liability (Proximate Cause)
1. General Principle
2. Overview
3. Unforeseeable or Remote or Indirect Consequences
    a. The Risk Principle
    b. The Direct Consequences Rule
    c. The Duty-Risk Rule
    d. Current Status of the Risk Principle
    e. Elasticity of "Foreseeable"
    f. Elasticity of "Hazard"
    g. Rescuers
    h. Physical Consequences (Eggshell Plaintiff)
    i. Intentional Torts; Strict Liability
4. Intervening Cause
    a. Definition
    b. General Rule
    c. Types of Intervening Causes
    d. Foreseeable Intervening Causes
        i. Weather
        ii. Negligence
        iii. Criminal Conduct or Intentional Torts by Third Parties
        iv. Self-Inflicted Harm
        v. Rescuers
        vi. Further Harm
    e. Foreseeable Consequences

D. Review Questions

I. The Negligence Cause of Action

"Negligence" is both the name of a primary tort cause of action and the descriptive term given to conduct that falls below the standard required by law. In other words, negligent conduct is one element of the negligence cause of action when a defendant breaches a standard of care. The prima facie elements of a negligence cause of action are:

(1) A *duty* owed by defendant to act or refrain from acting;

(2) A *breach* of that duty by defendant's failure to conform their conduct to the required standard of care they owed (i.e., defendant's negligent conduct);

(3) A sufficient *causal connection* between the defendant's negligent conduct and plaintiff's injury (i.e., both a factual connection (known as actual cause or cause-in-fact) and a jury willing to impose liability without concluding that the harm suffered is too remote as to be recoverable (known as proximate cause)); and

(4) The plaintiff suffered *harm* resulting from the defendant's breach in the standard of care (i.e., monetary harm that the law recognizes as measurable and compensable).

Cf. R.2d § 281; R.3d Liability for Physical & Emotional Harm § 6.

The subsequent sections of Part Two introduce Duty of Care, Breach-Failure to Conform with Standards of Care, and Causation. Part Three discusses Damages, Part Four covers Defenses to Negligence, and Part Five presents Advanced Duty Concepts.

Section 1

Duty of Care

I. Duty of Care Owed

(Dobbs §§ 225–230; R.2d §§ 314–324A)

A. Sweeping General Rule with Limitations

A putative defendant's duty of care to a plaintiff can best be analyzed as a general principle with exceptions and limitations, rather than as a collection of specific duties. Generally, a defendant's duty of care arises:

(a) out of a pre-existing relationship between the plaintiff and the defendant (e.g., doctor-patient, business-patron), or

(b) because the putative defendant could have foreseen that their conduct, if creating an unreasonable risk of harm, would endanger the plaintiff or plaintiff's property.

Thus, the putative defendant has a duty to exercise reasonable care to avoid subjecting others (and their property) to unreasonable foreseeable risks of physical harm, at least when the putative defendant's conduct is the source of the risk. See R.3d Liability for Physical & Emotional Harm § 7.

Specific limitations on that generalized duty are sprinkled throughout the law of torts. The most common general duty limitations are outlined in this subpart. Do not let the volume of remaining subsections setting out these limitations distort your understanding of the rule, however. The default rule is that a duty of care exists unless a limitation is triggered.

II. Duty Based on Special Relationship with Another

Certain pre-existing relationships will support a duty to aid or protect another when the risk arises within the scope of that relationship. Examples include carrier-passenger, innkeeper-guest, possessor of land-lawful entrant, landlord-tenant, employer-employee, jailer-detainee, school-student, parent-child, spouse-spouse, store-customer, and host-guest. R.2d §§ 314A, 314B; R.3d Liability for Physical & Emotional Harm § 40. This list is not exclusive.

A. Parent-Child

Parents are not vicariously liable for their children's torts. But a parent must exercise reasonable care to prevent tortious conduct by their dependent child, provided the parent knows or has reason to know that the child has the ability, and knows or should know of the necessity and opportunity to exercise such control due to some specific dangerous propensity of the child. R.2d § 316; R.3d Liability for Physical & Emotional Harm § 41(b)(1).

B. Employer-Employee

An employer has a similar duty with respect to an employee as a parent and a child. It includes providing reasonably safe working conditions, tools, and instrumentalities of the work. It includes adequate staffing, supervision, and training. This duty even extends to one acting outside the scope of their employment, if the employee is on the employer's premises or is using their chattel, or when the employment facilitates the employee's causing harm to third persons. R.2d § 317; R.3d Liability for Physical & Emotional Harm § 41(b)(3). The employer may also be liable to third persons on a separate theory of negligent hiring, retention, or supervision.

C. Person on Defendant's Land

Land possessors have a similar duty with respect to a person using their land or their chattel in their presence and with their permission. R.2d § 318.

D. Custodian of Dangerous Person

One who has custody of a person they know to have dangerous propensities (i.e. likely to cause bodily harm to others if not controlled) must exercise reasonable care to prevent them from doing such harm. R.2d § 319; R.3d Liability for Physical & Emotional Harm § 41(b)(2).

E. Persons in Custodial Care

The defendant has custody of plaintiff when the plaintiff is deprived of their normal power of self-protection or the plaintiff must associate with persons likely to harm him. Defendant has a duty to exercise reasonable care to prevent tortious conduct against the plaintiff in custodial care, provided the defendant knows or has reason to know they have the ability, and knows or should know of the necessity and opportunity for exercising such control. R.2d § 320. R.3d Liability for Physical & Emotional Harm § 40(b)(7) requires only that the custodian is required by law to take custody or voluntarily does so and has the superior ability to protect the person in custody.

1. Students in Primary and Secondary Schools

Students in primary and secondary schools who are abused by teachers or other school personnel of course have a cause of action against the abuser. But the school is not necessarily vicariously liable because the employee's acts are likely outside the scope of employment. The school, however, may be liable if school officials knew or should have known of the abuse but took no effective action. The school may also be liable for negligently failing to protect students from violence by other students or from attacks by intruders on school grounds.

It may also be liable for negligence in hiring, retaining, or supervising the abusers. The student may also have a civil rights claim if the school is a public school or a private school that receives federal financial assistance.

2. College Students

In general, colleges and universities have no duty to protect or guide students with respect to the dangers of sex, alcohol, or drugs. However, in cases where the school has specific knowledge of a specific danger or has undertaken to supervise or protect a particular activity, courts may impose a duty. For example, schools might be liable for an inadequate keycard entry system allowing intruders to enter.

F. Landlords Hold Limited Duties

Generally, courts have been slow to impose on landlords a duty to protect tenants and their guests from criminal attack by third persons. A duty may arise when the landlord has created, or is responsible for, a known defective condition on the premises that foreseeably enhances the risk of criminal attack—for example, defective lighting or nonworking locks.

In addition, a landlord who undertakes to provide security in common areas and other areas over which the landlord has control may be held to have assumed a duty to provide that security with reasonable care. The Restatement (Third) of Torts advocates an unqualified duty of reasonable care. See R.2d Liability for Physical & Emotional Harm § 40 cmt. *m*.

Some courts have also recognized a legal duty to tenants and even third persons to use reasonable care to protect them from dangerous tenants or their dangerous animals, to the extent the landlord has the power to do so.

G. Duties to Warn Third Parties

1. Mental Health Professionals' Duty to Warn of a Patient's Threat

In *Tarasoff v. Regents of Univ. of Cal.* (Cal. 1976), the California Supreme Court held that where a psychologist's patient, Poddar, had confided to the psychologist during treatment that he planned to kill Tarasoff, the psychologist had a duty to exercise reasonable care to warn Tarasoff of the danger if the psychologist, exercising proper professional judgment, in fact predicted or should have predicted that Poddar was likely to carry out the threat. Later cases make clear that the threat must be to a specific, identifiable person or small group of persons.

The *Tarasoff* duty has been accepted in many states. The Restatement (Third) of Torts includes the relationship of mental-health-professional and patient as one that gives rise to a duty of reasonable care for the protection of third persons, without qualification. R.3d Liability for Physical & Emotional Harm § 41(b)(4).

2. Health Care Professionals' Duty to Warn of Threats of Diseases or Treatments

Courts are split on whether a physician or other health care professional has a duty to warn their patient of dangers to third persons resulting from treatment or medication administered to the patient, or that the patient's communicable disease puts third persons at risk. Courts are also split on whether and when a health care professional has a duty to communicate such warnings to these third persons directly.

3. Land Possessors' Duty to Warn of Threats from Third Parties

In cases involving attacks upon patrons on business premises, instead of applying the general premises liability rules, courts have developed special tests to determine the duty issue. These tests focus on foreseeability.

Specific harm rule. Under this rule, a landowner does not owe a duty to protect visitors from violent acts of third persons unless the landowner is aware of specific, imminent harm. While such knowledge is sufficient to create a duty, it is no longer essential to liability.

Prior similar incidents rule. Under this test, foreseeability is established by evidence of previous crimes on or near the premises. The idea is that a past history of criminal conduct will put the landowner on notice of a future risk. Therefore, courts consider the nature and extent of the previous crimes, as well as their recency, frequency, and similarity to the crime in question.

Totality of the circumstances test. This test takes additional factors into account, such as the nature, condition, and location of the land, as well as any other relevant factual circumstances bearing on foreseeability.

Balancing test. This test balances the foreseeability of harm against the burden on the business of imposing a duty to protect against the criminal acts of third persons.

III. Limitations on Duties Owed

A. Duty to *This* Plaintiff

Negligence law has traditionally held that a putative defendant is not subject to liability to the plaintiff unless the defendant breached a duty owed to the plaintiff and not to someone else. Cf. *Palsgraf v. Long Island R. Co.* (N.Y. 1928).

B. Nature and Scope of the Risk

Conduct may be negligent because it foreseeably threatens property damage, but it instead causes some unforeseen personal injury. Conduct may also be negligent because it foreseeably threatens one type of harm to the plaintiff, but it actually causes another type of harm, as to which the risk was not unreasonable. Conduct may also be negligent because it creates a risk of injury to A, but unexpectedly injures B. While these scenarios raise questions similar to proximate cause (scope of liability) inquiries, some courts analyze such scenarios under the duty element and hold that there was no duty to protect against the harm that actually resulted. Other courts, however, reach the same result under proximate cause principles.

C. Limits on Certain Interests

Certain types of interests are given less than full protection against negligent invasion. A few are noted conceptually here and expounded upon in later chapters.

1. Economic Loss

3 Dobbs, Hayden & Bublick, The Law of Torts §§ 605–608 (2d ed. 2011).

a. In General

Tort law has been reluctant to extend liability for negligent conduct that results solely in economic harm to the plaintiff. This is notable in contrast to the freedom with which economic losses are recoverable in tort actions based on physical harm to a plaintiff. This may be seen as a duty limitation based on a policy consideration. Courts worry about the specter of astronomical liability, out of all proportion to the defendant's fault and beyond all reasonable limits—in effect, an economic death penalty. Courts reason that only a limited amount of *physical* damage will ordinarily ensue from a single act, whereas the number of economic interests a tortfeasor may destroy in a moment of carelessness is practically limitless.

b. Economic Loss Caused by Physical Harm to Another

In general, plaintiff cannot recover in negligence for economic loss resulting from physical harm to another or to property in which plaintiff has no proprietary interest. Unless there is some specific tort cause of action allowing recovery, plaintiff cannot recover for any other negligent conduct that results solely in economic loss. R.2d § 766C.

c. Negligent Misrepresentation

Generally, plaintiff may not recover for economic loss caused by reliance on a negligent misrepresentation that was not made directly to plaintiff or specifically on plaintiff's behalf. R.2d § 552.

d. Exceptions

A number of cases have allowed recovery for pure economic loss, but so far these cases defy easy categorization. A common thread, however, is that there is a special relationship between plaintiff and defendant.

i. Negligent Performance of a Service

In the case of negligence in the rendition of certain professional or business services, liability has been extended in favor of clients (and sometimes others) who foreseeably relied on the service or who were its intended beneficiaries. This group includes accountants and auditors, surveyors, termite inspectors, engineers, attorneys, notaries public, architects, weighers, and telegraph companies. Under R.2d § 552 and prevailing case law, such persons are liable for negligence in furnishing false information, but only to the person (or one of a limited, specific, and identifiable group of persons) for whose benefit and guidance the furnisher intends to supply the information, or where the furnisher knows that the recipient intends to rely on it. If a defendant has a public duty to furnish the information (e.g. a notary public, food inspector), defendant's liability extends to pecuniary loss suffered by any member of the class of persons for whose benefit the duty is created.

ii. Exercise of Public Right

In a few cases, a plaintiff whose business is based on the exercise of a public right (e.g., a commercial fisherman) has been allowed to recover for economic loss caused by the defendant's negligent interference with that right (e.g., by an oil spill).

2. Harm to the Unborn

(Dobbs §§ 288–293; R.2d § 869)

a. Child Born Alive

Traditionally, one who tortiously causes fetal harm is subject to liability for fetal harms if the child is subsequently born alive. R.2d § 869(1). The prevailing view is that the fetus need not have been viable at the time of the injury. If the fetus is born alive but then dies from the injury (however briefly the child was alive, and whether or not viable when born), a wrongful death action can be maintained.

b. Child Not Born Alive

If a defendant negligently causes fetal harm and the fetus dies from the injuries prior to birth, the authorities are divided, but most courts now allow the wrongful death action provided the fetus was viable at the time of the injury. See R.2d § 869(2). The pregnant person might also be allowed to recover emotional distress damages.

After the Supreme Court's decision in *Dobbs v. Jackson Women's Health Org.*, 597 U.S. 215 (2022), states are no longer bound by the viability line, which is leading restrictive abortion states to upend these traditional tort lines. It is likely that restrictive abortion states will vastly expand their tort liability based on adopting a fetal personhood model.

c. Damages for Unintended Children

i. Wrongful Conception

When a defendant's negligent conduct fails to prevent conception (e.g., negligence with respect to failed fertility management methods such as tubectomy, vasectomy, etc.) and results in an unplanned birth, the prevailing view is that the parents may recover, but their damages are limited to the cost of prenatal care and delivery and the associated pain and other general and special damages. Some courts have allowed, in addition, child-rearing expenses, most (but not all) requiring that such expenses be offset by the accompanying financial and emotional benefits to the parents.

ii. Wrongful Birth and Wrongful Life

(a) Description

Another category of claims arises when a defendant's negligence results in the unplanned birth of a child who is born with a physical or mental disability caused by a genetic (or other) disorder for which a defendant is not responsible.

Actions brought by the parents of such children for their damages (including damages for the ordinary and extraordinary costs of caring for such children and their mental distress) are usually referred to as "wrongful birth" claims. Actions brought by the child for their own damages (e.g., pain and suffering associated with the disability) are called "wrongful life" actions.

(b) Wrongful Birth

After initially rejecting wrongful birth claims, most courts now allow recovery. Some courts limit damages to the parents' pecuniary losses, but others now award damages for their emotional distress as well. In some jurisdictions, statutes bar wrongful birth actions.

(c) Wrongful Life

So far, almost all jurisdictions have rejected wrongful life claims. Courts find it too problematic to measure the value of life with a disability as compared to no life at all and find it philosophically difficult to support the child's claim that they should never have been born. A few courts have allowed such claims, the damages being limited to the child's extraordinary medical and care expenses (to the extent not recovered by the parents). The right is premised on the availability of medical care to terminate a pregnancy, so it is unlikely to prevail in states with abortion bans post-*Dobbs*.

3. Emotional Distress

a. Negligent Infliction of Emotional Distress (NIED)

If a defendant is subject to liability to plaintiff for negligence based on bodily injury (e.g., a broken leg), the plaintiff can recover not only for the physical injury but also their resulting pain, suffering, mental, and emotional harm. Plaintiff's mental damages are "parasitic" to their damages for physical harm. Suppose, however, that a plaintiff sustains no direct physical harm; plaintiff's injury is solely their severe emotional distress. In such cases, defendant's duty to plaintiff is limited.

The traditional view was that plaintiff had no standalone claim for negligent infliction of emotional distress under any circumstances. *Mitchell v. Rochester Ry. Co.* (N.Y. 1896). This is still the law in a very few jurisdictions. Everywhere else, however, the courts have gradually come to allow such claims with limiting principles attached.

b. The Impact Rule

The impact rule was the first small step away from *Mitchell*. Under this rule, if the defendant's negligent conduct resulted in any impact, however slight, with the plaintiff's body, that impact would support liability for plaintiff's emotional distress resulting from the same negligent conduct. R.2d §§ 456, 905. No impact meant no cause of action. A few states still adhere to this rule in some form, but most have abandoned it.

c. The Zone-of-Danger Rule

The Zone-of-Danger rule allows recovery for emotional distress when the defendant's negligent conduct threatens (but does not result in) bodily harm (impact) to the plaintiff (a "near miss" situation). Most courts that have adopted this approach will allow plaintiff to recover for *bodily harm* resulting from the fear, shock or other emotional disturbance caused by his presence in the zone of danger. R.2d § 436(2). Some courts no longer require bodily harm and allow recovery for the emotional distress itself.

Example: Defendant negligently drives through a red light and narrowly misses plaintiff, a pedestrian, crossing the intersection. Defendant is liable for plaintiff's bodily harm resulting from plaintiff's reasonable apprehension of being struck by defendant's car.

d. The Bystander Rule: Emotional Harm Caused by Witnessing Injury to Another

i. *Dillon* Factors

If plaintiff was not in the zone of danger but merely witnessed a shocking event in which defendant's negligent conduct caused serious physical harm or death to a third person, courts traditionally declined to hold defendant liable for plaintiff's severe emotional distress resulting from the shock.

Following *Dillon v. Legg* (Cal. 1968), however, most jurisdictions expanded liability to allow plaintiffs to recover in such situations under certain conditions. Typically, the plaintiff made their case for liability using factors considering whether (a) the actual injury to the third person was a serious one; (b) the plaintiff was a member of the immediate family of, or closely related to, the person in peril; (c) the shock resulted in serious emotional distress to plaintiff; and (d) the plaintiff actually witnessed the traumatic event, or at least comes upon the scene almost immediately and witnesses its aftermath. *Cf.* R.2d § 436(3); see Restatement (Third) of Torts: Liability for Physical and Emotional Harm § 48, cmt. *a* & *j*.

ii. The Restatement (Third) of Torts

R.3d Liability for Physical & Emotional Harm § 48 reframed the requirements of the bystander rule with more precision in its predictability: An actor who negligently causes sudden serious bodily injury to a third person is subject to liability for serious emotional harm caused thereby to a person who (a) perceives the event contemporaneously and (b) is a close family member of the person suffering the bodily injury.

iii. Zone of Danger, Fear for Another's Safety

In jurisdictions that have adopted the zone-of-danger rule but not the *Dillon* rule, most courts will allow plaintiff to recover for bystander shock under the circumstances stated in the preceding paragraph if plaintiff was also within the zone of danger.

e. Proximate Cause Limitations

i. Physical Manifestation Requirement

Absent impact, in some jurisdictions, plaintiff may recover only if their emotional distress results in physical illness or comparable objective bodily consequences. R.2d §§ 313, 436A. Most jurisdictions have now diluted or abolished the physical injury or objective manifestation rule, either generally or in specific situations.

ii. "Eggshell Plaintiff" Rule

Unless defendant has actual knowledge of some special sensitivity of plaintiff, defendant will be liable only to the extent that plaintiff's physical response to the emotional trauma was within the normal range of ordinarily sensitive persons. Defendant is not liable for unforeseeable physical consequences.

f. Fear of Future Harm from Toxic Exposure

When plaintiff has been exposed, or fears they have been exposed, to a toxic substance due to defendant's negligence additional duty rules apply. If, in fact, plaintiff was so exposed, there is a risk of serious future harm (e.g., cancer), but plaintiff has no present symptoms or diagnosis of the feared disease. The question is whether plaintiff can recover for the mental distress resulting from the fear of future harm, or for medical monitoring, until such time as it can be established that the risk of such future harm is zero.

If plaintiff can prove that they sustained any immediate physical harm, however slight, as a result of the exposure, the case fits within the traditional "impact" rule, and plaintiff can recover emotional distress damages parasitic to that injury. In most cases, plaintiff must show actual exposure to the toxic substance and not merely a fear (however reasonable) that such exposure occurred. If plaintiff can show actual exposure to the toxic substance but no immediate physical injury, many courts will allow plaintiff to recover for medical monitoring and emotional distress, but some courts require plaintiff to prove a greater-than-50% chance that they will contract the feared disease at some time in the future. "Actual exposure" means there must be a channel of exposure and a virus or toxin must be shown to exist. If plaintiff can only establish a possibility or fear of exposure and no present physical harm, almost all courts will deny recovery for emotional distress damages or medical monitoring.

g. Review Questions

[Answers Provided in Appendix A]

1. Driver negligently strikes a deer that is crossing a road in an area clearly marked as a deer crossing. Ranger, who is standing near the road, is struck by the deer as it ricochets off Driver's bumper. Is Driver liable for Ranger's emotional distress, even if Ranger suffered no significant physical injury?
2. Driver, making a futile attempt to avoid hitting the deer, veers far off the roadway, striking the deer and coming very close to Ranger, who observes the accident. Is Driver liable for Ranger's resulting emotional distress, even absent any bodily harm?
3. Ranger is exceptionally fond of deer and suffers severe bodily harm as a result of their witnessing Driver's accident. Is Driver liable for Ranger's bodily harm?

D. Misfeasance vs. Nonfeasance

Tort law distinguishes between "misfeasance" and "nonfeasance." Misfeasance is tortious conduct consisting of an affirmative act while nonfeasance is inaction which results in or allows harm to the plaintiff. Generally, the defendant is not liable for harm to the plaintiff resulting from mere failure to intervene, to aid, or to protect the plaintiff unless there is some pre-existing relationship between the plaintiff and defendant sufficient to create the duty, or unless the defendant is responsible for the plaintiff's peril. R.3d Liability for Physical & Emotional Harm § 37. In practice, however, this distinction is murkier than it seems. The next subsections outline some more concrete rules.

1. No General Duty to Rescue

Absent a pre-existing relationship between the plaintiff and the defendant or a duty to act arising from some other source (e.g., contract, statute), the defendant has no duty to protect or aid the plaintiff, who the defendant realizes is in a position of danger. R.2d § 314; R.3d Liability for Physical & Emotional Harm § 37. For example, a defendant might see a person who is visually impaired about to step into the path of an approaching car. Although the defendant *could* call out a word of caution or jump to the pedestrian's aid, the defendant is under no duty to do so.

2. No General Duty to Render First Aid

Absent a pre-existing relationship between the plaintiff and the defendant, or unless the defendant was responsible for plaintiff's injury, the defendant has no duty to render aid or assistance to an injured or otherwise needy plaintiff. R.3d Liability for Physical & Emotional Harm § 37.

3. Duty of Care Arises When Defendant Is Responsible for Peril or Injury

A duty of care does arise when the defendant is responsible for the plaintiff's injury or position of peril, whether or not the defendant was negligent. R.2d § 322; R.3d Liability for Physical & Emotional Harm § 39.

4. Duty of Care Arises When Voluntarily Assumed

R.3d Liability for Physical & Emotional Harm §§ 42–44

a. Reasonable Care Required When Rendering Aid

One who undertakes to render aid or to protect or take custody of the plaintiff, who reasonably appears to be imperiled and helpless or unable to adequately aid or protect themself, must do so with reasonable care. And, having undertaken this duty, they may not abandon the plaintiff and leave them worse off. R.2d § 324; R.3d Liability for Physical & Emotional Harm § 44. This rule has led to "Good Samaritan" statutes in many states, which relieve physicians (and others) who render emergency medical aid from all liability for negligence. Of course, if the defendant was the one responsible for the plaintiff's predicament, then the defendant has a duty of care arising from that negligent conduct.

b. Reasonable Care Required When Undertaking Services

When the defendant (gratuitously or otherwise) undertakes to render services which they know or should know are for the plaintiff's protection, the defendant must perform those services with reasonable care, at least if (a) their failure to do so increases the risk of harm to plaintiff, or (b) defendant has undertaken to perform a duty owed by another to the plaintiff, or (c) plaintiff's injury results from their reliance on the defendant. R.2d §§ 323, 324A; R.3d Liability for Physical & Emotional Harm § 43. Even a gratuitous promise to render such services may make the defendant subject to liability if there is reasonable detrimental reliance by the plaintiff.

The Restatement Third broadened the scope of liability to third persons of those undertaking to render services and applies to both gratuitous and contractual undertakings.

Example: City, owner of a monorail system, contracts with SMS to operate and maintain the system. City contracts with LTK to perform inspection and repairs on the system, which it did negligently. A resulting fire damaged certain trains, and SMS was required to pay for part of the restoration. SMS's insurer can recover tort damages from LTK, even though SMS was not a party to the contract between the City and LTK which gave rise to LTK's duties with respect to the system. *Affiliated FM Ins. Co. v. LTK Consulting Services* (Wash. 2010).

5. Duty Arising Ex Post Facto

If the defendant does an act, not tortious at the time, and later discovers that their act created an unreasonable risk of harm to the plaintiff, the defendant must exercise reasonable care to prevent the risk from taking effect. R.2d § 321; R.3d Liability for Physical & Emotional Harm § 39. For example, a duty arises if the defendant loans their car to the plaintiff reasonably believing it to be in good repair only to learn that the brakes are dangerously defective.

6. Statutory Duty of Protection

When a statute requires one to act for the protection of another, the court may (or may not) use the statute as a basis for an affirmative duty and its scope. R.3d Liability for Physical & Emotional Harm § 38. This is different from using a statute to establish the standard of care when a duty already exists. Such statutes are also to be distinguished from statutes that expressly or impliedly create a cause of action.

Most courts hold that a statutory requirement to report child abuse does not serve as a basis for tort liability for failure to report. A few courts have held that the reporting statute implies a private right of action or will support a negligence claim.

IV. Duties Arising from Contract

(Dobbs §§ 319–321; R.2d §§ 323, 324A)

One possible source of defendant's duty to plaintiff is a contract between them under which defendant agrees to perform certain services. If defendant breaches that contract and as a result plaintiff sustains physical or other harm, special rules apply to determine whether that breach may give rise to tort liability, as outlined in this subpart.

A. General Rule—Duty Owed in Tort for Misperformance Not Nonperformance

Where defendant's duty to act arises because of a contractual relation between the defendant and plaintiff, defendant is not liable in tort for harm caused by their breach of that contract where the breach consists merely of their failure to commence performance at all. But once defendant has begun to perform, they will be liable for their tortious misperformance, whether consisting of acts or omissions to act. Cf. R.2d § 323.

For example, defendant contracts to cut down a tree on plaintiff's premises. Defendant has not yet begun performance when the tree falls on plaintiff's house. Defendant is ordinarily not liable to plaintiff in tort, even though defendant could be found to have been negligent in failing to start the work. But once having appeared on the premises and begun performance, defendant is subject to liability for his negligence in performing or abandoning the work with the same result.

1. Misperformance and Nonperformance Distinguished

It is hard to distinguish the line between misperformance and nonperformance, and any distinction is often illusory. In general, the question is whether defendant's performance (as distinct from their promise or preparation) has gone so far that it has begun to affect the interests of plaintiff beyond the expected benefits of the contract itself and may be regarded as a positive act assuming the obligation beyond the mere promise to perform. In some cases, although the court finds no liability based on nonperformance, the real basis is a policy decision that liability would impose an unreasonable burden—in other words, a scope-of-liability problem.

2. The Contract Shapes the Scope of Duty

Assuming defendant's duty arises from the contract with plaintiff, defendant usually has no duty to notify plaintiff of, or repair, a dangerous condition that is outside the scope of the contractual duty, in most cases even if defendant actually discovers the condition. R.2d § 403; R.3d Liability for Physical & Emotional Harm § 42 cmt. *g* & Reporters' Note to cmt. *g*.

3. Exceptions Triggering Liability for Nonperformance

a. Public Callings

Those engaged in the public or "common" callings—common carriers, innkeepers, public warehouse workers, public utilities, and public officers—are subject to tort liability for nonperformance.

b. Other Relationships

Other relationships, which may be based on contract, impose a duty of affirmative conduct. A bailee, for example, must take affirmative steps to care for the goods. Employers must provide a safe place for their employees to work.

B. Contracts for Security Services

The Restatement (Third) of Torts provides that when a defendant contracts to provide security services intended to reduce the risk of physical harm, defendant is liable for failure to use reasonable care in doing so if the failure increases the risk of harm beyond that which otherwise would have existed, or the other person relies on the undertaking. R.3d Liability for Physical & Emotional Harm § 42.

C. Fraud

A promise made without any intent to perform it may be fraud for which a tort action in deceit will lie.

D. Third Persons Not Parties to the Contract

(*Cf.* R.2d § 324A; R.3d Liability for Physical & Emotional Harm § 43)

1. Common Law Privity Rule

The general common law rule was that plaintiff, not a party to a contract between defendant and another, had no cause of action in tort for harm sustained as a result of defendant's misperformance or nonperformance. This was because the plaintiff was not in "privity of contract" with defendant. A leading authority on this point is *Winterbottom v. Wright* (Exch. 1842).

2. Exceptions for Nonfeasance

In the case of nonfeasance, various exceptions to the privity rule have developed, thus creating a duty of care arising from nonperformance. For example, the nonperformance by an agent of their contractual duty (1) to supervise property or persons over which they has been given control (e.g., cattle), or (2) to take certain precautions for the safety of third persons (e.g., a crossing guard).

E. Dangerous Instrumentalities

Nonperformance of a contract to maintain, inspect, or repair an instrumentality which foreseeably creates a substantial risk of harm to third persons (e.g., elevator, scaffolding, boiler).

IV. Review Questions

[Answers Provided in Appendix A]

1. Defendant is an attorney. They gratuitously advise the checkout clerk at the local market on a speeding ticket problem. As a result of this advice, the clerk's license was suspended. Analyze in an IRAC structure whether the clerk has a claim for negligence against the attorney, even though the service was volunteered and gratuitous.

2. Angie, a child, was shopping with their mother when Angie struck and injured Patti, a passerby. Angie had never done such a thing before. Analyze whether Angie's mom has liability to Patti based on her parenting relationship. Answer in IRAC format.

3. Amaya inadvertently left her yard gate open, and her German Shepherd dog escaped through it. He darted across the road, causing a car to swerve and crash into a car coming the other direction. Amaya chased after her dog and ran right past the injured car driver. Advise Amaya on whether she had any duty to render aid. Answer in IRAC format.

Section 2

Breach—Failure to Conform with Standards of Care

I. General Standard of Reasonable Care

(Dobbs §§ 116–131; R.2d §§ 281–284, 289–309)

A. Reasonable Care Defined

"Negligence" is conduct which falls below the standard of care established by law for the protection of others against unreasonable risks of harm. R.2d § 282. A person is negligent when their conduct, given all the circumstances, is determined to fall short of reasonable care. R.3d Liability for Physical & Emotional Harm § 3.

The standard is "reasonable care" (sometimes called "ordinary care" or "due care") under the circumstances. The law does not require one to be perfect, but only to behave as a reasonably prudent person would behave in that situation. And they need only protect others against unreasonable risks of harm. R.2d § 298.

B. An Objective Test

Since negligence is conduct which fails to conform to the legal standard, the test for negligence is objective—not whether the actor intended to exercise due care, nor whether they did the best they could to be careful (subjective), but whether their conduct was that of a hypothetical reasonably prudent (or careful) person placed in the same or similar circumstances. R.2d §§ 283, 297.

C. When Is a Risk "Unreasonable"?

A risk is unreasonable when the foreseeable probability and gravity of the harm outweigh the burden to the defendant of alternative conduct that would have prevented the harm. Compare R.2d § 291; R.3d Liability for Physical & Emotional Harm § 3. This is sometimes referred to as the "Learned Hand" test (see *United States v. Carroll Towing Co.* (2d Cir. 1947) (L. Hand, J.) or the "risk-utility" test.

1. Magnitude of Risk

The foreseeable probability or likelihood that the harm will result, in conjunction with the gravity or seriousness of the potential harm, are placed on one side of the scale. The gravity of the harm includes both the extent of the damage and the relative societal value of the protected interest—e.g., personal security is more valuable than property. See R.2d § 293.

2. Burden of Alternative Conduct

The burden of reducing or eliminating the risk by alternative conduct is placed on the other side of the scale. Factors relevant in assessing this cost include:

a. the importance or social value of the defendant's activity;

b. the utility of the conduct as a means to that end;

c. the feasibility of alternative, safer conduct;

d. the relative cost of safer conduct;

e. the relative utility of safer conduct;

f. the relative safety of alternative conduct.

See R.2d § 292.

II. Juries Decide Standards of Care with Judges as Gatekeepers

Whether conduct was negligent is a question of fact for the trier of fact. R.2d §§ 328B, 328C; R.3d Liability for Physical & Emotional Harm § 8. In most cases, a jury is given only a short general definition of negligence and the reasonable person test, leaving it to the jury to apply its common experience to the evidence. R.2d § 285.

The judge, however, may enter summary judgment, direct a verdict, or otherwise take the case out of the jury's hands because the court decides whether the conduct in question was so clearly negligent that no reasonable person could reach any other conclusion. The trial court's decision to take such action is reviewable as an issue of law.

III. Attributes of the Reasonable Person

A. Knowledge, Experience, and Perception

In judging an actor's conduct, they will be charged with what they actually knew and observed, and also with those things that a reasonable person would have known and perceived. R.2d §§ 289, 290. And if they have superior intelligence, memory perception, knowledge, or judgment, they will be held to that standard. R.3d Liability for Physical & Emotional Harm § 12. But if they are deficient in any of these attributes, they are still held to the standard of the reasonable person. This approach incentivizes individuals to be mindful of their own ignorance and act accordingly. For example, one who drives a car is required to know and apply the laws and techniques necessary to do so with reasonable safety, beginning on their first day on the road. See R.2d §§ 299, 299A, 300.

B. Knowledge Common to the Community

The reasonable person knows those things which at that time are common knowledge in the community; e.g., commonly known qualities and habits of human beings and animals, and qualities, characteristics, and capacities of things. R.2d § 290.

C. Anticipating Conduct of Others

The reasonable person will regulate their conduct in light of what they can anticipate, expect, or foresee others will do. R.2d §§ 302A, 302B, 303. Thus, in particular circumstances they can expect negligent, or even criminal, conduct by others, or that their conduct will likely trigger conduct by another that will subject someone to an unreasonable risk of harm.

IV. Special Standards of Care—Modifications to the Reasonably Prudent Person

A. Elevated Standard Applied to Those with Specialized Skills and Knowledge

If one chooses to engage in an activity requiring specialized skills or knowledge, their conduct is measured against the hypothetical person who is reasonably skilled and knowledgeable in that activity. Beginners are held to the same standard. For example, one who undertakes to render services in the practice of a particular trade or profession must exercise the skill and apply the knowledge which a reasonably well-qualified and experienced member of that profession or trade would in similar circumstances. And one who undertakes to manufacture a product is deemed to have and must apply the knowledge and skill which a reasonably prudent manufacturer of that product would have and apply. See R.2d §§ 299, 299A, 300.

B. Modified Objective Standard for Physical Characteristics

The "reasonable person" standard is modified to the extent that defendant has a physical deficiency or disability. Defendant's conduct is then measured against that of a reasonably prudent person with those same physical characteristics. R.3d Liability for Physical & Emotional Harm § 11(a). For example, a person who is visually impaired is held to the standard of a reasonable person in the same or similar circumstances with a visual impairment. A person with exceptional strength, agility, or other physical prowess is held to the standard of a reasonably prudent person with such exceptional physical abilities.

C. Minors Can Be Liable for Negligence and Modified Objective Standard Applies

Below a certain age, a young child is incapable of negligence because they lack the mental maturity and experience to assess and respond to risks. In some jurisdictions, the trier of fact determines whether a particular child is capable of negligence, regardless of age. In others, children under the age of seven are incapable of negligence as a matter of law; children between seven and fourteen are presumed incapable but the presumption is rebuttable; and minors over the age of fourteen are presumed capable. R.3d Liability for Physical & Emotional Harm § 10(b) provides that children under five are incapable of negligence.

If the defendant is a minor that the law recognizes as capable of negligence, the test examines what is reasonable conduct for a child of that defendant's age, intelligence, and experience under the circumstances. R.2d § 283A; R.3d Liability for Physical & Emotional Harm §§ 10, 11(c).

The modified standard for minors does not apply to minors engaging in adult-like or inherently dangerous activities requiring special skills and training, such as driving a car, flying an airplane, operating a snowmobile or a motorboat, and the like. In those cases, the minor is held to the adult, objective standard of care because of the inherent dangerousness of the activity.

D. Professionals and Specialists

In most jurisdictions, the standard of care of medical professionals (and sometimes other professionals, such as architects, engineers, accountants, or lawyers) is *conclusively* established by the customary or usual practice of reasonably well-qualified practitioners in that field. Thus, the standard differs from that applied to other persons, where the customary practice in a particular trade, business, or other activity is merely *evidence* of the standard of care but not conclusive, and the jury is free to set a standard higher than that evidenced by the customary conduct.

Physicians or others who are certified specialists, or who hold themselves out as specialists, are held to the standards of that specialty, but again, in most cases the customary conduct of reasonably well-qualified specialists conclusively sets the standard of care.

E. Physicians—Medical Malpractice

Negligent conduct by persons practicing a profession or, in some cases, a skilled trade (physician or other skilled health care provider, dentist, optometrist, lawyer, accountant, engineer, architect, veterinarian, etc.) is commonly termed "malpractice." Special rules sometimes apply to professional negligence cases.

If a physician, hospital, or other health care provider negligently injures a patient but the negligence is not in the provision of medical services, the special medical malpractice rules do not apply, and the case is treated as an ordinary negligence case. For example, ordinary negligence would apply if a patient slips and falls on a slippery substance left on the hospital floor.

1. Locality Rule

At one time, the standard of care of medical professionals (and, occasionally, other professionals as well) was further limited by the so-called "locality rule." When this rule was applied, the standard of care was the customary practice of reasonably well-qualified similar professionals in that particular geographic locality, or alternatively, in similar localities.

Today, most jurisdictions have abandoned the locality rule. Even in those that still purport to follow the rule, its effect can be avoided by expert testimony that the applicable standard of care is uniform nationally, which it almost always is. Of course, the professional's geographic location, and the facilities and equipment available to them there, are necessarily part of the circumstances relevant to the jury's determination whether the conduct of the professional was negligent.

2. Proving Medical Malpractice

a. Expert Testimony Required

In most cases involving a claim of professional negligence, the plaintiff must provide expert testimony establishing (1) the relevant standard of care, (2) that defendant's conduct did not conform to that standard, and (3) that there was a causal relationship between defendant's breach and plaintiff's injury. Most courts now recognize that there can be substitutes for expert testimony.

b. Qualifications of Expert Witnesses

Although some states have adopted statutes regulating expert testimony in medical negligence cases (e.g., by requiring that the expert not be a mere testifying consultant or requiring that the expert have the same license and certification as the defendant), the common law applies the usual qualifying tests to such expert testimony.

c. Substitutes for Expert Testimony

In addition to proof by expert testimony, the standard of care and its breach in medical negligence cases can sometimes be established in other ways, such as by (1) admissions by the defendant, (2) authoritative medical literature, (3) statutes, (4) standards adopted by government or trade groups, such as hospital or nursing home licensing rules, (5) inspection reports, (6) hospital bylaws and rules, and (7) literature accompanying medical products that contains warnings and directions for use.

d. Res Ipsa Loquitur to Prove Malpractice

The doctrine of res ipsa loquitur is available in professional negligence cases to establish that the defendant's conduct was negligent. A common example is the case where a foreign object (sponge, towel, clamp) was left in the patient during surgery. In such "common knowledge" cases, no expert testimony is required to prove the defendant's negligence.

3. Statutory Remedies

Federal and state statutes may provide supplemental remedies for torts against patients. Many states have statutes directed against elder abuse and statutes providing remedies against nursing homes for injuries to residents caused by neglect or mistreatment.

4. The "Medical Malpractice Crisis" and Tort Reform

In the recent push for legislative tort reform, many states have adopted special rules to govern medical malpractice cases. These include modifications to the medical standard of care and medical res ipsa loquitur rules; partial abrogation or modification of the collateral source rule; special statutes of repose; restrictions on expert testimony; arbitrary limits on the amount recoverable in a medical malpractice action, either generally or for non-economic losses; requiring periodic payment of judgments; limits on attorney's fees; and mandatory submission of the case to arbitration or a screening panel prior to taking the case to court. Some of these reform measures have been held unconstitutional, and the mix and type of changes vary from state to state. Generally, one or more of these changes have been adopted in most jurisdictions.

F. Informed Consent

Under the doctrine of informed consent, a patient's consent to a particular treatment or procedure must be based on the professional's disclosure of the material risks and alternatives to the proposed treatment so that patient can make an informed decision as to whether to consent. Although the rule is most often applied in medical negligence cases, it appears equally applicable to other types of professional negligence.

The physician must disclose the risks and alternatives that a reasonable patient would want to know in order to make an intelligent choice, i.e., all risks material to the decision of the ordinary patient in the plaintiff's position. The plaintiff must prove that they would not have consented had they known this information.

G. Conduct in Emergencies

The fact that defendant is confronted with a sudden emergency that requires rapid decision is a factor that may be considered in determining the reasonableness of defendant's choice of action. R.2d § 296; R.3d Liability for Physical & Emotional Harm § 9. However, where defendant may have been negligent is in (a) failing to anticipate the emergency or (b) creating the emergency; as to such negligence, the foregoing rule would not be applicable. The emergency does not change the standard of care, and therefore (in most jurisdictions) no special jury instruction on conduct in an emergency is required or given.

H. Limited Modification for Sudden Incapacity

The conduct of defendant during a period of sudden incapacitation or loss of consciousness resulting from physical illness is negligent only if defendant sought to have foreseen such an incapacity and was negligent in failing to take reasonable precautions to prevent its occurrence. R.3d Liability for Physical & Emotional Harm § 11(b).

V. No Modifications to the Reasonably Prudent Person Standard

A. No Modified Standard for Reduced Mental Capacity

The prevailing rule is that tort law does not make allowance for deficiencies in defendant's mental capacity to conform to the "reasonable person" standard of care. The fact that the defendant is deficient in intelligence, judgment, memory, emotional stability, voluntarily intoxicated, or similar does not modify the standard of care. Their conduct is nonetheless measured against the reasonably prudent person. R.2d §§ 283B, 897J; R.3d. Liability for Physical & Emotional Harm § 11(c).

B. No Modified Standard for Elders

Tort law makes no modification for aging based on age alone. If, however, age produces a particular physical limitation, then the rules concerning physical limitations would modify the standard of care.

VI. Types of Breaches in the Standard of Care

Illustrations of types of negligent conduct are virtually limitless. Rather than try to catalog them, it may be more useful to conclude that, subject to duty and proximate cause limitations, any conduct may be negligent under the circumstances. Negligence may consist of an act or a failure to act (R.2d § 284), lack of competence (§§ 299, 299A), or lack of preparation (§ 300). A misrepresentation may be negligent conduct. R.2d § 304. It may be negligence to prevent protective action by another (R.2d § 305); to use an incompetent, defective, or inappropriate instrumentality (R.2d § 307); or to permit another to use a thing or engage in an activity under defendant's control so as to subject another to an unreasonable risk of harm (R.2d § 308). See R.3d Liability for Physical & Emotional Harm §§ 3, 18, 19; Scope Note to §§ 17–19.

A. Failure to Warn or Instruct

One type of negligence is a failure to warn or instruct another so that they can take proper precautions for their own safety. R.2d § 301. Conversely, defendant's exercise of reasonable care to give others an adequate warning of a danger does not necessarily prevent defendant's conduct (the subject of the warning) from being negligent. Generally, if there is an unreasonable risk of harm inherent in defendant's conduct, defendant must reduce that risk so far as reasonably possible; only then will an adequate warning of the remaining risk constitute "reasonable care."

B. Negligent Entrustment

It may be negligent to entrust a chattel—or any instrumentality, broadly defined—to a person defendant knows or should know is likely to use it in a dangerous way. R.3d Liability for Physical & Emotional Harm § 19. Liability for resulting injuries (assuming a duty is found) may include third persons injured by the entrustee, or the entrustee themself.

C. Negligent Hiring, Retention, or Supervision

Negligence may include failure to exercise reasonable care in the hiring, retention, or supervision of employees or independent contractors, whom defendant knew or should have known were dangerous, incompetent, or otherwise unfit for the work for which they were hired.

VII. Sources of Standards of Care

A. Statutes as Evidence of Standards of Care

(R.3d Liability for Physical & Emotional Harm § 14)

Federal and state statutes can set out standards of conduct to protect others. For tort law purposes, two types may be distinguished: legislation which (a) expressly or (b) by necessary implication creates a civil remedy for damages for violation (e.g., F.E.L.A., F.S.A.A.); and legislation which does not create a civil remedy (enforcement limited to criminal penalties or fines). As to the first type, if the statute creates a civil remedy, the court simply applies and enforces the statutory right. Courts routinely use legislation of the second type in negligence cases as evidence of, or as establishing, the standard of care defendant was required to meet, provided the court finds the appropriate legislative purpose.

B. Legislative Purpose to Protect This Class of Persons from This Harm

Legislation is relevant on the standard of care in a negligence case only if the statute was intended, at least in part, to protect a class of persons which includes plaintiff against the particular hazard and kind of harm which resulted. R.2d §§ 286, 288; R.3d Liability for Physical & Emotional Harm § 14.

Example: A statute requiring separate pens for animals transported by ship, intended to prevent the spread of disease, was not admissible in action where plaintiff's sheep were washed overboard at sea, even though the required pens (which were not provided) would have prevented the loss.

C. Statutory Standards That Impose New Duties

If the statute creates a wholly new obligation (but not a new cause of action) and defendant had no corresponding common law duty to plaintiff, courts tend to give the statute no tort law effect at all. In other words, the statute can supply the standard of care but does not itself create a duty that did not previously exist unless it creates a cause of action.

D. Licensing Statutes

Most courts hold that violation of a statute requiring a license to engage in a particular trade, profession or activity (e.g., physician, physical therapist, car driver) is not negligence *per se* and therefore the fact that defendant did not have a valid license is not admissible to show that defendant was negligent on a particular occasion. However, if defendant lacks a license because defendant failed necessary qualifications that have a safety purpose, the violation may be relevant and admissible on the negligence issue. See R.3d Liability for Physical & Emotional Harm § 14 cmt. *h*.

E. Effect of Statutory Violation

1. Majority Rule

The majority rule is that a relevant statute is prima facie proof of negligence or "negligence *per se*." If no evidence is introduced by defendant to excuse the violation, defendant's negligence is conclusively established. R.2d § 288B.

In most jurisdictions following the negligence *per se* rule, it is applied to violations of city ordinances and administrative regulations as well as to statutes. In a few, violation of an ordinance or administrative regulation is merely some evidence of negligence.

2. Minority View

In some jurisdictions, violation of a statute is merely *evidence* of negligence, which the jury can consider along with all other evidence in determining whether defendant was negligent. The violation does not per se establish negligence.

3. Cause

A violation does not *per se* establish a sufficient causal relation between the violation and plaintiff's injury. Proximate cause rules still apply, but some cases have adopted proximate cause rules more favorable to plaintiff.

4. Children

A minor's violation of a statute does not constitute negligence *per se* but may be introduced as evidence of the minor's negligence.

5. Defenses

Contributory negligence and assumption of risk defenses apply (if and to the extent otherwise available).

F. Excused Violations

1. Certain Safety Statutes

A few statutes having a strong safety purpose (e.g., Federal Safety Appliance Act, child labor laws, some factory and construction safety acts, pure food acts, some motor vehicle equipment and maintenance laws) permit no excused violations.

2. Other Statutes

As to most other statutes, courts will permit excuses for violations to be shown to rebut the *per se* or prima facie negligence. These include (a) physical circumstances beyond defendant's control; (b) innocent ignorance of facts which make the statute applicable; (c) sudden emergencies not of defendant's making; (d) situations in which it would be more dangerous to comply with the statute than to violate it; (e) violations that are reasonable in light of defendant's childhood, physical disability, or physical incapacity; and (f) defendant used reasonable care in attempting to comply with the statute. See R.2d § 288A; R.3d Liability for Physical & Emotional Harm § 15.

Of course, in jurisdictions where the statute is merely evidence of negligence, any proof tending to excuse or make reasonable the violation would be relevant.

G. Compliance with Statute

Defendant may also ordinarily show compliance with a statute as evidence of their reasonable care, but such compliance is not conclusive since a reasonable person might have taken precautions greater than the statutory minimum. R.2d § 288C; R.3d Liability for Physical & Emotional Harm § 16.

VIII. Proof of Negligence

A. Burden of Proof

1. Elements

Plaintiff must introduce sufficient evidence to tip the scales of probability in their favor with respect to each element of his cause of action—duty, negligence, causation, and damages. R.2d § 328A. Whether a duty exists is usually determined by the court, but in making that determination the court may have to resolve disputed fact issues. For plaintiff to recover, the trier of fact must find negligence, causation, and damages by a preponderance of the evidence—in other words, the factual basis of each essential element of plaintiff's claim must be found to be more probably true than not true.

2. Defenses

Any applicable defenses, such as plaintiff's contributory negligence, are affirmative defenses for defendant to plead and prove by the same standard of proof, more probably true than not true.

3. Circumstantial Evidence

Parties may prove any fact by circumstantial evidence (facts that support an inference of the fact the party seeks to prove) as well as by direct evidence (e.g., eyewitness testimony).

4. Role of Judge and Jury

It is the jury's task to determine, based on the evidence, whether plaintiff has proved each element of their cause of action by a preponderance of the evidence. But if the evidence on any essential element is so weak that no reasonable person could find that element established, the judge will decide the case and enter judgment for defendant. Conversely, if the judge finds that no reasonable person could find against the plaintiff on a particular element, the judge can direct a verdict for the plaintiff on that issue.

B. Presumptions

Each jurisdiction's tort law has its own set of legal presumptions, which are codified rules of circumstantial evidence.

C. Experts and Opinion Evidence

1. Expert Witnesses

In many tort cases, expert testimony is necessary or desirable to furnish the jury facts beyond its common knowledge. Expert testimony is usually required to establish the standard of care in professional negligence cases.

2. Opinions

Expert witnesses are permitted to testify to opinions or conclusions when they will be helpful to the jury. This even extends to opinions on an "ultimate issue"—i.e., an element of plaintiff's prima facie case (e.g., that the product was "unreasonably dangerous," causal relation). See Fed. Rules of Evid. 702–704.

Non-expert opinions are permitted in limited situations. See Fed. Rule of Evid. 701.

D. Res Ipsa Loquitur

Like presumptions, *res ipsa loquitur* ("the thing speaks for itself") is basically a rule of circumstantial evidence.

1. Rule

If plaintiff can establish a prima facie res ipsa loquitur case, they need not prove by direct or other evidence the specific conduct of defendant which was negligent. If plaintiff makes a prima facie showing that:

a. their injury was caused by an instrumentality or condition which was under defendant's exclusive management or control at the relevant time(s);

b. in the ordinary course of events, plaintiff's harm would not have occurred unless defendant was negligent;

then the jury is instructed on res ipsa loquitur and may infer that defendant was negligent and that defendant's negligence was the cause of plaintiff's injury without any more specific proof of what really happened. See R.2d § 328D; R.3d Liability for Physical & Emotional Harm § 17.

2. Control by Defendant

Although courts formerly required that defendant be in "exclusive" control of the instrumentality, it is now regarded as sufficient if defendant had the right to control and the opportunity to exercise it at the relevant time. In addition, defendant need not have been in control of the injury-causing instrumentality at the time of plaintiff's injury. Plaintiff need only establish that defendant's negligence, if any, must have occurred while the instrumentality was in defendant's control. Thus, defendant's control need only be "exclusive" in the sense that the negligence must have occurred, if at all, when defendant was in control or responsible for the instrumentality.

3. Multiple Defendants

The control requirement ordinarily precludes use of res ipsa loquitor against multiple defendants, because if more than one defendant could have been the responsible cause of plaintiff's injury, the inference of negligence does not point to the culpable defendant. However, in a few cases, the courts have applied a variation of the doctrine and shifted the burden of proof, requiring each defendant to prove that they were not the one who was negligent. In that case, all the defendants who failed to prove they were not negligent were held jointly and severally liable.

If there are multiple defendants but their relationship was such that they were jointly responsible for the instrumentality at the relevant time, or one would be vicariously liable for the conduct of the other, then the doctrine may be applied.

4. Inference of Negligence

Plaintiff need not show that defendant's negligence is the only possible explanation for the injury-causing occurrence, but only that the inference that it was defendant's negligence outweighs the sum of the other possible causes.

5. Plaintiff's Conduct

At one time there was a third element. plaintiff was required to prove that their injury was not due to any "voluntary act" by plaintiff, or that plaintiff's own conduct was not a significant causative factor, or, most recently, that plaintiff was not contributorily negligent. However, with the adoption of comparative negligence, this requirement has been eliminated in most jurisdictions. In comparative negligence jurisdictions, comparative fault applies to the same extent as in other negligence cases.

6. Procedural Effect

Once the court determines that plaintiff has established a prima facie res ipsa case, the issue becomes one for the jury to determine whether to draw the inference, taking into consideration defendant's contrary evidence (if any). The jury will be given a res ipsa instruction, but in most cases res ipsa is a permissible inference and not a presumption, so the jury is free to find against plaintiff even if it finds that plaintiff has proved the res ipsa elements. Both res ipsa and specific negligence theories may be submitted to the jury, so long as the two are not inconsistent.

7. Products Liability Cases

There is an analogous circumstantial evidence rule in strict product liability cases. Plaintiff need not prove the specific defect in the product, so long as the evidence tends to show that the product malfunctioned in such a way that the existence of a defect may be inferred and tends to exclude possible causes other than a product defect.

E. Custom and Character

1. Custom and Usage

a. General Rule

In determining whether conduct is negligent, the customary conduct of the community, industry, trade, business, or profession in similar circumstances is relevant but not conclusive. R.2d § 295A; R.3d Liability for Physical & Emotional Harm § 13; *The T.J. Hooper* (2d Cir. 1932). A typical use of such evidence is industry-wide practices introduced to show whether defendant's method of doing the same or a similar thing was negligent. Of course, to be relevant, plaintiff must show that the custom had a safety purpose.

Example: Defendant, a bottler, uses grade X glass. Plaintiff introduces evidence that all other bottlers use grade Y glass, which is more durable.

Such evidence might show that a risk is foreseeable, or that defendant knew or should have known of the risk, that the risk is an unreasonable one unless the customary precaution is taken, or that a particular safety precaution is feasible.

b. Exception

In professional negligence cases involving physicians and certain other professionals, the customary conduct of such professionals may conclusively establish the standard of care.

2. Character

Evidence that defendant or plaintiff was or was not a careful person is generally not admissible to prove that they acted carefully or negligently on the occasion in question.

F. Trade Rules and Standards

In some jurisdictions, rules and standards for the conduct of an activity promulgated by authoritative groups (e.g., accrediting agencies, trade associations, safety organizations), if relevant and recognized as authoritative, are like custom and are often admitted as some evidence of the standard of care.

G. Defendant's Own Rules and Standards

Often, courts will admit defendant's own rules and standards as some evidence of the standard of care, but they are not conclusive. R.3d Liability for Physical & Emotional Harm § 13 cmt. f.

IX. Degrees of Negligence

A. Degrees of Care

The duty of those who conduct certain dangerous activities is sometimes stated as greater than "ordinary" or "reasonable" care. See Dobbs § 141.

a. Some courts have held that common carriers (operators of airplanes, ships, buses, trains, taxicabs, and even elevators, escalators and amusement devices) are said to owe their passengers the "highest degree of care consistent with the mode of conveyance used and the practical operation of their business."

b. Some courts have held that persons responsible for certain dangerous instrumentalities (e.g., high-voltage electricity, explosives) must exercise a "high degree of care," commensurate with the danger, to protect others from harm.

There is a trend away from such special degrees of care. Analytically, such special duties are unsound. The standard negligence duty—"ordinary" or "reasonable" care under the circumstances—achieves the same result, since the "circumstances" include the high danger or special responsibility.

B. Degrees of Negligence

Occasionally, efforts have been made to subdivide the negligence concept into finer gradations—"slight," "ordinary," and "gross" negligence.

1. Light negligence is the failure to exercise great care.

2. Gross negligence is the failure to exercise even slight care. It shades into, and is usually indistinguishable from, reckless conduct. However, it will not support punitive damages, and contributory negligence is a defense to it.

These distinctions have proved unworkable and are rarely used.

X. Reckless Conduct ("Willful and Wanton Misconduct")

A. Definition

Conduct is in "reckless disregard of the safety of another" (also called "willful and wanton misconduct") when defendant knows or has reason to know that (1) it creates an unreasonable risk of harm and (2) the risk is relatively high, either in degree or in the probability that harm will occur. See R.2d § 500.

According to the R.3d Liability for Physical & Emotional Harm § 2, defendant's conduct is reckless if (1) they know that their conduct creates a risk of harm (or knows facts from which it should be obvious) and (2) the precautions that would reduce or eliminate the risk are so slight relative to the magnitude of the risk that defendant's conduct (in failing to take those precautions) shows a conscious indifference to the risk.

B. Distinguished from Negligent Conduct

Negligent conduct merely creates an unreasonable risk; no awareness of that risk is required. For conduct to be reckless, defendant must be conscious (or a reasonable person in defendant's situation would have been conscious) that it creates a relatively high risk of harm to another.

C. Distinguished from Intentional Torts

Conduct is intentional when defendant either intends to bring about the consequences or knows that they are substantially certain to occur. Reckless conduct lacks that certainty of result. For example, if defendant, intoxicated, drives their car 60 m.p.h. on a city street. Their conduct is probably reckless, even though they drive as carefully as possible, because they know or have reason to know that their conduct is creating a high risk of harm. But it is not intentional, because they do not intend to cause any harmful consequences, nor do they know that harmful consequences are substantially certain to occur.

D. When Required

Certain statutes (e.g., automobile and airplane guest statutes, governmental immunity acts, "Good Samaritan" laws) exempt defendant from liability for ordinary negligence, thereby requiring proof of reckless conduct for liability. It is also required by some common-law rules—e.g., in some jurisdictions a possessor of land is liable to a trespasser injured on the premises only for reckless conduct.

E. Effect

1. Proximate Cause

Broader rules of proximate cause may be applied if defendant's conduct is reckless. R.2d § 501(2); R.3d Liability for Physical & Emotional Harm § 33.

2. Defenses

In some jurisdictions, ordinary contributory negligence is not a defense or damage-reducing factor if defendant's conduct is found to be reckless. However, in most comparative negligence jurisdictions, plaintiff's contributory negligence will reduce their recovery even against defendant's reckless conduct. Assumption of the risk was formerly a defense to reckless conduct (R.2d §§ 502, 503), but in most jurisdictions it is now merely a damage-reducing factor.

3. Punitive Damages

In most jurisdictions, reckless conduct will support an award of punitive damages, the same as intentional torts.

XI. Review Questions

[Answers Provided in Appendix A]

1. As an act of self-defense, Plaintiff wires their clothing to give a severe electrical shock when touched. An Uber driver, injured when they attempted to help Plaintiff from their vehicle, seeks your legal advice. Explain to Plaintiff in a written IRAC structure what degree of negligence would likely govern.

2. City enacts an ordinance requiring all residents to clear snow from their sidewalks within 24 hours of a snowfall. Defendant violates the ordinance, and Plaintiff falls on Defendant's sidewalk. Plaintiff is legally intoxicated. Analyze whether, in a suit by Plaintiff against Defendant, Defendant's violation of the ordinance establishes a prima facie case of liability against Defendant.

3. An explosion and the resulting fire damage the kitchen in Plaintiff's house. At the time of the fire, Defendant (a carpenter) was alone in the house and was using an extremely flammable solvent to remove varnish from the cabinets. Analyze what Plaintiff must show to present a successful res ipsa loquitur argument that Defendant's negligence caused the damage to the kitchen.

Section 3
Causation

I. Causation of Harm

Plaintiffs must prove that the defendant's breach in the standard of care caused harm.

A. Overview of Causation Issues

Causation problems are common to many different torts (and to all torts involving physical harm).

Causation problems are among the most difficult, conceptually, in tort law. They may be analyzed in two categories:

1. Cause in fact (Factual Cause) exists when the "cause-and-effect" chain of events leading to plaintiff's injury includes defendant's tortious conduct.

2. Proximate cause, also called "legal cause" or "scope of liability." Proximate cause concepts are used to cut off defendant's liability when the court (or, in some cases, the jury) decides that it would be unjust under the circumstances, even though defendant's tortious conduct was a factual cause of Plaintiff's injury. Courts sometimes treat the same or similar scope of liability problems as duty issues or fault issues. Some courts and writers use the term "proximate cause" to encompass all causal relation issues (e.g., R.2d §§ 9, 43–45). Others distinguish between (a) proximate or legal cause and (b) cause in fact or factual cause (e.g., Dobbs, Chapters 9 and 10). Many now categorize proximate cause issues under the term "scope of liability," completely separating proximate cause issues from the issue of factual causation. This is the preferred approach, and the one used by the Restatement. See R.3d Liability for Physical & Emotional Harm § 26, cmt. *a*.

Many courts conflate "proximate cause" with "cause-in-fact." This outline will treat cause in fact as separate from proximate cause and use the latter term only to refer to scope of liability issues.

B. Cause in Fact

(Dobbs §§ 166–179; R.2d §§ 431–434; R.3d Liability for Physical & Emotional Harm §§ 26–28)

1. General Rule

Cause in fact is a question of fact, requiring proof that the injury would not have occurred "but for" defendant's conduct (the "sine qua non" rule). R.3d Liability for Physical & Emotional Harm § 26.

Example: Defendant drives his car negligently and collides with A's car, causing A's car to knock down a pole supporting electric wires. The wires break, causing a loss of electric power at a hospital six blocks away. The hospital's auxiliary power system fails, and Plaintiff, who was connected to an electric-powered life-support device, dies. "But for" Defendant's negligence, Plaintiff would still be connected to an electric-powered life support device.

Example: Defendant's cow kicks over a kerosene lantern, which Defendant negligently placed within her reach. The resulting fire destroys many city blocks of property. Defendant's negligence is a cause in fact of all of the fire damage.

In both examples, other rules (duty limitations, scope of liability limitations) may cut off Defendant's liability for these consequences, but Defendant's negligence was still a factual cause of the harm.

Earlier versions of the Restatement, and many courts, added a second element: that defendant's tortious conduct was a "substantial factor" (or sometimes "a material element") in bringing about plaintiff's injury. See, e.g., R.2d §§ 431, 432. Courts and torts scholars have discredited this element and have recognized that this factor was more appropriate to scope of liability ("proximate cause") questions.

Confusion between factual cause and proximate cause has been the norm, both in the courts and in the earlier Restatements, which regularly conflated the two concepts. In addition, the introduction of comparative fault has eliminated the need to screen out factual causes that are insubstantial. For an excellent discussion of this issue, see R.3d Liability for Physical & Emotional Harm § 26, cmt. *j*, and especially the Reporter's Note to cmt. *j*. Therefore, the current Restatement (and many courts) now reject the "substantial factor" element as part of the definition of factual causation. R.3d Liability for Physical & Emotional Harm § 26.

2. Proof

Circumstantial evidence that links plaintiff's injury to defendant's tortious conduct is usually all that is required to prove cause-in-fact. The question is whether plaintiff met their burden of presenting enough evidence to allow a rational factfinder to infer causation.

Example: Plaintiff's body is found at the bottom of Defendant's stairs, which were poorly lit and covered in debris. Whether Defendant's negligence in maintaining the stairs was a cause in fact of Plaintiff's death is a question of fact.

Where plaintiff's injury is closely linked to defendant's tortious conduct, courts are often lenient in permitting the trier of fact to infer factual causation.

In cases involving injuries by toxic substances, factual cause issues are very complex. See R.3d Liability for Physical & Emotional Harm § 28, cmt. *c* and Reporter's Note to cmt. *c*.

3. Multiple Causes

In life, most occurrences have more than one cause in fact. Defendant's conduct need only be "a" cause of plaintiff's harm. It does not need to be the sole cause or even the major or most important cause. See R.3d Liability for Physical & Emotional Harm § 26, cmts. *c* and *d*.

a. Concurrent Tortfeasors, Indivisible Injury

If the tortious conduct of multiple defendants coincides and both are causes in fact of plaintiff's injury, each or all defendants are subject to liability for plaintiff's damages. It does not matter that the defendants did not act together "in concert," or that no individual defendant's conduct by itself would have caused the injury.

Example: D1 and D2 both drive negligently and collide, and D2's car crashes into Plaintiff, a pedestrian. D1 and D2 are both subject to liability to Plaintiff.

Both D1 and D2 are also subject to liability to Plaintiff when either's tortious conduct alone would have caused Plaintiff's harm. R. 3d Liability for Physical & Emotional Harm § 27.

Example: D1 and D2, acting independently, negligently set separate fires. Both fires go out of control and combine to destroy Plaintiff's property. Plaintiff may sue either D1 or D2 or both for all of his damages, even though either fire alone would have caused the same result. N.B. The "but for" rule does not apply here.

This same rule applies even when one cause was tortious and the other was not. R.3d Liability for Physical & Emotional Harm § 27, cmt. *d*.

b. Concurrent Tortfeasors, Divisible Injury

i. General Rule

If multiple defendants each cause separate parts of plaintiff's harm, the defendants will each be liable only for the part an individual caused if it is possible to determine who caused which part. R.3d Liability for Physical & Emotional Harm § 28, cmt. *d*; R.3d Apportionment of Liability § 26.

Example: D1 and D2 each independently make defamatory statements about Plaintiff. D1 is liable only for that part of Plaintiff's damages attributable to his statement, and D2 is liable only for the damages attributable to his statement.

ii. Exceptions

(a) Concert of Action

All defendants are liable for all of Plaintiff's damages, even though divisible, if they were acting in concert or engaged in a joint enterprise.

Example: Dl and D2 work together to beat up Plaintiff. Dl breaks Plaintiff's right leg. D2 breaks the left. Plaintiff may sue either D1 or D2 to recover for both broken legs.

(b) Risk of Further Injury

If defendant's tortious conduct injures plaintiff and foreseeably exposes plaintiff to the risk of further injury by another, defendant is liable both for the injury defendant caused and for such further injury. For example, suppose the negligence of defendant caused plaintiff's injury, and the negligence of plaintiff's treating physician aggravated the injury. Defendant is subject to liability for both the original injury and the aggravation.

iii. Burden of Proof

A party alleging that damages are divisible has the burden to prove that they are divisible. R.3d Apportionment of Liability § 26, cmt. *h*; R.3d Liability for Physical & Emotional Harm § 26, cmt. *d*. If the alleging party cannot, the traditional rule is that they cannot recover against any. The modern and better view shifts the burden of proof on apportionment to defendants. See R.2d § 433B(2); R.3d Apportionment of Liability § 26; R.3d Liability for Physical & Emotional Harm § 28(b).

4. Concurrent Independent Tortfeasors, One Cause (Alternative Liability)

Suppose the tortious conduct of multiple defendants (acting independently) occurs so that each defendant (but not all) was the cause in fact of plaintiff's injury, but plaintiff cannot prove which one. Traditionally, plaintiff would lose. The modern and better view shifts the burden of proof to each defendant to prove that they were not the cause. See R.3d Liability for Physical & Emotional Harm § 28(b).

Example: Two hunters (D1 and D2), acting independently, each negligently fire their shotguns at the same time. A pellet from one of the guns strikes a third hunter, Plaintiff, in the eye. There is insufficient evidence to determine which shotgun's pellet hit Plaintiff. D1 and D2 each must prove that they did not cause Plaintiff's injury. If neither can, then both are liable to Plaintiff.

Example: Plaintiff's car is struck by a car negligently driven by D1. A car negligently driven by D2 then strikes both cars. Plaintiff cannot prove which collision caused Plaintiff's sprained neck. D1 and D2 then have the burden to prove whether either collision caused Plaintiff's sprained neck.

Of course, if D1 and D2 were acting in concert or engaged in a joint enterprise, both are subject to liability for the single harm.

5. Enterprise and Market Share Liability

In product liability cases involving an injury caused by a product from an unidentifiable manufacturer, some courts are willing to create new rules of causation when a plaintiff can prove that similar products were marketed during the relevant time by a group of manufacturers. The injury must have been caused by a common design feature of the similar products. In such cases, several manufacturers may be held jointly and severally liable to a plaintiff for an injury caused by a product manufactured and marketed by only one.

a. Enterprise Liability

A few courts may impose so-called "enterprise liability" when:

1) The injury-causing product was manufactured by one of a very small number of defendants in an industry;

2) The defendants had joint knowledge of the risks inherent in the product and possessed a joint capacity to reduce those risks;

3) Each defendant failed to take steps to reduce this risk, delegating this responsibility to a trade association; and

4) Most, if not all, of the manufacturers are joined as defendants.

Liability is joint and several. A manufacturer can escape liability only by proving that its product could not have been the one that injured the plaintiff.

b. Market Share Liability

So-called "market share" liability is sometimes used when plaintiff was injured by a fungible product (such as a drug) produced and sold by multiple manufacturers, but plaintiff cannot identify the particular manufacturer that sold the product that caused plaintiff's injury. In the small number of jurisdictions recognizing this rule, plaintiff must join manufacturers representing a substantial share of the relevant market at the time the product was used or consumed, and defendants who cannot be excluded are held *severally* liable for a proportional part of the plaintiff's damages. The operative details vary among jurisdictions, but in general the plaintiff must join enough manufacturers to encompass the great majority of the relevant market and prove their relevant market shares. A manufacturer can then escape liability by proving that its product could not have been the one that injured the plaintiff. There is some variation as to the effect of absent or escaped manufacturers on the shares of the remaining defendants. See R.3d Liability for Physical & Emotional Harm § 28, cmt. *o*; R.3d Apportionment of Liability § 26, Reporters' Note to cmt. *n*.

Many courts have disallowed market share liability altogether.

6. Liability for Reduced Chance

Suppose that defendant's tortious conduct does not *cause* plaintiff's harm in a "but for" sense but merely reduces plaintiff's chances of a favorable outcome. This issue often arises from a missed, and ultimately delayed, diagnosis. The negligence is in the timing or nature of the diagnosis, not in the medical condition itself. For example, had plaintiff been properly diagnosed with cancer when they first presented with the underlying symptoms, they had a 40% chance of survival. As a result of the defendant doctor's negligence in failing to make a prompt diagnosis, however, the patient's likelihood of survival was reduced to 25%, and Plaintiff eventually died.

Courts are split on whether defendant doctor is liable here. Some states deny all recovery unless the victim's chances were initially over 50% (the "traditional" rule). This is because the plaintiff cannot prove that the defendant's conduct was more likely than not the cause of plaintiff's outcome. In a few states the traditional rule is required by statute.

Other states allow damages if the jury finds that the defendant's negligence was a "substantial factor" in accelerating or triggering the adverse result. Finally, some states allow damages based on the percentage difference (in this case, 15%) attributable to the defendant's negligence times the plaintiff's total damages (the "value-of-the-chance" rule). See R.3d Liability for Physical & Emotional Harm § 26, cmt. *n*.

Some courts have also applied the loss-of-chance doctrine to cases in which plaintiff's enhanced injury did not result in death, or where defendant's negligence created an increased risk of future harm.

C. Scope of Liability (Proximate Cause)

(Dobbs §§ 180–197; R.2d §§ 9, 430, 435–461)

1. General Principle

Proximate cause or scope of liability rules limit defendant's liability to (a) persons and (b) consequences that bear some reasonable relationship to defendant's tortious conduct. Whether and how scope of liability rules shall be applied is a question of law for the court. However, in some instances the jury is allowed to decide whether the scope of liability in a particular case extends to plaintiff's harm. Proximate cause rules can be broadly grouped into two categories:

(a) unforeseeable or remote or indirect consequences; and

(b) intervening causes.

Earlier Restatements (and some courts) use the term "legal cause" to encompass both proximate cause and cause in fact. This usage is now obsolete, although some courts continue to use the term "proximate cause" to include both. To eliminate confusion and error, the better approach is to abandon both terms—"legal cause" and "proximate cause"—in favor of the terms "cause in fact" and "scope of liability." Nevertheless, the term "proximate cause" is still widely used to describe this category.

2. Overview

It is difficult to define proximate cause rules because different courts will use different approaches, sometimes even in the same jurisdiction and in similar types of cases. Focus on acquiring a broad skillset to argue and defend proximate cause arguments in varied ways depending on the facts of the case, the judge, or the jurisdiction.

Broadly defined, there are three typical approaches to the first category (unforeseeable or remote or indirect consequences): (a) the risk principle; (b) the direct consequences rule; and (c) the duty-risk rule. One of these approaches will be used, unless the case falls into a category of cases in which there is a fixed proximate cause or duty rule. Examples of the latter categories include liability to rescuers, greater-than-foreseeable harm due to plaintiff's preexisting condition that make plaintiff more vulnerable, and enhanced harm resulting from a third person's efforts to aid the injured plaintiff.

Special proximate cause rules have developed in certain situations involving an "intervening cause"—that is, a situation where defendant's negligence has created a risk of some future harm, but that risk would not have materialized into plaintiff's harm but for a later intervening cause that is completely independent of defendant. These rules determine whether defendant is liable to plaintiff or whether the intervening cause cuts off defendant's liability (in which case it is called a "superseding cause").

3. Unforeseeable or Remote or Indirect Consequences

(Dobbs §§ 187–189; R.2d § 435; R.3d Liability for Physical & Emotional Harm § 29)

a. The Risk Principle

Under the majority view, defendant's liability is limited (1) to those consequences, the foreseeability of which made defendant's conduct tortious in the first place, and (2) to persons within that foreseeable zone of danger. This is sometimes known as the "risk principle" or the "foreseeable-risk rule."

Example: Defendant negligently spills a large quantity of gasoline on the ground. Defendant is subject to liability for injuries to persons and property in the vicinity caused by the ensuing fire, even though it occurs hours later and the ignition source is unknown. But Defendant is arguably not liable for the death of Plaintiff's dog after Plaintiff's dog's, before the fire, wandered by and drank some of the gasoline. Courts will find that the death by poison was unforeseeable.

Example: Defendant's employees help a passenger board a train pulling out of the station, and in doing so negligently dislodge a package wrapped in newspaper. The train runs over the package which explodes, causing a scale located on the platform some distance away to tip over and injure Plaintiff. Defendant is arguably not liable to Plaintiff since an injury to Plaintiff was not a foreseeable consequence of the employees' negligence.

Under this test, we put ourselves in defendant's shoes, prior to the occurrence, and ask whether, if we were a reasonable person in defendant's position, the risk of what happened to plaintiff would have been sufficiently foreseeable that defendant was negligent in not taking sufficient care to obviate that risk. This is a "foresight"-oriented test because we are judging what defendant ought to have foreseen prior to the occurrence. Defendant may have been negligent with respect to other risks, but if defendant was not negligent with respect to the risk that resulted in plaintiff's harm, defendant is not liable to plaintiff for that harm.

This is the test favored by R.3d Liability for Physical & Emotional Harm § 29: "[L]iability is limited to those harms that result from the risks that made the actor's conduct tortious."

b. The Direct Consequences Rule

Under the direct consequences rule (a minority view), defendant is subject to liability for those consequences that are a direct result of defendant's tortious conduct, whether or not foreseeable. The result is direct if it follows in an unbroken natural sequence from the effect of defendant's act upon conditions existing and forces already in operation at the time, without the intervention of any external forces which were not then in active operation. Thus, the direct consequences rule embodies a hindsight test rewinding from the harm that resulted to the breach in the standard of care.

Example: Defendant's dockhands negligently cause a wooden plank to fall into the hold of a ship. Unexpectedly, the plank strikes a spark, which ignites gasoline vapor in the hold, and the ship is destroyed. Defendant is subject to liability for the loss, even if the risk of the plank striking a spark and igniting the vapor was totally unforeseeable. This is because it followed an unbroken natural sequence directly connected to defendant's negligence without the intervention of any other forces.

Under the direct consequences rule, defendant can be liable to plaintiff if defendant was negligent with respect to any risk, even if that was not the risk that resulted in plaintiff's injury, as long as the injury-producing event is not too remote or indirect from defendant's negligent conduct. Courts using this test typically permit the jury to determine whether defendant's negligence was a "natural and probable" result of defendant's negligence, subject to the court's right to decide the issue if it concludes that such a finding would be unreasonable. A leading example of this test is Judge Andrews' dissenting opinion in the *Palsgraf* case.

The Restatement (Second) of Torts adopted a modified direct consequences rule. According to R.2d § 435, defendant is subject to liability if defendant could have foreseen any harm from their tortious conduct, even though the manner or extent of the harm was unforeseeable, unless the court finds it "highly extraordinary" that the conduct should have brought about the harm. This rule has been replaced by R.3d Liability for Physical & Emotional Harm § 29.

c. The Duty-Risk Rule

Both the risk principle and the direct consequences rule have been criticized as being too easily manipulated to reach a result desired on other grounds. Some commentators have proposed that all questions of scope of liability or "proximate cause" should be treated as duty issues, to be decided by the court based on a variety of factors: social policy, fairness, expediency, etc. This approach, known as the "duty-risk rule," has won few adherents in principle, but it is not uncommon for courts to rule against plaintiffs on the ground that a defendant had no "duty" to protect plaintiff against a particular risk or that a defendant owed no "duty" to a plaintiff—an analysis consistent with the duty-risk rule. See, e.g., Judge Cardozo's opinion in the *Palsgraf* case. From a civics perspective, the difference in approaches is noteworthy because the "duty" question keeps the case from the jury whereas the "scope of risk" question is more often directed to the jury. Note that this approach (duty rules specific to a particular case) is also inconsistent with other duty rules, which are rules of more general application.

Example: Defendant, a physician, prescribes a drug for A but negligently fails to warn A that A should not drive a car after taking the drug because it will make A drowsy. A, having taken the drug, is driving their car in which Plaintiff is a passenger when A passes out. The car crashes and Plaintiff is injured. Although Defendant's negligence is clearly a cause in fact of Plaintiff's harm, and injury to Plaintiff is foreseeable, the court held that Defendant was not liable to Plaintiff because Defendant owed no duty to Plaintiff.

d. Current Status of the Risk Principle

Although most courts follow Judge Cardozo's approach in the *Palsgraf* case and limit defendant's liability to the foreseeable risks that made defendant's conduct negligent, many tend to allow juries to determine when the harm realized is too remote from defendant's negligence. They tend to see all causation issues as for the jury, and questions as to whether the risk realized is too disproportionate or different from the risk that made defendant's conduct tortious as questions for the court.

e. Elasticity of "Foreseeable"

Under the majority view, courts can expand or contract the bounds of Defendant's liability by expansive or constrictive rulings on the foreseeability question. Courts may find particular results foreseeable (or not), and thereby reach a decision preferred on policy grounds. Courts sometimes reach a desired outcome by characterizing the result as "not unforeseeable."

f. Elasticity of "Hazard"

The bounds of defendant's liability may also be expanded or contracted depending on how the court defines the hazard or risk that makes defendant's conduct tortious. See R.2d § 281, cmts. *f*, *g*.

Example: Even though Defendant's tortious conduct created a foreseeable risk only of damage to Plaintiff's property, most courts will hold Defendant liable for Plaintiff's personal injuries resulting from the same conduct, even if unforeseeable. Thus, if Defendant poisons Plaintiff's dog and the poison infects and kills Plaintiff, Defendant is subject to liability for Plaintiff's death even though any injury to Plaintiff themself was in fact unforeseeable. See R.2d § 281, cmt. *j*.

g. Rescuers

Rescuers benefit from a fixed scope of liability rule. Courts usually hold that the intervention of would-be rescuers is foreseeable as a matter of law, and therefore when defendant's tortious conduct endangers anyone (including themself), they are subject to liability to plaintiff who is injured in attempting a rescue, so long as the harm arises from a risk inherent in the effort to provide aid. R.3d Liability for Physical & Emotional Harm § 32. Note that professional rescuers are often treated differently under what is known as the "firefighters' rule"—a professional rescuer (police, fire, and emergency personnel) cannot sue defendant in tort if defendant's only tort was creating the risk that resulted in the occasion for the response, and sometimes also risks associated with the condition of the premises.

h. Physical Consequences (Eggshell Plaintiff)

Under another fixed rule, the so-called "thin-skulled" or "eggshell" plaintiff rule, defendant is liable for the full consequences of plaintiff's injury even though, due to plaintiff's peculiar susceptibility to harm (of which defendant was unaware)—plaintiff's physical or mental condition or other characteristics—those consequences were more severe than they would have been in others. This rule is often stated as, "You take your plaintiff as you find them." R.3d Liability for Physical & Emotional Harm § 29 cmt. *p*, § 31.

Examples: Defendant negligently rides their bicycle and runs into Plaintiff, a pedestrian, knocking Plaintiff down. Unknown to Defendant, Plaintiff has an unusually thin skull, which strikes the pavement. Plaintiff dies from multiple skull fractures.

Plaintiff has hemophilia, as a result of which Plaintiff bleeds to death from a laceration. Defendant is subject to liability for Plaintiff's death, even though other plaintiffs would have suffered injuries far more minor.

Defendant negligently throws a dart, blinding Plaintiff in Plaintiff's right eye. Unknown to Defendant, Plaintiff was already blind in their left eye. Defendant is subject to liability for Plaintiff's total blindness.

i. Intentional Torts; Strict Liability

Courts tend to expand the limits of foreseeability when defendant's conduct amounts to an intentional tort and conversely confine liability to foreseeable consequences when liability is strict. See R.2d §§ 435A–B, 504(3)(c), 524A; R.3d Liability for Physical & Emotional Harm § 33.

4. Intervening Cause

(Dobbs §§ 190–96; R.2d §§ 440 461; R.3d Liability for Physical & Emotional Harm § 34)

a. Definition

An intervening cause is conduct by some third person, or an event, which occurs after defendant's tortious conduct, and operates with or upon defendant's conduct to produce plaintiff's injury.

Example: Defendant negligently spills a quantity of gasoline upon the ground and departs. Sometime later, a third person negligently discards a cigarette, and the gasoline ignites. Or the gasoline is ignited by a bolt of lightning and Plaintiff is badly burned. The act of the third person and the lightning are intervening causes of the resulting injury to Plaintiff.

b. General Rule

If (1) an intervening cause was foreseeable, or (2) the intervening cause was not foreseeable but the consequences were of the type which defendant could foresee as resulting from their conduct, the intervening cause will not operate to relieve defendant of liability. But if both the intervening cause and the resulting consequences were not foreseeable, it is called a superseding cause and defendant's tortious conduct is not a proximate cause of plaintiff's injury. R.3d Liability for Physical & Emotional Harm § 34.

c. Types of Intervening Causes

An intervening cause may consist of either human conduct or any other natural force or event (e.g., action of weather, animals).

d. Foreseeable Intervening Causes

Foreseeable intervening causes may include:

i. Weather

Non-extraordinary weather conditions or changes, such as those typical for the geography and forecasted to the community.

ii. Negligence

Negligence by a third party is normally foreseeable. Note that in such cases, Defendant and Third Party may both be liable to Plaintiff. For example, it is foreseeable that a hospitalized patient from a car accident might further contract a staph infection due to hospital negligence.

iii. Criminal Conduct or Intentional Torts by Third Parties

At one time, many courts held that an intervening intentional tortious or criminal act by a third party that was the immediate cause of plaintiff's harm broke the chain of causation.

Today, it is recognized that criminal conduct or intentional torts by third parties may be foreseeable if defendant's negligent conduct exposes plaintiff to a greater-than-normal risk of such conduct, or if the exposure to such risks is what makes defendant's conduct tortious.

Example: Defendant negligently leaves Plaintiff's car unlocked with the keys in the ignition. When a thief proceeds to steal the car, this act cannot be recognized as a superseding cause.

Example: Defendant negligently leaves their car unlocked with the keys in the ignition in the heavily-populated bar district of a college town. An intoxicated student steals the car and negligently drives it, injuring Plaintiff. Neither the theft nor the negligence of the driver is a superseding cause of Plaintiff's injury.

Example: Defendant negligently spills a large quantity of gasoline. Third Party, an arsonist, seeing the gasoline puddle, throws a match into it for the purpose of causing it to ignite. The ensuing explosion injures Plaintiff. Defendant is subject to liability to Plaintiff if the foreseeable risk of Third Party's conduct was one of the things that made Defendant's conduct negligent in the first place.

Example: Plaintiff is a guest at Defendant's hotel. Returning to their room, Plaintiff is assaulted by Third Party, who was able to gain entrance to Plaintiff's room because the lock on the door was easy to break. Plaintiff sues Defendant claiming negligence in providing inadequate locks for guest rooms. Assuming Defendant is found negligent in maintaining adequate locks, these Third Party criminal acts are not a superseding cause of Plaintiff's harm.

iv. Self-Inflicted Harm

The same analysis (as in 3 above) applies to plaintiff's self-inflicted harm, such as suicide or attempted suicide.

Example: Defendant, knowing of Plaintiff's suicidal state of mind, negligently leaves a loaded gun where Plaintiff can access it. In some jurisdictions, Defendant's negligence can be found to be a proximate cause of the injury resulting from Plaintiff's attempted suicide.

v. Rescuers

Acts, even negligent ones, by rescuers and others who render aid reasonably required by plaintiff's injury are foreseeable. R.3d Liability for Physical & Emotional Harm § 35.

vi. Further Harm

Disease contracted or subsequent physical or mental injuries sustained because of the impairment of plaintiff's health resulting from the original injury caused by defendant's tortious conduct are foreseeable. R.2d §§ 458, 459.

e. Foreseeable Consequences

If the resulting harm is foreseeably within the risk created by Defendant's tortious conduct, then even an unforeseeable intervening cause ordinarily does not supersede defendant's liability. R.3d Liability for Physical & Emotional Harm § 34.

Example: Defendant negligently spills a large quantity of gasoline, which is ignited by fragments of a falling meteor. Defendant is subjcct to liability.

If the intervening cause is culpable human conduct, then comparative fault rules may apply and both defendant and the intervening actor may be liable to plaintiff.

D. Review Questions

[Answers Provided in Appendix A]

Marcus's northbound car crosses the line into the southbound traffic lane. Southbound Brianna, who is driving too fast for weather conditions, swerves to the right to avoid a collision with Marcus. Brianna is injured when her car strikes an electric pole. The resulting power disruption causes Phil, a patient in a nearby hospital, permanent brain damage when his respirator ceases to work. Analyze, in IRAC form, the following issues:

1. Whether Marcus's negligence was the cause in fact of Phil's injury.

2. Whether Marcus's negligence is a proximate (legal) cause of Phil's injury. 3. In a joint-and-several liability jurisdiction, if a jury finds that the negligent actions of both Marcus and Brianna proximately caused Phil's injury, who can be held liable for the full amount of damages?

4. Is Marcus liable for any aggravation of Brianna's injury resulting from any negligent medical treatment?

5. Are Marcus and Brianna liable for Phil's brain damage?

6. Craig rushes to rescue Brianna from her burning car. Craig is burned. Is Marcus liable for Craig's injury?

7. In attempting to rescue Brianna, Craig exacerbates Brianna's injury. Is Marcus liable?

8. While Phil is experiencing complications from the respirator ceasing to work, robber Xavier enters his room, takes Phil's money and property, and hits Phil on the head. Is Marcus liable for Phil's head injury?

Part Three

Damages

■ ANALYSIS

I. Damages

(Dobbs §§ 377, 380–384, 385–390; R.2d §§ 875–886B, 901–932; R.3d Apportionment of Liability)

A. Compensatory Damages

1. Categorizing General Damages vs. Special Damages

a. General Damages or Noneconomic Loss

General damages are compensatory damages for a type of harm, like pain and suffering or loss of companionship, because they so frequently result from the tort involved that such damages are anticipated and hence need not be alleged with specificity for plaintiff to prove and recover them. Today, such damages are more often categorized as noneconomic loss because they are losses not supported with itemized receipts.

b. Special Damages or Economic Loss

Special damages are those awarded for all other compensable harms, such as medical expenses or lost wages. These damages are usually called "economic loss" or "pecuniary loss," but sometimes are referred to as "specials."

2. Nominal Damages

Nominal damages are a trivial sum (e.g., one dollar) awarded to a litigant who has established a cause of action but has not established that they are entitled to compensatory damages. R.2d § 907. Some tort actions, such as negligence, do not support nominal damages.

3. Damages for Personal Injury

When a plaintiff proves a compensable personal injury, they may recover for all foreseeable adverse physical and mental consequences of that injury, past and future, in the following categories. R.2d § 924.

a. Past and Future Pecuniary or Economic Loss and Out-of-Pocket Expenses

1) Medical, hospital, rehabilitative, and similar costs;
2) Lost wages, earnings or profits;
3) Substitute labor;
4) Custodial care;
5) Medical monitoring (in some situations);
6) Any other specifically identifiable pecuniary losses resulting from the injury (e.g., travel to obtain medical care).

b. Noneconomic or Nonpecuniary Damages

1) Conscious physical pain and suffering (past and future);

2) Mental or emotional distress

Different jurisdictions will define this category of mental or emotional distress in different ways. Some examples include:

a) Fright and shock sustained during the occurrence;

b) Anxiety about the future;

c) Loss of peace of mind, happiness, mental health in the present;

d) Humiliation, embarrassment, or loss of dignity, including disfigurement;

e) Loss of the ability to enjoy a normal life, sometimes referred to as "disability" (not to be confused with loss of earning capacity);

f) Inconvenience in performing the daily activities of life.

c. Physical Impairment

To the extent not recoverable under one of the foregoing, plaintiff may recover for physical impairment of some portion of the body. This is usually categorized under the "disability" element.

4. Defendant Responsible for Pre-Existing Conditions

Defendant is responsible in damages for all the consequences of plaintiff's injury, including those caused or aggravated by some pre-existing condition, predisposition, or vulnerability of the plaintiff that others would not have sustained, even if that condition was unknown to the defendant. This is an aspect of the so-called "eggshell" or "thin-skulled" plaintiff rule.

5. Awarding Future Losses at Present

a. Pecuniary Losses Awarded at Present Value

If a plaintiff is awarded damages for pecuniary losses which they will incur in the future, the amount of such damages must ordinarily be reduced to present cash value. R.2d § 913A.

b. Some Jurisdictions Consider Inflation for Future Losses

Some jurisdictions still do not allow the jury to consider the effects of future inflation in calculating damages for future economic losses. A growing number do.

6. Collateral Source Rule

a. General Rule

Under the general rule, payments made to, or benefits conferred on, a plaintiff from sources other than the defendant are not credited against the defendant, even though they cover all or part of the damages for which the defendant is liable. R.2d § 920A(2). This issue can arise through the coverage of expenses by private health and accident insurance, worker's compensation, social security, disability insurance, wage continuation plans, sick leave, veterans' benefits, public aid, or free medical or nursing services provided as a matter of professional courtesy.

b. Rationale

Although the plaintiff's net loss may have been reduced because of such payments, that benefit to the injured party should not be shifted to become a windfall for the defendant. The defendant still holds responsibility to compensate the plaintiff for all foreseeable harms they caused.

c. Trend Toward Statutory Abolition

Statutes in an increasing number of jurisdictions have either abolished or modified the collateral source rule. Some courts will credit a defendant with medical charges waived by a health-care provider (e.g., the hospital's bill was $10,000, but it agreed to accept $5,000 for whatever reason). Many states allow the defendant a partial credit in some or all cases, which can be further offset by the insurance premiums or other payments the plaintiff has paid for the collateral source benefit for a specified period.

7. Limitations on Damages or "Caps"

As a result of tort reform legislation, about half of the states place statutory caps (e.g., $250,000 maximum) or other limits on the amount of noneconomic damages recoverable, either in personal injury actions generally, or in medical malpractice cases only. Some statutes limit liability for certain types of defendants, such as alcohol providers. In some jurisdictions, these statutes have been held unconstitutional; in others, they have not. Constitutional challenges include the right to a jury trial, equal protection, due process, and separation of powers grounds.

If multiple defendants in a single case are found liable, the better rule (statute permitting) is that the cap applies to each defendant individually. For example, if the cap is $250,000, and Plaintiff recovers a joint-and several judgment of $500,000 against Defendant 1 and Defendant 2, Plaintiff can collect $250,000 from each. Also, the cap is per injured plaintiff (or group of plaintiffs recovering for a single death).

If the plaintiff's damages are reduced because of plaintiff's contributory fault, that reduction should occur *before* the cap is applied, not after.

Statutes can also cap damages in tort cases against governmental units, in certain statutory tort actions, or where alternate compensation funds exist.

Judges also hold the power of remittur to reduce a damage award that exceeds that which a reasonable juror could award.

8. Plaintiff's Duty to Mitigate Damages

Plaintiffs must make reasonable efforts to mitigate the consequences of their injury and to take reasonable steps to prevent further harmful consequences from developing. R.2d § 918. For example, a plaintiff may need to seek alternate employment or undergo surgery. If part of plaintiff's damages are attributable to their failure to mitigate or to reasonably facilitate their recovery, the traditional rule is that the plaintiff cannot recover that part. Under this view, "avoidable consequences" is really a causal apportionment rule—that is, damages are apportioned according to who caused them.

The Restatement (Third) Apportionment of Damages § 3 provides for comparative responsibility in this situation. Defendant is solely responsible for all damages not attributable to the plaintiff's failure to mitigate. As to the damages caused by plaintiff's breach of their duty to mitigate, that part of plaintiff's damages is apportioned between the plaintiff and defendant based on the applicable comparative fault rules.

9. Damages Awards Not Generally Taxed

Damages for personal injuries involving physical harm are generally not subject to federal income taxation. However, other kinds of tort damages are taxable, such as damages for purely emotional injuries and punitive damages.

Although a growing minority of jurisdictions disagree, the prevailing rule is that the nontaxability of compensatory damages may not be the subject of evidence, argument, or instructions to the jury. R.2d § 914A.

B. Punitive Damages

(Dobbs §§ 381–384)

1. Rationale

In most jurisdictions, the trier of fact may award punitive damages when the defendant's misconduct is sufficiently serious, to punish defendant and to deter the defendant and others from similar conduct in the future. R.2d § 908.

2. Conduct Required

States that allow punitive damages have heightened requirements regarding the qualifying conduct. Defendants generally must have acted from a wrongful motive, or at least with gross or knowing indifference to the rights or safety of another. Defendant's conduct must have an element of outrage, similar to criminal conduct. An intentional tort will usually suffice. Most jurisdictions also allow punitive damages in all cases of reckless or willful and wanton misconduct. Others require a kind of malice, which means a conscious and deliberate disregard of a high probability of harm.

3. Limitations on Punitive Damages

a. Constitutional Limitations

United States Supreme Court decisions have established due process limits on awards of punitive damages. *BMW of N. Am., Inc. v. Gore* (U.S. 1996) (due process limits amount of punitive damages); *Honda Motor Co. v. Oberg* (U.S. 1994) (due process requires judicial review of punitive damages award); *Cooper Indus. v. Leatherman Tool Grp., Inc.* (U.S. 2001) (constitutionality of punitive damages award is subject to de novo standard of review); *State Farm Mut. Auto. Ins. Co. v. Campbell* (U.S. 2003) ($145 million award excessive). Under these cases, review of punitive damages by the trial and reviewing courts is constitutionally required, using three guideposts:

(1) the degree of reprehensibility of the defendant's misconduct;

(2) the disparity between plaintiff's actual or potential harm and the punitive damages award; and

(3) the difference between the punitive damages awarded and any applicable civil penalties for similar misconduct.

Defendant cannot be punished for conduct that bears no relation to plaintiff's harm, such as similar conduct that occurred elsewhere, or similar conduct that occurred in other cases, or harm to nonparties. However, such evidence may be relevant as to the defendant's culpable state of mind.

b. Statutory Limitations

There may be limits on how much can be awarded in punitive damages. For example, state statutes might have award caps by statutory ratios, multiples, or dollar figure caps. They might require a higher level of judicial scrutiny or set a higher burden of proof than for other damages (e.g., clear and convincing evidence). They are also limited by the type of conduct, as described in B.2. (e.g., malicious, wanton, or reckless conduct).

c. Discretionary Variations and Judicial Limitations

Whether to award punitive damages at all and the amount of the award is typically within the discretion of the trier of fact and may be subject to review for excessiveness. Particularly in personal injury cases, many courts require that punitive damages bear some reasonable relation to the compensatory damages awarded, or at least to the seriousness of the injury or potential injury. Evidence of defendant's wealth is ordinarily admissible as a relevant factor. Punitive damages are not reduced by plaintiff's comparative fault.

Although some cases spend considerable effort analyzing ratios, and the U.S. Supreme Court has said that few awards exceeding a single-digit ratio between punitive and compensatory damages to a significant degree will satisfy due process, the fact is that courts still sustain punitive damages awards with much larger ratios based on the unique facts of the case. In short, there is no one-size-fits-all formula but there is widespread judicial review.

d. Cause of Action Limitations

Punitive damages may not be available against an employer for any tort committed by their employee for which the employer is vicariously liable. Other jurisdictions follow the Restatement (R.2d § 909) and refuse to allow them against the employer unless:

(a) the employer authorized the doing and the manner of the act,

(b) the employee was unfit, and the employer was reckless in employing them,

(c) the employee was working in a managerial capacity, or

(d) the employer or one of their managerial agents ratified or approved the act.

In theory, punitive damages should not be awarded if the sole basis for plaintiff's claim is strict liability, but some courts permit them in such cases if there is also a showing of the necessary conduct and state of mind.

Typically, punitive damages are not allowed in wrongful death actions.

Statutory causes of action typically permit only compensatory damages, although some allow double or treble damages.

C. Derivative Claims for Spouse, Parent, and Child

Derivative actions can be brought by a spouse or parent that are independent of the injured spouse's or child's action. In these claims, the defendant may also invoke any defense (e.g., contributory negligence) that would have been available in a suit brought by the injured person directly, as well as defenses available against the plaintiff. Some courts require these actions to be brought in the same lawsuit with the injured person's action for their damages.

1. Spouse (Loss of Consortium)

In most jurisdictions, if defendant's tort has injured one spouse, the other spouse has a separate cause of action against the defendant for the damages resulting from their loss of the injured spouse's society, love, companionship, affection, and marital relations. Sometimes this broader framing of harms is referred to as "loss of consortium"; sometimes the term "consortium" refers only to intimacy. Dobbs § 310; R.2d §§ 693, 694, 694A.

2. Parent's Loss of Child's Services

A parent can recover damages for reasonable loss of the services of their minor child resulting from an injury to the child caused by the tortious conduct of defendant. In addition, some courts permit damages for loss of the child's society, companionship, love, and affection. R.2d §§ 703, 704, 704A.

3. Child's Loss of Parent's Services

Except in a few jurisdictions, a child has no action for loss of their parent's care, support, training, guidance, companionship, love, and affection resulting from a tortious injury to the parent. R.2d § 707A.

D. Review Questions

[Answers Provided in Appendix A]

1. Draft a one-paragraph email explaining to a client whether punitive damages may be awarded in your state. Some brief research may be necessary. Advise the client on what punitive damages are, what proof requirements govern, and what damage caps might apply.
2. Draft a one-paragraph email to a parent who lost their child (age 16) in a car accident explaining what claims the parent might have derivatively for the underlying negligence that took the life of their child.
3. Piper Plaintiff (a passenger) suffered a neck injury after her friend (the driver) was texting and driving and their vehicle struck a jaywalking pedestrian. As a result, Piper suffered an injury caused by two potential tortfeasors. Piper Plaintiff was confined to the hospital for three weeks and incurred a hospital bill

of $4800. This sum was paid directly to the hospital by Plaintiff's insurance. In a suit against the tortfeasors, explain what relevance this insurance payment will have on Piper's recovery in a one-paragraph email to Piper. Can she still recover the $4800?

4. Defendant negligently struck Palmer Pedestrian, causing Palmer severe injuries which resulted in him being hospitalized for twenty days and which left him unable to work for eight months because of which he lost eight months of wages. Palmer incurred numerous other medical expenses, such as physical therapists, medications, and surgeries. Palmer experienced intense pain and suffering and is now fearful of going out of his home for fear of being struck by another car. He will never be able to work overtime or long hours like he did before the accident because of their injuries. Identify in the chart below the categories of damages that are recoverable in a negligence suit brought by Palmer against the Defendant driver.

Category of Damages	Facts that Support Pleading for this Category of Damages

Part Four

Defenses to Negligence

■ ANALYSIS

I. **Contributory and Comparative Negligence**
   A. Defined
   B. Causation
   C. Effect of Plaintiff's Contributing Fault
      1. Terminology
      2. Contributory Negligence
      3. Comparative Negligence
         a. Pure Comparative Negligence
         b. Modified Comparative Negligence
      4. Trier of Fact Assigns Relative Fault
      5. Intentional or Reckless Conduct
      6. Strict Liability
      7. Serious Misconduct or Fault
      8. Public Policy Exceptions
   D. Imputed Contributory Negligence
      1. Negligence of Third Parties Not Generally Imputed to Plaintiff
         a. Employee's Conduct Imputed to Employer
         b. Conduct Imputed to Members of a Joint Enterprise
         c. Conduct Will Be Imputed for Relational Damage Claims
      2. Fault May Be Imputed for Driving an Automobile with Owner's Permission
   E. Plaintiff's Fault May Arise from Negligent Failure to Exercise Control
      1. General Rule
      2. Parent

II. **Last Clear Chance**
   A. Historical Rule Mitigating Harshness of Contributory Negligence
   B. Doctrine Limited to Subsequent Negligence, Not Antecedent Negligence
   C. Relevant Scenarios
      1. Helpless Plaintiff
      2. Inattentive Plaintiff
      3. Observant Defendant
      4. Inattentive Defendant
      5. Application to Relevant Scenarios
   D. Comparative Negligence Subsumes Last Clear Chance Doctrine

I. Contributory and Comparative Negligence

A. Defined

If plaintiff creates an unreasonable risk of harm to themselves, their contributory fault can combine with the defendant's negligence to cause plaintiff's injury. R.2d §§ 463, 466. This set of circumstances triggers an affirmative defense. R.2d § 477. In general, the factfinder may use the same rules and tests to determine whether plaintiff's own conduct contributed to their harm as it uses to determine if conduct is negligent. R.2d §§ 464, 469, 476.

B. Causation

The same rules of causation apply to plaintiff's contributing fault as to defendant's negligent conduct. R.2d § 465. The defendant must prove that the plaintiff's harm resulted from the plaintiff's conduct. R.2d § 468. For example, if a plaintiff is negligent for standing on an unstable platform, that conduct is not the cause of injuries if the plaintiff is instead injured by an adjacent wall collapsing.

C. Effect of Plaintiff's Contributing Fault

1. Terminology

"Contributory negligence" is when the legal rules adopted in a state yield a complete bar on plaintiff's recovery. "Comparative negligence" or "comparative fault" is when the legal rules of the state merely reduce plaintiff's recovery by their own percentage of fault.

2. Contributory Negligence

Under the traditional common law rule, plaintiff's contributory negligence was a complete defense and totally barred any recovery against a negligent defendant. R.2d § 467. This is now the minority rule that remains in just five jurisdictions: Alabama, Maryland, North Carolina, Virginia, and the District of Columbia (allowing some exceptions for suits brought by pedestrians and cyclists).

3. Comparative Negligence

Comparative negligence is the modern and majority rule. Plaintiff's contributing fault is not a complete bar to recovery; it merely reduces plaintiff's damages *pro tanto*. Plaintiff's damages are calculated and then reduced by the relative percentage of plaintiff's own fault. Thus, if defendant's negligence contributed 75% to plaintiff's harm and plaintiff's conduct contributed 25% to their injury, plaintiff will recover $75,000 of a $100,000 damage award.

a. Pure Comparative Negligence

In a pure comparative negligence jurisdiction, adopted in 12 states, plaintiff may recover any portion of damages no matter how great their relative fault is. This means that plaintiff will recover only $20,000 of a $100,000 damage award if the plaintiff was 80% at fault and the defendant was 20% at fault.

b. Modified Comparative Negligence

The majority rule, adopted in 33 states, follows a modified comparative negligence approach, in which plaintiff recovers nothing if their negligence was as great as (50%) or greater than (51%) that of the defendant or defendants. Thus, if plaintiff was 51% at fault and the defendant was 49% at fault, plaintiff recovers nothing.

4. Trier of Fact Assigns Relative Fault

These rules reveal the importance of the trier of fact assigning the relative percentage of fault. According to § 8 of R.3d Apportionment of Liability, the trier of fact should consider (1) the nature of the risk-creating conduct (including any awareness of the risk or indifference to it, and any intent to harm) and (2) the causal connection between the risk-creating conduct and the harm.

5. Intentional or Reckless Conduct

Traditionally, ordinary contributory negligence was not a defense to an intentional tort or to reckless conduct (but contributory reckless conduct was a defense to the latter). R.2d §§ 481, 482. In most comparative negligence jurisdictions, plaintiff's fault will reduce their recovery even though defendant's conduct was reckless, but not if defendant's conduct was intentional. R.3d Apportionment of Liability § 1 calls for all application of comparative fault rules to all claims for physical harm, but it takes no position on whether a plaintiff's comparative fault reduces their recovery against an intentional tortfeasor. The Restatement leaves this to substantive law. The Restatement does capture rules governing apportionment of liability among intentional and negligent defendants, as discussed in the Joint Tortfeasors chapter. Some comparative negligence states do not permit the plaintiff's ordinary fault to reduce plaintiff's damages if defendant's tortious conduct was reckless ("willful and wanton").

6. Strict Liability

Prior to the adoption of comparative negligence, contributory negligence was not a defense to a strict liability action, except when that conduct amounted to assumption of the risk. R.2d § 484. Today, some of the jurisdictions adopting comparative negligence permit plaintiff's ordinary contributory negligence to reduce plaintiff's damages. Others do not. The only damage-reducing defense is plaintiff's assumption of the risk.

7. Serious Misconduct or Fault

In some jurisdictions, if plaintiff's contributory fault was seriously unlawful conduct, they will be barred from recovery altogether. And in some cases, plaintiff's serious fault is considered a superseding cause of plaintiff's own harm. These latter cases are arguably inconsistent with comparative fault principles.

8. Public Policy Exceptions

Courts have sometimes refused to permit defendant to assert the defense of contributory negligence in cases where an overriding public policy prevails. For example, where a statute ensuring safe working conditions is intended to protect workers against economic pressure which might force them into unsafe employment, defendant employers cannot assert the defense that plaintiff employees consented to such unsafe conditions.

Some courts have refused to consider plaintiff contributorily negligent for engaging in some activity involving a right or entitlement, even though that conduct involves a risk of harm. For example, crossing a crosswalk without looking both ways when the walk sign is on, dining at a restaurant where outdoor seating abuts a busy road, or in-person meetups to exchange items sold online.

D. Imputed Contributory Negligence

1. Negligence of Third Parties Not Generally Imputed to Plaintiff

With three exceptions, a third party's negligence will not be imputed to plaintiff to reduce or bar plaintiff's recovery for injuries caused by defendant's negligence, despite the existence of some relationship between plaintiff and the third party. R.2d §§ 485–92; R.3d Apportionment of Liability § 5. For example, the negligence of a spouse is not imputed to the other spouse (R.2d § 487), nor a child to a parent (R.2d § 488).

a. Employee's Conduct Imputed to Employer

An employer's recovery against a negligent defendant is reduced or barred by the negligence of an employee acting within the scope of their employment. R.2d § 486.

b. Conduct Imputed to Members of a Joint Enterprise

Joint enterprises trigger an exception to the general rule. If plaintiff is a member of a joint enterprise and is injured by defendant's concurrent negligence, a third party outside the enterprise, and a member of the enterprise, plaintiff's recovery against defendant is reduced by the member's negligence. R.2d § 491. Plaintiff in that scenario also has a cause of action against the member of the joint enterprise.

c. Conduct Will Be Imputed for Relational Damage Claims

Where plaintiff has a cause of action based upon personal injuries to another, plaintiff's recovery is reduced by the other individual's contributory negligence. R.2d § 494; R.3d Apportionment of Liability § 6. For example, if one spouse has a cause of action against defendant for loss of the other spouse's consortium, the spouse's recovery is reduced by the other spouse's contributory negligence.

2. Fault May Be Imputed for Driving an Automobile with Owner's Permission

Some state statutes make the owner of a vehicle vicariously liable for the negligence of a person they allow to drive it. The R.3d Apportionment of Liability § 5, Comment c, notes that the driver's negligence is not imputed to the owner when the owner is the plaintiff. Injured parties might also have a direct negligence claim against the owner for negligent entrustment.

E. Plaintiff's Fault May Arise from Negligent Failure to Exercise Control

1. General Rule

If plaintiff has a duty to control the conduct of A and negligently fails to do so, A's contributory negligence (combined with that of plaintiff bringing the suit) reduces or bars plaintiff's recovery (depending on whether in a comparative or contributory jurisdiction) against defendant whose negligence was also a cause of plaintiff's injury. R.2d § 495. The rationale underlying this rule is that of self-preservation. For example, passengers can generally trust the driver, but in exceptional circumstances passengers might have a duty to call excessive speed to the driver's attention.

2. Parent

A parent's ability to recover for injuries to plaintiff's child caused by a third party's negligence is reduced by the parent's negligence in protecting or supervising their child, who was too young to be responsible for their own safety. R.2d § 496; R.3d Apportionment of Liability § 6(a). Parents are barred from recovery if the child is too young to care for itself, the child contributed to their own harm, and the parent failed to exercise reasonable care to prevent the child from being in the dangerous situation.

II. Last Clear Chance

A. Historical Rule Mitigating Harshness of Contributory Negligence

The "last clear chance" doctrine now only survives in a dwindling minority of jurisdictions. It was intended to ameliorate the harsh effects of the contributory negligence bar, and it was primarily an intermediate stop on the road to comparative fault. Most jurisdictions adopting comparative fault have also abolished this doctrine. However, it may still apply in jurisdictions that have not adopted comparative fault and might be relevant in assessing the parties' relative fault.

The "last clear chance" doctrine applies only when defendant's negligent act occurs later than plaintiff's contributorily negligent act. In essence, plaintiff (or plaintiff's property) is in a zone of danger from which they cannot escape in time, leaving defendant with the last opportunity to prevent the harm which otherwise will occur. If defendant then negligently fails to act to prevent the harm, they are not permitted to use plaintiff's prior negligence as a defense.

B. Doctrine Limited to Subsequent Negligence, Not Antecedent Negligence

The "last clear chance" doctrine applies only when defendant's negligence occurs after that point in time when they discover (or should have discovered) plaintiff's peril. For example, if defendant's negligence was failing to keep their brakes in repair and this was the reason they could not stop in time to prevent plaintiff's injury, the doctrine would not apply to this antecedent negligence.

C. Relevant Scenarios

Jurisdictions vary with respect to the fact situations in which they will permit application of the rule depending on (1) the nature of plaintiff's predicament and (2) the state of defendant's attentiveness to plaintiff's peril.

1. Helpless Plaintiff

The helpless plaintiff is one who has negligently placed themself in a position of peril from which they are now helpless to escape in time to avoid the harm. For example, a helpless plaintiff is one in the path of defendant's moving vehicle who cannot move because their foot is stuck, they are unconscious, or they have been injured by a third person.

2. Inattentive Plaintiff

The inattentive plaintiff has negligently placed themself in a position of peril and has failed to observe the danger. For example, a plaintiff is jogging down the middle of a road, oblivious to the approach of defendant's car from behind.

3. Observant Defendant

The observant defendant sees plaintiff in time to act to avoid the harm (assuming that defendant has a duty to so act under the circumstances), and observes plaintiff's helpless or inattentive condition, but thereafter is negligent in failing to act to prevent plaintiff's harm. Defendant's conduct need not be the source of plaintiff's danger.

The better rule is that plaintiff need not prove that defendant actually perceived plaintiff's helplessness or inattentiveness; it is sufficient to show that defendant saw plaintiff and that any normal person in defendant's situation would have realized that plaintiff was helpless or inattentive.

4. Inattentive Defendant

The inattentive defendant is one under a duty to maintain a lookout such that they would have seen the plaintiff in time to avoid the harm, and (had they been looking) would have perceived their helpless or inattentive condition and exercised reasonable care to avoid the harm. But due to defendant's negligence in failing to maintain the necessary lookout, they fail to see plaintiff in time and the injury occurs.

5. Application to Relevant Scenarios

The case of the "helpless plaintiff" versus the "observant defendant" is the classic "last clear chance" situation, and all jurisdictions which accept the doctrine will apply it here.

In cases of the "helpless plaintiff" versus the "inattentive defendant" or the "inattentive plaintiff" versus the "observant defendant," most jurisdictions recognizing the "last clear chance" rule will apply it in these situations. See R.2d §§ 479, 480.

In cases of the "inattentive plaintiff" versus the "inattentive defendant," however, no jurisdiction applies the doctrine here.

D. Comparative Negligence Subsumes Last Clear Chance Doctrine

The doctrine does not survive the adoption of comparative negligence; it is subsumed.

III. Assumption of Risk

A. Traditional Rule

Under the traditional common law rule, if plaintiff voluntarily assumes a risk of harm arising from the negligent or reckless conduct of defendant, plaintiff cannot recover for such harm. R.2d § 496A.

B. Relevance in Comparative Negligence Jurisdictions

Prior to the widespread adoption of comparative negligence, most jurisdictions recognized this defense, some by a different name. A few have limited it to (1) employer-employee cases and (2) express assumption of risk cases. Some courts analyze plaintiff's assumption of risk as affecting defendant's duty, e.g., negating defendant's duty to exercise care for plaintiff's safety.

There is a strong trend to abolish the defense of implied assumption of risk as a separate defense in negligence cases because it overlaps completely with the doctrine of contributory negligence. When jurisdictions adopt comparative negligence, they frequently merge the contributory negligence and assumption of risk defenses under a general "comparative fault" concept. Whether retained as a separate doctrine or merged with contributory negligence, the two doctrines become functionally the same when the courts treat them both as damage-reducing factors.

C. Express Assumption of Risk

1. Defined

If plaintiff, by contract or otherwise, expressly agrees to accept a risk of harm arising from defendant's negligent or reckless conduct, plaintiff cannot recover for such harm, unless the agreement is invalid as contrary to public policy. R.2d § 496B; R.3d Apportionment of Liability § 2.

Example: Plaintiff joins Defendant's health club. Plaintiff signs a written contract containing a prominent provision by which Defendant is relieved of liability for negligence in the operation of the club. The contract is probably valid and therefore Plaintiff has "assumed the risk."

2. Construction

Such agreements are strictly construed against defendant and are not enforceable if plaintiff reasonably was ignorant of that term. They are unenforceable as to intentional torts, and most courts will not enforce them as to reckless conduct.

3. Public Policy

Such agreements are unenforceable when contrary to public policy. Generally, they will not be enforced in favor of employers against employees, those charged with a duty of public service against their customers/patients (e.g., common carriers, innkeepers, health care providers), and those having a significantly superior bargaining position as compared to plaintiff. However, in some cases, those rendering a public service may limit their liability to a fixed sum, provided plaintiff is given the option to purchase full protection.

Most courts have held that a parent's pre-injury release of a child's rights is invalid.

D. Implied Assumption of Risk

1. Defined

If plaintiff knows, appreciates, and understands the risk of harm created by defendant's negligent or reckless conduct, and nevertheless voluntarily subjects themself to the risk by conduct which impliedly manifests their consent to accept the risk, then they are subject to the assumption of risk defense. Compare R.2d § 496C, which is broader and covers several meanings of "assumption of risk." The effect of the defense varies by jurisdiction.

Example: Defendant negligently furnishes Plaintiff Painter a scaffold with a frayed rope. Plaintiff discovers the rope's condition, decides to use the scaffold anyway, and is injured. Plaintiff has "assumed the risk" that the rope would break.

2. Proving Manifestation of Consent

The essence of the defense is consent to accept the risk, and therefore plaintiff's conduct must impliedly manifest that consent. The defendant asserting the defense bears the burden of proof.

Example: Plaintiff Pedestrian attempts to dash across the street ahead of Defendant's speeding car. Plaintiff's conduct does not manifest consent to relieve Defendant of his duty to exercise reasonable care for Plaintiff's safety and therefore is not assumption of the risk (although it may be contributory negligence).

3. Proving Knowledge and Appreciation of Risk

The defendant must also prove knowledge and appreciation of the risk. The consent must be informed. Defendant must show that plaintiff knew of the existence of the risk and understood and appreciated its unreasonable character. R.2d § 469D.

Example: Plaintiff installs their TV antenna near Defendant's uninsulated power line, not appreciating (1) that it contained 12,000 volts, or (2) that the current could arc from one to the other. Plaintiff will only be charged with knowledge of risks that are matters of common knowledge or are readily ascertainable by observation.

4. Proving Voluntariness

Plaintiff's assumption of the risk must be voluntary. R.2d § 496E.

a. Reluctance

Plaintiff's conduct in proceeding into the zone of danger, even reluctantly or under protest, may ordinarily be deemed voluntary. Even if plaintiff has no reasonable alternative but to encounter the risk, plaintiff's doing so is voluntary unless one of two exceptions applies. Plaintiff does not voluntarily encounter the risk if defendant's tortious conduct is responsible for plaintiff's predicament and plaintiff must encounter the risk to avert harm to themself or another. Plaintiff does not voluntarily encounter the risk if it requires plaintiff to exercise or protect a right or privilege of which defendant has no right to deprive him.

b. Independent Circumstances

Defendants are not liable for independent circumstances that compel a plaintiff to assume risk, even if the plaintiff believes they have no other choice. The assumption of risk is still voluntary because the compulsion does not come from the defendant's tortious conduct.

c. Public Policy Limits

The same public policies which negate an express assumption of risk should similarly prevent the finding of an implied assumption. See R.2d § 496C, Comment j.

5. Violation of Statute

Plaintiff's assumption of risk bars or reduces their recovery based on defendant's violation of a statute unless this result would defeat a policy of the statute to place the entire responsibility for such harm on defendant. R.2d § 496F. Some statutory torts, such as the Federal Employers Liability Act (FELA) governing the rights of railroad workers injured at work to sue for damages, expressly exclude the defense.

6. Distinguished from Contributory Negligence

Implied assumption of risk and contributory negligence can have some overlap as defenses. In theory, implied assumption of the risk is plaintiff's implied voluntary consent to encounter a known danger created by defendant's negligence. Contributory negligence is unreasonable conduct. The former is a subjective test; the latter is objective.

Example: Defendant negligently offers Plaintiff a seat in Defendant's chair, which has a defective leg. The chair collapses and Plaintiff is injured. If Plaintiff knew the leg was broken, Plaintiff probably assumed the risk of that defect.

Plaintiff may *also* have been contributorily negligent if a reasonably prudent person would not have used the chair.

If Plaintiff did not actually know of the defect, they did not assume the risk, even though they may have been contributorily negligent if a reasonably prudent person would have inspected the chair or discovered the defect before using it.

In contrast, contributory negligence applies when plaintiff voluntarily enters a *relationship* with defendant knowing that there is a risk that defendant will act negligently.

Example: Plaintiff agrees to ride with Defendant, an intoxicated or known reckless driver. Here, the true basis of Plaintiff's fault is their unreasonable conduct in entering into the relationship and hence should be restricted to the defense of contributory negligence.

E. No Liability for Inherent Hazards Not Arising from Negligence

Plaintiff chooses to engage in an activity that has certain inherent and commonly accepted risks, even though the others involved exercise proper care—e.g., hazardous employment, spectators and participants in some sporting events. As to these risks, there is no negligence, and therefore no assumption of the risk of negligent conduct. Thus, the doctrine does not properly apply. Some courts call this "primary" assumption of the risk. These are "no duty" or "no negligence" cases.

IV. Review Questions

[Answers Provided in Appendix A]

1. Write a summary for a lay reader explaining the difference between contributory and comparative negligence.
2. Contributory negligence will *not* be imputed in which of the following circumstances?
   a. A child's negligence to their parent.
   b. An employee's negligence to their employer.
   c. One member of a joint enterprise to another.
   d. A parent's negligence to their child.
3. Plaintiff, a tightrope walker, signs a contract with their employer, a circus owner, which expressly relieves the employer of liability for negligence in the circus operation. That contract provision is unenforceable under which of the following circumstances?
   a. The tightrope breaks because of negligent maintenance.
   b. The tightrope breaks because a competing tightrope walker cuts it in a fit of jealousy.
   c. The tightrope breaks because the maintenance crew used substandard materials, which they should have known presented an unreasonable risk of great harm.
   d. The language of the provision was so convoluted that plaintiff reasonably did not understand it.
   e. In all the above, because such agreements are generally held unenforceable in favor of employers as contrary to public policy.
4. Plaintiff accepts a ride home from an office party with Defendant, who has been drinking heavily and is unsteady on their feet. On the way home, Defendant drives their car into a large tree, severely injuring Plaintiff. In a jurisdiction that permits the assumption of risk defense in negligence cases, Plaintiff sues Defendant and Defendant claims that Plaintiff impliedly assumed the risk that Defendant's negligence would injure them. What result in each of the following factual scenarios?

a. Plaintiff was not near Defendant at the party and did not observe their drinking or unsteadiness.

b. Plaintiff had no money with them and could not have paid cab fare.

c. Plaintiff becomes unconscious at the party, and their friends load them into the car.

d. Plaintiff believes Defendant when they said that they have had nothing to drink.

5. Runner is jogging alone late at night wearing dark clothing. Runner cuts across a dark alley to reach their home. Neighbor is backing down the alley from their garage and strikes Runner. Runner sues Neighbor who raises the defense of Runner's contributory negligence. Runner argues that Neighbor had the last clear chance to prevent Runner's harm. The case goes to trial in a comparative negligence jurisdiction. The jury returns a verdict for Runner. It finds Runner and Neighbor equally negligent. Explain the resulting case outcome to each client.

6. Discuss how the result in the case described in Question 5 would change under the following circumstances.

   a. If Neighbor was Runner's spouse.

   b. If Neighbor was Runner's child.

   c. If Neighbor was Runner's sibling.

   d. If Neighbor was the Mayor of City and was driving to their office.

   e. If Neighbor was incompetent.

Part Five

Advanced Duty Topics

■ ANALYSIS

I. **Owners and Occupiers of Land**
   - A. Possessors of Land Can Be Liable for Conditions and Activities on the Premises
   - B. Liability Arises from Conditions and Activities on the Premises
   - C. Traditional Liability Rules Governing Categories of Persons Entering the Premises
     - 1. General Rule
     - 2. Artificial vs. Natural Conditions
       - a. Traditional Rule
       - b. Modern Variations on the Traditional Rule
     - 3. Adjacent Public Ways
       - a. Traditional Rule
       - b. Modern Approach in Restatement (Third)
   - D. Trespassing Adults
     - 1. Trespasser Defined
     - 2. Traditional Rule
     - 3. Exceptions to General Rules
       - a. Frequent Trespassers on Limited Area
       - b. Discovered Trespassers
         - i. Rule
         - ii. Duty to Rescue
     - 4. Restatement (Third) Distinguishes Between Flagrant and Non-Flagrant Trespasser
   - E. Trespassing Children ("Attractive Nuisance" Doctrine)
     - 1. Rule (Factors)
       - a. Knowledge of Child Trespassers
       - b. Shift from Child "Attracted" by Condition to the Foreseeability of Child Trespassers
       - c. Knowledge of Condition
       - d. Artificial Condition
       - e. Child's Lack of Knowledge of Risk
       - f. Utility to the Defendant
       - g. Defendant's Conduct Is Not Reasonable
     - 2. General Duty of Reasonable Care as Alternate Rule
   - F. Licensees
     - 1. Licensee Defined

2. Duty to Licensees
   a. Intentional and Reckless Conduct
   b. Active Operations (Latent Dangers)
   c. Latent Conditions

G. Invitee
1. Invitee Defined
   a. Public Invitee
   b. Business Visitors Are Invitees
   c. Scope of Invitation Can Be Express or Implied
   d. Incidental Visitors Included
   e. Social Guests Are Licensees
   f. Exceeding Scope of Invitation Changes Status
2. Duty to Invitees
   a. Rule
   b. Open and Obvious Dangers
   c. Acts of Third Persons

H. Other Privileged Entrants
1. General Rule
2. Public Employees Are Invitees
3. Fire and Police Personnel Are Licensees
4. Professional Emergency Responders
5. Recreational Entrants

I. Modern Trend to Reject Categories in Favor of General Duty of Ordinary Care

J. Lessors
1. General Rule
2. Exceptions
   a. Latent Hazards
      i. Lessor's Knowledge
      ii. Latency
      iii. Persons Protected
   b. Persons Outside the Premises
      i. Pre-Existing Conditions
      ii. Conditions and Activities During Lease
      iii. Contract to Repair
   c. Public Admission
      i. Lessee's Agreement
      ii. Scope
   d. Retained Control
      i. Scope
      ii. Lease Exculpatory Clause
      iii. Criminal Violence
   e. Agreement to Repair
      i. Scope
      ii. Notice
      iii. Consideration
      iv. Services
   f. Negligent Repairs

g. Independent Contractors
h. General Duty of Reasonable Care
i. Statutes May Impose Further Duties

K. Review Questions

II. Employer's Liability to Employees

A. Common Law Duties of Employer to Employee
1. Safe Place to Work
2. Defenses

B. Workers' Compensation
1. Workers' Compensation Acts
a. Introduction
b. Type of Occurrence
c. Exclusive Remedy Against Employer
d. Benefits
e. Third-Party Actions
f. Arbitration

C. Review Questions

III. Alcoholic Beverages

A. Commercial Vendors of Alcohol
1. Common Law Liability
2. Dram Shop Acts

B. Social Hosts

C. Review Questions

I. Owners and Occupiers of Land

Certain activities are governed by special tort liability rules. In some cases, these rules are merely special applications of the general principles of tort liability previously discussed. In other cases, these rules expand or contract the duty that a defendant would otherwise have had under those general principles.

The category of rules captured in this subpart is often alternatively called "premises liability." American law inherited from England's common law an approach to premises liability that classified persons entering a defendant's land as trespassers, licensees, or invitees. The duty owed by a defendant to these categories of entrants varied greatly. These rules can best be understood by identifying the policy considerations underlying them.

Just under half the states continue to follow these traditional common law rules grounded in categorization of entrants. In states following the traditional rules, the status of the entrant (plaintiff) determines the duty (if any) owed to them by a defendant. See R.3d Liability for Physical & Emotional Harm § 51 Reporters' Note. Although these traditional limited duty rules have been significantly modified in many jurisdictions, the traditional rules are still relevant even in those jurisdictions where they have been reformed.

As a procedural matter, these special duty rules often have the effect of taking questions that would have been jury issues, if analyzed under the general rules of tort liability, and shifting them to questions of law for the court to resolve.

A. Possessors of Land Can Be Liable for Conditions and Activities on the Premises

The possessor is a person in actual occupation and control of the land, or if there is no such person, a person entitled to immediate occupation and control. "Possessor" accordingly includes renters as well as owners. If there are no such persons, it is the last person who occupied and controlled the land. R.3d Liability for Physical & Emotional Harm § 49.

Possessors also include persons on the premises acting on behalf of the possessor, such as contractors or agents, and members of the possessor's household. R.3d Liability for Physical & Emotional Harm § 49 cmts. *e*, *f*, *i*.

B. Liability Arises from Conditions and Activities on the Premises

The following special duty rules apply to claims against possessors of land for injuries resulting from either a condition of the premises or an activity being conducted on the premises. The benefits and burdens of these special rules apply to (1) the possessor of the land, (2) activities carried on by members of the possessor's household, and (3) activities conducted by and conditions created by another who is acting for the possessor.

C. Traditional Liability Rules Governing Categories of Persons Entering the Premises

1. General Rule

A possessor must exercise reasonable care to see that activities (conduct) and artificial conditions on the land do not harm their neighbors or passers-by on adjacent ways. R.2d §§ 364–366, 370–371; R.3d Liability for Physical & Emotional Harm § 54.

2. Artificial vs. Natural Conditions

a. Traditional Rule

The traditional rule has been that a defendant's liability to persons off their premises was limited to dangers created by artificial conditions or activities on their land. If a defendant altered the natural condition of the land to create or aggravate the risk, the defendant was subject to liability for unreasonable risks thereby created. Defendants were not liable for physical harm to persons outside the premises or to adjoining land resulting from natural conditions. Thus, there would be no liability for the natural flow of surface water off the land, natural accumulations of ice and snow on adjacent public ways, or dead trees that fall from defendant's land off the premises. There would, however, be liability where a structure on defendant's land is so erected or maintained that water, snow or ice is discharged or unnaturally accumulates on a public way or the land is landscaped so as to change the natural flow or surface water.

b. Modern Variations on the Traditional Rule

Modern courts have been increasingly willing to alter this rule with respect to urban land. For example, an urban landowner may be liable for negligence in failing to inspect and maintain their trees to prevent an unreasonable risk of harm to passers-by on adjacent public ways. R.2d § 363(2). The Restatement (Third) adopts an even broader rule.

3. Adjacent Public Ways

a. Traditional Rule

Under traditional common law doctrine, several rules governed a defendant's liability to persons traveling on public ways adjacent to their property. For example, a defendant could not negligently create or maintain an artificial condition or activity dangerous to passers-by. R.2d § 368. In some cases, a defendant could even be subject to liability to persons who deviated from a public way onto their property if such deviations were foreseeable. R.2d § 368–369, 371.

b. Modern Approach in Restatement (Third)

The modern view is that a defendant's duty is the same to all persons outside the premises, with two exceptions. As to adjacent walkways, the Restatement (Third) provides that a possessor of land adjacent to a public walkway has no duty with respect to a risk posed by the condition of the walkway if the possessor did not create the risk. R.3d Liability for Physical & Emotional Harm § 54(c). The Restatement (Third) provides that a possessor, however, "(1) has a duty of reasonable care if the land is commercial; and (2) otherwise has a duty of reasonable care only if the possessor knows of the risk or if the risk is obvious."

D. Trespassing Adults

1. Trespasser Defined

A trespasser is one who enters or remains upon the defendant's land without the defendant's consent or other legal privilege. R.3d Liability for Physical & Emotional Harm § 50.

2. Traditional Rule

Under the traditional common law rule, a possessor is under no duty to exercise reasonable care (1) to make the premises reasonably safe for a trespasser (or to warn trespasser of hidden dangers), or (2) to carry on activities on the premises so as not to endanger a trespasser. But a defendant's immunity from liability to trespasser does not extend to intentional torts or to harm caused by a defendant's reckless ("willful and wanton") misconduct.

3. Exceptions to General Rules

Under the traditional common-law rules, courts often hold that a defendant owes a duty of reasonable care to an adult trespasser in certain fact situations. Note that the same result can usually be reached in these fact situations by applying the "willful and wanton" conduct rule, which is what some courts (and the Restatement (Third)) do in lieu of recognizing these specific exceptions.

a. Frequent Trespassers on Limited Area

When a defendant knows (or from facts within their knowledge ought to be aware) that trespassers constantly intrude upon a limited area of their premises, the defendant is subject to liability to such trespasser if they fail to exercise reasonable care (1) in the conduct of active operations on the premises which create a risk of serious bodily harm to a trespasser (R.2d § 334) and (2) to warn a trespasser of a dangerous artificial condition on the land (created or maintained by the defendant) which the defendant has reason to believe a trespasser will not discover and which creates a risk of serious bodily harm (R.2d § 335).

Example: The defendant railroad knows that pedestrians regularly cross its tracks at a certain point. Although the path is on railroad land and is not a designated crossing, and despite warning signs that trespassers at this point will be prosecuted, a defendant must operate its trains past this point in the exercise of reasonable care for a trespasser's safety.

b. Discovered Trespassers

i. Rule

Once a defendant discovers the presence of a trespasser on their land, the defendant must exercise reasonable care to (a) conduct their activities with regard to the trespasser's safety (R.2d § 336), (b) warn trespassers of an artificial condition which poses a risk of serious bodily harm, if a defendant knows or has reason to know that a trespasser is in dangerous proximity to it and that a trespasser will probably not discover the danger or realize the risk (R.2d § 337), and (c) control those forces within their control which threaten a trespasser's safety, or give a trespasser an adequate warning of them (R.2d § 338).

ii. Duty to Rescue

A defendant may have to exercise reasonable care to come to the aid of a discovered trespasser who is injured or in peril on the defendant's premises, even though the defendant is not responsible for the trespasser's situation.

4. Restatement (Third) Distinguishes Between Flagrant and Non-Flagrant Trespasser

The Restatement (Third) creates a new classification: the flagrant trespasser. R.3d Liability for Physical & Emotional Harm § 52. The Restatement's duty to a flagrant trespasser is the same as the traditional common law duty to all trespassers—not to injure them by intentional or "willful and wanton" conduct.

The Restatement provides no definition of the term "flagrant," but the comment discusses its meaning, summarized as "egregious or atrocious." The concept is that the presence of certain trespassers on another's land is so antithetical to the rights of the land possessor to exclusive use and possession of the land that the land possessor should not be subject to liability for failing to exercise the ordinary duty of reasonable care otherwise owed to them as entrants on the land. It stems from the idea that when a trespass is sufficiently offensive to the property rights of the land possessor, it is unfair to subject the possessor to liability for mere negligence.

Section 52 thus creates an exception to § 51, which creates a broad duty of reasonable care owed to all entrants on the land, including non-flagrant trespassers. See R.3d Liability for Physical & Emotional Harm § 51 cmt. *j*.

According to R.3d, flagrant trespassers are the only entrants not owed a duty of reasonable care; but if the flagrant trespasser reasonably appears to be imperiled and (1) helpless or (2) unable to protect themselves, the possessor *does* owe the flagrant trespasser that duty.

E. Trespassing Children ("Attractive Nuisance" Doctrine)

(Dobbs § 236; R.2d § 339)

1. Rule (Factors)

Most (but not all) jurisdictions have special rules applicable to child trespassers, sometimes called the "turntable" or "attractive nuisance" doctrine. The component rules vary among jurisdictions, but the courts have increasingly relied upon R.2d § 339 and it now represents the most widely held version.

A possessor of land is subject to liability for physical harm to trespassing children caused by an artificial condition upon the land if a defendant fails to exercise reasonable care to eliminate the danger to such children or otherwise protect them. Courts consider the following factors.

a. Knowledge of Child Trespassers

A defendant knows or has reason to know that the place where the condition exists is one where children are likely to trespass. It is not enough that child trespassers are merely foreseeable. A defendant need not inspect the premises to see if children trespass or if such dangerous conditions are present. A defendant is held to what they know about the premises and what they can reasonably anticipate based on that knowledge.

b. Shift from Child "Attracted" by Condition to the Foreseeability of Child Trespassers

Courts previously held that the child must be attracted onto the premises by the condition that injured them (hence the doctrine's name). This is no longer required. It is now enough that children who do foreseeably trespass can be expected to encounter the condition. It need not be an open and obvious condition, and the child need not even discover it prior to their injury.

c. Knowledge of Condition

A defendant must know or have reason to know of the condition and must realize or should realize that it involves an unreasonable risk of death or serious bodily harm to such children. A defendant need not have created the condition but merely maintained it or permitted it to exist.

d. Artificial Condition

The doctrine applies only to artificial conditions (not activities or natural conditions) upon the land.

Some courts have codified this rule, creating categories of "common hazards" as to which a defendant is not liable, or limiting a defendant's liability to injuries caused by "dangerous instrumentalities." Under this view, a defendant is not liable for dangers such as fire, falling from a height, drowning in water, visible machinery in motion, piles of lumber, etc., which almost all children are held to appreciate. However, the better view is that whether the risk is unreasonable depends on the facts and circumstances of each case.

e. Child's Lack of Knowledge of Risk

The child, because of their youth, does not (a) discover the condition or (b) realize the risk. While some courts have established arbitrary age limits (e.g., 14), the better (and Restatement) view does not. Nonetheless, the younger the child, the more dangers they will not understand or appreciate.

f. Utility to the Defendant

Courts weigh the risks of the condition against the utility of a condition when considering the burdens on the defendant. Courts consider whether the burden of eliminating the danger is outweighed by the risk to the children involved.

g. Defendant's Conduct Is Not Reasonable

The defendant fails to exercise reasonable care to eliminate the danger or otherwise protect the children.

2. General Duty of Reasonable Care as Alternate Rule

The duty created by R.2d § 339 approximates that which would be imposed by a general duty to exercise reasonable care toward children whose trespasses can be anticipated. A few courts have opted for this approach. The Restatement (Third) contains no special rule on child trespassers on the theory that §§ 51 and 52 will serve the same purpose. See R.3d Liability for Physical & Emotional Harm § 51 cmt. *l*.

F. Licensees

1. Licensee Defined

A "licensee" is a person who has a privilege to enter or remain on a defendant's land but is not an invitee. Licensees include a person who enters a defendant's land with consent but solely for the entrant's own purpose, such as social guests attending a party. A defendant's consent may be express or implied from their conduct, or from custom, usages in the community, or prior dealings.

Section 330 of the Restatement limits this term to those whose privilege is based on the defendant's consent, but courts sometimes use the term to encompass persons with other privileges (e.g., public employees).

2. Duty to Licensees

A defendant's duty to a licensee is similar (but not identical) to that owed to a discovered trespasser.

a. Intentional and Reckless Conduct

A defendant is subject to liability to a licensee for intentional and reckless ("willful and wanton") misconduct.

b. Active Operations (Latent Dangers)

In conducting their activities on the premises, a defendant must exercise reasonable care for the safety of licensees, provided (i) licensors expect that licensees will not discover or realize the danger and (ii) licensees do not know or have reason to know of the defendant's activities and the risk involved. R.2d § 341.

c. Latent Conditions

A defendant is subject to liability for physical harm caused to a licensees by a condition of the land if (i) the defendant knows or has reason to know of the condition, and should realize that it involves unreasonable risk of harm, and that the licensees will not discover or realize the danger, (ii) the defendant fails to exercise reasonable care to make the condition safe, or to warn the licensee of the condition and the risk involved, (iii) the licensees do not know or have reason to know the condition and risk involved. R.2d

§ 342. A defendant must have actual knowledge of the condition (or of facts which are the equivalent of such knowledge). They have no duty to inspect or discover such conditions.

G. Invitee

1. Invitee Defined

An "invitee" is either a public invitee or a business visitor. R.2d § 332.

a. Public Invitee

A public invitee is a person who is invited to enter or remain on land as a member of the public for a purpose for which the land is held open to the public. For example, persons attending free public meetings, lectures, church services, free public amusements, or using public or private land held open to the public for a recreational or social purpose.

b. Business Visitors Are Invitees

A business visitor is a person who is invited to enter or remain on a defendant's land for a purpose directly or indirectly connected with business dealings with the possessor of the land. For example, customers in stores; patrons of theaters, banks, places of amusement; employees and independent contractors entering to perform their work. Invitees include persons entering only for the purpose of potential or future business dealings—persons entering a store only to browse, or even to return merchandise.

c. Scope of Invitation Can Be Express or Implied

The invitation may be expressly or impliedly limited, as to (a) duration, (b) purpose, or (c) the portion of the premises to which the invitation extends. The invitation may be either express, or implied from a defendant's conduct, prior dealings, usages in the community, etc.

d. Incidental Visitors Included

Invitees include persons whose visit is for the convenience, or arises out of the necessities of, others who are on the land for a business purpose—e.g., a child taken by its parent to a shop; a plaintiff going to a hotel to visit a guest; a plaintiff going to an airport to meet a passenger; a plaintiff in common areas of an apartment building on their way to visit a tenant.

e. Social Guests Are Licensees

Traditionally, a social guest in a defendant's home was a licensee, despite incidental services performed by the guest or an incidental business motive behind the invitation (e.g., the boss invited to dinner).

f. Exceeding Scope of Invitation Changes Status

If a plaintiff exceeds the scope of the invitation, they become a trespasser or licensee, depending upon whether the defendant consents to their remaining or the plaintiff has some other privilege to remain.

2. Duty to Invitees

a. Rule

As to invitees, there is no duty limitation. A defendant must exercise reasonable care for their safety with respect to the conduct of activities and the maintenance of the premises. R.2d §§ 341A, 343.

b. Open and Obvious Dangers

Until recently, there was one limitation on the duty to invitees. It was commonly held that even as to invitees, a defendant was not liable for "open and obvious" dangers (R.2d §§ 341A, 343(b), 343A) unless the defendant should have anticipated the harm despite the condition's obviousness. The emerging and better view is that the obviousness of the danger is merely one fact bearing on whether a defendant was negligent or on a plaintiff's contributory fault or assumption of risk and is not per se a duty limitation.

c. Acts of Third Persons

A defendant must exercise reasonable care to warn and protect their business invitees against foreseeable harm by third persons on the premises, and to discover that such acts by third persons are being done or are likely to occur. R.2d § 344. While some courts have held that, on particular facts, a defendant's duty does not extend to protection against criminal violence by third persons, many other courts hold that in such cases a defendant's negligence is a question of fact for the jury.

H. Other Privileged Entrants

1. General Rule

Courts ordinarily classify one who enters a defendant's land by virtue of a privilege other than that created by the defendant's consent as a licensee. R.2d § 345(1).

2. Public Employees Are Invitees

Public employees who are required by law regularly to enter a defendant's premises to make inspections, deliveries, or collections necessary to the defendant's operations—e.g., sanitary and safety inspectors, garbage collectors, meter readers, postmen, revenue collectors—are invitees.

3. Fire and Police Personnel Are Licensees

Firefighters, police, and other professional emergency responders have a privilege to enter premises in the course of their work but are typically classified as licensees. In instances where the premises are open to the public (R.2d § 345(2)), emergency responders are invitees. The rationale being that if the public has been invited onto the premises, an emergency responder can reasonably assume that the land has been prepared for reception of the public and is therefore safe for them.

4. Professional Emergency Responders

The possessor's duty to professional emergency responders may be limited by the so-called "firefighter's rule." In many jurisdictions, the possessor has no general duty of reasonable care to such entrants, at least with respect to the risks that occasioned the emergency response, and in some cases with respect to conditions of the premises. The rationale is that the professional emergency responder assumes these risks as part of their employment, trains for encountering these risks, and receives medical, disability, and other benefits for on-the-job injuries. However, this no-duty rule is subject to numerous exceptions and limitations. See 2 Dobbs, Hayden & Bublick, The Law of Torts ch. 30 (§§ 362–365) (2d ed. 2011); R.3d Liability for Physical & Emotional Harm § 51 cmt. *m*. Typically, the rule limits only a defendant's negligence liability, and in some jurisdictions operates only to bar a plaintiff with respect to injuries caused by the misconduct that created the risk which necessitated a plaintiff's presence on the premises.

5. Recreational Entrants

Most states now have statutes that negate any duty of reasonable care to persons permitted to come upon a defendant's land for recreational purposes (e.g., hunting, fishing, swimming), provided the defendant makes no charge to, or receives no consideration from, the visitor.

I. Modern Trend to Reject Categories in Favor of General Duty of Ordinary Care

Beginning with *Rowland v. Christian* (Cal. 1968), about half the states have abolished the tedious classification of entrants upon land. Some states have done this completely by merging the licensee and invitee categories. This approach substitutes a general duty of ordinary care under the circumstances, with one of the circumstances being the status of a plaintiff on the land. Some states have done so by judicial decision, others by statute. Most states retain the limited-duty-to-trespassers rules in some form, even if they have eliminated the special licensee rules. See Reporters' Note to R.3d Liability for Physical & Emotional Harm § 51.

Section 51 of the new Restatement (Third) of Torts: Liability for Physical & Emotional Harm, entitled "General Duty of Land Possessors," provides that, except for flagrant trespassers (covered in § 52), the possessor owes a duty of reasonable care with regard to virtually all risks—those created by activities on the land, artificial conditions, natural conditions, and other risks when any of the affirmative duties apply.

J. Lessors

1. General Rule

Under the traditional rule, a lessor of real property is not liable to their lessee (or anyone else on the premises with the lessee's consent) for physical harm sustained by such persons during the term of the lease because of a condition of the leased premises, whether that condition arose or existed before or after the lessee took possession. R.2d §§ 355–356.

2. Exceptions

a. Latent Hazards

When the lessor knows or has reason to know of a condition, whether natural or artificial, involving unreasonable risk of harm at the time the lessee takes possession, and fails to make the lessee aware of the condition, is subject to liability for physical harm sustained as a result of that condition. R.2d § 358.

i. Lessor's Knowledge

The lessor need not inspect the premises to discover such conditions. They must know or have reason to know of the condition and realize or should realize the risk involved.

ii. Latency

The danger must be latent, in the sense that it may be expected that the lessee will not discover the condition or the extent of the risk. A defendant's duty is only to disclose the existence of the condition. There is no liability for open and obvious hazards, however dangerous.

iii. Persons Protected

A defendant's liability extends to the lessee and all persons on the premises with their consent or by their right.

b. Persons Outside the Premises

i. Pre-Existing Conditions

If there is a condition on the land existing at the time the lessee takes possession, which the lessor realizes or should realize may unreasonably endanger persons outside the premises, the lessor's liability to such persons survives the transfer of possession to the lessee. R.2d § 379.

ii. Conditions and Activities During Lease

The lessor is generally not liable for conditions on the premises that come into existence after the lessee takes possession (R.2d § 377) or for the lessee's activities on the premises. But if the lessor knows at the time the lease is executed that the lessee intends to conduct an activity on the premises that will subject persons off the premises to the risk of actionable harm and nevertheless consents to that activity or fails to require proper precautions, the lessor is subject to liability for foreseeable resulting harm to such persons. R.2d §§ 379A, 837.

iii. Contract to Repair

In some jurisdictions, negligent failure to perform the lessor's contract to repair the premises subjects them to liability to persons off the premises. R.2d § 378.

c. Public Admission

When the lessor leases their premises for a purpose which involves the admission of the public, they must exercise reasonable care to inspect the premises and remedy unreasonably dangerous conditions which exist when possession is transferred, if they have reason to expect that the public will be admitted before the lessee has remedied the condition. R.2d § 359.

i. Lessee's Agreement

The lessee's agreement to make the repair does not exonerate the lessor unless the lessor could reasonably expect them to perform in time.

ii. Scope

A plaintiff need not be a business invitee of the lessee or lessor, nor need there be an admission charge. But a defendant's liability is limited to those parts of the premises open to the public under the lease, and to persons entering for the contemplated purpose.

d. Retained Control

i. Scope

The lessor is subject to liability for physical harm caused by a dangerous condition located on a part of the premises which the lessee is entitled to use and over which the lessor has retained control, provided the lessor by the exercise of reasonable care could have (1) discovered the condition and the unreasonable risk and (2) made it reasonably safe. R.2d § 360.

Examples include common areas used by tenants and their visitors, such as approaches, entrances, hallways, common stairways, elevators, yards, garages, common rooms, and basements. Other examples include appliances and other appurtenances necessary to the use of the premises, such as heating and air conditioning systems, water and water heating systems, electrical systems, and common laundry facilities. In some cases, the scope can include structural components of the building, such as foundations.

ii. Lease Exculpatory Clause

A clause in the lease exonerating the lessor from this liability may or may not be effective as to the tenant but is always ineffective as to third persons not party to the lease.

iii. Criminal Violence

The cases are divided on whether a landlord is subject to liability to their tenants for criminal violence by third persons occurring in common areas of the building based on their failure to provide adequate security.

e. Agreement to Repair

i. Scope

The lessor's liability extends to the tenant and all others on the premises with the tenant's consent. The extent of their duty is defined by the contract.

ii. Notice

Unless otherwise provided by the lease, the lessor's duty is only to exercise reasonable care to make the repairs after they have notice of the need for them. They need not inspect the premises.

iii. Consideration

The contract to repair must be supported by consideration. As yet, there is no liability for failure to perform a gratuitous promise to repair.

iv. Services

The lessor may be liable for failure to provide a service required by the lease (e.g. heat, light) where the premises cannot be safely used without it.

f. Negligent Repairs

A lessor who undertakes (or purports to undertake) repair of the leased premises is subject to liability for physical harm resulting from the condition if (1) the lessee neither knows nor should know that (2) the repairs made the land more dangerous for use or gives the deceptive appearance of safety. R.2d § 362.

g. Independent Contractors

The lessor cannot escape their responsibilities by delegating the work to an independent contractor. They are liable for the contractor's negligence in performing the foregoing duties to the same extent as if the contractor were their employee. R.2d §§ 419–421.

h. General Duty of Reasonable Care

Several states have abolished the foregoing limited rules and substituted the rule that the lessor is under a general duty of reasonable care under the circumstances, either generally or only for residential leases. Section 53 of the Restatement (Third) of Torts: Liability for Physical & Emotional Harm reflects this view. It provides that lessors have a duty of reasonable care for a) the portions of the leased premises over which the lessor retains control, b) conduct of the lessor creating risks to others, and c) disclosure of certain dangerous conditions. A landlord also has a duty based on applicable statutes, contractual or voluntary undertakings, and compliance with an implied warranty of habitability.

i. Statutes May Impose Further Duties

Statutes and ordinances in many jurisdictions impose duties on lessors which have the effect of expanding their common law tort duties, particularly their duty to keep the premises in repair. Violation of these statutes can subject the lessor to liability for resulting physical harm. Section 53 of the Restatement (Third) of Torts: Liability for Physical & Emotional Harm also recognizes that a landlord has a duty based on applicable statutes.

K. Review Questions

[Answers Provided in Appendix A]

1. Maxwell has constructed an impressive array of spooky Halloween animated decorations that are visible from the street and sidewalk to passersby. He has told sightseers and neighbors not to go in the yard and has numerous "no trespassing" signs posted. Nolan Neighbor sees the decorations and decides to get a closer look. Nolan is injured by a low hanging branch that is protruding from Maxwell's neighbor's land onto Maxwell's property. What result do you predict in a case by Nolan versus Maxwell? Discuss the standard of care that Maxwell owed Nolan and whether Maxwell breached that standard in a one-paragraph IRAC format.
2. Same facts as Question 1. Instead, Caroline Child (age 9) enters Maxwell's property and trips over an extension cord between an animatronic and the electrical outlet. What result do you predict in a case by Caroline versus Maxwell? Discuss the standard of care that Maxwell owed Caroline and whether Maxwell breached that standard in in a one-paragraph IRAC format.
3. Opal Owner owns a piece of property adjacent to a stretch of public highway that is currently closed for repairs. Tatiana Traveler is driving along the highway unaware that the road ahead is closed because vandals have defaced the warning and detour signs. Opal assumes that no one will be on the road because of the construction. Opal fells several large trees bordering the highway just before the stretch of closed road. Tatiana is injured when her car strikes one of the trees. Discuss the standard of care that Opal owed Tatiana and whether Opal breached that standard in in a one-paragraph IRAC format.
4. Trevor Traveler is injured when a rotten and decaying tree on Owen Owner's property is blown down by the wind into the path of Trevor's car, which is traveling on a public highway. Discuss the standard of care that Owen owed Trevor and whether Owen breached that standard in in a one-paragraph IRAC format.
5. An old treehouse exists in one of the trees on Olivia Owner's land bordering the public highway. Olivia just purchased the property a few weeks ago and has not yet inspected the land to even discover the existence of the tree house. Cory Cyclist (7 years old) is biking along the bike path adjacent to the highway when they see the treehouse and decide to inspect it. They climb over a low fence and ignore the "private property" signs. The ladder leading to the treehouse collapses and Cory is injured when they fall from the tree. Discuss the standard of care that Olivia owed Cory and whether Olivia breached that standard in a one-paragraph IRAC format.

6. Lenny Landlord has recently purchased a rental property containing six apartments and some common spaces (e.g., mail room, outdoor patio). Lenny is new to the landlord role. He has hired you to advise him on what his liabilities are to the guests of his lessees. He understands that the lease agreement governs his liability to renters. He wants to know what other liabilities he might face to others who come on the property. Advise Lenny.

II. Employer's Liability to Employees

A. Common Law Duties of Employer to Employee

1. Safe Place to Work

An employer's common law duty to their employees is analogous to the duty of a possessor of land to business invitees. The employer must provide their employee with reasonably safe working conditions and warn the employee of unsafe conditions which the employer should anticipate will not be discovered by the employee. Specifically, this includes a duty to:

a. Provide safe premises, tools, equipment, structures, appliances, and instrumentalities for the work;

b. Provide a sufficient number of competent fellow employees;

c. Promulgate and enforce plans and rules for the conduct of the work and of the employees to make the work reasonably safe;

d. Provide adequate supervision; and

e. Properly instruct the employee and give them suitable work.

2. Defenses

The employer's defenses include:

a. Assumption of risk

b. Contributory negligence

c. Co-worker negligence (also known as the "fellow servant rule"). In most jurisdictions, an employer is not vicariously liable for an injury to an employee caused solely by the negligence of a co-worker in the performance of the operative details of the work.

B. Workers' Compensation

1. Workers' Compensation Acts

a. Introduction

The employee's common law tort action against their employer proved inadequate, due mainly to these three defenses. It has been replaced in all states and several other jurisdictions by workers' compensation acts, which make the employer strictly liable to pay scheduled benefits for most employee injuries occurring "in the course of" and "arising out of" the employment. These scope-of-employment issues are often litigated.

With minor exceptions, workers' compensation coverage is mandatory for all employers with a certain number of employees. Exceptions may include "casual workers," domestic workers, and agricultural workers.

b. Type of Occurrence

Ordinarily workers' compensation is available only for "accidental" injuries. If a plaintiff's injury was caused by environmental conditions over a period of time, their remedy arises under an occupational diseases act. However, an intentional tort by a fellow employee can be a compensable accidental injury as to the plaintiff if it arises out of the employment.

c. Exclusive Remedy Against Employer

If an employee's injury occurs in the course of, and arises out of, an employment covered by a workers' compensation act, their remedy under the act is their exclusive remedy against the employer, even if for some reason the particular injury is not compensable. The employee has no common law tort action against their employer, except in rare instances when (a) the employer's conduct amounts to an intentional tort or certain criminal violations, or (b) plaintiff is a minor employed in violation of labor laws. In such cases, the plaintiff-employee may elect between the workers' comp and tort remedies. But if the injury-producing facts fall outside the scope of the act, the employee may have a common law or statutory tort claim against the employer. Several federal statutes create workers' remedies which are not barred by any state workers' compensation statutes. State discrimination laws or wrongful termination laws may also apply and are not barred by the workers' compensation statute.

d. Benefits

In exchange for strict liability and a relatively speedy remedy, the employee's compensation is limited to a statutory schedule of limited benefits, usually a percentage of the plaintiff's average weekly wage for a specified number of weeks which varies according to the severity of the injury. The employee receives more or less unlimited medical benefits, benefits for partial or total disability (temporary or permanent), and—in the event of a job-related death—the plaintiff's survivors receive death benefits.

e. Third-Party Actions

In most jurisdictions, the workers' comp act does not bar the employee from bringing a tort action and recovering full damages, even though the employee's injury is compensable under the act, if the employee can find a third party (other than their employer) whose tort contributed to the employee's injury. An example would be a products liability action against the manufacturer of the tool that caused an employee's injury. If the employee is successful against the third party, then the employee must ordinarily repay the workers' compensation that the employee has received. In a few states, the third party may have a contribution claim against the employer if the employer's fault contributed to the injury.

In states applying several liability, the law may allow a finding as to the employer's fault to be included in the mix, in which case the third party would only have to pay their comparative fault share.

f. Arbitration

Workers' compensation issues are tried in an arbitration system, rather than through a civil lawsuit.

C. Review Questions

[Answers Provided in Appendix A]

1. Employer assigns employees Anthony and Margaret to a window-washing job requiring scaffolding. Anthony is injured on the job. In representing Anthony in his common law tort action against Employer, what questions do you prepare for your initial client meeting with Anthony? What are your anticipated arguments? What possible defenses do you think Employer might raise?

III. Alcoholic Beverages

A. Commercial Vendors of Alcohol

1. Common Law Liability

The general common law rule was that one who sold intoxicating beverages was not liable to third persons injured by the person thereby intoxicated, whether directly (e.g., reckless driving) or indirectly (e.g., the family's loss of support). Many courts held that furnishing alcohol was not a "proximate cause" of Plaintiff's injury, but others have opined that this is just a "no-duty" rule based on public policy. In a few states, this immunity is statutory.

A few jurisdictions have overturned this rule in cases where the application of ordinary negligence principles would support liability, particularly where the sale was unlawful because the purchaser was a minor or was already intoxicated or nearly so.

2. Dram Shop Acts

A number of states have enacted statutes called dram shop acts which impose civil liability on commercial sellers in favor of third persons injured by an intoxicated person. Some statutes require that the sales have been illegal because the purchaser was a minor or visibly intoxicated. Other statutes merely require that the beverage sold have caused or contributed to the intoxication, effectively a form of strict liability. Some statutes apply only to those who sell alcohol for consumption on the premises. Others include package liquor sales. Typically, the dram shop statute is the exclusive remedy against commercial vendors of alcohol.

B. Social Hosts

Most courts have refused to impose liability on persons who are not licensed dram shops who furnish alcoholic beverages to others with resulting physical harm, even where the application of ordinary negligence principles would justify recovery.

Example: Tina hosts an after-work wine tasting party for her employees, including a minor, Erin, who becomes intoxicated with Tina's knowledge and consent. Tina permits Erin to get in her car to drive home, and en route Erin's intoxication results in a collision in which Patrick is injured. Most courts hold that Patrick has no cause of action against Tina.

Some jurisdictions are beginning to find liability, based on (1) violation of a liquor control statute as negligence per se, or (2) common law negligence principles such as negligent entrustment or negligent supervision or ordinary duty rules. Some states allow social host liability upon a showing of reckless conduct in serving alcohol but not mere negligence.

C. Review Questions

[Answers Provided in Appendix A]

1. Bartender sells Underage liquor illegally, and Underage becomes intoxicated. On Underage's way home, Underage drives their car up onto a sidewalk and injures Jogger. Using the IRAC method, discuss Bartender's liability under the common law and dram shop act.

2. Host sponsors a holiday party in Host's home. Host provides Guest free liquor. Guest becomes intoxicated, drives, and hits Bicyclist, who is injured from the collision. Using the IRAC method, discuss Host's liability to Bicyclist.

Part Six

Strict Liability

■ ANALYSIS

I. Strict Liability for Animals

A. Intruding Animals

1. General Rule

Owners or possessors of all animals, including domesticated ones such as fowl, livestock, birds, and reptiles are strictly liable for physical harm resulting from the trespass of their animals on the property of another. R.2d § 504; R.3d Liability for Physical & Emotional Harm § 21.

2. Exceptions

a. Cats and Dogs

Except where imposed by statute or ordinance, possessors of dogs and cats are not strictly liable for their intrusions under the general rule. This is because they are believed to be less likely to do substantial harm upon intrusion.

b. Livestock Straying on Highways vs. Driven to Highway

Owners or possessors of livestock that *stray* onto a public highway are not strictly liable when the animals contribute to a highway accident. Rather, negligence rules apply in the majority of jurisdictions, thus allowing for consideration of the driver's conduct, the owner's conduct, and other factors. R.3d Liability for Physical & Emotional Harm § 21 comment *h*. In contrast, when possessors of livestock *drive* the livestock on a highway, strict liability applies to resulting harms. R.2d §§ 504(3)(b), 505; R.3d Liability for Physical & Emotional Harm § 21 comment *i*.

c. Liability for Livestock on Property ("Fencing Statutes")

The traditional English rule holds possessors of livestock strictly liable for their intrusions on the property of others. This is popularly known as a "fence in" requirement because of the functional incentives that strict liability creates toward fencing animals in. Many jurisdictions follow this approach as does the Third Restatement.

Other jurisdictions follow a "fence out" rule allowing an affirmative defense asserting that the plaintiff should have protected their property by fencing out livestock intrusions. The latter rule functionally embraces the roaming of livestock. Finally, some jurisdictions have negotiated these tensions by adopting a negligence standard. R.3d Liability for Physical & Emotional Harm § 21.

B. Other Harm Caused by Animals

1. Domestic Animals

Owners or possessors of domestic animals are generally held to a negligence standard for harms caused, reflecting the rationale that these animals are not generally abnormally dangerous. Strict liability will only apply if (a) the owner or possessor knew or had reason to know that the animal had a harmful or dangerous propensity or trait, and (b) that particular trait or propensity was the cause of the harm. R.2d §§ 509, 518; R.3d Liability for Physical & Emotional Harm § 23. Statutes in some jurisdictions impose strict liability for certain kinds of harm (e.g., dog bites), irrespective of the keeper's knowledge of any propensity to cause that harm.

2. Wild Animals

Wild animals are generally defined as those that are not generally domesticated in that geographic region and those that, if unrestrained, would likely cause physical harm. Both the owners and possessors of wild animals are strictly liable for all harm done by the animal as a result of a harmful or dangerous propensity or characteristic of such animals. R.2d § 507; R.3d Liability for Physical & Emotional Harm §§ 21–22.

3. Scope of Strict Liability

According to the Restatement (Second) of Torts, plaintiffs cannot recover if they "knowingly and unreasonably" subjected themself to the risk. R.2d § 515. The Restatement (Third) (which does not recognize assumption of the risk as a separate defense) provides that strict liability does not apply (a) if the plaintiff suffers physical harm as a result of making contact with or coming into proximity to defendant's animal for the purpose of securing some benefit from that contact or that proximity, or (b) if the defendant maintains ownership or possession of the animal pursuant to an obligation imposed by law, such as a common carrier or a public official taking possession of a dangerous dog. R.3d Liability for Physical & Emotional Harm § 24. In these cases, negligence liability may be appropriate.

4. Comparative Fault

If the plaintiff was negligent in failing to take reasonable precautions, then the plaintiff's recovery in a strict liability claim is reduced in proportion to their comparative fault. This approach avoids the harshness of contributory negligence. R.3d Liability for Physical & Emotional Harm § 25.

II. Strict Liability for Abnormally Dangerous Activities

A. *Rylands v. Fletcher*: The Original Rule

Strict liability for abnormally dangerous activities originated in the 1868 English case of *Rylands v. Fletcher*, which held the Defendant strictly liable for damage to Plaintiff's mine caused by water which escaped from Defendant's reservoir. The court reasoned that because a reservoir was a "non-natural use" of land in that area and the Plaintiff's harm was caused by the "escape" of the water from Defendant's land, strict liability governs.

B. *Rylands v. Fletcher*: The Modern Rule

1. General Rule

Defendants may be held liable for harm resulting from "abnormally dangerous activities" (formerly called "ultrahazardous" activities) on their property. R.2d § 519; R.3d Liability for Physical & Emotional Harm § 20. It is no longer necessary that the activity was conducted on the defendant's land, or that the harm was caused by something which "escapes."

2. The Second Restatement Factors

The Second Restatement deploys a list of factors to determine whether an activity is abnormally dangerous. Courts consider the factors holistically. No one factor is dispositive.

a. Extent of Risk

Courts consider whether there is a high degree of risk or harm to others, and whether it is likely that the harm will be great.

b. Ability to Eliminate Risk

Courts consider whether the risk can be eliminated by the exercise of reasonable care. If, despite defendant's reasonable care, the risk remains, there is greater justification for strict liability. This factor is distinctly valuable to courts analyzing whether strict liability should apply.

c. Common Usage

Courts consider whether the activity is a matter of common usage. The more unusual the activity, the greater the justification for strict liability. For example, automobiles and electricity are a common usage; while moving a two-story house down the road is not.

d. Location

Courts consider whether the activity is inappropriate to the place where it is being conducted. For example, courts might differ on managing the risks of an oil well in rural Texas versus a densely populated urban area.

e. Social Utility

Courts consider whether the activity's value to the community is outweighed by its dangerous attributes. For example, courts might think very differently about the transmission of electricity or water reservoirs because they serve the whole community.

3. The Third Restatement Centers Two Factors

The lengthier list of factors from the Second Restatement yields questions of predictability and consistency. The Third Restatement pares it down to two core inquiries: (1) whether the activity creates a foreseeable and highly significant risk of physical harm even when all actors exercise reasonable care; and (2) whether the activity is not one of common usage. R.3d Liability for Physical & Emotional Harm § 20(b).

Under this formulation, the location at which the activity is conducted does not independently determine if it is abnormally dangerous but could be relevant under either or both criteria. And the social utility of the activity is no longer a separate factor; it is reflected in its commonness. R.3d Liability for Physical & Emotional Harm § 20, comment *k*.

4. Activities Likely to Be Subject to Strict Liability

Few activities necessarily give rise to strict liability in all cases. Much depends on the facts and circumstances. However, blasting or the use of explosives are said to be typical examples of such an activity. Other activities that are good candidates for strict liability include crop dusting, pest control and fumigation, the escape of hazardous wastes, other high-energy activities (e.g., rocket testing, pile driving, oil well blowouts), and perhaps large fireworks displays. The overarching question is whether reasonable care is enough to manage risk.

5. Alternative Theories: Trespass or Nuisance

A dwindling minority of U.S. jurisdictions rejects the rule by name but usually reach the same result via trespass or nuisance theories. For example, in blasting cases some jurisdictions once rejected strict liability for concussion damage because there was no physical trespass; today, such artificial limits generally do not exist.

C. Liability Limitations

1. Scope of Liability

The harm must result from the risk that gives rise to the abnormal danger. R.2d § 519(2). It is generally no defense that it was precipitated by an unforeseeable intervening cause. R.2d § 522 (some states *contra*). Thus, the defendant will not be held strictly liable if the plaintiff intentionally or negligently trespasses on the defendant's land where the activity is being conducted. And the defendant is not strictly liable to the extent that the plaintiff's harm results from the abnormally sensitive characteristics of the plaintiff. R.3d Liability for Physical & Emotional Harm § 24 provides that strict liability does not apply if the plaintiff suffers physical harm as a result of coming into proximity to the abnormally dangerous activity for the purpose of securing some benefit from that proximity, or (b) if the defendant carries on the abnormally dangerous activity pursuant to an obligation imposed by law. See also R.2d § 517. The comments to R.3d Liability for Physical & Emotional Harm § 20 make it clear that this form of strict liability applies only when others (besides the plaintiff) impose the strict liability risks, so that if the plaintiff is a participant in the activity, they cannot assert a strict liability claim.

2. Defenses and Apportionment of Liability

According to R.2d §§ 523, 524, assumption of the risk is a defense, but contributory negligence is not except when the plaintiff "knowingly and unreasonably subjects himself to the risk." According to R.3d Liability for Physical & Emotional Harm § 25, if the plaintiff has been contributorily negligent in failing to take reasonable precautions, the plaintiff's recovery in a strict liability claim for physical harm is reduced by the plaintiff's proportionate share of comparative fault. R.3d AL (and, by implication, R.3d Liability for Physical & Emotional Harm § 25) does not recognize assumption of the risk as a separate defense. This modern view thus allows the fact finder to assign shares of fault or responsibility to all parties, including a party that is strictly liable. R.3d Liability for Physical & Emotional Harm § 25; Restatement (Third) of Torts: Apportionment of Liability § 1.

3. Federal Tort Claims Act

There is no strict liability under the FTCA.

III. Review Questions

[Answers Provided in Appendix A]

1. Your homeowner client has a pet cat that frequently escapes out of the family's dog door to meander the neighborhood. Advise your client in a one paragraph email whether they will face any liability for the cat intruding on the neighbor's land. Use an IRAC structure to draft your answer.
2. Advise your homeowner client on the liability they might face after their pet skunk sprays an Amazon driver delivering a package. Use an IRAC structure to draft your answer.
3. Defendant, a salesperson, enters the Plaintiff's property. Under which of the following conditions is the Defendant liable if their dog attacks Plaintiff?
    a. If a statute or ordinance imposes strict liability for dog bites.
    b. If Defendant knew that the dog was vicious.
    c. If Defendant is negligent and this negligence results in Plaintiff's injury.
    d. All of the above.
4. Plaintiff ignores the "KEEP OUT! DANGEROUS ANIMALS!" signs and enters Defendant's property. Plaintiff sees a large bear tethered to a tree. Nearby a sign warns of the bear's sharp claws and great strength. Despite these warnings, Plaintiff pokes and taunts the bear until the animal pulls loose from its tether and swats them. Plaintiff is suing the Defendant homeowner. Advise Defendant on the defenses you might offer in answering the complaint.
5. As a publicity stunt, Defendant plans to drive cross-country with a 20 feet tall helium-filled balloon shaped like their company's product tethered to their car's bumper. At the first intersection, the balloon tangles with several heavy-duty power lines, which fall to the ground electrocuting Plaintiff. Draft a persuasive argument for the court on behalf of Plaintiff arguing why strict liability should apply:
    a. Under the list of factors from the Second Restatement.
    b. Applying the two central factors of the Third Restatement
6. Plaintiff's house is damaged by blasting conducted by Defendant coal company. Plaintiff's house suffered cracked walls. Advise the homeowner on their likely recovery. What theory of liability will govern and what result?
7. Plaintiff is moving their rare collection of custom-made glass vases from one room to another, when they are frightened by an explosion set off in one of Defendant coal company's tunnels. Plaintiff was unusually jumpy and scared by the noise beyond that of an ordinary person. Advise Defendant on their likely liability for the resulting property damage.

Part Seven

Products Liability

■ ANALYSIS

ii. Manufacturing Defects
iii. Defects in Warnings or Instructions for Use (Informational Defects)
(a) No Duty to Warn of Open and Obvious Risks
(b) Plaintiff Must Also Prove Causation
(c) Limited to Known or Knowable Risks
(d) The Learned Intermediary Rule
(e) Sophisticated Users
b. Tests to Prove a Product Is "Unreasonably Dangerous"
i. Risk-Benefit Balancing Test
(a) Proving a Feasible Alternative Design
(b) Consumer Expectation Test
(c) Presumed Seller's Knowledge Test
c. Unavoidably Unsafe Products
d. Food Products
e. Intrinsically Dangerous Products
f. Circumstantial Evidence Admissible to Prove a Defective Product
7. The Restatement (Third) of Torts: Products Liability
a. Revised Approaches to Proving a Defective Product
b. Prescription Drug and Medical Device Liability
8. Types of Harms Recoverable
9. Defenses
a. Contributory Negligence
b. Implied Assumption of Risk
c. Unforeseeable Misuse of the Product
d. Statutes of Limitations and Repose
e. Disclaimers Do Not Block Claims
f. State of the Art Design
g. Preemption
h. Statutory Presumption of Non-Defectiveness
10. Nondelegable Duties
11. Post-Sale Duties

II. Review Questions

I. Overview of Products Liability

(Dobbs §§ 351–376; R.2d §§ 388–408; R.3d Products Liability)

Liability for physical harm caused by an unsafe product may be based on one or more of three legal theories: negligence, breach of warranty, or strict tort liability. In most cases, a plaintiff injured by a product may elect any or all of these theories in the same lawsuit, to the extent supported by the facts.

A. Injuries Arising from Products Can Be Pleaded as Negligence

Ordinary negligence principles apply to claims arising from product injuries that are pleaded under a negligence theory (as compared to claims pleaded under warranty or strict products liability).

1. Historic Privity Limitations

Prior to *MacPherson v. Buick Motor Co.* (N.Y. 1916), the general rule was that the manufacturer or other seller of an unsafe product was not liable in negligence to the user or consumer absent privity of contract between plaintiff and defendant (*Winterbottom v. Wright*)—that is, unless plaintiff had bought the product directly from defendant.

Exceptions arose (1) when the unsafe condition was fraudulently concealed by the seller, and (2) for products "inherently" or "imminently" dangerous to human life or health (e.g., poisons, guns, explosives). Following some expansion of these exceptions, *MacPherson* (per Cardozo, J.) held that lack of privity is not a defense when it is foreseeable that the product, if negligently made, is likely to cause injury to a class of persons which includes the plaintiff. This historic case effectively abolished the privity limitation. Eventually all jurisdictions followed *MacPherson*.

2. Modern Defendants Liable to Purchasers and Foreseeable Users or Consumers

Absent these historic privity limitations, modern product defendants are subject to liability not only to the ultimate purchaser or lessee of the product but also to all foreseeable users or consumers, and to all other persons foreseeably exposed to the risk it creates. R.2d §§ 395, 406. Usual proximate cause rules apply.

Further, most jurisdictions allow recovery by "bystanders" (persons other than the above) whose exposure to the risk of injury was foreseeable (e.g., a third person injured in a crash caused by a defect in the car's braking system).

3. Potential Product Defendants in Negligence

a. Product Manufacturers

Negligence in the manufacturing process includes negligent design (R.2d § 398); errors or omissions during production (R.2d § 395); failure to properly test or inspect; unsafe containers or packaging; inadequate warnings or directions for use; and misrepresentation. A subsequent seller's failure to inspect does not relieve the manufacturer of liability for its negligence. R.2d § 396.

b. Subsequent Product Sellers

Subsequent sellers (e.g., distributors, retailers) may also be negligent in failing to warn of the existence of an unsafe condition or otherwise protect the user. R.2d § 401. Under the majority view, such seller is liable only for dangers of which it knew or had reason to know. It has no duty to inspect or test the product to discover latent dangers. R.2d § 402.

c. Other Product Suppliers

Commercial lessors, and others who furnish chattels (tangible personal property) commercially, are liable for negligence in furnishing an unsafe chattel; their duty includes a duty to inspect. R.2d §§ 391–393, 408. Other suppliers (e.g., donors, gratuitous bailors) are subject to liability if they knew or had reason to know that the product was unsafe. R.2d § 388–389, 405. Supplying a chattel to one knowing or having reason to know they will incompetently use it also subjects the supplier to liability for resulting physical harm. R.2d § 390.

d. Independent Contractors

Contractors who make, rebuild, or repair a chattel are subject to similar rules. R.2d §§ 403–404.

e. Ostensible Suppliers

One who puts out as its own a chattel manufactured by another is subject to the same liability as though it were its manufacturer. R.2d § 400.

B. Product Harms May Also Yield Breach of Warranty Claims

1. Types of Warranties

Warranty is not a tort concept. Breach of certain warranties gives rise to an action for resulting physical harm, which makes warranty claims part of the law of "products liability." The following warranties, codified by the Uniform Commercial Code, are relevant.

a. Express Warranty (UCC § 2–313)

Express warranties are promissory assertions of fact or descriptions that are explicitly part of the basis of the bargain in purchasing the product. For example, a car manufacturer issues an express warranty when it states that its car has a fuel efficiency of 25 miles to the gallon.

b. Implied Warranty of Merchantability (UCC § 2–314)

The implied warranty of merchantability implies minimum standards of product quality including safety. Defendant must be a "merchant" with respect to goods of that kind. For example, a vehicle purchaser expects the transmission to work and the wheels to be affixed properly, even if not expressly warranted.

c. Implied Warranty of Fitness for a Particular Purpose (UCC § 2–315)

This warranty arises when the buyer relies on the seller to furnish goods suitable for a particular specified use. For example, a car purchaser tells the seller they plan to competitively race the vehicle at speeds of 100+ mph, and the seller recommends a vehicle model for that purpose.

2. Strict Liability Applies to Breach of Express and Implied Warranties

Liability for breach of warranty is strict. The consumer need not prove negligence or other fault.

3. Limitations to Pursue Breach of Warranty Claims

The principal limitations on liability for breach of warranty are:

(1) the seller must be given prompt notice of the breach,

(2) the buyer must have relied upon the warranty, and

(3) the seller in certain cases can limit or disclaim these warranties (but see UCC § 2–719(3)).

4. Historic Privity Limitations on Warranty Claims Lifted

As in the case of negligence, liability for breach of warranty was once limited to the parties to the contract of sale. The first exception was in cases involving products intended for human consumption, and then for intimate bodily use. *Baxter v. Ford Motor Co.* (Wash. 1932) signaled the end of the privity limitation as to express warranties. Beginning in *Henningsen v. Bloomfield Motors, Inc.* (N.J. 1960), courts abolished the privity limitation as to the implied warranties.

C. Strict Tort Liability for Defective Products

Urged by legal writers and led by Justice Traynor's concurring opinion in *Escola v. Coca Cola Bottling Co.* (Cal. 1944), strict tort liability for defective products was first adopted in *Greenman v. Yuba Power Products, Inc.* (Cal. 1963). Shortly thereafter this principle was codified in R.2d § 402A, and it is now the governing law in most jurisdictions.

1. Rule

Product defendants are strictly liable for any resulting physical or property harms to plaintiff caused by a defective condition of a product which renders it unreasonably dangerous, if (1) the product was in the same condition as when it left defendant's control, and (2) defendant is engaged in the business of furnishing such products. R.2d § 402A.

2. Product Defendants in Strict Liability

Strict products liability extends to (1) the producer (manufacturer, processor, assembler, packager, or bottler) of the product and of the defective component part, and (2) all those in its distribution chain—wholesaler, distributor, retailer, and commercial lessors and bailors. Defendant must be "engaged in the business" of dealing in that product, but such product need not be their principal business.

Courts usually refuse to extend liability to dealers in used products or "casual sellers" (businesses that are not in the business of regularly selling that product but do so on a one-time or occasional basis).

3. Rationales for Strict Products Liability

Support for strict products liability is based on some combination of these rationales.

a. Consumer Expectations and Reliance

By placing a product on the market, the seller impliedly represents that it is reasonably safe and healthy, and consumers justifiably rely on that implied representation.

b. Enterprise Liability

The most economically efficient means of distributing the costs resulting from injuries caused by defective products is to place those costs on the manufacturer or seller, who can spread those costs among all purchasers of their products.

c. Problems of Proof

Although manufacturers of defective products will often have been negligent, it is difficult and costly for the purchaser or consumer to prove negligence, and therefore too many valid negligence claims will be lost or deterred.

d. Deterrence

Strict liability provides the necessary incentive for manufacturers to make their products as safe as reasonably possible.

e. Litigation Practicalities

A series of warranty actions can already accomplish strict liability, but such extended litigation is wasteful and needless.

f. Manufacturer Position and Power

The manufacturer is in a better position than the consumer to protect against harm from defective products and to insure against such liability.

g. Fairness

The manufacturer imposes nonreciprocal risks on the consumer and reaps a significant economic benefit from placing its products on the market. Therefore, it is fair for the manufacturer to be held responsible for the risks it creates, rather than to impose the costs of those risks on the victim or on society at large.

4. Product Defined

"Product" includes all forms of tangible personal property (chattels). With rare exceptions, courts have not extended "product" to include sales of other commodities (e.g., human blood, electricity after it has been delivered to the consumer, or intangibles). In addition to manufactured products, "product" includes those which undergo little or no processing (e.g., bottled water). The doctrine has not generally been extended to transactions which, although incidentally involving a product, are essentially the rendition of a service.

5. Elements of Plaintiff's Claim

In a strict products liability claim, plaintiff must prove that

(1) the product was "defective" (and perhaps also that the defect made the product "unreasonably dangerous");

(2) the defect was a factual and proximate cause of plaintiff's harm; and

(3) the product was defective when it left defendant's possession and control.

6. Proving a Product Is Defective

a. Types of Defects

In most jurisdictions, defendant is subject to liability to plaintiff only if the product contains a "defect" which renders it "unreasonably dangerous" to the user or consumer. The defect may be in the product itself, in its container or packaging, or in the documentation accompanying the product.

The types of defects include:

i. Design Defects

Design defects are those that are inherent in the product's design and thus are common to every unit of the product on the market (e.g., the use of inadequate materials or the absence of feasible safety devices). In design defect cases, the product is manufactured and sold exactly as the manufacturer intended it to be. The plaintiff's argument therefore is that the manufacturer's intended design was flawed and unsafe.

ii. Manufacturing Defects

A manufacturing defect is one that occurs in a particular product unit because of an error or omission in manufacturing, assembly, or processing. The product was *not* marketed or sold in the condition the manufacturer intended (e.g., an automobile power steering mechanism with an anomalous missing bolt that causes the steering to lock up on one car).

iii. Defects in Warnings or Instructions for Use (Informational Defects)

A product may be defective and unsafe because of inadequate directions for use or inadequate safety warnings (e.g., informational defects). This is also a type of design defect. Warnings and directions for use may be defective if they do not adequately and effectively communicate not just that there is a danger but its nature and extent, the possible consequences of encountering the risk, and, if applicable, alternatives that will minimize or negate the risk. See R.3d Products Liability § 2(c).

(a) No Duty to Warn of Open and Obvious Risks

A product that fails to warn of an open and obvious danger, or a danger that is common knowledge, may not be defective. But if defendant can anticipate harm despite the obviousness of the danger, the product could be defective if it could have been made safer, or if a warning could be found to have effectively prevented the harm.

(b) Plaintiff Must Also Prove Causation

Plaintiff must still prove causation—that is, that they would have read, understood, and heeded the warning or instructions that should have accompanied the product if the manufacturer had provided them. But courts often allow an inference that plaintiff would have read the proposed warning or instructions, and defendant will have the burden of rebutting that inference.

(c) Limited to Known or Knowable Risks

Almost all courts have held that a manufacturer has no duty to warn of risks that were not known or knowable when it sold the product. This means that there is no strict liability for failure to warn. The risk must have been reasonably foreseeable.

(d) The Learned Intermediary Rule

When a physician buys prescription drugs or medical devices with physician-appropriate warnings, the manufacturer ordinarily can rely on the physician to protect the ultimate user. The manufacturer has no duty to provide a warning aimed at, or communicated to, the consumer. However, the rule may be otherwise if the manufacturer markets its drugs directly to consumers. The Products Liability Restatement provides that warnings about the health risks of prescription drugs and medical devices must be given directly to consumers only when the manufacturer knows or has reason to know that the learned intermediary will not be able to reduce the risks of harm in accordance with the instructions or warnings. R.3d Products Liability § 6(d).

(e) Sophisticated Users

Similar rules apply to "sophisticated users"—those users who are already aware or should be aware of the product's dangers (e.g., members of a trade or profession who are presumed to have common knowledge of the risks).

b. Tests to Prove a Product Is "Unreasonably Dangerous"

Most jurisdictions follow the Restatement (Second) of Torts § 402A and require that the product be not only "defective" but also "unreasonably dangerous." A few states (e.g., California) consider these two concepts synonymous; on this basis, one or two states have rejected the "unreasonably dangerous" requirement as redundant. However, jurisdictions differ as to the test to determine when a product's design is "unreasonably dangerous." While this issue can apply to all types of defects, it usually arises in design defect cases.

i. Risk-Benefit Balancing Test

The popular "risk-benefit" or "risk-utility" test requires the trier of fact to balance:

(1) the safety risks of the product as designed, and

(2) the utility and other benefits of the product as designed, against

(3) the safety risks and benefits of the product if it had been designed as plaintiff claims it should have been.

In practice, this is the same kind of "Learned Hand Test" balancing that would occur if the cause of action were based on negligence. The difference is that the focus is on the *product* and not on the *conduct* of the manufacturer. Thus, in theory, it does not matter whether the manufacturer's design choice was objectively reasonable at the time it made that choice if the trier of fact concludes that the product could have been designed to be safer (and thus have prevented plaintiff's injury) without incurring unreasonable additional costs.

The seven factors proposed by Dean John Wade are often used in this test:

(1) the usefulness and desirability of the product as designed;

(2) the likelihood and probable seriousness of injury from the product as designed;

(3) the availability of an alternative product or design that would meet the same need and not be as unsafe;

(4) the manufacturer's ability to eliminate the danger without impairing the product's usefulness or making it too expensive;

(5) the user's ability to avoid the danger;

(6) the user's anticipated awareness of the danger; and

(7) the feasibility of the manufacturer's spreading the risk of loss by pricing or insurance.

In some jurisdictions, more than one of these tests are available, sometimes in a single case.

(a) Proving a Feasible Alternative Design

As part of plaintiff's risk-utility case, plaintiff will usually try to show that there was a feasible alternative design—that is, some practicable, cost-effective, and reasonable way to have designed the product that would likely have prevented plaintiff's harm. In some situations, plaintiff risks defeat in a design defect case without such proof. A qualified expert witness is almost always required, and in some cases, the expert's proposed alternative design was held inadequate because the expert had not built and/or tested it. However, plaintiff is not required to build a prototype.

(b) Consumer Expectation Test

Another popular test is the "consumer expectation" test, derived from the language of § 402A comment *i*, requiring the product to be dangerous "to an extent beyond that which would be contemplated by the ordinary consumer who purchases it, with the ordinary knowledge common to the community as to its characteristics." This is like the UCC's standard of "merchantability." This test is adequate in many situations, but sometimes the ordinary consumer does not have enough information to have a reasonable expectation as to the product's design safety. In addition, this test sometimes insulates manufacturers from liability for open and obvious design defects.

(c) Presumed Seller's Knowledge Test

Another test implements the strict liability standard directly: would the seller have been negligent in marketing the product if the seller had known of its harmful or dangerous condition? This test, often applied in design defect cases, is actually just another form of the risk-benefit test, since it requires the same kind of "Learned Hand Test" balancing of the risks and benefits of the design chosen by defendant vs. the safer design proposed by plaintiff.

c. Unavoidably Unsafe Products

Under comment *k* to R.2d § 402A, some highly useful products (e.g., certain drugs and vaccines) may be "unavoidably unsafe" because of inherent dangerous side effects which "in the present state of human knowledge" cannot be eliminated. Such products, "properly prepared, and accompanied by proper directions and warnings," are not defective or unreasonably dangerous.

Key issues as to which the courts disagree include whether this provision applies (1) only to design defects, and (2) to unknowable dangers, or only to known but preventable dangers.

As to prescription drugs and medical devices, R.3d Products Liability § 6 goes beyond comment *k*. If a reasonable healthcare provider, knowing the benefits and risks of the product, would prescribe it, then the manufacturer is not liable.

d. Food Products

In the case of food products that contain a harm-causing ingredient (e.g., a sharp one-inch chicken bone in a chicken enchilada, a piece of glass in a serving of slaw), most courts (and the Restatement) hold that the ingredient constitutes a defect if a reasonable consumer would not expect the food product to contain that ingredient, regardless of whether the ingredient is foreign (the glass) or natural (the chicken bone). R.3d Products Liability § 7 thus retains the consumer expectation test for food products. A few courts allow strict products liability if the ingredient is foreign but not if it is natural. These courts permit recovery for natural ingredients on a negligence theory.

e. Intrinsically Dangerous Products

Certain intrinsically dangerous products (e.g., tobacco, firearms, and ammunition) are not per se defective even if they could be made safer or not sold at all. The risks arise from the intended use of the product, not from anything wrong with it. A federal statute (the PLCAA) prohibits most claims against federally licensed gun manufacturers, sellers, and importers.

f. Circumstantial Evidence Admissible to Prove a Defective Product

In a strict products liability case, plaintiff may use circumstantial evidence to show the existence of an unspecified manufacturing defect, analogous to the use of *res ipsa loquitur* in a negligence case. R.3d Products Liability § 3, states the rule: It may be inferred that a product defect existing at the time of sale or distribution caused the harm plaintiff sustained, without proof of a specific defect, when the incident that harmed plaintiff (a) was of a kind that ordinarily occurs as a result of product defect, and (b) was not, in the particular case, solely the result of causes other than product defect existing at the time of sale or distribution.

7. The Restatement (Third) of Torts: Products Liability

a. Revised Approaches to Proving a Defective Product

The new products liability provisions in the Restatement (Third) of Torts: Products Liability, which supersede § 402A, now explicitly recognize the three categories of product defects outlined in section 5(a): manufacturing defects, design defects, and informational defects (warnings and directions for use).

Sellers remain strictly liable for manufacturing defects, but the Restatement's proposed liability for design defects is close to a negligence standard, imposing liability only for "foreseeable risks of harm" that could have been avoided by the adoption of a "reasonable alternative design" (§ 2(b)) or by "reasonable instructions or warnings" (§ 2(c)). Thus, as a general rule, under this provision a product is not defectively designed unless plaintiff can prove that there was a feasible alternative design at the time the manufacturer made the product, and that the manufacturer knew or should have known about the risk created by the product as designed. Similarly, there is no duty to warn under this provision unless plaintiff can prove that the manufacturer knew or should have known of the risk about which plaintiff claims they should have been warned. However, if the product's design is "manifestly unreasonable" because of its negligible utility and high risk of danger, plaintiff can prove defectiveness even without proof of an alternative design (e.g., a dangerous toy gun).

As an alternative, plaintiff can recover if they can prove that the product as designed, or the warning, failed to comply with an applicable safety statute or administrative regulation (§ 4(a)). On the other hand, as evidence that the product was not defective, defendant can prove the product's compliance with an applicable safety statute or administrative regulation, although such compliance is not conclusive on the issue of defectiveness (§ 4(b)).

Only a small number of jurisdictions have adopted the Restatement (Third) approach to products liability.

b. Prescription Drug and Medical Device Liability

The Restatement (Third) further restricts liability for defective prescription drugs and medical devices. Under § 6(c), a prescription drug or medical device is not defective in design unless the foreseeable risk of harm is so "great in relation to its foreseeable therapeutic benefits that reasonable health-care providers, knowing of such foreseeable risks and therapeutic benefits, would not prescribe the drug or medical device for any class of patients." Under § 6(d), manufacturers need only warn "health care providers" unless the manufacturer "knows or has reason to know that health-care providers will not be in a position to reduce the risks of harm in accordance with the instructions or warnings." Only in that case does the manufacturer owe an adequate warning to the patient.

Strict liability will still apply to drugs and medical products for manufacturing defects.

8. Types of Harms Recoverable

Strict products liability is almost always limited to damages for physical harm to persons or other property, and consequential damages resulting from physical harm, attributable to the defect. Pecuniary loss resulting from a defect in the product without an accidental injury to persons or other property or resulting from non-accidental physical damage confined to the product itself is recoverable only under a breach of warranty or contract theory. This is known as the "economic loss" rule.

Example: Strict products liability applies when a toaster has an electrical short that causes a house fire. It does not apply when the toaster has an electrical short that only destroys the toaster or merely renders the product non-functional.

9. Defenses

a. Contributory Negligence

Prior to the adoption of comparative fault, most jurisdictions held that plaintiff's "ordinary" contributory negligence was not a defense to strict products liability. In other words, if plaintiff's fault was only in failing to discover the defect or to guard against the possibility of a defect, such fault was not a defense. Today, some jurisdictions adopting comparative negligence permit that type of contributory negligence to reduce plaintiff's damages; others continue to hold that such negligence is not a damage-reducing factor.

b. Implied Assumption of Risk

Prior to the adoption of comparative fault, in most jurisdictions, implied assumption of the risk—that is, unreasonably proceeding to use the product after discovering the defect—was a complete bar to recovery under strict products liability. Today, in most comparative fault jurisdictions, implied assumption of the risk is only a damage-reducing factor, and in many, it is not even a separate concept, having been merged into contributory fault. It remains a complete bar in a few states. According to R.3d Products Liability § 17, whatever comparative fault system a given jurisdiction generally uses, it should also use in products liability cases.

c. Unforeseeable Misuse of the Product

Plaintiff's misuse of the product is not a defense at all but is relevant in plaintiff's prima facie case. If an unforeseeable misuse of the product causes plaintiff's injury, defendant is not liable, since either the product was not defective, or any defect was not a cause in fact of plaintiff's harm. But if plaintiff's use, even though not an intended use of the product, was a foreseeable misuse (e.g., standing on a chair, a child putting a toy in their mouth), the product may be found defective because it was not designed to be reasonably safe in light of the foreseeable misuse. On this basis, car crashes are generally regarded as a foreseeable misuse of the car, and cars must be designed so as not to subject occupants to enhanced injuries from unreasonably dangerous design features of the car during a collision.

Of course, plaintiff's foreseeable misuse may be contributory fault, in which case it will be a damage-reducing factor, and in some cases may completely bar recovery. In some cases, plaintiff's serious misuse may be a superseding cause of plaintiff's harm, breaking the chain of causation and exonerating defendant.

In certain cases, a particular misuse might be unforeseeable because the product seller can rely on the user to follow warnings or instructions, or to guard against obvious or generally known dangers. In some states, subject to certain conditions, statutes immunize product manufacturers and sellers from liability for foreseeable uses or misuse if the dangers of the product are common knowledge.

d. Statutes of Limitations and Repose

If plaintiff's claim is for personal injury and based on a tort theory, the statute of limitations does not begin to run until the product injures plaintiff. This can result in liability for some very old products. In claims based on a breach of warranty theory, the UCC statute will usually apply, and typically the statute starts to run on the date of the new product's sale to the purchaser. Generally, plaintiff can choose to claim under either theory (or both), even if the statute has run as to one.

Legislation in some jurisdictions imposes an additional limitation period, called a "statute of repose," which runs from the date of the product's manufacture or first sale. Although statutes of repose are typically long (e.g., 12 years), they can have the effect of barring a claim before it even arose.

e. Disclaimers Do Not Block Claims

A purported disclaimer of strict products liability is ineffective. R.3d Products Liability § 18.

f. State of the Art Design

In some jurisdictions, defendants can defend a design defect case by showing that they designed the product in accordance with the "state of the art" practices at the time they manufactured and first sold it.

g. Preemption

Federal preemption is an increasingly important defense in products liability cases. Under the supremacy clause of the U.S. Constitution, federal law is supreme over state law. Thus, when federal legislation or regulations expressly or impliedly preempt a particular field (e.g., statutes governing cigarette warnings, certain medical products), state tort law either cannot regulate the field at all or cannot impose a higher standard than the applicable federal law. Whether (and the extent to which) a federal statute or regulation is preemptive is a question of statutory interpretation for the court. Preemption can apply in negligence and strict products liability cases.

h. Statutory Presumption of Non-Defectiveness

Some state statutes provide that when a product complies with a federal or state regulation concerning that product, there is a rebuttable presumption that the product is not defective with respect to its design or informational characteristics.

10. Nondelegable Duties

The manufacturer is usually not liable unless the product was defective when it left its control. An exception applies where the manufacturer places in the stream of commerce an unfinished or unassembled product that must be assembled or finished by its dealer, who in doing so, creates the defect. A manufacturer cannot delegate to its purchaser the duty to select and purchase optional safety devices without which the product is not reasonably safe.

11. Post-Sale Duties

In some jurisdictions, when a defective condition arises post-sale, a manufacturer may be subject to liability for failure to retrofit a previously marketed product with safety devices (or to provide appropriate warnings). This obligation arises if locating current users and furnishing such devices or warnings is not an unreasonable burden compared to the risk of injury inherent in the product without them. This liability arises even though the product was arguably not unsafe when the manufacturer first marketed it. See R.3d Products Liability § 10.

II. Review Questions

[Answers Provided in Appendix A]

1. Henry Homeowner buys a riding lawnmower manufactured by the Acme Lawn Company and sold at Home Depot. Henry allows his six-year-old son, Sampson, to ride the machine on a hillside, despite warnings that the machine is not to be driven on hills and that no one under the age of sixteen should be allowed to drive the machine. Acme expressly disclaims any liability for injuries resulting from the use of its mower. Sampson is injured when the mower flips over, and the blade severely cuts his leg. Identify all possible defendants that can be sued and each possible cause of action. For the strict products liability action, analyze the claim using an IRAC structure. What defenses will the defendant(s) assert?

2. Following the lawsuit described in Question 1, the General Counsel at Acme Lawn Company hired you to revise its product warnings. Currently, all product warnings are affixed by a sticker with writing in eight-point font on the engine of the lawnmower. What recommendations do you have to strengthen the warnings? What relevance do the learned intermediary rule or the sophisticated consumer doctrines have, if any?

Part Eight

Survival and Wrongful Death

■ ANALYSIS

I. Survival and Wrongful Death

(Dobbs §§ 294–301; R.2d §§ 493, 494, 925, 926)

A. Survival of Tort Actions

1. Common Law Rule

Historically, no cause of action for personal torts survived the death of either the tortfeasor or the person injured, regardless of the cause of death.

2. Statutory Modifications

All jurisdictions have altered the common law rule through statutory modifications. About one-third of the states provide that either (a) all tort actions or (b) all tort actions except defamation survive the death of either a plaintiff or a defendant. The rest have a wide variety of inclusions and exclusions.

3. Personal Injury Actions

Personal injury actions survive in almost all jurisdictions, but sometimes with limitations on the damages recoverable. In a few states, personal injury actions do not survive the injured person's death unless as part of an action for that death. Actions for consequential damages sometimes do not survive. In most states, wrongful death actions survive the death of the tortfeasor.

4. Damages

Damages are generally measured as if no one had died, except that the victim's death terminates the accumulation of certain kinds of future damages (pain and suffering, mental distress, medical expenses, loss of earnings, disability, etc.) that the victim otherwise could have recovered based on their life expectancy. R.2d § 926. Survival statutes sometimes contain other limitations. A few states also allow "loss of life" damages, i.e., the loss of the value that the decedent would have placed on their life.

5. Punitive Damages

A plaintiff's right to seek punitive damages may cease if a defendant dies. In some states however, if the injured person's death may do the same, but in many jurisdictions, the estate of the decedent may seek punitive damages.

6. Medical, Funeral, and Burial Expenses

In some cases, funeral, burial expenses, and the decedent's last medical expenses may be elements of damages in the survival action, or, in the alternative, in the wrongful death action. In some jurisdictions, medical, funeral, and burial expenses are a separate claim altogether.

Decedent's estate would have no claim for medical, funeral, or burial expenses against a defendant to the extent that these expenses are causally unrelated to decedent's cause of action against defendant.

7. Defenses

A survival action is just a continuation of the decedent's tort case, so all the same defenses or liability limitations will apply. The fact that a beneficiary's negligence contributed to the death is not relevant and does not affect the damages recoverable. However, in a joint-and-several liability jurisdiction the defendant can seek contribution from the negligent beneficiary, thereby indirectly reducing or negating his share. In a several liability jurisdiction, fault will be apportioned, so defendant's proportional share may be lower due to the fault of a beneficiary, thereby reducing the estate's recovery. See R.3d Apportionment of Liability § 6(b).

B. Wrongful Death

1. Common Law Rule

Since *Baker v. Bolton* (Eng. 1808), the general common law rule has been that one whose tortious conduct results in the death of a person is not liable to that person's survivors (Hawaii alone to the contrary).

2. Statutory and Other Modifications

Beginning in 1846, statutes were passed in England (Lord Campbell's Act) and American jurisdictions creating a remedy for wrongful death, also known as "death statutes." R.2d §§ 493. A few cases have reversed the common law rule e.g., *Moragne v. States Marine Lines, Inc.* (U.S. 1970) (common law wrongful death action recognized in admiralty cases); *Gaudette v. Webb* (Mass. 1972). Various federal statutes also provide actions for wrongful death or other death benefits.

3. Basis

Any tort theory that would have supported a personal injury action will support an action for wrongful death. The usual scope-of-liability rules apply.

4. Types of Statutes

There are two basic types of wrongful death acts.

a. Lord Campbell's Act

Most states have adopted a wrongful death act modeled after the 1846 English statute that creates a new cause of action for the benefit of specified near relatives of the decedent. This would be because the decedent would have had a cause of action had they been merely injured and not killed in the tortious act.

b. Survival

A few jurisdictions have a "survival"-type statute which preserves the cause of action that vested at decedent's death and expands it to include the damages resulting from the death itself.

c. Statutory Torts

Most statutory tort actions (F.E.L.A., dram shop acts) have their own provisions for recovery in the event of death. If not, then an appropriate general death act will apply.

5. Concurrence of Remedies

If a plaintiff survived their injuries for a time before dying from them, in most jurisdictions either a survival action or a wrongful death action or both may be brought independently or in the same lawsuit. In some, the causes of action merge. In others, plaintiff's survivors must elect one or the other. In a few others, the survival action abates in whole or in part.

6. Beneficiaries

The beneficiaries are the relatives or classes of relatives designated in the wrongful death statute. Decedent's spouse and children, if any, receive the award to the exclusion of all other surviving relatives. If there is no surviving spouse or children, then typically certain other close relatives (parents, siblings, grandparents) may be able to claim pecuniary (monetary) loss but only if and to the extent they can show that they have been receiving, or probably would have received, support or services from the decedent. In some cases, parents or siblings may be able to recover nonpecuniary loss.

In most jurisdictions, stepchildren and unmarried cohabitants do not qualify as beneficiaries. However, some wrongful death statutes include domestic partners who have legal status, and a few include stepchildren.

Generally, a wrongful death claim survives the sole beneficiary who dies prior to judgment in the wrongful death case.

7. Damages

A wide variety of rules govern the elements of damages recoverable. The general types of statutes are:

a. Loss to the Survivors

Elements of damages include:

i. Pecuniary Loss

Many statutes include "pecuniary loss," which involves at the very least the present value of the loss of support, services, and contributions the beneficiaries would have received in the future but for the death. In some jurisdictions, this includes loss of a probable inheritance.

ii. Nonpecuniary Loss

Nonpecuniary loss—loss of plaintiff's society, companionship, love and affection—is recoverable in some jurisdictions, either by specific statutory language or by judicial construction of the term "pecuniary loss." A few allow recovery for the survivor's mental anguish (bereavement). In the case of decedents whose earnings were small or zero at the time of death (minor children, elderly parents), the entire claim may be based on nonpecuniary loss.

iii. Medical and Other Expenses

Medical and other expenses, such as funeral and burial costs, ordinarily may be recovered by the survivor paying them, either as part of the death action or separately.

b. Loss to the Estate

A minority of jurisdictions measure damages by the loss to the estate—decedent's future earnings minus their personal expenses, or their probable future accumulations or net savings. A few jurisdictions permit recovery of both the loss to survivors and the loss to the estate (i.e., loss of inheritance).

c. Punitive Wrongful Death Acts

In two states, damages are determined without reference to decedent's earnings or their family's needs but are based solely on defendant's fault.

d. Punitive Damages

Jurisdictions are split on whether punitive damages may be recovered in a wrongful death action. In a few states, they are expressly allowed by statute.

e. Limits

At one time, almost half the states had specific dollar limits on wrongful death awards. Today, most jurisdictions have removed such limits, but a few jurisdictions limit elements of damage, or limit damages as to certain beneficiaries. Additionally, wrongful death awards may be subject to limits that apply to damages generally.

8. Defenses

In wrongful death cases, the same defenses are available as if decedent had lived (e.g., decedent's contributory negligence or assumption of risk can reduce or negate the beneficiaries' claim). R.2d § 494; R.3d Apportionment of Liability § 6. In addition, a beneficiary's negligence that contributed to the death bars or reduces that beneficiary's recovery (but not that of other beneficiaries) consistent with the governing contributory and comparative fault rules. Remarriage of decedent's spouse does not mitigate the spouse's damages. The intra-family immunities generally are not available as defenses in wrongful death actions.

Regarding the statute of limitations, courts are split as to whether beneficiaries are barred from bringing a wrongful death action which otherwise would have been viable if the statute of limitations applicable to decedent's cause of action had expired by the time the decedent died, or after they died before suit could be filed. Many, but not all, hold that the statute begins running at the time of death. Courts are also divided as to the application of the discovery rule in wrongful death cases.

C. Procedure

1. Survival Actions

The plaintiff is the executor or administrator of the decedent's estate, and the surviving cause of action is an asset of the estate. Any recovery in the survival action goes to the estate and is distributed based on the decedent's will, if any, or the applicable law governing intestacy. As such, it is subject to the claims of the estate's creditors.

2. Wrongful Death Actions

A wrongful death cause of action is an independent claim by the beneficiaries. It is not an asset of the decedent's estate and does not pass through the estate. In some jurisdictions, the plaintiff is the executor or administrator of the estate, but it is brought on behalf of the beneficiaries, and any recovery goes directly to them. It is not subject to claims of the estate's creditors. In some jurisdictions, the plaintiff is one of the beneficiaries or their representative who sues on behalf of all the beneficiaries. If there is more than one beneficiary for whom damages are awarded, the recovery is divided in accordance with applicable local procedure.

Part Nine

Nuisance

■ ANALYSIS

I. Introduction

"Nuisances," public and private, are two distinct fields of tort liability. In essence, nuisance is not a particular kind of tortious conduct. Rather, it is a form of action for particular kinds of harm. It is the extent of the invasion to plaintiff's interest, not the conduct of the defendant, which determines whether plaintiff has an action for nuisance. Liability can be based on intentional conduct, negligence, or strict liability.

II. Private Nuisance

A. Definition

A private nuisance is a thing or activity which substantially and unreasonably interferes with the plaintiff's use and enjoyment of their land. Interferences can have a physical effect on the land itself, such as by vibration, objects thrown upon it, destruction of crops, flooding, or pollution of its water or soil (see R.2d §§ 832, 833). Interference can affect the comfort, convenience or health of the occupant, as by foul odors, smoke, dust, insects, noxious gases, excessive noise, excessive light, or high temperatures. Conditions on adjoining land which impair plaintiff's mental tranquility by the fear or offensive nature of their mere presence, such as a house used for drug manufacture and/or distribution, a waste processing plant, stored explosives, or a wild animal can also be considered interferences.

An interference with the plaintiff personally, but not their use and enjoyment of their land, is not a private nuisance.

B. Relation to Trespass to Land

A trespass is an invasion of plaintiff's interest in the exclusive possession of land (e.g., by entry upon it). A nuisance is an interference with plaintiff's interest in the private use and enjoyment of the land, which does not require interference with their exclusive possession; but, unlike trespass, the interference must be unreasonable and cause substantial harm. Plaintiffs may proceed on either or both theories.

C. Basis of Liability

1. Fault

Liability is not absolute. Absent a statute, a defendant's interference with a plaintiff's protected interest must be intentional, reckless, negligent, or the result of an abnormally dangerous activity such that principles of strict liability will apply. R.2d §§ 822, 824, 825. Many ongoing nuisances can be classified as intentional torts because the defendant knows or has reason to know that their conduct is interfering with the plaintiff's use and enjoyment of their land but persists in the conduct anyway.

2. Substantial Interference

Nuisance liability requires substantial harm, of a type which would be suffered by an ordinary person in the community, or by property in normal condition and used for a normal purpose. R.2d § 821F. A plaintiff cannot, by devoting their land to an unusually sensitive use, make a nuisance out of conduct which would otherwise be relatively harmless.

3. Continuing or Recurring Interference Not Required

At one time it was thought that a nuisance did not exist unless the interference was continuing or recurring. There is no such requirement now, although some interferences will not be sufficiently substantial unless they are.

4. Interference Must Be Unreasonable

The interference must be unreasonable, which generally means that either (a) the gravity of a plaintiff's harm outweighs the utility of the defendant's conduct, or (b) if intentional, the harm caused by a defendant's conduct is substantial and the financial burden of compensating for this and other harms does not render unfeasible the continuation of the conduct. R.2d § 826.

Illustrations of unreasonable conduct include:

(a) conduct inspired solely by hostility or a desire to cause harm to the plaintiff, or which is contrary to common decency (R.2d § 829);

(b) harm which is substantial and greater than a plaintiff should be required to bear without compensation (R.2d § 829A);

(c) harm which is substantial and the defendant can avoid the harm in whole or in part without undue hardship (R.2d § 830); and

(d) harm which is substantial, plaintiff's use or enjoyment is well suited to the character of the locality, and defendant's conduct is unsuited to the character of that locality (R.2d § 831).

a. Weighing the Gravity of the Harm

Courts review the gravity of the harm by considering factors such as the

(i) extent of the harm,

(ii) character of the harm,

(iii) the social value of plaintiff's use or enjoyment it affects,

(iv) the suitability of that use or enjoyment to the locality, and

(v) the burden for the plaintiff to avoid the harm. R.2d § 827.

b. Weighing the Utility of Defendant's Conduct

Courts review the utility of a defendant's conduct by considering factors such as the

(i) social value of the defendant's conduct,

(ii) its suitability to the locality,

(iii) the feasibility of preventing or avoiding the interference, and

(iv) the practicability of continuing the defendant's activity if it is required to bear the cost of compensating for the interference. R.2d § 828.

D. Remedies

1. Who Can Recover

Anyone whose use and enjoyment of any interest (possessory or non-possessory) in the land is affected can maintain the action. R.2d § 821E.

2. Damages

The usual remedy is damages. If the nuisance is permanent, all damages must be recovered in one action. If the nuisance can be abated, plaintiff recovers all damages at the time of trial. If a defendant then fails to abate, future invasions give rise to a new cause of action.

3. Injunction

If the nuisance threatens to continue and the plaintiff has no adequate legal remedy, equitable relief may be sought. The court will then balance:

(i) the relative economic hardship to the parties from granting or denying the injunction, and

(ii) the public interest in continuing the defendant's activity.

Thus, the court can require a defendant to pay damages but deny injunctive relief.

4. Self-Help

There is a limited privilege to enter another's land (or trespass upon their chattel) to abate a private nuisance. R.2d §§ 201, 264.

E. Persons Liable

Liability includes one who carries on or participates in a nuisance-creating activity. In some cases, it can also include lessors and possessors who fail to prevent or abate a nuisance carried on by third persons on their land.

F. Defenses

1. Contributory Negligence and Assumption of Risk Are Viable Defenses

A plaintiff's contributory negligence or assumption of risk is a nuisance defense to the same extent as in other tort actions. R.2d §§ 840B, 840C.

2. Coming to the Nuisance

The fact that a plaintiff has acquired or improved their land after a nuisance has come into existence is not itself sufficient to bar their action but is a factor to be considered in determining whether the nuisance is actionable. R.2d § 840D.

3. Others Contributing to the Nuisance

Except as it may affect the character of the locality, the fact that others contribute to a nuisance is not a bar to a defendant's liability for their own contribution. R.2d § 840E. This is true even though no one person's activity, by itself, would have been sufficient.

4. Legislation

Legislation authorizing a particular activity or use of land (e.g., zoning laws, licenses) may be used to establish that it is not a nuisance, but such authority is usually narrowly construed to include only reasonable conduct.

III. Public Nuisance

A. Definition

A public nuisance is an unreasonable interference with a right common to the general public. R.2d § 821B. It is a collection of minor crimes, now mostly statutory. For example, interference with the public health (e.g., pollution of a water supply, keeping diseased animals); interference with the public safety (e.g., storage of explosives, harboring a wild animals); interference with public morals (e.g., a house of prostitution, gambling, indecent exhibitions, illegal liquor establishment); interference with the public peace; and interference with public comfort or convenience (e.g., smoke, dust, vibrations, assembly of large crowds, obstructing a public street or navigable stream).

B. Public Right

The right interfered with must be common to the public as a class, and not merely that of one person or even a group of citizens.

C. Remedies

Available remedies include a criminal prosecution or suit to enjoin or abate the nuisance by public authorities or others on behalf of the public. A private citizen has no civil remedy for the harm they have sustained resulting from a public nuisance if that harm is of the same kind as that suffered by the general public, even though they have been harmed to a greater degree than others. A private citizen may sue for harm caused by a public nuisance only if their harm is different in kind from that suffered by other members of the public. R.2d § 821C.

D. Concurrence of Remedies

If a public nuisance also interferes with a plaintiff's use and enjoyment of their land, the plaintiff may sue for their damages under either public or private nuisance theories.

IV. Review Questions

[Answers Provided in Appendix A]

1. A group of concerned Citizens brings a suit against a large chemical company that has a factory located near their residences. Several times over the past few years, the factory has experienced failures of various types, resulting in the release of poisonous gases into the air. These gases have drifted onto Citizens' property, damaging the paint on their cars and homes and causing them discomfort from the noxious odors and smoke. Discuss Citizens' cause of action under private nuisance. Use an IRAC structure to frame your answer.

2. Same facts as Question 1. Discuss Citizens' cause of action under public nuisance. Use an IRAC structure to frame your answer.

Part Ten

Misrepresentation, Defamation, and Privacy

■ ANALYSIS

5. Justifiable Reliance
    a. Materiality
    b. Duty to Investigate
    c. Opinion of Adverse Party
    d. Opinion of Apparently Disinterested Person
6. Damages
7. Physical Harm

C. Negligent Misrepresentation
1. Elements
2. Physical Harm
3. Pecuniary Loss
4. Scope of Liability
    a. Interest in Transaction
    b. Actual Knowledge of Plaintiff
    c. Foreseeable Harm to One Remote User
    d. Public Duty to Furnish Information
    e. Transaction
5. Contributory Negligence
6. Damages

D. Innocent Misrepresentation (Strict Liability)
1. Physical Harm: Products
2. Pecuniary Loss: Sale, Rental, or Exchange Transaction

E. Review Questions

II. Defamation

A. General Rules
1. Elements of Cause of Action
2. What Is Defamatory?
3. Truth
4. Who May Be Defamed
    a. Deceased Persons
    b. Entities
5. Meaning of Communication
    a. Understanding of Recipient
    b. Extrinsic Circumstances
6. Application to Plaintiff
7. Group Defamation
8. Types of Defamatory Communications
    a. Fact
    b. Opinion
    c. Ridicule
    d. Verbal Abuse
    e. Fabricated Quotation

B. Libel and Slander Distinguished
1. Libel Defined
2. Slander Defined
3. Relevant Factors

C. Defamation Actionable Without Proof of Special Damages
  1. Libel
  2. Libel Per Quod
  3. Slander
    a. Criminal Conduct
    b. Communicable Disease
    c. Business, Trade, Profession, or Office
    d. Sexual Misconduct
  4. Special Damages
D. Publication
  1. Definition
  2. Fault
  3. Agent
  4. Multiple Publications
  5. Wills
  6. Liability of Republisher
  7. Causation: Liability of Original Publisher for Republication
E. Fault
  1. Common Law
  2. First Amendment
  3. Public Official, Public Figure
    a. Public Official
    b. Public Figure
    c. Public Concern
    d. Fault
    e. Private Communications
  4. Private Persons
    a. Effect of *Gertz*
    b. Majority Rule
    c. Minority Rule
    d. Burden of Proof
F. Defenses to Actions for Defamation
  1. Consent
  2. Absolute Privileges
    a. Judicial Proceedings
    b. Legislative Proceedings
    c. Executive and Administrative Officers
    d. Spousal Privilege
    e. Publication Required by Law
  3. Conditional or Qualified Privileges
    a. In General
    b. Protection of the Publisher's Interest
      i. Rule
      ii. Value of Defendant's Interest
    c. Protection of Interest of Recipient or Third Person
      i. Rule
      ii. Decent Conduct

iii. Examples
d. Protection of Common Interest
e. Family Relationships
f. Public Interest
g. Inferior State Officers
h. "Abuse" (Loss) of the Privilege
i. Knowledge, Recklessness, or Negligence Concerning Falsity
ii. Rumor
iii. Purpose
iv. Excessive Publication
v. Unprivileged Matter
i. Fair Comment on Matters of Public Concern
4. Special Types of Privilege
a. Report of Official Proceeding or Public Meeting
b. Providing Means of Publication
G. Damages
1. Types Recoverable
2. Nominal Damages
3. General Damages
a. Rule
b. Exception
4. Special Damages
5. Emotional Distress and Bodily Harm
6. Punitive Damages
7. Mitigation
8. Right of Reply
H. Review Questions

III. **Privacy**
A. Introduction
B. Appropriation
1. Rule
2. Commercial Use
3. Appropriation
C. Intrusion
1. Rule
2. Form
3. Publication
4. Private Matters
5. Substantial Interference
6. Government Intrusion
D. Public Disclosure of Private Facts
1. Rule
2. Publicity
3. Private Facts
4. Legitimate Public Concern or Interest
a. Constitutional Limitations
b. Public Figures

I. Misrepresentation

A. Introduction

1. Definition

Words or conduct asserting the existence of a fact constitute a misrepresentation if the fact does not exist. Misrepresentation is often an element of some torts claims and other causes of action. However, there is a tort action called "misrepresentation" where defendant, in the course of some transaction (usually a bargaining situation) makes a false statement to plaintiff (or another), plaintiff acts in reasonable reliance on the statement, and plaintiff therefore sustains pecuniary loss.

2. Basis

At common law, this action was called "deceit" and would exist only if defendant's misrepresentation was fraudulent—i.e., made with "scienter." Today, liability is recognized for some types of negligent misrepresentations.

B. Deceit

1. Elements

The elements necessary to establish a prima facie case in an action for deceit are: (1) Defendant made a false representation, ordinarily of a fact. (2) Defendant must have known that the statement was false, or else they must have made it consciously or with reckless disregard for whether it was true or false. (3) Defendant must have intended that plaintiff act (or refrain from acting) in reliance upon the representation. (4) Plaintiff must have justifiably relied upon the representation in acting or failing to act. (5) Plaintiff must have sustained actual damage as a result of their reliance.

a. Representation

Defendant made a false representation, ordinarily of a fact.

b. Scienter

Defendant must have known that the statement was false, or else they must have made it consciously or with reckless disregard for whether it was true or false.

c. Intent to Induce Reliance

Defendant must have intended that plaintiff act (or refrain from acting) in reliance upon the representation.

d. Justifiable Reliance

Plaintiff must have justifiably relied upon the representation in acting or failing to act.

e. Damages

Plaintiff must have sustained actual damage as a result of their reliance.

See R.2d § 525.

2. Fraudulent Misrepresentation

A misrepresentation is "fraudulent" (i.e., made with "scienter") if defendant

1) knows or believes that the character of the representation is not as they represent it to be,

2) does not have the confidence in the accuracy of their representation that they state or imply, or

3) knows that they do not have the basis for their representation that they state or imply. R.2d § 526.

Benjamin Cardozo explained, in *Ultramares Corp. v. Touche, Niven & Co.*, 255 N.Y. 170, 180 (1931), "Fraud includes the pretense of knowledge when there is none." Pretending to have knowledge when you do not is fraud.

3. Form of Representation

a. Misrepresentation of Fact, Not Opinion

In general, the representation must be of a fact. It may be by words or conduct. Statements that represent only defendant's opinion or prediction are not generally actionable. However, an opinion may be understood as an implied representation concerning its underlying facts. R.2d § 539.

Statements of quantity ordinarily may be taken as statements of fact. But statements of quality and value traditionally have been classified as opinions where no reliance can reasonably be placed, unless sufficiently specific.

In the past, statements of law were deemed opinions and therefore not actionable. Today, some specific representations as to the state of law may be representations of fact, and even if opinion, may be actionable if reasonably understood as implying a statement of fact.

b. Ambiguous Representations Can Be Actionable

A representation capable of two interpretations, one true and the other false, is actionable if made with the intent that it be understood in the false sense or with reckless indifference as to how it will be understood. R.2d § 527.

c. False Statements of Intent Are Actionable

A statement that the speaker or another person currently intends to do (or not do) something in the future is typically seen as a statement of fact which is actionable if untrue. R.2d §§ 530, 544.

d. Incomplete Statements Are Actionable

A representation stating the truth that the maker knows or believes to be materially misleading because of the maker's failure to state additional or qualifying matter, is actionable. R.2d § 529.

e. Fraudulent Concealment Is Actionable

If defendant conceals or otherwise prevents plaintiff from acquiring material information, defendant is liable as though they had stated its nonexistence. R.2d § 550.

f. Nondisclosure Not Generally Actionable

At one time, mere silence could not amount to a misrepresentation. Parties to a transaction were free to knowingly take advantage of the other's ignorance of material facts. This rule is now subject to several significant exceptions:

i. Fiduciary or Confidential Relations

Fiduciary or confidential relations, such as principal-agent, guardian-ward, executory-beneficiary, bank-depositor, attorney-client, physician-patient, and parties to certain contracts (suretyship, insurance, partnership), carry with them the duty to make disclosure of all material facts.

ii. Active Concealment

The rule does not apply where defendant actively conceals material information or prevents investigation.

iii. Subsequently Acquired Information

Subsequently acquired information which makes the prior statement untrue or misleading must be disclosed if defendant knows or believes that plaintiff is still acting on the basis of the original statement.

iv. Newly Discovered Reliance

If defendant makes a statement without expecting that plaintiff will rely upon it (therefore, not actionable) and Defendant later discovers that plaintiff, in a transaction with them, is about to rely upon it, they have an affirmative duty to disclose its falsity.

v. Material Facts Known to Defendant, Not Plaintiff

There is a growing trend to find an affirmative duty to disclose material facts known to defendant, where those facts are peculiarly and exclusively within defendant's knowledge or when defendant has special access to those facts which plaintiff does not, and plaintiff is not in a position to discover the facts for themself. The rule may be relaxed in other cases where there is some reason why nondisclosure would be unconscionable or at least very unfair.

vi. Statutory Duty to Disclose

Securities laws, consumer protection laws, and other statutes may impose an affirmative duty to disclose. R.2d § 551.

4. Scope of Liability

The scope of defendant's liability for a fraudulent misrepresentation is as follows.

a. Persons

Defendant is liable to the specifically identifiable person(s) or group of persons they (1) intend to act or (2) have reason to expect, will act (or refrain from acting) in reliance upon their representation. R.2d §§ 531, 534.

b. Third Persons

If defendant intends or has reason to expect that their representation will be communicated to a specific third person, and that it will influence their conduct in the type of transaction involved, they are subject to liability to that third person. R.2d § 533.

c. Type of Transaction

Plaintiff's reliance must ordinarily be in the transaction or type of transaction in which defendant intends or has reason to expect that plaintiff's conduct will be influenced. R.2d § 531.

d. Actual and Proximate Cause

Defendant's representation must have been a substantial factor in influencing plaintiff's conduct (R.2d §§ 546, 547), and plaintiff's loss from the reliance must have been reasonably foreseeable (R.2d § 548A). Defendant is not liable if plaintiff uses the information in an entirely unexpected way.

5. Justifiable Reliance

Plaintiff can recover only if they in fact relied on the representation, and their reliance was justifiable. R.2d § 537. The standard is a subjective one. R.2d § 545A cmt. b.

a. Materiality

Reliance is not justifiable unless the matter misrepresented is material. R.2d § 538.

b. Duty to Investigate

Plaintiff may justifiably rely on the other's statements without further investigation even when their falsity could have been easily and quickly discovered, unless something known to them or apparent in the situation at hand should have served as a warning to them that the statement should not to be accepted without further inquiry. R.2d §§ 540, 541, 541A. Reliance may also be justified without investigation if defendant somehow prevents or deters further inquiry.

c. Opinion of Adverse Party

Plaintiff cannot justifiably rely on Defendant's statement in the form of an opinion, unless the fact to which the opinion relates is material and (1) Defendant claims to have special knowledge, (2) Defendant stands in a fiduciary or confidential relation to plaintiff, or (3) Defendant has some other special reason to expect that plaintiff will rely on defendant's opinion. R.2d § 542.

d. Opinion of Apparently Disinterested Person

Plaintiff can justifiably rely on the opinion of an apparently disinterested person if the fact that they hold the opinion is material. R.2d § 543.

6. Damages

Damages for fraudulent misrepresentations are measured by plaintiff's pecuniary loss, including the difference between the value of what they paid and the value of what they actually received, plus consequential damages.

7. Physical Harm

Defendant may also be liable for physical harm caused by reasonable reliance on an intentional, affirmative misrepresentation if defendant intends or knows it will induce reliance that involves a risk of physical harm to plaintiff, and if defendant knows that the statement is false or does not have the knowledge they profess. R.2d § 310.

C. Negligent Misrepresentation

1. Elements

Even though defendant honestly believed his mistaken statement to be true, they may have been negligent in (a) failing to exercise reasonable care to ascertain the true facts, or (b) failing to possess or apply the skill and competence required by their business or profession (e.g., attorney, accountant, surveyor, product manufacturer), or (c) expressing their assertion as they did (R.2d § 528).

2. Physical Harm

If Defendant's negligent misrepresentation proximately causes physical harm, ordinary negligence principles apply. R.2d § 311.

3. Pecuniary Loss

Most jurisdictions recognize a limited form of liability for such negligent misrepresentations as a separate tort action. R.2d § 552. Some courts have barred negligent misrepresentation actions under the economic loss rule, except in cases where defendant is in an information business or profession (e.g., attorney, accountant, etc.).

4. Scope of Liability

a. Interest in Transaction

Defendant is not liable for their negligent misrepresentation (causing only pecuniary loss) unless made in the course of their business, profession or employment, or other transaction in which they had a pecuniary interest. R.2d § 552. Some courts limit recovery for negligent misrepresentation to cases where defendant was in the business of supplying information.

b. Actual Knowledge of Plaintiff

At first, defendant was liable only to the specific person or persons for whose benefit and guidance they intended to supply the information. Today, many courts have extended defendant's liability to include persons in a limited group, even though not specifically known to defendant, if defendant knows that one or more persons in that group will receive and rely upon that information, R.2d § 552(2), even though Defendant had no knowledge of their specific identity or the particulars of the transaction in which it would be used.

c. Foreseeable Harm to One Remote User

Where defendant knows that the information they furnished will be used by a succession of persons whose specific identity is presently unknowable, but only one such person will suffer loss (the person using the information at the time the error is discovered), some courts have extended defendant's liability to all who will foreseeably use and rely upon the information (e.g., surveyors; title abstracters).

d. Public Duty to Furnish Information

Certain kinds of statutes (e.g., securities laws, recording acts) require defendant to furnish, file, or publish information for the protection of a class of persons. If such information is negligently erroneous, a member of that class who relies upon it to their detriment may recover. R.2d § 552(3).

e. Transaction

Liability is limited to the transaction for which the information was furnished or a substantially similar transaction.

5. Contributory Negligence

Plaintiff's contributory negligence in relying upon a negligent misrepresentation is a defense. R.2d § 552A. Comparative negligence rules, if any, apply.

6. Damages

Damages for negligent misrepresentation include plaintiff's out-of-pocket loss and consequential damages, but not the benefit of the bargain. R.2d § 552B.

D. Innocent Misrepresentation (Strict Liability)

1. Physical Harm: Products

If defendant is engaged in the business of selling a certain product, they are subject to strict liability for physical harm resulting from a misrepresentation made to the public concerning the character or quality of that product they sold. R.2d § 402B; R.3d Products Liability § 9.

2. Pecuniary Loss: Sale, Rental, or Exchange Transaction

The Restatement (Second) § 552C proposes strict liability for pecuniary loss sustained as the result of a misrepresentation made by defendant in a sale, rental or exchange transaction with plaintiff, upon which plaintiff justifiably relied. Damages would be limited to the difference between the value of what plaintiff received and the value of what Plaintiff gave. So far, only a few cases support this rule. Traditionally, contract, equitable, or restitutionary remedies have been applied in this situation.

E. Review Questions

[Answers Provided in Appendix A]

1. Defendant, a car salesperson, tells Plaintiff that a car in which Plaintiff has expressed interest was owned by an infrequent and cautious driver who only drove it 25,000 miles total and never over 30 miles an hour. These statements are all true. However, Defendant also knows that the oil was never changed, and that the car was in three major accidents and spent six months at the bottom of a lake. Defendant gives Plaintiff the former owner's phone number, but Plaintiff does not bother calling. Instead, Plaintiff buys the car and without inspecting it drives off. Three days later, while Plaintiff is driving the car, the bent and rusted front axle breaks, and Plaintiff has an accident which results in the total destruction of the car and in serious injury to Plaintiff.

   a. Plaintiff cannot recover any damages for misrepresentation because Defendant misrepresented nothing.

   b. Plaintiff cannot recover any damages for misrepresentation because Plaintiff could have easily discovered the defect by looking or by phoning the former owner.

   c. Plaintiff can recover the difference between what Plaintiff paid for the car and what it was worth before the accident.

   d. Plaintiff can recover the difference between what Plaintiff paid for the car and its value before the accident. Plaintiff can also recover for the damage to the car and their injuries from the accident if these were proximately caused by their reliance on Defendant's statements.

II. Defamation

A. General Rules

1. Elements of Cause of Action

The elements of a common-law defamation action are: (1) A false and defamatory statement concerning another. (2) An unprivileged publication to a third party, the publication being intentional or at least negligent on the part of defendant. (3) Depending on the status of the defendant, plaintiff may have to show some degree of fault on the part of defendant in knowing or failing to ascertain the falsity of the statement. (4) Some defamatory statements are actionable without proof of special damages (i.e., are actionable "per se"); others are not.

2. What Is Defamatory?

A communication is defamatory if it tends to harm plaintiff's reputation in the community, either by (1) lowering others' estimation of them, or (2) deterring others from associating or dealing with them. R.2d § 559.

These communications include those that expose plaintiff to hatred, contempt, ridicule; which reflect unfavorably on their morality or integrity; which impair their financial reputation; or which impute that plaintiff has a disease or other physical or mental attribute or deficiency such that others will be deterred from associating with them.

A communication is defamatory if a substantial and respectable minority of plaintiff's community or associates would so regard it; it is not necessary that all or a majority would. However, it is not defamatory if the minority's views on that subject are so anti-social or extreme that it would not be proper for the courts to recognize them.

3. Truth

A defamatory statement is not actionable unless it is false. R.2d § 681A. Traditionally, truth has been regarded as an affirmative defense on which defendant has the burden of proof. In cases involving issues of public interest, however, the First Amendment now requires plaintiff to bear the burden of proving falsity. Additionally, the law now requires plaintiff to establish defendant's fault with respect to the falsity of the statement in at least some, if not all, defamation cases.

4. Who May Be Defamed

a. Deceased Persons

Unless a statute otherwise provides, no libel or slander action lies for the defamation of a deceased person. R.2d § 560. Whether the action survives plaintiff's death (where plaintiff was defamed while alive) depends on the local survival statute.

b. Entities

Corporations, partnerships, and unincorporated associations may be defamed. R.2d §§ 561.

5. Meaning of Communication

a. Understanding of Recipient

A communication is defamatory only if the recipient understands it in a defamatory sense and understands that it was so intended. R.2d § 563. If the recipient reasonably so understood it, it does not matter that they were mistaken. The context of the statement is considered.

b. Extrinsic Circumstances

Extrinsic facts and circumstances known to the recipient are considered.

6. Application to Plaintiff

The communication must have been understood by the recipient (correctly, or mistakenly but reasonably) as intended to refer to plaintiff. R.2d § 564. The applicability of the defamatory matter to plaintiff may depend upon extrinsic facts or circumstances known to the recipient.

7. Group Defamation

Generally, no action lies for the publication of defamatory words concerning a large group or class of persons, since they cannot reasonably be understood as applying to any one individual.

***Example*:** "All the lawyers in this town are fraudsters." (there being 150 lawyers).

But a member of a small group may recover if the statement may reasonably be understood as applying to them specifically. And so may a member of any size group if the circumstances indicate that it is intended to apply to them.

***Example*:** "That jury was bribed." "Most of the players on that team are on drugs."

***Example*:** "All lawyers are fraudsters," where Plaintiff is the only lawyer present and Defendant's remarks may reasonably be understood as directed at Plaintiff. R.2d § 564A.

8. Types of Defamatory Communications

a. Fact

Typically, a defamatory communication consists of a statement of fact. R.2d § 565. It may be direct or indirect, as where words or pictures imply a defamatory meaning about plaintiff without so stating directly.

b. Opinion

At common law, a defamatory statement of opinion (if not privileged) was actionable the same as one of fact. This rule appears to have been modified by constitutional law interpretations. R.2d § 566.

If the defamatory opinion is based entirely on facts (a) known to those making and receiving the statement, or (b) stated as a predicate to the opinion, the First Amendment permits one to express one's opinion, however misguided or debatable, without defamation liability. "Under the First Amendment, there is no such thing as a false idea." *Gertz v. Robert Welch, Inc.*, 418 U.S. 323, 339 (1974).

On the other hand, if and to the extent that the opinion implies the allegation of undisclosed defamatory facts as the basis for the opinion it may be actionable. *Milkovich v. Lorain Journal Co.*, 497 U.S. 1 (1990).

c. Ridicule

Humorous writings, verses, cartoons, or caricatures which may be understood as making a statement about plaintiff are similarly protected, at least to the extent that they represent merely negative opinions not implying false facts. *Hustler Magazine v. Falwell*, 485 U.S. 46 (1988).

d. Verbal Abuse

Profanity and similar statements, directed at plaintiff in anger and obviously intended as mere vituperation or abuse, ordinarily cannot be taken literally and therefore are not defamatory.

e. Fabricated Quotation

To attribute a fabricated quotation to plaintiff may be defamatory.

B. Libel and Slander Distinguished

1. Libel Defined

Libel is the publication of defamatory matter by (1) written or printed words, or (2) embodiment in physical form (e.g., photos, cartoons, sculpture, film, videotape, sound recordings), or (3) any other form of communication that has potentially harmful characteristics comparable to those of written or printed words.

2. Slander Defined

Slander is the publication of defamatory matter by spoken words, transitory gestures, or other form of communication not amounting to a libel.

3. Relevant Factors

The relevant factors in distinguishing libel and slander are the area of dissemination, the deliberate and premeditated character of the publication, and the persistence or permanency of the publication.

C. Defamation Actionable Without Proof of Special Damages

1. Libel

In most jurisdictions, any libel is actionable per se, that is, without proof that plaintiff sustained any special harm or damage from the publication. Even if plaintiff cannot or does not prove actual damages, the trier of fact can infer harm sufficient to support an award of compensatory or nominal damages.

2. Libel Per Quod

In a minority of U.S. jurisdictions, a libel which is not defamatory on its face but requires reference to extrinsic facts to establish its defamatory meaning is not actionable without proof of special harm. This is sometimes called libel per quod.

3. Slander

Publication of a slander is not actionable without proof of special damages unless it defames plaintiff in one of four ways. If actionable without proof of special damages, it is called "slander per se"; if not, it is "slander per quod."

a. Criminal Conduct

It imputes to plaintiff conduct that constitutes a crime punishable by imprisonment or involving moral turpitude. R.2d § 571.

b. Communicable Disease

It imputes that plaintiff has a sexually transmitted disease or "other loathsome and communicable disease." R.2d § 572.

c. Business, Trade, Profession, or Office

It imputes to plaintiff conduct, characteristics or a condition that would adversely affect his fitness for the proper conduct of his business, trade, profession, or office. R.2d § 573.

d. Sexual Misconduct

It imputes serious sexual misconduct, regardless of gender. R.2d § 574.

4. Special Damages

In this context, special harm or damages refers to the loss of something having economic or pecuniary value resulting from the harm to plaintiff's reputation. It does not include plaintiff's emotional distress and resulting bodily harm, which may, however, be compensated if the defamation is otherwise actionable.

D. Publication

1. Definition

Publication is the communication of defamatory matter by defendant to someone other than plaintiff. R.2d § 577.

2. Fault

Even at common law (i.e., before *Gertz*), and today, defendant is not liable for unintended or accidental publication. The publication must have been intentional or the result of defendant's negligence.

3. Agent

In most jurisdictions, publication to defendant's agent is sufficient (but may be privileged). If dictated with the intent that it will be reduced to writing (a letter), it is libel. And defendant is liable for a publication by their agent where they directed or procured it.

4. Multiple Publications

Each of several communications to a third person by the same defendant is a separate publication. A single communication heard at the same time by two or more third persons is a single publication. One edition of a book or newspaper, or one radio or TV broadcast, one exhibition of a motion picture, or a similar aggregate publication is a single publication.

For each single publication, only one action can be maintained in which plaintiff must claim all damages resulting from that publication. This raises issues of venue, statute of limitations, and choice of law when the publication is received in more than one state.

5. Wills

Generally, an action will lie against defendant's estate for libelous matter published in their will after his death.

6. Liability of Republisher

One who repeats or otherwise republishes a defamation is subject to liability to the same extent as if he had originally published it. R.2d § 578.

Where a libel is published in a newspaper, magazine, or book, the author, editor, printer, publisher, and owner are all subject to liability as publisher. One who broadcasts defamatory matter by radio or TV is subject to the same liability as an original publisher (R.2d § 581(2)).

One who only delivers or transmits defamatory matter published by a third person, such as those who deliver newspapers or mail, is subject to liability only if they know or have reason to know of its defamatory character. This exception does not apply to broadcasters. R.2d § 581.

By federal law, information published on the Internet is treated as published only by the content provider and not by the internet service provider or one who merely provides the web site. See 47 U.S.C.A. § 230(c)(1).

7. Causation: Liability of Original Publisher for Republication

Defendant is liable for the republication of his defamatory statement by another if (a) the third person was privileged to repeat it, or (b) defendant authorized or intended the repetition, or (c) the repetition was reasonably foreseeable. Cf. R.2d §§ 576, 662A. Ordinarily, defendant is not liable for a repetition by plaintiff.

E. Fault

1. Common Law

At common law, defamation liability was strict. Defendant did not have to be aware of the falsity or defamatory character of the statement or even be negligent in ascertaining these things; nor need they have intended or foreseen any harm, or that the statement could be understood as referring to plaintiff. The only fault required was with respect to its publication. Defendant had to intentionally or negligently publish the matter.

2. First Amendment

The Supreme Court has held that the First Amendment to the U.S. Constitution imposes fault requirements, at least in the case of defamatory matter concerning public officials, public figures, or matters of public concern when defendant is exercising the freedom of the press protected by that amendment. These decisions have led some states to impose fault requirements as common law rules, even where not strictly required by constitutional law.

3. Public Official, Public Figure

Under *New York Times Co. v. Sullivan*, 376 U.S. 254 (1964), one who publishes a false and defamatory communication concerning a public official or a public figure with regard to their conduct, fitness, or role in that capacity is subject to liability only if defendant (a) knows that the statement is false and that it defames plaintiff, or (b) acts in reckless disregard of these matters. R.2d § 580A.

a. Public Official

A public official is a governmental employee who has (or appears to have) responsibility for or control over the conduct of governmental affairs, and may include even relatively low-ranking personnel, such as police officers. To receive the benefit of this special First Amendment protection, the defamatory statement must concern the official's fitness for or performance in the office.

b. Public Figure

A public figure is one who has achieved a degree of fame or notoriety, either generally or as to a particular public issue or controversy (e.g., candidates for public office, professional athletes). The voluntary nature of plaintiff's participation is a relevant factor. The statement must affect plaintiff in their public capacity.

c. Public Concern

Whether a matter is one of public concern depends on its content, form, and context.

d. Fault

The requisite fault is "actual malice" (sometimes described as "constitutional malice"). Here, malice does not have its literal meaning. "Actual malice" means nothing more than knowledge of the statement's false and defamatory character or a reckless disregard of these matters, as when a statement is published despite a high degree of awareness of its probable falsity, or with serious doubts as to its truth. Actual ill will need not be proved. The availability of time and opportunity to check the truth of the statement may be relevant. Proof of defendant's fault must be clear and convincing.

e. Private Communications

The cases that impose the foregoing fault requirement so far have involved public statements in the press, media and books. It remains to be seen whether these fault requirements apply to other forms of communication, though most jurisdictions do not distinguish between media and non-media cases in applying these rules.

4. Private Persons

Under *Gertz v. Robert Welch, Inc.*, 418 U.S. 323 (1974), one who publishes a false and defamatory communication concerning a private person, or concerning a public official or public figure with regard to a purely private matter (i.e., not affecting his conduct, fitness or role in their public capacity) is subject to liability only if defendant (a) knows that the statement is false and that it defames plaintiff, or (b) acts in reckless disregard of these matters, or (c) acts negligently in failing to ascertain them. R.2d § 580B.

a. Effect of *Gertz*

After *Gertz*, strict liability for defamation published in the press, media, and possibly books is unconstitutional, regardless of the status of plaintiff. However, the states are free to determine the degree of fault required for defamation actions by persons described above, so long as at least negligence is required.

b. Majority Rule

Most states have followed the *Gertz* criteria, so that in those jurisdictions all those persons described above need only prove that defendant was negligent in ascertaining the falsity and defamatory character of the statement.

c. Minority Rule

In some jurisdictions, if the defamation concerns a matter of general or public interest, even those persons described above are required to prove that defendant either (1) knew that the statement was false and that it defames plaintiff, or (2) acted in reckless disregard of these matters (i.e., same as for public officials and public figures).

d. Burden of Proof

Those persons described above must prove falsity and the requisite fault by a preponderance of the evidence.

F. Defenses to Actions for Defamation

1. Consent

Plaintiff's consent to the publication of defamatory matter concerning them is a complete defense. R.2d § 583. Defendant may be liable for a republication that results from plaintiff's honest inquiry or investigation to ascertain the existence, source, content, or meaning of the defamatory publication. R.2d § 584.

Defendant may be liable for a republication that results from plaintiff's honest inquiry or investigation to ascertain the existence, source, content, or meaning of the defamatory publication. R.2d § 584.

2. Absolute Privileges

a. Judicial Proceedings

While performing their functions in judicial proceedings, judges and judicial officers, attorneys, parties, witnesses, and jurors are absolutely privileged to publish defamatory matter that has some relation to the proceeding. R.2d §§ 585–589.

b. Legislative Proceedings

A member of Congress or a state or local legislative body is absolutely privileged to publish defamatory matter in the performance of his legislative functions. A witness is absolutely privileged to publish defamatory matter as part of a legislative proceeding in which he is testifying or in communications preliminary to the proceeding, if the matter has some relation to the proceeding. R.2d §§ 590, 590A.

c. Executive and Administrative Officers

An executive or administrative officer of the U.S., or a governor or other superior executive officer of a state, is absolutely privileged to publish defamatory matter in communications made in the performance of their official duties. R.2d § 591.

d. Spousal Privilege

Spouses are absolutely privileged to publish defamatory matter to the other. R.2d § 592.

e. Publication Required by Law

One who is required by law to publish defamatory matter is absolutely privileged to publish it, such as a newspaper required to publish an official notice. R.2d § 592A.

3. Conditional or Qualified Privileges

a. In General

At common law, certain defamatory communications are conditionally or qualifiedly privileged, so that defendant is not liable provided defendant meets all the conditions or qualifications. R.2d § 593. As to these privileges, the chief limitation is that defendant must (1) believe their statement to be true, and (2) (a) in some jurisdictions, have reasonable grounds for believing it to be true, or (b) in other jurisdictions, not have acted recklessly in failing to ascertain its truth or falsity. But the *N.Y. Times* and *Gertz* cases, when applicable, require plaintiff to prove that defendant acted either recklessly or negligently in ascertaining the truth or falsity of the statement. Thus, if and to the extent that *N.Y. Times* and *Gertz* apply, the existence of a conditional privilege is partly or totally irrelevant. Therefore, the following privileges apply only when and to the extent that they are not superseded by the *N.Y. Times* or *Gertz* rules.

b. Protection of the Publisher's Interest

i. Rule

Defendant's defamatory communication is conditionally privileged when the circumstances cause defendant to correctly or reasonably believe that (1) the information affects a sufficiently important interest of defendant, and (2) the information will be of service to the recipient in the lawful protection of that interest. R.2d § 594.

ii. Value of Defendant's Interest

Interests of defendant worthy of protection include, for example, (a) any lawful business or pecuniary interest, *other than* their interest in competition for prospective advantage (e.g., defamation to obtain customers), (b) their bodily security, (c) their present interest in land, chattels, or intangible property, (d) their family, and (e) their own reputation. In each case, the value of defendant's interest is to be balanced against the harm to plaintiff's reputation if the defamatory matter is false.

c. Protection of Interest of Recipient or Third Person

i. Rule

Defendant's defamatory communication is conditionally privileged when the circumstances cause defendant to correctly or reasonably believe that (1) the information affects a sufficiently important interest of the recipient or a third person, and (2) the recipient is one to whom (a) defendant is under a legal duty to publish it or (b) its publication is otherwise within generally accepted standards of decent conduct. R.2d § 595.

ii. Decent Conduct

Important factors in determining whether the publication is within generally accepted standards of decent conduct include whether (a) it is in response to a request, rather than volunteered by defendant, or (b) a family or other relationship exists between the parties. R.2d § 595.

iii. Examples

Fiduciaries discharging their duties; reports to proper authorities that defendant believes plaintiff is about to commit a crime against another; communications among members of a trade association; reports to an employer about the character or conduct of a present or prospective employee.

d. Protection of Common Interest

Defendant's defamatory communication is conditionally privileged when the circumstances cause defendant to correctly or reasonably believe that another who shares a common interest is entitled to know it. R.2d § 596.

***Examples*:** Business partners and associates in a business enterprise exchanging information about employees and others. Co-owners of real or personal property, concerning their common interest in that property. Members of religious, fraternal, and charitable organizations discussing the qualifications of officers, other or prospective members, and association activities.

e. Family Relationships

Defendant's defamatory communication is conditionally privileged when the circumstances cause defendant to correctly or reasonably believe that: (1) the recipient's knowledge will help protect the well-being of a member of defendant's immediate family; or (2) the recipient's knowledge will help protect the well-being of a member of the immediate family of the recipient or a third person, and the recipient has requested the information or is a person to whom its communication is otherwise within generally accepted standards of decent conduct. R.2d § 597.

f. Public Interest

Defendant's defamatory communication is conditionally privileged when the circumstances cause defendant to correctly or reasonably believe that a sufficiently important public interest requires its communication to a public officer or other person who is authorized or privileged to act if it is true. R.2d § 598.

Examples: Reporting a crime or anticipated crime (unless absolutely privileged, see judicial proceedings); reporting misconduct or incompetence by a public official or employee; petitions for legislative action.

g. Inferior State Officers

Lower-level state or local government employees who are not entitled to an absolute privilege have a conditional privilege for communications required or permitted in the performance of their duties. R.2d § 598A.

h. "Abuse" (Loss) of the Privilege

i. Knowledge, Recklessness, or Negligence Concerning Falsity

Negligence

Prior to *Gertz,* in some jurisdictions a conditional privilege was lost if defendant did not honestly believe the truth of his statement, or if he did not have "reasonable grounds" to believe in its truth. It remains to be seen whether this rule has any purpose after *Gertz.*

Recklessness

Other jurisdictions have held that a conditional privilege is lost only if defendant knows that the statement is false or acts in "reckless disregard" as to its truth or falsity. Where *Gertz* or *N.Y. Times* applies, any conditional privilege will be irrelevant. R.2d § 600 adopts this version of the rule.

ii. Rumor

Defendant may be privileged to publish a defamatory rumor or suspicion, even though defendant believes or knows that it is untrue, provided: (a) they state the defamatory matter as a rumor or suspicion and not as a fact; and (b) the publication is reasonable, considering the relation of the parties, the importance of the interests affected, and the harm likely to be done. R.2d § 602.

iii. Purpose

There is no conditional privilege unless defendant publishes the defamatory matter for the purpose of protecting the interest which gives rise to the privilege, R.2d § 603, and reasonably believes the publication to be necessary for that purpose, R.2d § 605.

iv. Excessive Publication

There is no conditional privilege to the extent that defendant knowingly publishes the defamatory matter to a person outside its scope, unless defendant reasonably believes that such publication is a proper means of communicating it to a proper person. R.2d § 604.

v. Unprivileged Matter

The privilege is lost to the extent that defendant adds unprivileged matter to the communication. If not severable, the entire privilege is lost. R.2d § 605A.

i. Fair Comment on Matters of Public Concern

At common law, there was a qualified privilege for what was called "fair comment" (i.e., publicly expressing one's opinion) on matters of public concern. This former privilege appears to have been subsumed under the constitutional right to express such opinions without defamation liability. See R.2d § 566.

4. Special Types of Privilege

a. Report of Official Proceeding or Public Meeting

Defendant is privileged to publish defamatory matter in a report of an official action or proceeding or of a meeting open to the public that deals with a matter of public concern, provided the report is accurate or a fair abridgment of the occurrence reported. R.2d § 611. Although the Restatement omits this limitation, the privilege probably does not extend to matter published solely for the purpose of harming the person defamed. As a matter of constitutional law, as applied to the press and news media, plaintiff must also establish defendant's fault (as defined in *N.Y. Times* and *Gertz*) in failing to make a fair and accurate report.

b. Providing Means of Publication

One who provides a means of publication of defamatory matter published by another is privileged to do so if the other is privileged to publish it. R.2d § 612(1). However, internet service providers are probably not liable for mere transmission of the matter regardless of the privilege.

G. Damages

1. Types Recoverable

Damages which may be recoverable in a defamation action include (a) nominal damages, (b) general (or "presumed") damages for harm to reputation, (c) damages for proved special harm caused by the harm to plaintiff's reputation, (d) damages for emotional distress and resulting bodily harm, and (e) punitive damages.

2. Nominal Damages

One who is liable for a libel or slander actionable per se is liable for at least nominal damages. R.2d § 620.

3. General Damages

a. Rule

At common law, once defendant's liability was established, the jury could award plaintiff general damages for harm to their reputation, whether plaintiff proved actual harm or not. In most jurisdictions these are known as "presumed" damages. In the absence of such proof, the jury could compensate plaintiff for the harm to their reputation that normally would be assumed to flow from a defamatory publication of the nature involved. However, *Gertz* holds that the First Amendment prohibits the states from permitting recovery for presumed damages unless plaintiff proves defendant's knowledge of the defamation's falsity or their reckless disregard for its truth; otherwise, proof of actual harm is required. "Actual harm" is not limited to pecuniary loss; it includes such intangibles as harm to plaintiff's reputation and emotional distress. No specific dollar value of such harm need be shown.

b. Exception

In *Dun & Bradstreet, Inc. v. Greenmoss Builders, Inc.*, 472 U.S. 749 (1985), the Supreme Court held that a state could award presumed damages when plaintiff was a private figure and the speech did not involve any issue of public interest or concern.

4. Special Damages

Special damages (i.e., economic or pecuniary loss) resulting from the defamation may always be recovered. In the case of slander per quod (and libel per quod in some jurisdictions), such damages are a prerequisite to liability. R.2d § 622.

5. Emotional Distress and Bodily Harm

Once defendant's liability is established, damages for emotional distress and resulting bodily harm are recoverable. R.2d § 623.

6. Punitive Damages

The common law generally allows punitive damages in a defamation action when defendant's conduct involves "actual malice," which usually means an intent to harm plaintiff or a reckless disregard of whether they will be harmed. In addition, the constitution prohibits punitive damages, at least against the press and media defendants, unless plaintiff proves defendant's knowledge of the statement's falsity or their reckless disregard for its truth.

7. Mitigation

By statute in some jurisdictions and common law in most others, a retraction by defendant is not a complete defense, but may be considered in mitigation of plaintiff's damages. Other mitigating circumstances may also be considered.

8. Right of Reply

Statutes requiring a newspaper to publish plaintiff's reply to a defamatory statement previously printed in it are unconstitutional.

H. Review Questions

[Answers Provided in Appendix A]

1. Defendant defames a neighbor at a neighborhood barbecue by falsely alleging that the neighbor had an extramarital affair. Defendant retracts this defamatory statement later in the party. Does the neighbor have a claim for defamation against Defendant?

2. Defendant dictates a letter containing defamatory statements about Plaintiff to their secretary. Before mailing the letter, they change their mind and destroy the letter. Advise Defendant whether they face any liability. Use an IRAC format to structure your answer.

3. Plaintiff applies to Employer for a job and puts down Defendant as a reference. As a result, Employer calls Defendant and asks him about Plaintiff. Defendant states that Plaintiff is a liar, a thief, and is generally incompetent. Advise Plaintiff of the most likely outcome in their suit against Defendant. Use an IRAC format to structure your answer.

4. While testifying as a witness in court Defendant falsely and gratuitously refers to their neighbor, who is not in court, who is not a witness, and who is not a party to the suit, as a loud, obnoxious, stupid, fool whose rantings disturb the neighborhood. Which of the following is accurate?

   a. Plaintiff cannot recover damages from Defendant because the statement was made in court.

   b. Plaintiff cannot recover damages because they did not themself hear the statement.

   c. Plaintiff cannot recover damages unless they can show special damages because this is not a slander per se.

d. Plaintiff cannot recover under the *Gertz* rule unless he shows that Defendant was at least negligent.

III. Privacy

A. Introduction

The tort action for invasion of privacy did not develop until the 20th century, stimulated by an 1890 Harvard Law Review article by Samuel Warren and Louis Brandeis. At present, the tort encompasses four distinct wrongs (R.2d § 652A):

1. Appropriation of one's name or likeness;
2. Intrusion upon another's privacy or private affairs;
3. Public disclosure of private facts about plaintiff; and
4. Placing plaintiff in a false light in the public eye.

Other forms (or variations on these forms) may develop in the future; these categories are not limitations.

The action for invasion of privacy is recognized in most jurisdictions (but not in all forms). In some it is affected by statute.

B. Appropriation

1. Rule

Defendant is subject to liability for appropriating the name or likeness of plaintiff for their own use or benefit. R.2d § 652C. This is often called the "right of publicity," and primarily protects the right to control the commercial value of one's identity.

***Example*:** Without permission, defendant uses the name and photograph of plaintiff, a famous baseball player, in an advertisement of defendant's cereal.

2. Commercial Use

Unless otherwise required by statute, the use need not be for business or commercial purposes. Many states, however, do impose a business or commercial purpose requirement. Commercial uses are mainly uses associated with sales. An advertisement is a commercial use (feature stories, biographies, news, and creative works are not a commercial use). Plaintiff's identity may be used in noncommercial works, both because the right of publicity does not extend to such uses and because of constitutional free speech rights.

3. Appropriation

Plaintiff must prove that defendant used plaintiff's name or identity for the purpose of taking advantage of plaintiff's reputation, prestige, or other value associated with plaintiff's name or likeness. Merely adopting a name identical to that of another, or using another's name in a communication or publication, is not an invasion of privacy unless the purpose is to appropriate the benefit of its commercial value.

C. Intrusion

1. Rule

Defendant is subject to liability for intrusion (physical or other) upon the solitude, seclusion, or private life and affairs of another, provided the intrusion would be highly offensive to a reasonable person. R.2d § 652B.

2. Form

The forms of intrusion are varied—unpermitted entry into plaintiff's home or hospital room; an illegal search of plaintiff's person or property; tapping plaintiff's telephone; using mechanical aids to observe plaintiff's private activities in his home; opening plaintiff's personal mail; hacking plaintiff's email account; and persistent and unwanted communications or close physical presence. Whether recording a conversation between plaintiff and defendant (or plaintiff and others) under various circumstances is an unlawful intrusion may depend on state eavesdropping laws.

3. Publication

The tort is complete when the intrusion occurs. No publication or publicity of the information is required.

4. Private Matters

The intrusion must be into what is, and is entitled to remain, private. Photographing or watching plaintiff in a public place, or inspecting or copying nonprivate records, is not actionable.

5. Substantial Interference

The intrusion must be highly offensive to the ordinary person, resulting from conduct to which the reasonable person would strongly object.

6. Government Intrusion

The courts are beginning to recognize a constitutional right of privacy, to be free from excessive or unreasonable governmental intrusion.

D. Public Disclosure of Private Facts

1. Rule

Defendant is subject to liability for giving publicity to some private fact about plaintiff, provided the fact publicized would be highly offensive to a reasonable person and is not a matter of legitimate public concern. R.2d § 652D.

2. Publicity

The information about plaintiff need not be "published." It is sufficient if it is disclosed so as to be likely to become public knowledge.

3. Private Facts

In this case, the facts disclosed are true. Thus, there is no liability for facts which are already known by, or available to, the public. The facts must be intimate or at least private details of plaintiff's private life, the disclosure of which would be embarrassing, humiliating or offensive. And plaintiff's right to keep these facts private is balanced against the legitimate interest of the public. Thus, there are fewer "private" facts of the famous and those in high positions.

4. Legitimate Public Concern or Interest

a. Constitutional Limitations

The First Amendment freedoms of the press and speech are a further limitation of this tort, and permit, to an extent yet to be fully developed, publication of private facts which are matters of legitimate public concern or interest—i.e., "news."

b. Public Figures

Persons who have voluntarily become public figures, and even those involuntarily in the public eye by being part of a newsworthy event, cannot complain of the publication of facts, otherwise private, which are of legitimate public concern or interest in connection with that person, activity, or event. This legitimate concern may even extend to the family and close friends of the public figure, and to some facts about persons who were public figures at some time in the past.

E. False Light in the Public Eye

1. Rule

Defendant is subject to liability for giving publicity to a matter which places plaintiff before the public in a false light, provided (a) the false light would be highly offensive to a reasonable person, and (b) Defendant had knowledge of the falsity of the matter and the false light it created, or acted in reckless disregard of these matters. R.2d § 652E.

2. Relation to Defamation

In this case, the information communicated about plaintiff is false. Thus, if it is also defamatory, an action for libel or slander may be an alternative remedy. However, it is not necessary to this action that plaintiff be defamed. It is enough that they have given unreasonable and highly objectionable publicity that attributes to their characteristics, conduct, or beliefs that are false.

Example: A photograph of plaintiff, an honest taxi driver, is used to illustrate a newspaper article on the practices of taxi drivers who cheat the public. Plaintiff has an action for both libel and invasion of privacy.

Because it largely overlaps defamation claims, some courts have rejected false light claims.

3. Highly Offensive

The matter must be highly offensive to a reasonable person. Relatively minor inaccuracies or fictions in an otherwise accurate and favorable story about plaintiff are not actionable.

4. Constitutional Limitations

Time, Inc. v. Hill, 385 U.S. 374 (1974) extended the *N.Y. Times* rule to this type of invasion of privacy action, requiring plaintiff to prove by clear and convincing evidence that defendant knew of the statement's falsity or acted in reckless disregard of its truth or falsity. Whether the *Gertz* case has modified this rule (to include negligence in the case of private individuals), and the extent to which this limitation applies to others than the press and media, has yet to be decided.

F. Privileges

To the extent applicable, the absolute, conditional and special privileges to publish defamatory matter are also available in invasion of privacy cases. R.2d §§ 652F, 652G.

G. Damages

In an action for invasion of privacy, plaintiff can recover damages for: (1) harm to the interest in privacy; (2) mental distress, if of a kind that normally results from such an invasion; and (3) special damages.

H. Persons Who May Sue

Unless otherwise provided by statute, and except for appropriation, an action for invasion of privacy can be maintained only by a living individual whose privacy is invaded. R.2d § 652I. Whether an action survives plaintiff's death depends on the local survival statute.

I. Review Questions

[Answers Provided in Appendix A]

1. Patrice, 32-years-old, lives in Illinois with her spouse and two children. When she was 18, she lived briefly in Minnesota where she was arrested several times for petty theft and possession of controlled substances. She was never convicted of any of these offenses and has never been arrested for anything else. She never told anyone about her arrests in Minnesota and no one else knew until Denny came upon a reference to the arrests in an old newspaper. He reproduced the newspaper page and sent copies to Patrice's spouse, children, and neighbors. Can Patrice recover damages from Denny for invasion of her privacy?
2. Sarah is a freelance photographer who sells her photos to news outlets. Sarah constantly follows Diego on public streets. Diego is an A-list celebrity. Sarah photographs his movements on sidewalks, roads, and outside his home. Can Diego recover damages from Sarah for invasion of his privacy?
3. The same facts as Question 2, but Sarah, acting without Diego's permission, furnishes pictures of Diego to tourists and other persons who will buy them as souvenirs and curios. Is Sarah liable to Diego for appropriation of his likeness?

Part Eleven

Vicarious Liability

■ ANALYSIS

I. Introduction

A. General Rule

A person who, while acting on behalf of another, commits a tortious act and thus subjects themselves to tort liability may also thereby subject the person on whose behalf they are acting to tort liability. The latter person may be vicariously liable to the plaintiff.

B. Relationships Giving Rise to Vicarious Liability

Three types of relationships give rise to vicarious liability: (1) employer-employee (the archaic phrase "master-servant" is sometimes still used to reference this relationship); (2) principal-agent; and (3) employer-independent contractor. For purposes of tort law, there is little distinction between the liability rules governing employer-employee and principal-agent relationships. However, the vicarious liability of one who employs an independent contractor is significantly different.

II. Employers and Employees

A. Vicarious Liability

If, at the time of their negligent or reckless act, the employee-tortfeasor acted in the scope of their employment, then their employer is vicariously liable to the plaintiff for their employee's tort. This principle of vicarious liability in the context of employer-employee relationships is sometimes still referred to by the Latin phrase *respondeat superior*.

B. Defining an Employee

An employee is an agent whose principal controls or has the right to control the manner and means of the agent's work performance. Sometimes the employer-employee relationship is not clear, as this type of work can range from the formal (a full-time salaried hire at a company) to the informal (a person who agrees to dog-sit a friend's dog). R.3d of Agency § 7.07(3)(a) and cmt. *f*.

Typically, agency law is used to determine whether the actor is the employee of another. According to the Restatement (Second) of Agency § 220(2), in determining whether one acting for another is an employee or an independent contractor, the following factors, among others, are considered:

1. the extent of control which the principal may exercise over the details of the work in their agreement;
2. whether the person doing the work is engaged in a distinct occupation or business;
3. whether that type of occupation, in the locality, is usually done under the direction of an employer or by a specialist without supervision;
4. the skill required in the particular occupation;
5. whether the employer or the workman supplies the instrumentalities, tools, and workplace for the person doing the work;
6. the length of time for which the person is employed;
7. the method of payment, whether by the time or by the job;

8. whether the work is a part of the regular business of the employer;
9. whether the parties believe they are creating the relationship of employer and employee; and
10. whether the principal is or is not in business.

One can be an employee even without payment or the promise of payment for their services (for example, an unpaid intern), provided the other incidents of the relationship are sufficient. R.3d of Agency § 7.07(3)(b).

C. Scope of Employment

Whether the employee was acting in the scope of their employment is a question of fact, which depends upon:

(a) the employee's job description and assigned duties,

(b) the time, place and purpose of the employee's act,

(c) the similarity of their conduct to the things they were hired to do, or which are commonly done by such employees, and

(4) the foreseeability of their act. See R.2d of Agency §§ 228–229.

The Restatement (Third) of Agency § 7.07 adopts a simpler version. It provides that "[a]n employee acts within the scope of employment when performing work assigned by the employer or engaging in a course of conduct subject to the employer's control. An employee's act is not within the scope of employment when it occurs within an independent course of conduct not intended by the employee to serve any purpose of the employer."

The fact that the employee disregarded the employer's instructions or work rules does not necessarily, in and of itself, remove the employee from the scope of his employment. The test is whether, at the relevant time, the employee was performing a service in furtherance of the employer's business, not whether it was done in exact observance of the detail prescribed by the employer.

D. Employees in Transit

Under the "going-and-coming" rule, an employee is normally outside the scope of their employment when in transit to and from work. However, where the trip involves some incidental benefit to the employer, not common to commuting trips by ordinary workers, or where the employee is traveling away from home on the employer's business, the employee may be found within the scope of their employment during the trip. This may include attending to personal matters or socializing if somehow related to the purpose of the trip. It may also include travel time where the employee is being reimbursed for their travel expenses, at least when the employee at the time is traveling within the scope of the employer's expectations. Nevertheless, some courts hold that, to find the employee was within the scope of their employment, the employee must have received compensation for travel time at the time of the incident.

E. Frolic and Detour

An employee who is in transit during working hours on the employer's business, such as traveling from one job site to another, is still within the scope of employment if they make a minor or trivial deviation from the assigned travel for personal reasons (a "detour"). However, if the employee makes a substantial deviation, in time or space, from the expected route (a "frolic"), they may be found outside the scope of employment during that deviation. See R.3d of Agency § 7.07 cmt. *e.*

An employee on a "frolic"—and therefore outside the scope of employment—reenters the employment when they have once again started performing assigned work and taken actions incidental to it. See R.3d of Agency § 7.07 cmt. *e.*

F. Intentional Torts

Usually, an employer is not vicariously liable for the intentional torts of their employees. However, an employer may be vicariously liable for their employee's intentional torts committed in the scope of employment and in furtherance of the employer's business, at least if the employee's act was foreseeable. See R.3d of Agency § 7.07 cmt. *c.* And where there is some special relationship between the employer and the plaintiff such that the employer owes the plaintiff a duty of protection, the employer is subject to vicarious liability for their employee's intentional torts, even if committed for personal reasons.

Statutory and other special relationships may also expand liability for acts that might otherwise be outside the scope of employment, such as assisted living facility employees, scout leaders, priests, police officers, or daycare employees.

G. Employer's Liability

An employer may be directly (not vicariously) liable for torts committed by their employee based upon the employer's own negligence or other conduct. Thus, the employer may have been negligent in selecting, hiring, instructing, or supervising the employee; or the employer may have commanded, authorized, or ratified the employee's tortious act.

H. Partnerships, Joint Ventures

Partners and joint venturers acting in the scope of the business subject the other partners and joint venturers to vicarious tort liability to third persons just as if they were employees.

All members of a joint enterprise are jointly and severally liable to third persons injured by the tort of any member when engaged in the enterprise.

I. Employee's Liability

Even though the employer may be vicariously or otherwise liable for the tort of the employee, the employee (or contractor) is also subject to liability. If the employer is held vicariously liable, the employer may have a claim for indemnity from the employee.

J. Concert of Action

All who expressly or impliedly agree to jointly participate in tortious conduct are jointly and severally liable to third persons injured by any of the participants.

K. Independent Contractors

1. General Rule

An employer is not vicariously liable for physical harm caused by the tortious conduct of his independent contractor or their contractor's employees. R.2d § 409; R.3d Liability for Physical & Emotional Harm § 57.

An independent contractor is a person who contracts with another to do something for them but who is not controlled by the other nor subject to the other's right to control with respect to their physical conduct in the performance of the undertaking. R.2d of Agency § 2(3).

The Restatement (Third) of Agency disdains use of the term "independent contractor" (R.3d of Agency § 1.01 cmt. *c*), preferring to use only agency concepts. But it is doubtful that the courts (or lawyers!) will abandon the independent contractor category and rules, and the Restatement (Third) of Torts continues this tradition. R.3d Liability for Physical & Emotional Harm §§ 55–65.

2. Exception: Employer's Own Negligence

a. Negligent Selection, Retention

An employer must exercise reasonable care to select a reasonably competent, experienced, careful, and properly equipped contractor, and is subject to liability for physical harm resulting from their failure to do so. R.2d § 411; R.3d Liability for Physical & Emotional Harm § 55 and cmt. *a*.

b. Negligent Instruction

An employer is subject to liability for the negligence of an independent contractor acting in accordance with the employer's instructions. R.2d § 410; R.3d Liability for Physical & Emotional Harm § 55 and cmt. *a*.

c. Failure to Inspect Completed Work

An employer has a duty to inspect their contractor's completed work, at least where they have a duty to third persons to maintain the land or chattels for their protection. R.2d § 412; R.3d Liability for Physical & Emotional Harm § 55 and cmt. *a*.

d. Failure to Require Precautions

If the work will create a foreseeable danger to third persons, the employer must require (in the contract or otherwise) that appropriate precautions be taken for their safety. R.2d 413, 414A; R.3d Liability for Physical & Emotional Harm § 55 and cmt. *a*.

e. Retained Supervision and Control

To the extent that the employer retains or exercises supervision or control over the work of the contractor, they must do so with reasonable care. R.2d § 414; R.3d Liability for Physical & Emotional Harm § 56(b).

f. Duty as Possessor of Land

A possessor of land held open to the public must exercise reasonable care to protect that public from unreasonably dangerous conditions or activities of an independent contractor on the land. R.2d § 415; R.3d Liability for Physical & Emotional Harm § 55 and cmt. *a*.

3. Exception: Nondelegable Duties

Where the safe performance of some duty is of sufficient importance to the community, an employer is vicariously liable for the negligence of their independent contractor in performing that duty which results in physical harm. In other words, these duties are personal to the defendant and are not "delegable" to an independent contractor so as to relieve the defendant of tort liability if they are negligently performed. Examples include:

a. Work done in a public place (R.2d § 417; R.3d Liability for Physical & Emotional Harm § 64);

b. Construction or maintenance of public highways or other governmental premises held open to the public (R.2d § 418; R.3d Liability for Physical & Emotional Harm § 64);

c. The various duties owed by the possessor or lessor land to lessees and visitors (R.2d §§ 419–421, 425; R.3d Liability for Physical & Emotional Harm § 62);

d. Construction, repair, or other work on the possessor's land or a structure on the land, if he has possession during the work or after he has resumed possession of the land upon its completion (R.2d § 422; R.3d Liability for Physical & Emotional Harm § 62);

e. Activities involving a trespass, nuisance, or withdrawal of lateral or subjacent support (R.3d Liability for Physical & Emotional Harm § 61);

f. The duty of the lessor or bailor of a chattel, or one furnishing a chattel for their own business purposes (e.g., an employer furnishing tools to their employees) (R.2d § 425; R.3d Liability for Physical & Emotional Harm § 62);

g. Making or repair of instrumentalities used in highly or abnormally dangerous activities (R.2d § 423, 427A; R.3d Liability for Physical & Emotional Harm §§ 59–60);

h. Precautions required by statute or regulation (R.2d § 424; R.3d Liability for Physical & Emotional Harm § 63);

i. Work done pursuant to the employer's franchise (R.2d § 428; R.3d Liability for Physical & Emotional Harm § 64); and

j. Work given to the employer in reliance upon the employer doing the work himself (R.2d § 429; R.3d Liability for Physical & Emotional Harm § 65).

4. Exception: Inherently Dangerous Work

When the contracted work involves a special danger to others which the employer knows or has reason to know is inherent in, or normal to, the work, or which is contemplated at the time of the contract, the employer is vicariously liable for physical harm caused by the independent contractor's failure to take reasonable precautions against such danger. R.2d 416, 427; R.3d Liability for Physical & Emotional Harm § 59. For example, this exception would apply to an independent contractor hired to transport gasoline.

L. Apparent Agency

If a principal creates the appearance that someone is their agent or employee, they are not permitted to deny the agency if a third party, who does not know otherwise, reasonably relies on the apparent agency. There is some difference among the authorities as to the meaning of "reliance." Some courts do not require reliance at all, just that the defendant-employer created the appearance that the person providing the service was their agent. See R.3d Liability for Physical & Emotional Harm § 65.

III. Review Questions

[Answers Provided in Appendix A]

1. Restaurant Owner owned a top-rated restaurant and employed Host as its on-site manager. One day, Host greeted Diner at the restaurant. After Diner went to the restroom to wash their hands, Host intercepted Diner in the hallway of the restaurant, grabbed Diner's face, and kissed Diner on the mouth. Diner considered this to be unwelcome touching.

   If Diner brings a lawsuit against Restaurant Owner, can Restaurant Owner be held liable for Host's conduct toward Diner?

   a. Restaurant Owner may be liable for Host's conduct toward Diner because Restaurant Owner is Host's employer.

   b. Restaurant Owner cannot be liable because an employer cannot be subject to liability for the intentional torts of its employees.

   c. Restaurant Owner may be liable for Host's conduct because Host's conduct was foreseeable.

   d. Restaurant Owner cannot be liable because Hosts and Diners have a special relationship.

2. Summer Camp Organization ran a summer camp for children. Summer Camp Organization employed Camp Counselor to help run the summer camp. When Summer Camp Organization hired Camp Counselor, there was nothing raising concern in Camp Counselor's background check, and Camp Counselor reasonably believed that there were no risks associated with Camp Counselor performing the job. One day, during the summer camp, Camp Counselor became annoyed with one Child and pinched Child on the arm, injuring Child.

   If Child's Parents bring a lawsuit against Summer Camp Organization on behalf of Child, can Summer Camp Organization be held liable for Camp Counselor's conduct toward Child?

   a. Summer Camp Organization may be liable for Camp Counselor's conduct toward Child because Summer Camp Organization is Camp Counselor's employer.

   b. Summer Camp Organization cannot be liable because an employer cannot be subject to liability for the intentional torts of its employees.

   c. Summer Camp Organization may be liable for Camp Counselor's conduct because Camp Counselor's conduct was foreseeable.

   d. Summer Camp Organization may be liable because Summer Camp Organization has a special relationship with children who participate in their programs and therefore owe children-participants a duty of protection.

3. Aero Airlines learned that a passenger infected with the highly contagious B1C2 virus traveled on its flight. Aero Airlines contracted with Spotless Cleaners, Inc. (SCI) to sanitize and clean the plane in which the infected passenger flew. SCI was indisputably negligent in its clean-up efforts causing Polly Passenger to further contract the virus on a subsequent flight. Polly sued Aero Airlines. Which of the following is the most likely outcome in this suit?

   a. Aero Airlines is not liable because it hired an independent contractor.

   b. Aero Airlines is not liable because of corporate immunity.

   c. Aero Airlines is liable because the independent contractor was negligent.

   d. Aero Airlines is liable because of the non-delegable duty doctrine.

Part Twelve

Joint Tortfeasors

■ ANALYSIS

I. Apportionment Among Joint Tortfeasors

(Dobbs §§ 385–390; R.2d § 876; R.3d Apportionment of Liability, Topics 2–3, 5)

Many cases yield the division of liability among various actors. This broader inquiry can be a causal apportionment by which a factfinder concludes that one actor was responsible for a certain percentage of the harm and another actor for the remainder. Apportionment broadly can occur across the 'v.' between plaintiff and defendant(s) or on the same side of the 'v.' among multiple defendants. This section considers apportionment among joint tortfeasors specifically. This is a particularly noteworthy topic when a harm simply cannot be divided among tortfeasors and the law might allow one party to be held to pay the full damage award.

II. Joint and Several Liability

A. Joint and Several Liability Defined

There is a jurisdictional split between several liability, joint and several liability, and hybrid approaches. In joint and several liability jurisdictions, when two or more tortfeasors are responsible for the same harm to the plaintiff, all whose tortious conduct is found to be a legal and factual cause of that harm are *jointly* and *severally* liable for all of plaintiff's recoverable damages. The plaintiff may sue one, some, or all who are liable. The plaintiff may obtain judgements for the full amount of recoverable damages and may collect that judgement from one or any combination of those found liable.

As long as the judgment is not satisfied in full, plaintiff can continue to bring further suits or collection proceedings. Pure joint and several liability is the minority rule today. Joint and several liability has the effect of offering the plaintiff multiple sources of funds for recovery, but the plaintiff will never recover more than one satisfaction of the judgment.

B. Bases for Joint and Several Liability

There are three factual scenarios that trigger joint and several liability.

1. Acting in Concert

Persons acting in concert are liable for harm to a plaintiff if they

(a) committed the tortious act pursuant to a common plan or design,

(b) know the other's conduct constituted a breach of duty and gave substantial aid or encouragement, or

(c) gave substantial aid to the other to accomplish the tortious result and their own conduct, when separately considered, constituted a breach of duty to the plaintiff. R.2d § 876.

When persons are liable because they acted in concert, all persons are jointly and severally liable to the plaintiff for the resulting harm. R.3d Apportionment of Liability § 15.

Example: Defendants 1 and 2 drag race their respective cars down a residential street. Defendant 1 negligently skids out of control and strikes Plaintiff's vehicle. Defendant 2 comes to a careful stop and makes no contact with Plaintiff's vehicle. Defendant 2 is fully liable to Plaintiff as a joint tortfeasor, even though their conduct did not directly cause the Plaintiff's injury, because Defendant 2 acted in concert with Defendant 1.

2. Indivisible Injury

Joint and several liability can also apply when two negligent acts combine to create one indivisible injury. Here, each tortfeasor is liable for the entire judgment (not to exceed a single satisfaction).

3. Vicarious Liability

If Defendant 1's liability is entirely vicarious, or imputed, based on the tortious conduct of Defendant 2, Defendant 1 is jointly and severally liable for whatever share of the fault is assigned to Defendant 2. In other words, Defendant 1 and Defendant 2 are jointly responsible for a single share. If Defendant 1 pays that share to Plaintiff, Defendant 1 ordinarily has a right to obtain indemnity from Defendant 2. R.3d Apportionment of Liability § 13.

C. Joint and Several Liability Triggers a Right to Contribution

1. Common Law Rule—No Right to Contribution

When a plaintiff obtains a judgment against two or more tortfeasors in a joint and several liability jurisdiction, that plaintiff can collect that full judgment from any one defendant, all, or any combination of defendants. The common law rule in most jurisdictions was that the defendant who paid the plaintiff more than their proportionate share of the judgment, was not entitled to obtain contribution from the other joint tortfeasors. The "no contribution" rule originally applied only to intentional torts, but most U.S. jurisdictions extended it to negligence and strict liability actions. This rule was fundamentally unfair to the defendant where the other defendants were available and economically viable.

2. Modern Status—Contribution Applies to Joint and Several Liability

Contribution among joint tortfeasors is now the rule in joint and several liability jurisdictions. There is no right to contribution by or against a party who is only severally liable because the precondition of paying more than their proportionate share cannot occur.

3. Amount of Contribution

In most jurisdictions, the damages are allocated among the joint tortfeasors in proportion to their relative fault as determined by the trier of fact, and those shares determine contribution liability. R.3d Apportionment of Liability § 23. In a few jurisdictions, damages are divided pro rata. A defendant (having made a successful contribution claim against other tortfeasors) who then pays a plaintiff more than the defendant's proportional share of the judgment has a right to recover the excess amount over their proportional share from the other contribution defendants.

Example: Plaintiff sues Defendants 1, 2, and 3 for an indivisible injury sustained in an automobile accident. Plaintiff obtains a judgment against Defendant 1, Defendant 2, and Defendant 3 whereby they are jointly and severally liable to Plaintiff for $100,000. The factfinder assigns responsibility to Defendant 1 (50%), Defendant 2 (30%), and Defendant 3 (20%). Defendant 1 pays Plaintiff the entire judgment. Defendant 1 may recover contribution from Defendant 2, Defendant 3, or both, for a total of $50,000 ($100,000 × .50), because Defendant 1's satisfaction of the judgment extinguished Defendant 2's and Defendant 3's liability to Plaintiff.

Example: Same facts, except that Defendant 1 pays Plaintiff $80,000 of the $100,000 judgment, and Defendant 2 and Defendant 3 pay Plaintiff the remaining $20,000. Plaintiff can obtain contribution from Defendant 2 or Defendant 3 for a total of $30,000 ($100,000 × .50 minus the $20,000 that Defendant 1 did not have to pay).

4. Contribution Available Absent Judgment

Defendant can even seek contribution against other joint tortfeasors not sued by the plaintiff.

a. Immune Tortfeasors

There is a split of authority as to whether contribution can be obtained against a tortfeasor who is immune from suit by the plaintiff. Most require the defendant to prove that the tortfeasor was subject to liability to the plaintiff, so the defendant cannot seek contribution if the tortfeasor is immune with respect to the plaintiff.

b. Settlement

A tortfeasor who settles prior to trial can obtain contribution, provided they settle for all tortfeasors and they can prove the others' liability, the amount of the damages, and the reasonableness of their settlement. They need not prove that they would have been found liable to plaintiff, only that there was a potential for such liability. The prevailing view is that a tortfeasor who settles only their own liability cannot be sued for contribution, nor can they obtain contribution from others.

5. Intentional Tortfeasors

In some jurisdictions, intentional tortfeasors cannot seek contribution, but R.3d Apportionment of Liability § 23, comment *l*, says they can.

III. Several Liability

With the advent of comparative fault, some jurisdictions now make a joint tortfeasor only "severally liable" to the plaintiff—i.e., their liability is limited to their proportional share of the total liability. R.3d Apportionment of Liability § 11. Several liability has the effect of placing the risk of an uncollectible judgment on the plaintiff. There is no right to contribution because the defendant cannot overpay beyond their apportioned harm.

Example: Defendant 1's proportional share of Plaintiff's $100,000 recoverable damages is found to be 30%. Plaintiff will be awarded a judgment against Defendant 1 for only $30,000. Under joint and several liability, their judgment against Defendant 1 could have been $100,000.

IV. Hybrid Allocation of Damages Approaches

Many U.S. jurisdictions have adopted a mixture of joint and several liability and several liability. The approaches vary widely and resist simple categorization, and some systems have characteristics of more than one category. Broadly defined, they can be described as:

A. Reallocation of Uncollectible Shares

This category begins with joint and several liability for independent tortfeasors who cause an indivisible injury to the plaintiff. It places the risk of a tortfeasor's uncollectible judgment on all parties who bear responsibility for the plaintiff's damages, including the plaintiff. An insolvent tortfeasor's comparative share of responsibility is reallocated to the other parties in proportion to their comparative responsibility. A very similar result is obtained by starting with a rule of several liability but then providing for reallocation in the event a share is uncollectible.

B. Joint and Several Liability Threshold

All tortfeasors whose percentage of comparative responsibility exceeds a specified threshold are jointly and severally liable. Tortfeasors whose percentage falls below that threshold are only severally liable. The threshold serves to impose the risk of uncollectability on the plaintiff as to all tortfeasors below the specified threshold.

C. Type of Harm

In this category, the variable that determines joint and several liability or several liability is the type of harm suffered by the plaintiff. Independent tortfeasors are jointly and severally liable for damages for certain harms (e.g., economic or pecuniary harms, or pollution damage) but are severally liable for compensatory damages awarded for other types of harm.

D. Type of Defendant

In some jurisdictions, joint and several (or several) liability is restricted to certain categories of defendants.

E. Whether Plaintiff Was Free from Contributory Fault

In some cases, the plaintiff gets the benefit of joint and several liability only if they are free from contributory fault.

V. Joint and Several Liability Applies to Intentional Tortfeasors

Intentional tortfeasors are jointly and severally liable for any indivisible injury caused by the tortious conduct, regardless of the jurisdiction's approach for nonintentional torts. R.3d Apportionment of Liability § 12. Thus, if Defendant 1 and Defendant 2 are both intentional tortfeasors with respect to the plaintiff's indivisible injury, both are jointly and severally liable.

If Defendant 1 is negligent because of their failure to take precautions to protect Plaintiff against the specific risk created by Defendant 2 (the intentional tortfeasor) then Defendant 1 is jointly and severally liable for the share of comparative responsibility assigned to Defendant 2 as well as the share assigned to Defendant 1. R.3d Apportionment of Liability § 14.

Example: Plaintiff is a guest at a hotel operated by Defendant 1. Defendant 1 is negligent in failing to provide adequate door locks and other security. This negligence results in Defendant 2 gaining access to the Plaintiff's room, where Defendant 2 strikes Plaintiff and steals Plaintiff's property. Defendant 1 is liable to Plaintiff for the comparative responsibility assigned to both Defendant 1 and Defendant 2. If Defendant 1 pays more than their share, they can obtain contribution from Defendant 2 if Defendant 2 is financially viable as a defendant.

Whether the negligence of Defendant 1 can be compared with the intentional or willful tort of Defendant 2 depends on interpretation of the comparative fault statute (if any). If there is no such statute, the Restatement (Third) permits this comparison. Courts rarely permit the plaintiff's contributory negligence to reduce their recovery from an intentional tortfeasor.

VI. Effect of Settlement of Plaintiff's Claim(s)

The existence of multiple tortfeasors dramatically changes the dynamics of the case strategy for the defendants. Some defendants might be motivated to get out of the case sooner and those resources might also be invaluable to plaintiffs facing a long litigation timeline. This section outlines some of these agreements that defendants can enter with plaintiffs, and their effects on the remaining tortfeasors.

A. Settlement Agreements Are Contracts

A plaintiff may enter into a settlement agreement with the defendant(s) by which the plaintiff settles their claim(s) against the defendant(s) for a fixed sum. The agreement may take the form of a release, covenant not to sue, or loan receipt agreement. Ordinary rules of contract interpretation apply. Settlement agreements may be set aside for fraud, duress, incapacity, or mutual mistake. A dispute may arise as to whether the settlement should be set aside due to mutual mistake when it later develops that the plaintiff's injuries are much more serious, or of a different type, than the parties believed when the settlement was reached, particularly if the release by its terms extended to "unknown" injuries. Some courts will look beyond the terms of the release to see if one or both settling parties were mistaken about the nature of the injury, and if so, provide relief. Others will not.

The prevailing view is that a settlement by the plaintiff during their lifetime (or a judgment during the plaintiff's lifetime for either party) will bar a wrongful death action by the plaintiff's survivors when the death results from the same injuries.

B. Release

A release is a form of settlement agreement whereby the plaintiff completely surrenders their claim against one or more potential defendants. Historically, the general rule was that a release executed in favor of one tortfeasor released all other tortfeasors potentially liable for the same harm. The modern rule is that a release which is not indented as a full satisfaction, and contains a reservation of rights against others, does not *ipso facto* discharge others of their potential liability to the plaintiff. Under the Restatement view, no such reservation of rights is required; a release is only effective as to the party released, unless it is intended as a full satisfaction of all of plaintiff's claims arising out of the occurrence in question. R.2d § 885; R.3d Apportionment of Liability § 24.

C. Covenant Not to Sue

A covenant not to sue (or not to execute) is a settlement device designed to avoid the former effects of a release. It is a contract by which the plaintiff does not release their claim against the defendant but merely promises to forego any further attempts to enforce it. It does not discharge other potential defendants, even if it contains no reservation of rights against them, unless it is expressly intended as a satisfaction of all plaintiff's claims. R.2d § 885(2); R.3d Apportionment of Liability § 24.

D. Mary Carter Agreements

Some courts have approved settlement with one potential defendant by a loan receipt agreement, known as a Mary Carter Agreement, whereby a defendant "loans" a plaintiff a sum, without interest, to be repaid only if and to the extent that the plaintiff is successful in their claims against other joint tortfeasors, and only from the proceeds of any amount which the plaintiff eventually collects from the others. Although such agreements were at one time valid in many jurisdictions, they are now increasingly disapproved as against public policy. This is because such agreements distort the trial dynamics in ways that are perceived as unfair to the remaining defendants with one party appearing as a defendant adversarial to the plaintiff, when their interests are actually financially aligned with the plaintiff's case. For that reason, if allowed, such an agreement must be disclosed at trial so that the jury can evaluate defendant's credibility.

Some settlement agreements provide the settling tortfeasor with a financial interest in the plaintiff's recovery. In an acquired interest settlement, the settling tortfeasor obtains a release from liability but also acquires a partial interest in the plaintiff's claim against nonsettling tortfeasors.

E. High-Low Agreements

Another type of settlement is a "high-low" agreement. The plaintiff and a defendant (or the sole defendant) contract for a minimum and maximum amount, depending on the jury's verdict. The settling defendant remains in the case. Such agreements are often entered into during trial. Since the agreement could affect how the case is tried, and might impact credibility determinations, most courts require that it be disclosed immediately to the court and all other parties.

Example: Plaintiff and Defendant 1 agree that Plaintiff will receive a minimum of $300,000 and a maximum of $1 million. If the jury's verdict against Defendant 1 is $0 or anything less than $300,000, Plaintiff receives $300,000. If the verdict is over $1 million, Plaintiff receives $1 million. If the jury's verdict is anything in between those figures, Plaintiff receives the amount of the verdict. There may be other terms too.

F. Effect of Partial Settlement on Remaining Defendants in Joint and Several Liability Jurisdictions

Partial settlements with one tortfeasor yield a credit to remaining joint defendants. If a plaintiff has a claim against more than one joint tortfeasor subject to joint and several liability, the plaintiff can settle with one tortfeasor prior to obtaining a judgment against the remaining joint tortfeasor(s), reserving the plaintiff's right to proceed against the others. If the plaintiff then succeeds in their remaining claim(s), the tortfeasor(s) against whom the plaintiff obtained a judgment receive a credit based on the plaintiff's prior settlement with the first tortfeasor. There are different approaches to handling that credit:

1. Dollar Credit

In some jurisdictions, the credit is the dollar amount of the settlement with Tortfeasor 1. This is called the "pro tanto" or dollar credit rule.

Example: Plaintiff has a claim against Tortfeasor 1, Tortfeasor 2, and Tortfeasor 3 for an indivisible injury. Plaintiff settles prior to trial with Tortfeasor 1 for $50,000 and proceeds to trial against Tortfeasor 2 and Tortfeasor 3. Plaintiff obtains a $300,000 judgment against Tortfeasor 2 and Tortfeasor 3, and the jury apportions fault as one-third each to Tortfeasor 1, Tortfeasor 2, and Tortfeasor 3. The court will enter a joint and several judgment against Tortfeasor 1 and Tortfeasor 2 for $250,000. Tortfeasor 2 and Tortfeasor 3 cannot seek contribution against Tortfeasor 1, but they can seek contribution between themselves if either pays more than their proportional share, which is $125,000.

In most pro tanto or dollar credit jurisdictions, Tortfeasor 1 will be immune from contribution, but only if the court finds that the settlement was in "good faith," i.e., an arm's length bargain and a bona fide (not a collusive) settlement.

2. Proportional or Percentage Credit

In some jurisdictions, the credit is the settling tortfeasor's (Tortfeasor 1's) proportional share of the common liability, regardless of the dollar amount of the settlement with Tortfeasor 1. This is called the proportional or percentage credit rule. This is the rule favored by R.3d Apportionment of Liability § 16.

Example: Plaintiff has a claim against Tortfeasor 1, Tortfeasor 2, and Tortfeasor 3 for an indivisible injury. Plaintiff settles prior to trial with Tortfeasor 1 for $50,000 and proceeds to trial against Tortfeasor 2 and Tortfeasor 3. Plaintiff obtains a $300,000 judgment against Tortfeasor 2 and Tortfeasor 3. The jury apportions fault as one-third each to Tortfeasor 1, Tortfeasor 2, and Tortfeasor 3. The court will enter a joint and several judgment against Tortfeasor 1 and Tortfeasor 2 for $200,000. Tortfeasor 2 and Tortfeasor 3 cannot seek contribution against Tortfeasor 1, but they can seek contribution between themselves if either pays more than their proportional share, which is $100,000.

Note that Plaintiff will recover only $250,000 of their $300,000 verdict, because Plaintiff settled with Tortfeasor 1 for what turned out to be less than Tortfeasor 1's share.

Example: Plaintiff has a claim against Tortfeasor 1, Tortfeasor 2, and Tortfeasor 3 for an indivisible injury. Plaintiff settles prior to trial with Tortfeasor 1 for $150,000 and proceeds to trial against Tortfeasor 2 and Tortfeasor 3. Plaintiff obtains a $300,000 judgment against Tortfeasor 2 and Tortfeasor 3, and the jury apportions fault as one-third each to Tortfeasor 1, Tortfeasor 2, and Tortfeasor 3. The court will enter a joint and several judgment against Tortfeasor 1 and Tortfeasor 2 for $200,000. Tortfeasor 2 and Tortfeasor 3 cannot seek contribution against Tortfeasor 1, but they can seek contribution between themselves if either pays more than their proportional share, which is $100,000. Note that Plaintiff will recover a total of $350,000, even though their verdict was only $300,000. Plaintiff is entitled to the benefit of their settlement with Tortfeasor 1 even though it turned out to be greater than Tortfeasor 1's proportional share.

3. Pro Rata Credit

A third, little-used approach, the "pro rata" method, gives a nonsettling tortfeasor a credit against the judgment equal to the settling tortfeasor's share of damages, which is determined by dividing the recoverable damages by the number of liable parties.

G. Effect of Partial Settlement on Remaining Defendants in Several Liability Jurisdictions

If a settling tortfeasor is only subject to several liability, any nonsettling tortfeasors simply pay their proportional share(s) as determined by applicable apportionment rules. The settling tortfeasor has settled their several liability, and it matters not whether the settlement is more or less than the amount of their proportional share as later determined.

Example: Plaintiff, a passenger in Tortfeasor 1's car, is injured in a collision with Tortfeasor 2's car. Plaintiff settles with Tortfeasor 1 for $25,000. Plaintiff's case against Tortfeasor 2 proceeds to verdict ($170,000), but the jury assesses Tortfeasor 1's fault at 99% and Tortfeasor 2's fault at 1%. Plaintiff recovers $1,700 from Tortfeasor 2 and nothing further from Tortfeasor 1, for a total recovery of $26,700.

VII. Non-Party Tortfeasors

If a particular tortfeasor is not joined as a defendant or third-party defendant, the courts are split as to whether the factfinder can allocate that tortfeasor's proportional share of the total fault and included in the responsible fault calculation. Whether a tortfeasor is included or not may depend on the purpose of the calculation. A tortfeasor may be a nonparty because:

(1) Tortfeasor cannot be identified by name, such as a hit-and-run driver;

(2) Tortfeasor is immune from suit;

(3) Tortfeasor has settled with the plaintiff before trial;

(4) Tortfeasor cannot be served with process;

(5) Tortfeasor is plaintiff's employer and plaintiff's injury occurred in the course and scope of plaintiff's employment; or

(6) Plaintiff simply chose not to sue Tortfeasor for some other reason (e.g., Tortfeasor is uncollectible).

A. Joint and Several Liability

If all tortfeasors are subject to joint and several liability and there is no contribution claim, then there is no reason to allocate fault among multiple tortfeasors, whether joined or not. However, whether a tortfeasor is included could still make a difference in determining a plaintiff's share of the fault if the plaintiff is found contributorily at fault.

Example: Plaintiff, a factory worker, is injured while working on a machine. They bring a products liability claim against Defendant, the manufacturer of the machine. Plaintiff's employer, Tortfeasor, could be found negligent in failing to properly maintain the machine. If Plaintiff is found contributorily negligent, Plaintiff's share of the fault might vary depending on whether it is compared only to Defendant's fault or to the combined fault of Defendant and Tortfeasor.

For purposes of calculating plaintiff's share, the total fault should include all tortfeasors, whether joined as a defendant or not. R.3d Apportionment of Liability § 7, comment *g*. Not all states agree; in some jurisdictions, tortfeasors who are not parties to the suit are not included.

B. Several Liability

If some or all defendants are potentially subject only to several liability, then the factfinder must allocate fault proportionally, and it makes a difference whether a tortfeasor's fault is included in the fault calculation.

Example: Plaintiff is injured in an automobile accident. Plaintiff brings a products liability claim against Defendant 1, the auto's manufacturer, and joins a negligence claim against Defendant 2, the driver of the car. Tortfeasor, the driver of another car involved in the collision, was also negligent and was identified, but has since disappeared and cannot be located. If the jury finds all (Plaintiff, Defendant 1, Defendant 2, and Tortfeasor) equally at fault, and Plaintiff's damages are $100,000, then judgment will be entered for Plaintiff against Defendant 1 and Defendant 2 for $25,000 each. But if Tortfeasor's fault is not included, and the jury finds Plaintiff, Defendant 1, and Defendant 2 equally at fault, then judgment will be entered for Plaintiff against Defendant 1 and Defendant 2 for $33,333 each.

Jurisdictions are split. Some require Tortfeasor to be included if there is enough evidence from which the factfinder can assess fault against Tortfeasor. In others, only those who are party to the lawsuit can be included in the fault calculation. The Restatement rule is that the calculation may include such nonparties if they can be sufficiently identified. R.3d Apportionment of Liability § D19(a) and comment *k*.

C. Successive or Enhanced Injury Cases

These non-party rules differ for successive or enhanced injuries. Suppose Tortfeasor 1 drives negligently and crashes into a tree, injuring Plaintiff, their passenger. Plaintiff sues Defendant, the manufacturer of the car, on the theory that the design of the car enhanced their injuries or caused a fire that resulted in further injuries not sustained in the initial crash. Plaintiff's expert witness testifies and allocates the damages between Tortfeasor 1 and Defendant. In this case, Tortfeasor 1's share of the total fault is not considered with respect to the liability of Defendant. Defendant is liable for all of Plaintiff's recoverable separate or enhanced damages. Of course, Tortfeasor 1 is jointly and severally liable for all Plaintiff's damages, including those caused by the car's defective design.

Similarly, in a medical malpractice case, Defendant (the physician) is liable for any enhanced injury resulting from Defendant's negligent treatment, without reduction for any fault by Tortfeasor 1 that caused the initial injury for which Plaintiff is being treated.

However, if Plaintiff's injuries are indivisible, then fault will be apportioned between Defendant and Tortfeasor 1 in accordance with the applicable apportionment rules.

D. Contribution

Where contribution is available to some or all of the defendants (or in a separate action for contribution), it becomes necessary to allocate fault among tortfeasors. For this purpose, the calculation is restricted to the tortfeasors who are party to the action in which contribution is being sought. In most cases, contribution may not be sought from settling tortfeasors.

VIII. Indemnity

(R.3d Apportionment of Liability § 22)

A. Distinguished from Contribution

Contribution is an equitable sharing of the loss among joint tortfeasors. Indemnification is a shifting of the entire loss from one tortfeasor to another. Indemnity can occur by law, based on equitable considerations, or through a prior agreement of the parties.

B. Indemnity by Agreement—Subject to Some Limitations

A contract in which Tortfeasor 2 agrees to indemnify Tortfeasor 1 if Tortfeasor 1 is held liable to Plaintiff is frequently enforceable, although in some instances agreements to indemnify for Tortfeasor 1's own negligence may be void by statute or as against public policy. Agreements to indemnify Tortfeasor 1 for Tortfeasor 1's liability for reckless or intentional misconduct are usually unenforceable.

C. Implied Indemnity (Indemnity by Operation of Law)

Implied indemnity is indemnity based on the concept of unjust enrichment. It is available when Tortfeasor 1 and Tortfeasor 2 are both liable for the same harm to Plaintiff, and (1) Tortfeasor 1's liability is based entirely on Tortfeasor 1's vicarious liability for the tort of Tortfeasor 2, or (2) Tortfeasor 1 is the seller of a product (e.g., a retailer), the product was supplied to Tortfeasor 1 by Tortfeasor 2 (e.g., the manufacturer), and Tortfeasor 1 is held liable to Plaintiff solely because they sold the product to Plaintiff (i.e., Tortfeasor 1 was not independently culpable). If Tortfeasor 1 satisfies Plaintiff's judgment, Tortfeasor 1 is entitled to indemnity from Tortfeasor 2 for the amount paid to Plaintiff plus reasonable legal expenses.

Example: Tortfeasor 2 is Tortfeasor 1's employee. Tortfeasor 2, driving a company car on company business, negligently injures Plaintiff. Tortfeasor 1, being vicariously liable for Tortfeasor 2's negligence, is joined as a defendant in Plaintiff's lawsuit and Plaintiff recovers a judgment against Tortfeasor 1, which Tortfeasor 1 pays. Tortfeasor 1 is entitled to indemnity from Tortfeasor 2.

Example: A hardware store (Tortfeasor 1) sells a leaf blower manufactured by Tortfeasor 2 to Plaintiff. The leaf blower has a defect that results in an injury to Plaintiff. Plaintiff sues the seller (based on strict products liability) and recovers a judgment against seller, but Plaintiff did not join Tortfeasor 2 (the manufacturer). The seller pays the judgment.

Assuming the hardware store is free from fault, it is entitled to indemnity from the product manufacturer.

D. "Active-Passive" Implied Indemnity

Prior to the adoption of comparative contribution, implied indemnity was also available when there was a significant or qualitative difference between the blameworthiness of Tortfeasor 1 and Tortfeasor 2, both of whom are nevertheless legally liable to Plaintiff for their injury, such that the primary responsibility for the harm rests upon the defendant against whom indemnity is sought. This was often called "active-passive" indemnity, because the fault of the indemnitor was "active" or major and the fault of the indemnitee was "passive" or minor. In those jurisdictions adopting comparative contribution, contribution is usually deemed to supersede the "active-passive" form of implied indemnity

IX. Review Questions

[Answers Provided in Appendix A]

1. Piper Plaintiff suffered a neck injury as a passenger after her friend was texting and driving and their vehicle struck a jaywalking pedestrian. As a result, Piper suffered an injury caused by two potential tortfeasors (their texting and driving friend and the jaywalking pedestrian).

   (a) In a joint and several liability jurisdiction, explain to Piper whether she can be made whole without suing her friend who was texting and driving. Draft a one-paragraph email to the client.

   (b) How would that legal advice differ in a several liability jurisdiction? Draft a one-paragraph email to the client.

Part Thirteen

Defenses to Liability—General

■ ANALYSIS

I. Statutes of Limitations and Repose

A. Statutes of Limitations

1. In General

A statute of limitations is a statutory period within which the plaintiff must file their lawsuit. There are statutes of limitations for all causes of action. In tort cases, the time is usually short, typically one to three years. By contrast, for example, property damage actions may be longer, e.g., five years.

Statutes of limitations are designed to promote stability and avoid the uncertainties and burdens inherent in defending stale and possibly fraudulent claims. The price of this protection, however, is the extinguishment of valid claims.

2. Procedural Effect

A statute of limitations does not automatically extinguish the cause of action. It must be asserted by the parties as an affirmative defense. If the parties do not assert the defense, it is waived.

3. Starting the Statute of Limitations Clock

a. Begins at Cause of Action Accrual

The statute of limitations begins to run on the date the cause of action "accrues." In tort cases, this is usually the date on which the injury occurs since compensable injury is a necessary element of the cause of action.

b. Concealment or Nondisclosure Tolls the Statute of Limitations

If defendant fraudulently, actively conceals or misrepresents the existence of the cause of action from plaintiff, the statute of limitations is tolled. Mere nondisclosure is not enough unless there is a fiduciary relationship between the parties.

c. Continuing Duty Can Extend the Statute of Limitations

In some contexts, the courts will extend the available time by finding a continuing duty to disclose or continuing negligence or other tort. In medical negligence cases, some courts hold that that the statute does not begin to run until plaintiff's course of treatment has concluded. If defendant's conduct constitutes a continuing nuisance, the statute may not start to run until defendant's conduct in creating the nuisance ceases, or it may not start to run as long as the harm continues.

d. Discovery Rule Tolls the Statute of Limitations

Strict application of the statute of limitations can be especially harsh in certain cases where plaintiff justifiably failed to discover that they even had a cause of action until after the limitation periods had expired. In response to this factual problem, courts (and sometimes legislatures) have created a "discovery" rule whereby the statute is tolled and does not commence to run until plaintiff discovers (or by the exercise of reasonable care should have discovered) that (a) they are injured and (b) the injury is the result of someone's tortious conduct. The issue usually is whether and when plaintiff knew or should have known enough facts to begin an investigation as to whether defendant might have caused an actionable injury.

This "discovery" rule was first applied in medical malpractice cases. Today, it is often extended to other areas, such as product liability and other forms of professional negligence. Some apply the discovery rule broadly. Whether plaintiff meets the requirements for the discovery rule is normally a question of fact for the jury.

e. Latent Potential Harm

Plaintiff, because of defendant's negligence, may have been exposed to a toxic material resulting in no present symptoms or minor symptoms but a measurable risk that plaintiff may contract a serious or fatal illness at some uncertain time in the future. If the plaintiff sues early for the minor harm, some courts will allow recovery now for the present symptoms or medical monitoring and either (1) award damages for the potential future harm times the probability of its occurrence or (2) allow a later suit if the potential future harm actually occurs. These claims are necessary because the cause of action begins to accrue when the plaintiff suffers some symptoms.

f. Repressed Childhood Sexual Abuse

Most courts have permitted the statute of limitations to be tolled during the time when plaintiff has repressed memories of childhood sexual abuse (assuming the repression began before the applicable statute expired and the plaintiff can prove repression factually). A few courts have rejected the defense. Some legislatures have adopted extended statutes of limitations in sexual abuse cases.

g. Minors

A statute of limitations normally does not begin to run if plaintiff is a minor when the cause of action accrues. It commences when plaintiff reaches legal adulthood.

h. Others Lacking Capacity

A statute of limitations normally does not begin to run if plaintiff is under some legal disability or lacks legal capacity when the cause of action accrues. It commences when plaintiff is no longer under any disability. In this context, lacking capacity usually means that the individual is unable to manage their business affairs or estate, or to comprehend their legal rights or liabilities. The appointment of a guardian for the disabled person may or may not start the running of the statute, depending on the state.

i. Statute of Limitations in Wrongful Death

In wrongful death cases, the statute begins to run on the date of death, even though the fatal injury occurred earlier. In death cases, the statute of limitations is often regarded as an intrinsic part of the cause of action rather than as a mere affirmative defense.

4. Estoppel to Assert

If defendant actively induces plaintiff not to take timely legal action on a claim, and plaintiff reasonably relies on defendant's inducement, defendant may be estopped to assert the statute of limitations defense.

B. Statutes of Repose

Statutes of repose are special limitation periods which supplement and override statutes of limitations, the discovery rule, and other similar rules and exceptions. Their purpose is to set an outer limit beyond which defendant can no longer be held responsible for a completed activity, irrespective of whether an injury has occurred for which defendant might be subject to liability. They reflect the successful lobbying efforts of various interest groups, such as product manufacturers seeking to set such limits.

Sometimes, particularly in product liability cases, statutes of repose merely create a presumption of nonliability. The most common forms of these statutes are in the areas of (1) medical malpractice (X years after the allegedly negligent treatment), (2) product liability (Y years after defendant manufactured the product or placed it in the stream of commerce), and (3) professional negligence of builders, architects, and engineers (Z years after completion of the structure). These statutes may have the effect of barring a lawsuit before the cause of action even accrues. Despite this, most courts have held that these statutes are constitutional.

C. Notice of Claim Statutes

In suits against state or local governments, statutes sometimes require plaintiff to give notice, in a specified form, to the potential defendant within a certain period (typically six months or a year, but sometimes as little as 60 or 90 days) after the date of the injury, or prior to filing suit, as a further condition on the right to sue. Dobbs §§ 216–223.

II. Immunities

A. Liability of the Government and Its Employees

(Dobbs §§ 260–278)

1. Immune at Common Law

At one time, all levels of government (federal, state, local, and their agencies) were entirely immune from tort liability.

2. United States Government

a. Federal Tort Claims Act

In the Federal Tort Claims Act (FTCA), the United States has waived its tort immunity for personal or property damage "caused by the negligent or wrongful act or omission of any employee of the Government while acting within the scope of his office or employment, under circumstances where the United States, if a private person, would be liable to the claimant in accordance with the law of the place where the act or omission occurred." 28 U.S.C.A. § 1346(b). *See* R.2d § 895A.

b. Exceptions to the Federal Tort Claims Act

In addition to exceptions for specific activities (e.g., tax collection, failure to deliver mail, military combat in time of war, actions arising in foreign countries), there are several other important general exceptions:

i. Specified Torts

The United States is not liable for (1) assault, battery, false imprisonment, false arrest, or malicious prosecution, except in the case of investigative or law enforcement officers; or (2) abuse of process, libel, slander, misrepresentation, deceit, or interference with contract rights.

ii. Discretionary Acts

The United States is not liable for acts done with due care in the execution of a statute or regulation (even though invalid), or for "an act or omission . . . based upon the exercise or performance or the failure to exercise or perform a discretionary function or duty . . . whether or not the discretion be abused."

iii. Strict Tort Liability

The United States is not subject to strict tort liability in any form.

iv. The *Feres* Doctrine

The United States is not liable for injuries to members of the armed forces on active duty if the injury is "incident to service." This rule arises from a Supreme Court case, *Feres v. United States*, 340 U.S. 135 (1950), as compared to a statutory exception. Many critics argue that this rule goes too far and deters accountability for government wrongdoing. The doctrine does not bar recovery by the service member's spouse or child if that person is *directly* injured by government negligence. In 2019, as part of the National Defense Authorization Act, Congress created a compensation fund allowing recovery for medical malpractice liability through a Pentagon review process, an alternative to the tort system.

3. States

Most states have largely abolished state sovereign immunity. The rest provide some limited means of making a claim. Many states have comprehensive tort immunity legislation which limits the state's liability for certain governmental functions. Immunity is generally preserved for judicial and legislative acts, and for the exercise of high-level administrative discretion. R.2d § 895B.

4. Local Governments

After a period during which the immunity of local governments was eroded, as by holding them liable for "proprietary" (as opposed to "governmental") functions, where the entity had purchased liability insurance, and for other activities (e.g., operation of vehicles), a strong trend has developed to abolish immunity entirely, often by judicial decision and then by a statute that re-establishes limited immunities. Liability is now the rule in a majority of states, subject to various immunities for certain types of governmental functions. Both the common law and statutes exempt judicial and legislative functions, and exempt executive and administrative policy or planning decisions. R.2d § 895C.

5. Public Duty Rule

Under the public duty doctrine, public entities and officers are not liable for failure to perform a duty owed to the public at large, rather than to a particular individual or group. A special relationship, which can overcome the public duty limitation and give rise to liability, can arise when the officer or entity takes affirmative action that endangers plaintiff specifically, or where a statute creates a special duty to a particular group, or when an agent of the entity has taken action or made a promise on which plaintiff justifiably relied.

6. Governmental Officers and Employees

Governmental officers and employees (state and federal) are immune from tort liability when exercising a judicial or legislative function. The highest executive officers of state and federal governments are absolutely immune, except where they have so far exceeded the scope of their official discretion as to be acting clearly beyond the bounds of their authority. Lower-level executive and administrative employees have qualified immunity for the good faith exercise of a discretionary function but are liable for tortious ministerial acts. Various statutes increasingly alter the scope of governmental officers' and employees' liability.

B. Charities

At one time, all but one or two states held that charitable, educational, religious, and benevolent organizations and enterprises were immune from tort liability. These courts sought to avoid diverting charitable funds beyond the charitable mission. Today, that immunity has been generally abolished. Some vestiges of immunity remain, however, in the form of other liability limitations, such as caps on damages. Dobbs §§ 282–83; R.2d § 895E. Increasingly, legislation is recreating specific immunities for particular charitable activities or for individuals engaged in certain charitable activities.

C. Immunity in Family Relationships

(Dobbs §§ 279–281; R.2d §§ 895F–895H)

1. Spousal Immunity

At one time, the general common law rule was that spouses were each immune from tort liability to the other spouse for torts committed during coverture. Under coverture, courts reasoned that the married couple was one legal entity under the male spouse's legal control. More than half the states have now abolished this immunity. R.2d § 895F. Many of the remaining states (a few of which have statutes expressly preserving it) recognize exceptions, as for suits brought after the marriage has been terminated, intentional torts, torts occurring in a business activity, and suits against persons vicariously liable for the spouse's tort. The states that have not abolished immunity express concern regarding fraudulent claims and destroying marital harmony.

2. Parental Immunity

The general common law rule was that a parent (or someone *in loco parentis*) and their unemancipated minor child were each immune from suit by the other for a personal tort, whether intentional or negligent. The historic reason for the immunity was rooted in the duty of children to obey their parents. Today, a substantial minority of the states have abolished this immunity altogether (R.2d § 895G). In the remainder, the number of exceptions is increasing, such as for (a) intentional or reckless conduct, (b) torts occurring during defendant's business activity, (c) breach of a duty external to the family relationship (e.g., child-driver runs over pedestrian-parent), and (d) suits after the parent-minor child relationship has ended, as by emancipation of the child or the death of either party. Some states have abolished the immunity in certain classes of cases (e.g., motor vehicle accidents). Among the states that have abolished the immunity, some hold that the parent cannot be held liable for negligent supervision, or the exercise of parental authority, or where the negligent act involves the exercise of parental discretion with respect to the provision of food, clothing, housing, medical and dental services, and other care.

3. No Immunity for Siblings and Other Kin

Brothers, sisters, and other kin are not, by reason of their relationship, immune from tort liability to one another. R.2d § 895H.

D. Minors and Legal Incompetency

(Dobbs § 120; R.2d § 895I, 895J)

1. No *Per Se* Immunity for Minors

If plaintiff can establish the requisite mental state (if any), an infant or minor is not immune from tort liability, unless the liability depends upon the enforceability of a contract the infant is privileged to disaffirm. R.2d § 895I.

2. Legal Incompetency

One who has a mental disability is not, for that reason alone, immune from tort liability. R.2d § 895J. Particularly in torts involving physical harm, a defendant with a mental disability is held to the same standard as others. However, defendant's mental health condition may be relevant in determining whether any tort has been committed. Dobbs § 225; R.2d §§ 895A–895D.

III. Preemption

Under the supremacy clause of the U.S. Constitution, federal law is supreme over state law. Thus, when a federal statute or regulation expressly or impliedly preempts a particular field (e.g., regulations governing railroad crossing warnings, statutes governing cigarette warnings), state tort law either cannot regulate the field at all or cannot impose a lower standard than the applicable federal law. Whether (and the extent to which) a federal statute or regulation is preemptive is a question of statutory interpretation for the court.

IV. Review Questions

[Answers Provided in Appendix A]

1. Donnie Dad was texting while watching his children play on a trampoline in the backyard. The trampoline was only safe for one child at a time. While he was distracted, all four children climbed into the trampoline. Two of the children, Carl and Cassie, collided into each other and Carl suffered a concussion from the impact. If Carl were to try to sue his own father for the injuries they suffered, what would be the result? Use an IRAC rule structure to write-up your analysis.

2. When Millie Mom is delivering her infant, Matthias, Matthias suffers shoulder dystocia from the doctor's negligent extraction of Matthias from the birth canal. Matthias is currently four years old. The statute of limitations for negligence is one year. What is Matthias' best argument were he to try to sue when he reaches the age of majority for the harms that he suffered at birth? Use an IRAC rule structure to write-up your analysis.

3. Parker Parishioner was sexually abused by Phillip Priest between the ages of 4–7. He is now 34 years old. News coverage has exposed that Phillip also abused other children around the same time. This sends Parker into counseling. While working with a licensed psychotherapist, Parker remembers for the first time that he too was sexually abused as a child.

   a. What is Parker's best argument to bring a claim against Phillip Priest in his personal capacity? Use an IRAC rule structure to write-up your analysis.

   b. Advise Parker on whether he could possibly bring a claim against the parish itself?

4. A United States military doctor committed negligence in an emergency appendectomy procedure at Ft. Knox performed on a soldier. Which of the following statements is the most accurate?

   a. Since the government waived sovereign immunity, the patient can proceed with a lawsuit for negligence.

   b. The longstanding doctrine of sovereign immunity prohibits suit here.

   c. The patient's sole remedy arises under the Workers' Compensation statutes because it happened in the course of employment.

   d. The patient is barred from suing the federal government for malpractice under the *Feres* doctrine exception.

5. The National Highway Traffic Safety Commission (NHTSC), a federal government agency, has authority to mandate manufacturer recalls of products that it concludes pose an unreasonable risk of harm to consumers. The NHTSC received reports of 13 deaths relating to the deaths of drivers due to an ignition switch malfunction in Lamar Motors vehicles, but it took no action. The families of victims have filed a lawsuit against the NHTSC. What is the NHTSC's strongest defense to this suit?

   a. That the claim is expressly preempted by state law.

   b. That the claim is impliedly preempted by state law.

   c. That the agency is immune because it is a federal government agency.

   d. That the agency is immune under the discretionary function exception.

Appendix A

Answers to Review Questions

PART ONE. INTENTIONAL TORTS

I. LIABILITY RULES FOR INTENTIONAL TORTS

Review Questions

1. The issue is whether Defendant is liable for false imprisonment. False imprisonment is the intentional confinement of another where the plaintiff is either aware of confinement or harmed by it. Here, there was intent because Defendant locked Plaintiff in the dorm room on purpose, as indicated by the later change in Defendant's mind when they later decided to open the door. Confinement occurs when there is a barrier, threat, or force with no reasonable means to escape. Here, there was confinement because Defendant locked Plaintiff in a room, which is a physical barrier comprised of walls and a locked door. There is no evidence of a reasonable means of escape because Defendant stood outside the only door, which was locked. The next issue is whether Plaintiff was harmed by the confinement or had awareness of the confinement. Here, Plaintiff did not have awareness of the confinement at the time of confinement because Plaintiff was sound asleep. However, Plaintiff experienced actual harm because of the confinement when they broke their wrist, as Plaintiff's wrist break was caused by the process of pushing on the door (the means of confinement). Finally, Plaintiff is "another" person because Plaintiff is a human being who is not Defendant. Because all elements are met, there is a prima facie case for false imprisonment. There do not seem to be any viable defenses. Therefore, Plaintiff is likely to succeed in their false imprisonment claim and Defendant would be liable.

2. The issue is whether Defendant is liable for battery. Battery is an intentional harmful or offensive contact with another. The issue is whether Defendant's contact was intentional. Intent is purpose to cause a result or knowledge to substantial certainty that a result will occur. Here, while Defendant did not seem to have the purpose to cause Plaintiff's contact with the ground, Defendant arguably satisfies the knowledge type of intent because Defendant felt the door pushing, so they knew that by yanking the door open, Plaintiff would fall. Therefore, intent is met. The next element of battery is contact. Contact may be direct (between Defendant and Plaintiff) or indirect. Here, there was an indirect contact, as Plaintiff was not touched by Defendant, but—due to Defendant's action of yanking open the door—Plaintiff's wrist made contact with the ground. Battery also requires that the contact be harmful or offensive. Here, the contact was harmful because Plaintiff suffered the harm of a broken wrist because of the fall. Therefore, the element of harmful contact

was met. Finally, battery also requires contact be to another. Another is a human being other than Defendant. Here, Plaintiff is a person other than Defendant. Because all elements were met, there is a prima facie case for battery. There do not seem to be any viable defenses. Therefore, Plaintiff is likely to succeed in their battery claim and Defendant would be liable.

3. Use IRAC to reason through each of the conclusions below.

   a. The issue is whether Defendant's actions resulted in conversion or trespass to chattels. Conversion of chattels is the intentional exercise of dominion or control over a chattel that so seriously interferes with the right of another to control the chattel. Trespass to chattels is the intentional interference or dispossession over a chattel in the possession of another. Here, the element of intent is met because the facts tell us that Defendant stole Plaintiff's hat, which indicates purpose to interfere with or control the chattel. Here, we also know that the "another" element is met because the facts tell us that the hat was "Plaintiff's," and Plaintiff is a human being who is not the Defendant. The key distinction between these two torts is whether the interference with the chattel was so serious that it warrants damages in the full amount of the chattel (which would be conversion). Here, this element is missing, as there is no evidence that the hat was physically destroyed or dispossessed for a substantial amount of time. Because the dispossession was a short five minutes, there was only mild interference with the chattel. Therefore, this would be trespass to chattels, not conversion. The measure of damages would be limited to diminuition in value.

   b. The issue is whether Defendant's actions resulted in conversion or trespass to chattels. Conversion of chattels is the intentional exercise of dominion or control over a chattel that so seriously interferes with the right of another to control the chattel. Trespass to chattels is the intentional interference or dispossession over a chattel in the possession of another. The issue is whether Defendant's interference or control over the chattel of another was intentional. Intent is purpose to cause a result or knowledge to substantial certainty that a result will occur. For both of these property torts, the relevant result for intent is interference with the chattel; in other words, the relevant intent is intent to interfere or control, not intent to trespass or convert. Accordingly, it is irrelevant that Defendant mistook Plaintiff's hat for their own. The element of intent is met because Defendant voluntarily took the hat from the hat rack, which indicates purpose to control or interfere with the hat. Here, we also know that the "another" element is met because the facts tell us that the hat was "Plaintiff's," and Plaintiff is a human being who is not the Defendant. The key distinction between these two torts is whether the interference with the chattel was so serious that it warrants damages in the full amount of the chattel (which would be conversion). Here, Plaintiff was permanently dispossessed of the hat, given that the hat went down a sewer and is unlikely to be recovered. This is the functional equivalent of total destruction of the hat, which warrants damages in the amount of the full value of the hat. Accordingly, conversion is the appropriate cause of action here.

   c. The issue is whether Defendant's actions resulted in conversion or trespass to chattels. Conversion of chattels is the intentional exercise of dominion or control over a chattel that so seriously interferes with the right of another to control the chattel. Trespass to chattels is the intentional interference or dispossession over a chattel in the possession of another. The issue is whether Defendant's interference or control over the chattel of another was intentional. Intent is purpose to cause a result or knowledge to substantial certainty that a result will occur. For both of these property torts, the relevant result for intent is interference with the chattel; in other words, the relevant intent is intent to interfere or control, not intent to trespass or convert. Accordingly, it is irrelevant that Defendant mistook Plaintiff's hat for their own. The element of intent is met because Defendant voluntarily took the hat from the hat rack, which indicates purpose to control or interfere with the hat. Here, we also know that the "another" element is met because the facts tell us that the hat was "Plaintiff's," and Plaintiff is a human being who is not the Defendant. The key distinction between these two torts is whether the interference with the chattel was so serious that it warrants damages in the full amount of the chattel (which would be conversion). Here, Plaintiff cannot prove this element, as there is no evidence that the hat was physically destroyed or dispossessed for a substantial amount of time. Because the dispossession was a short five minutes, there was only mild interference with the chattel. Therefore, this would be trespass to chattels, not conversion.

4. Multiple Choice: Defendant Homeowner builds a garage on what they and Plaintiff Neighbor both believe to be Defendant's land. Later a resurvey of the land establishes that the garage extends 2 inches into Plaintiff Neighbor's land. What outcome?

   a. Defendant Homeowner is not liable to Plaintiff Neighbor for trespass because Homeowner does not live in the garage and thus is not occupying Plaintiff Neighbor's land.

   b. Defendant Homeowner is not liable to Plaintiff Neighbor for trespass because the invasion of Plaintiff Neighbor's land is minimal.

   c. Defendant Homeowner is not liable to Plaintiff Neighbor for trespass because Homeowner had no intent to enter onto Plaintiff Neighbor's land.

   d. Defendant Homeowner is liable to Plaintiff Neighbor for trespass because Homeowner built on Plaintiff Neighbor's property.

   e. Defendant Homeowner is liable to Plaintiff Neighbor for trespass because Homeowner was negligent in not searching the title and surveying the land before building.

IV. DEFENSES TO LIABILITY FOR INTENTIONAL TORTS: PRIVILEGES

Review Questions

1. Traveler has a limited privilege to enter upon Owner's land only if it reasonably appears to be necessary. Here, an alternate route was available via a detour, and there was no emergency justifying the trespass. The Owner may therefore have a valid claim. It is unlikely that Traveler has a viable defense.

2. Owner may be liable to Traveler for exceeding reasonable force here. Owner may only use force or threat of force that is *minimally* necessary to prevent or terminate Traveler's intrusion. Force likely to cause death or serious bodily injury is not privileged. Here, the use of a gun likely exceeds the scope of a defense of property claim. Even though the Traveler was not actually injured, the force is likely to cause serious bodily injury.

3. Traveler is privileged to come to the defense of any other person and may use so much force as reasonably appears to be immediately necessary to protect Child against imminent physical harm. Here, the Owner can likely prevail because there was no longer a threat of imminent harm. Further, Owner was likely privileged to apply such reasonable force upon their child or another child entrusted to his care and training as they reasonably believe to be necessary for the child's proper control, training, or education. It is likely that the Owner will recover for battery without a valid defense protecting Traveler.

4. Owner's gestures ordinarily would be interpreted as consent, even though Owner's actual state of mind was to the contrary. The Traveler will likely prevail with the defense of consent.

5. The Owner will likely prevail in this claim. Traveler's privilege was impliedly limited in scope. Traveler's shift into four-wheel drive and their aggressive driving patterns went beyond that to which Owner had consented.

6. Owner's consent was given under duress and was not effective.

7. Patient's consent was obtained by fraud in the inducement, and not merely the failure to disclose risks or alternatives. Hence, Patient's consent was ineffective, and Doctor's conduct constituted a battery. If Doctor had merely failed to mention the risks involved in the surgery, his conduct would have been negligent under the doctrine of informed consent but not a battery.

8. This defense will likely prevail. Absent evidence that the punch exceeded the scope of conduct in a boxing match, the facts seem to fall squarely within the sport of boxing. Plaintiff's battery claim will likely fail due to Defendant's successful assertion of a consent privilege.

9. In the absence of a statute or a provision in the contract of sale, Seller has no privilege to repossess the car. It was rightfully acquired but is merely being tortiously withheld from Seller. Since Seller has no privilege to retake the car by self-help methods, Buyer was privileged to defend his own possession of it. The Buyer was entitled to use reasonable force to terminate the intrusion. However, Buyer's actions in beating and tying up Seller exceeded the scope of Buyer's privilege, and therefore Buyer is likely liable to Seller for assault, battery, and false imprisonment.

PART TWO. NEGLIGENCE

SECTION 1. DUTY OF CARE

C.3.g. Review Questions (Emotional Distress)

1. If Driver's negligent conduct results in any impact with Ranger, that impact is sufficient "bodily harm" to support liability for Ranger's emotional distress.

2. Ranger was within the zone of danger. Driver's negligence threatened bodily harm to Ranger. Driver would be liable to Ranger for bodily harm that resulted from their emotional distress, and in most jurisdictions, for emotional distress even if it did not cause some physical illness or comparable physical consequences.

3. Driver would be liable for Ranger's physical harm resulting from their emotional distress, but only if such consequences were reasonably foreseeable. Unless Driver has actual knowledge of Ranger's special sensitivity, Driver will be liable only to the

extent that Ranger's physical response to the emotional trauma was within the normal range of ordinarily sensitive persons.

III. LIMITATIONS ON DUTIES OWED

Review Questions

1. The issue is whether the attorney owes a duty of care to the clerk for the gratuitous legal advice provided and the clerk can establish a negligence claim. A duty of care arises when a defendant undertakes to render services for the protection of the plaintiff, including gratuitous and voluntary services. Even a gratuitous promise to render such services may make a defendant subject to liability if there is reasonable detrimental reliance by a plaintiff. Here, the attorney assumed a duty to act with reasonable care because the attorney provided the clerk with gratuitous services voluntarily when they advised the clerk on a speeding ticket problem. The clerk's reliance on the advice and the resulting harm (suspension) satisfy the causation and damages elements of negligence. Therefore, the clerk likely has a claim for negligence because the attorney assumed a duty by giving gratuitous legal advice and the clerk relied upon that advice to their detriment.

2. The issue is whether Angie's mom is liable for Patti's injury based on her parenting relationship with Angie. Generally, there is no vicarious liability for a child's torts unless the parent was negligent in supervising or controlling the child, creating a foreseeable risk of harm. Here, Angie's act of striking Patti appears to be a one-off incident with no history of similar behavior. The facts do not suggest that Angie's mom failed to supervise Angie or had reason to foresee the harm Angie caused. Without prior incidents or knowledge of potential danger, Angie's mom likely owed no duty to Patti related to her child's conduct. Therefore, Angie's mom is likely not liable to Patti and Patti does not have a negligence claim against Angie's mom.

3. The issue is whether Amaya owed a duty to render aid to the injured car driver after her dog caused a car accident. A defendant owes a duty of care to render aid if they are responsible for the plaintiff's position of peril or injury. Absent such responsibility, there is generally no duty to render aid unless the defendant voluntarily assumes such a duty. Here, Amaya's act of leaving her gate open led to her dog's escape and caused the accident, which placed the driver in a position of peril. This created a duty for Amaya to render aid. Her failure to assist the injured driver after causing the peril constitutes a breach of that duty. Accordingly, Amaya likely had a duty to render aid to the injured driver because her negligent conduct (leaving the gate open) caused the driver's injury, and her failure to assist may expose her to liability.

SECTION 2. BREACH—FAILURE TO CONFORM WITH STANDARDS OF CARE

VI. TYPES OF BREACHES IN THE STANDARD OF CARE

Review Questions

1. Plaintiff's conduct in wiring their clothing is such that Plaintiff should have been aware that it created more than a relatively high risk of harm to another; Plaintiff should have known that harm was substantially certain to occur. Hence, a jury will likely find their conduct to be negligent.

2. Normally, a violation of this type of ordinance constitutes negligence per se or at least evidence of negligence. However, a violation does not automatically establish a sufficient causal relation between the violation and Plaintiff's injury. Plaintiff has the burden of proving that the violation of the statute was a cause in fact of his injury. If Plaintiff cannot, or if Defendant is able to persuade the trier of fact that the snow did not contribute to Plaintiff's injury, then the violation of the ordinance would be irrelevant, and Defendant would prevail.
3. Plaintiff must make a prima facie showing that the damage to the kitchen was caused by Defendant's use of the solvent, which was under Defendant's control, and that the occurrence in question was of the type which would not have occurred unless Defendant was negligent. The modern view is that Plaintiff need not prove that Plaintiff's conduct did not contribute to the explosion and fire as part of Plaintiff's prima facie case. It may be relevant on the issue of contributory fault.

SECTION 3. CAUSATION

Review Questions

1. The issue is whether Marcus' negligence was the cause in fact of Phil's injury. To determine case in fact, we apply the but-for test by asking, "But for Defendant's conduct, would Plaintiff's injury have occurred?" Here, but for Marcus crossing the border line into the southbound traffic lane, Phil's injury probably would not have occurred. Phil's injury was brain damage due to the failed respirator, which probably would not have occurred when it did had Brianna not hit the electric pole. Brianna hit the electric pole because they were swerving to avoid Marcus's negligent driving (Though Brianna was driving too fast for weather conditions, they probably would not have struck the pole if not for avoiding Marcus). But for Marcus's negligence, the chain of events leading to Phil's injury would not have occurred. Accordingly, Marcus was the cause in fact of Phil's injury.
2. The issue is whether Marcus was the proximate cause of Phil's injury. The rule is that a Defendant is liable for proximate cause if their actions were within the scope of foreseeable risk. To determine whether Defendant's conduct was within the scope of foreseeable risk, we apply the class of persons type of harm test by asking if Defendant should have foreseen the type of harm that occurred to a class of persons that included the Plaintiff. Here, a person would not reasonably foresee that, by causing a car accident, the collision would impact patients at a hospital due to electric failure. This type of harm was not in the natural sequence of events of a car accident. Therefore, it is likely that the harm to Phil was too remote and not the result of a foreseeable risk of Marcus's negligent conduct. Accordingly, Marcus's negligence is not the proximate cause of Phil's injury.
3. In a joint-and-several liability jurisdiction, if a jury finds that both Marcus and Brianna proximately caused Phil's injury, Phil is entitled to collect full damages from both parties or either party.
4. Yes, Marcus would be liable for both Brianna's injury and for further injury by negligent medical treatment. This is because injury invites treatment. The subsequent negligence is itself foreseeable.
5. No, neither is liable because both were negligently driving. Both Marcus and Brianna were negligent in that they breached a standard of care. Neither were exercising

reasonable care. Marcus crossed the center line into opposing traffic. Brianna was driving too fast for weather conditions. Both are a cause in fact of Phil's injury, but neither are a proximate cause of Phil's injury. This is because the type of harm Phil suffered was not reasonably foreseeable to a person in either Marcus's or Brianna's position at the time of their negligence. A person would not reasonably foresee that, by causing a car accident, the collision would impact patients at a hospital due to electric failure.

6. Yes. The intervention of would-be rescuers, like Craig, is usually deemed foreseeable as a matter of law. Therefore, when Marcus's negligent conduct of driving over the center line endangered others, Marcus was subject to liability to Craig, who was injured in attempting to rescue Brianna, especially since Craig's harm arose from a risk inherent in the effort to save Brianna from the burning car.

7. Likely, yes. Marcus's negligent conduct injured Brianna and foreseeably exposed her to the risk of further injury by another, such as a rescuer like Craig. Marcus is liable both for the injury they caused and for this further injury.

8. No. The injury caused by Xavier's criminal act was completely independent of Marcus. Xavier is likely a "superseding cause" because it was not foreseeable.

PART THREE. DAMAGES

Damages for Physical Harm

Review Questions

1. Answers will vary depending on the state. Punitive damages generally require a heightened mental state (e.g., reckless), a heightened burden of proof (e.g., clear and convincing evidence), and are sometimes limited by claims (e.g., no punitive damages for vicarious liability.

2. Consequential damages are damages that a plaintiff can recover as a consequence of an injury to someone such as a parent, spouse, or child, with whom he has a close relationship. These could be loss of society, comfort, and companionship, funeral expenses, and lost income (if applicable). These are likely brought through a wrongful death claim.

3. In the tort claim, these payments have no relevance. Payments made or benefits conferred on Piper from sources other than the tortfeasors do not reduce defendants' liability. Here even though the money was paid directly to the hospital it reduces Piper's debt to the hospital and thus was a benefit conferred on Piper. Piper can still recover the $4800. The collateral source rule bars admission of this information.

4.

Category of Damages	Facts that Support Pleading for This Category of Damages
Past medical damages	Hospital bills, physical therapy, and medications are a type of compensable economic loss.
Future medical expenses and lost wages	Recoverable, if proven.

Past pain and suffering	Twenty days of hospitalization plus eight months of recovery is a compensable loss.
Past and future mental distress	Mental distress including anxiety about the future is a compensable loss.
Lost wages (past)	Missing eight months of work is compensable.
Lost earning capacity (future)	The loss of overtime is recoverable.

PART FOUR. DEFENSES TO NEGLIGENCE

Review Questions

1. In contributory negligence jurisdictions, the person who suffered the harm will not be able to recover any damages if their negligence played even a small part in the injury. In comparative fault jurisdictions, however, the person who suffered the harm will be able to recover damages even if their negligence played a part in the injury, but their damages will be reduced based on how negligent they were in their own harm. Furthermore, in modified comparative fault jurisdictions, the injured party may not be able to recover if their negligence was as great as or greater than the defendant's.

2. Contributory negligence will *not* be imputed in which of the following circumstances?

   a. A child's negligence to their parent.

   b. An employee's negligence to their employer.

   c. One member of a joint enterprise to another.

   d. A parent's negligence to their child.

3. Plaintiff, a tightrope walker, signs a contract with their employer, a circus owner, which expressly relieves the employer of liability for negligence in the circus. That contract provision is unenforceable under which of the following circumstances?

   a. The tightrope breaks because of negligent maintenance.

   b. The tightrope breaks because the strong man cuts it in a fit of jealousy.

   c. The tightrope breaks because the maintenance crew used substandard materials, which they should have known presented an unreasonable risk of great harm.

   d. The language of the provision was so convoluted that plaintiff reasonably did not understand it.

   e. In all of the above, because such agreements are generally held unenforceable in favor of employers as contrary to public policy.

   [Notes: This type of employer-employee contract provision is generally found to be unenforceable as against public policy. However, even if it were enforceable generally, it would not be under b, c, and d. This type of agreement will be enforced in cases of intentional torts (b), and, in some jurisdictions, reckless torts (c). It is also unenforceable if plaintiff was reasonably ignorant of its provisions (d).]

4. Plaintiff accepts a ride home from an office party with Defendant, who has been drinking heavily and is unsteady on their feet. On the way home, Defendant drives their car into a large tree severely injuring Plaintiff. In a jurisdiction that permits the defense of assumption of the risk in negligence cases, Plaintiff sues Defendant and Defendant claims that Plaintiff impliedly assumed the risk that Defendant's negligence would injure them. What result in the following cases:

   a. Plaintiff cannot be said to have assumed the risk in this case. The consent to ride with Defendant was not "informed," because Plaintiff did not know that Defendant was drunk, and therefore could not have understood and appreciated the risk of accepting a ride with Defendant.

   b. Even though Plaintiff did not have the funds to pay cab fare, their decision to ride with Defendant cannot be said to have been made under economic duress. (Even if it had, some courts would not recognize this as a factor making Plaintiff's consent involuntary.) There may have been other alternatives available to Plaintiff. Since Plaintiff's consent to ride with Defendant was voluntary, they may be found to have assumed the risk if that consent was informed, as described in the answer above.

   c. Here Plaintiff clearly did not assume the risk. Since they were unconscious, Plaintiff gave no consent, informed or otherwise. No consent. No assumption of the risk.

   d. Plaintiff will be charged with knowledge of those facts that are readily ascertainable by observation. If Defendant were so drunk that it was clear from observing them that they were in no condition to drive, Plaintiff could be said to have assumed the risk. If, however, Defendant were able to conceal their drunken state, Plaintiff would not have assumed the risk.

5. Runner's last clear chance argument will not succeed in a comparative negligence jurisdiction. The amount of damages will depend upon whether the jurisdiction adopted pure or modified comparative negligence. In a pure comparative negligence jurisdiction, Runner will recover their damages reduced by 50%, the proportion that Runner's fault bears to the total causative fault of their harm. If the jurisdiction has adopted modified comparative negligence, Runner will recover either half their damages or nothing, depending upon the comparative negligence statute.

6.

   a. At one time, Runner would not have been unable to bring suit against their spouse as long as they were still married and living together. However, today, in most jurisdictions, spousal immunity has been abolished in negligence cases—especially in auto cases.

   b. In some jurisdictions, this suit, too, would be barred by a common-law immunity. Some jurisdictions that still observe this immunity recognize exceptions in the following cases: intentional or reckless conduct, torts occurring during Defendant's business activities, wrongful death actions, and suits after the parent-minor child relationship has ended.

   c. There are no common law or statutory immunities for siblings.

   d. In most jurisdictions, Mayor would be liable. Mayor's act in driving to work was not an executive or judicial function, so it would not be protected under a common law or statutory immunity.

e. Neighbor's incompetence would not affect their liability in this case.

PART FIVE. ADVANCED DUTY TOPICS

I. OWNERS AND OCCUPIERS OF LAND

Review Questions

1. The issue is whether Maxwell is liable to Nolan. Nolan is a trespasser, and the facts provided do not specify if Nolan frequently trespassed or if Maxwell discovered Nolan before the incident. In most jurisdictions, Maxwell is under no duty to make his property reasonably safe for trespassers. Therefore, Maxwell is not liable here.

2. The animatronic arguably might constitute an "attractive nuisance." Maxwell is liable for physical harm to children trespassing on their land caused by an artificial condition if (1) they know or have reason to know that children are likely to trespass; (2) the cord created a risk of serious bodily harm or death; and (3) Caroline does not realize the risk. However, the jury would also have to find Maxwell negligent as to Caroline in maintaining the condition. The visibility and common nature of the cords are important factors supporting Maxwell's defense.

3. Tatiana was traveling a public highway and Opal is liable if they negligently conducted an activity that subjected Tatiana to an unreasonable risk of harm. Traveler's trespass was a foreseeable deviation, and Opal is likely liable if they negligently conducted an activity that subjected Traveler, a foreseeable trespasser, to an unreasonable risk of harm.

4. If Trevor knew or should have known of the tree's condition, then they are likely liable. The answer might depend on the location. If Owen or any predecessor planted the tree close to the road as part of their landscaping, or if Owen's land was located in an urban area, Trevor may be more likely to be liable if they had knowledge of the condition. If the tree is in a rural setting with an extended property line, perhaps not.

5. Olivia must know or have reason to know of the condition and realize that it presents a risk of harm to children. The recent purchase of the property cuts against likely liability.

6. Where the lessor knows of a concealed unreasonably dangerous condition existing on the premises at the time the lessee takes possession and fails to warn the lessee, they are liable. However, the lessor need not inspect the premises to discover the condition, and the danger must be latent.

   Lessor is also liable for physical harm caused by dangerous conditions in parts of the premises which lessee is entitled to use and over which lessor retains control, provided lessor by the exercise of reasonable care could have (1) discovered the condition, and (2) made it reasonably safe. Liability does not extend to areas where lessees and their guests are forbidden.

   In some jurisdictions, a lessor may also be liable for negligent failure to repair the leased premises, or for negligent repairs under certain conditions, where the repair is required by the lease or applicable statute or ordinance.

II. EMPLOYER'S LIABILITY TO EMPLOYEES

Review Questions

1. Anthony may argue that Employer failed to provide safe equipment and appliances, to provide a sufficient number of competent fellow servants, to promulgate and enforce safety rules, or to adequately supervise or instruct. Employer might argue that Anthony was contributorily negligent or that they assumed the risk. Also, if Anthony was injured by Margaret while both were performing their jobs, the fellow servant rule applies, and Employer is not liable.

III. ALCOHOLIC BEVERAGES

Review Questions

1. The first issue is whether Bartender is liable under the common law rule. The general common law rule was that one who sold intoxicating beverages was not liable to third persons injured by the person intoxicated, whether directly or indirectly, as furnishing the alcohol was not a proximate cause of Jogger's injury. Here, Bartender sold the intoxicating beverage of liquor to Underage, and Underage, through driving, directly injured a third person, Jogger. Thus, under operation of the common law rule, Bartender was not the proximate cause of Jogger's injury and therefore is not liable.

   The second issue is whether Bartender is liable under the dram shop act. This statute imposes civil liability on commercial sellers in favor of third persons injured by an intoxicated person. Some statutes require that the sales be illegal (as to an underage person), and others require that the beverage sold be the cause of the intoxication. Here, both prongs are met. The facts tell us that Bartender's sale of the intoxicating beverage was illegal, and the facts suggest that Underage became intoxicated because of the liquor sold by Bartender. Therefore, under operation of the statute, Bartender is liable to Jogger because Jogger was a third person injured by an intoxicated person—Underage.

2. The issue is whether Host is liable to Bicyclist. Most courts have refused to impose liability on persons who are not licensed dram shops who furnish alcoholic beverages to others with resulting physical harm—even where the application of ordinary negligence principles would justify recovery. Here, Host is not a dram shop and is providing liquor inside their home. There was resulting physical harm, as Guest hit Bicyclist, but nevertheless, Host would not be liable under the majority rule—because Host is not a licensed dram shop. Therefore, Host is not liable here.

PART SIX. STRICT LIABILITY

I. STRICT LIABILITY FOR ANIMALS

Review Questions

1. The issue is whether the homeowner faces liability for a cat intruding on the property of another without further harm. Except where imposed by statute or ordinance, possessors of dogs and cats are not strictly liable for their trespasses. Here, the mere fact of escaping from the family home and entering the property of another, would not be enough to impose liability.

2. The issue is whether an Amazon driver can recover for the harms caused by the client's pet skunk spraying the driver. One who possesses animals not customarily domesticated in the region is strictly liable for all harm done by the animal as a result of a harmful or dangerous propensity characteristic of such animals. Therefore, the homeowner will be liable for all resulting harms from the skunk spraying the driver.

3. Defendant, a salesperson, enters the Plaintiff's property. Under which of the following conditions is the Defendant liable if their dog attacks Plaintiff?

   a. If a statute or ordinance imposes strict liability for dog bites.

   b. If Defendant knew that the dog was vicious.

   c. If Defendant is negligent and this negligence results in Plaintiff's injury.

   d. All of the above.

4. The Defendant can assert a defense of assumption of risk. As a general rule, one who possesses animals not customarily domesticated in that region is strictly liable for all harm done by the animal as a result of a harmful propensity characteristic of such animals. However, if Plaintiff voluntarily brings themself into proximity with the animal and provokes the attack, this may be found to be the voluntary assumption of a known particular risk.

5.

   a. Plaintiff will rely on the list of factors from the Second Restatement to advocate for strict liability. Here, Plaintiff will argue that the act of driving a helium-filled balloon tethered to a car presented a high degree of risk to others that could not be eliminated with due care. Plaintiff will argue that this activity is not a matter of common usage, and it is not appropriate for the geography where it occurred because of the presence of pedestrians and heavy-duty power lines. Finally, Plaintiff will argue that the activity had no social utility. A mere publicity stunt does not support this degree of risk.

   b. Plaintiff will rely on the two factors in the Third Restatement. The Plaintiff will argue that the activity of driving a helium-filled balloon tethered to a car created serious risks that were foreseeable and could not be mitigated by reasonable care. This activity was unique and not a matter of common usage.

6. Blasting is the iconic example of an activity that qualifies for strict liability in all jurisdictions. Knowing that it qualifies for strict liability, the only question remaining is whether the harm that Plaintiff suffered resulted from the blasting. Here, the facts do not give any indication that there are any issues connecting the blasting to the cracked walls causally. The homeowner will likely recover for the resulting damages.

7. The issue is whether the property damage resulted from the abnormally dangerous activity or not. Defendants are not strictly liable to the extent that Plaintiff suffers harm resulting from Plaintiff's abnormal sensitivity. It is thus unlikely that Defendant will be liable here based on the facts stating that Plaintiff was unusually jumpy.

PART SEVEN. PRODUCTS LIABILITY

Products Liability

1. Henry can bring suit on behalf of Sampson against Acme Lawn Company and Home Depot (the seller and the product manufacturer). Against both, Sampson will argue that the mower was unreasonably dangerous for two reasons: (1) it was defectively designed, in that it tipped over when used on slopes; and (2) the warnings against using on hillsides and driving by children were inadequate. The product defendants will deny these allegations and will argue that Henry and Sampson misused the product by using it in a manner expressly proscribed in the directions.

   Misuse is not a defense when it is foreseeable. The disclaimer is ineffective as against public policy. The manufacturer can be strictly liable under R.2d § 402A if the product's design is "defective" causing it to be "unreasonably dangerous." However, under modern products liability rules, in most jurisdictions Acme will be liable for a design defect only if the risk of harm was foreseeable to Acme, and in some jurisdictions the plaintiff must prove that there was a feasible alternative design that would have prevented the harm.

   Products liability can include inadequate warnings (for example, warnings that do not specify consequences) and directions for use, but Sampson must show that the Defendants knew of the danger and then failed to provide a warning.

   If the jury finds liability here, it extends also to Home Depot, regardless of its knowledge of the mower's alleged defects. The defenses of contributory negligence (if and to the extent applicable in products liability cases) and assumption of the risk may apply to reduce or bar any damages sought by Henry but do not reduce Sampson's recovery.

   Henry will also argue that the mower was negligently designed and that the warnings were inadequate. Home Depot will defend that it was unaware and had no reason to know of the alleged defects in the mower. Acme will deny the allegations and argue that Sampson was not a foreseeable user. The standard of care for negligent design (including negligent failure to warn) is similar to the "unreasonably dangerous" standard under strict product liability. Acme will also argue that Henry's damages must be reduced by his own contributory negligence or assumption of the risk. Sampson is too young to be subject to those defenses, and Henry's fault is not imputable to him.

2. General Counsel should advise Acme to make its warnings more accessible. Larger font, including images of an X over an image of the lawnmower on a hill would be helpful. The warnings might also be placed closer to the seat, the ignition, or the keys to ensure visibility.

   The learned intermediary doctrine and the sophisticated consumer doctrine do not likely have any relevance here. The product is sold at Home Depot without a learned intermediary (such as a doctor) intervening in the selection. It is used by everyday consumers as well as more sophisticated consumers, such as professional landscapers.

PART NINE. NUISANCE

Review Questions

1. A private nuisance is an activity which substantially and unreasonably interferes with a Citizen's use and enjoyment of his land. Here, the interference affected both the property itself and Citizens' comfort and health. It may also have impaired Citizens' mental tranquility. Liability is not strict, so Citizens must prove that the company's interference with their interest was intentional, reckless, negligent, or the result of an abnormally dangerous activity such that principles of strict liability will apply. The interference was likely recurring, substantial, and unreasonable since the gravity of Citizens' harm was probably greater than the utility of the company's conduct. Citizens will likely recover damages, and if the nuisance continues, a court may issue an injunction.
2. Company's activities have interfered with the public's rights to health, safety, and comfort. These rights are common to the public as a class, and not merely to the group of Citizens. Their remedy is a criminal prosecution or suit to enjoin the nuisance by public authorities. They can recover under a public nuisance theory only if their harm is different in kind from that suffered by all members of the public as a class.

PART TEN. MISREPRESENTATION, DEFAMATION, AND PRIVACY

I. MISREPRESENTATION

Review Questions

1. Defendant, a car salesperson, tells Plaintiff that a car in which Plaintiff has expressed interest in was owned by an infrequent and cautious driver who only drove it 25,000 miles tota and never over 30 miles an hour. These statements are all true. However, Defendant also knows that the oil was never changed, and that the car was in three major accidents and spent six months at the bottom of a lake. Defendant gives Plaintiff the former owner's phone number, but Plaintiff does not bother calling. Instead, Plaintiff buys the car and without inspecting it drives off. Three days later, while Plaintiff is driving the car, the bent and rusted front axle breaks, and Plaintiff has an accident which results in the total destruction of the car and in serious injury to Plaintiff.

    a. Plaintiff cannot recover any damages for misrepresentation because Defendant misrepresented nothing.

    b. Plaintiff cannot recover any damages for misrepresentation because Plaintiff could have easily discovered the defect by looking or by phoning the former owner.

    c. Plaintiff can recover the difference between what Plaintiff paid for the car and what it was worth before the accident.

    d. Plaintiff can recover the difference between what Plaintiff paid for the car and its value before the accident and, in addition, Plaintiff can also recover for the damage to the car and their injuries from the accident if these were proximately caused by their reliance on Defendant's statements.

Even though Defendant did not make any false statements, liability can be predicated on the fact that Defendant knew their statements were so factually incomplete that they were misleading. It also seems clear that Defendant intended for Plaintiff to rely on Defendant's representations and that Plaintiff in fact did so. Under the modern rule Plaintiff's failure to call the former owner and their failure to check the condition of the car are of no consequence even though Plaintiff could easily have done these things. Plaintiff can recover the difference between what they paid for the car and its actual value at that time and, in addition, because it was foreseeable that an accident could result, the damage to the car and their personal injuries that proximately resulted from the accident.

II. DEFAMATION

Review Questions

1. Yes, the neighbor has a claim for defamation against Defendant and will recover at least nominal damages. Defamation requires a statement about Plaintiff be published and resulting damage to Plaintiff's reputation. Here, the neighbor made a statement, and the statement was published to attendees of the barbecue. The statement was defamatory in that having an extramarital affair is likely to lower others' estimation of Defendant in the community. The facts also tell us that the statement is false. Fault is also required for defamation depending on the status of the defendant. There is nothing here to indicate that Defendant was a public figure or public official, so actual malice is not required. Even while the time was short before the neighbor's retraction, the injury of lowered esteem in the community was accomplished for that appreciable time.

2. The issue is whether Defendant faces any defamation liability for dictating a letter containing defamatory statements to their secretary. Defamation requires a defamatory statement about Plaintiff be published and resulting damage to Plaintiff's reputation. There were defamatory statements, according to the facts. The element at issue here would be publication, which generally requires only that the defamatory statements be communicated to a third party. In most jurisdictions, publication to defendant's agent is sufficient, and if the communication is dictated for a writing, the conduct is libel. Here, there is sufficient publication because Defendant communicated the defamatory statements to their agent (the secretary), and those statements were intended to be reduced to writing, making this libel.

3. The issue is what the most likely outcome of a defamation suit against Defendant will be. There are conditional or qualified privileges for defamation. One such privilege is protection of interest of a recipient or third party. Defendant's defamatory communication is conditionally privileged when the circumstances cause Defendant to correctly believe that the information affects a sufficiently important interest of the recipient. One scenario covered by this privilege is reporting to an employer about the character or conduct of a prospective employee, i.e., serving as a job reference. An important factor that weighs in favor of applying this privilege is that the statements were in response to a request, rather than volunteered by Defendant. Here, assuming Defendant's statement is defamatory, the qualified privilege of protection of interest of recipient applies because Defendant was acting as a job reference and relaying information that affected the employment interest of Employer. Application of the privilege is supported by the fact that Employer called Defendant and requested information about Plaintiff. Defendant did not volunteer the information on their

own. Therefore, the likely outcome of a defamation suit against Defendant would be that Defendant will not be liable.

4. While testifying as a witness in court Defendant falsely and gratuitously refers to their neighbor, who is not in court, who is not a witness, and who is not a party to the suit, as a loud, obnoxious, stupid, fool whose rantings disturb the neighborhood. Which of the following is accurate?

   a. Plaintiff cannot recover damages from Defendant because the statement was made in court.

   b. Plaintiff cannot recover damages because they did not themself hear the statement.

   c. Plaintiff cannot recover damages unless they can show special damages because this is not a slander per se.

   d. Plaintiff cannot recover under the *Gertz* rule unless they show that Defendant was at least negligent.

   (d) is wrong because *Gertz* probably applies only to defamation in the press, media, or in books. (b) is wrong as a matter of law. (a) is wrong because the absolute immunity for statements made during judicial proceedings does not apply where the statement has no relation to the proceeding.

IV. PRIVACY

Review Questions

1. In most jurisdictions, a cause of action for the public disclosure of true private facts can be maintained where, as here, the facts are embarrassing or humiliating, were previously unknown to the general public, and are not matters of legitimate public interest.

2. Photographing or watching a person from a public place, even if offensive, is not actionable because there is no intrusion into the person's private life (assuming Sarah does not intrude too closely into Diego's personal space).

3. In most jurisdictions a person who appropriates the name or likeness of another for their own use or benefit is liable to the other.

PART ELEVEN. VICARIOUS LIABILITY

Review Questions

1. Restaurant Owner owned a top-rated restaurant and employed Host as its on-site manager. One day, Host greeted Diner at the restaurant. After Diner went to the restroom to wash their hands, Host intercepted Diner in the hallway of the restaurant, grabbed Diner's face, and kissed Diner on the mouth. Diner considered this to be unwelcome touching.

   If Diner brings a lawsuit against Restaurant Owner, can Restaurant Owner be held liable for Host's conduct toward Diner?

   a. Restaurant Owner may be liable for Host's conduct toward Diner because Restaurant Owner is Host's employer.

b. Restaurant Owner cannot be liable because an employer cannot be subject to liability for the intentional torts of its employees.

c. Restaurant Owner may be liable for Host's conduct because Host's conduct was foreseeable.

d. Restaurant Owner cannot be liable because Hosts and Diners have a special relationship.

2. Summer Camp Organization ran a summer camp for children. Summer Camp Organization employed Camp Counselor to help run the summer camp. When Summer Camp Organization hired Camp Counselor, there was nothing raising concern in Camp Counselor's background check, and Camp Counselor reasonably believed that there were no risks associated with Camp Counselor performing the job. One day, during the summer camp, Camp Counselor became annoyed with one Child and pinched Child on the arm, injuring Child.

   If Child's Parents bring a lawsuit against Summer Camp Organization on behalf of Child, can Summer Camp Organization be held liable for Camp Counselor's conduct toward Child?

   a. Summer Camp Organization may be liable for Camp Counselor's conduct toward Child because Summer Camp Organization is Camp Counselor's employer.

   b. Summer Camp Organization cannot be liable because an employer cannot be subject to liability for the intentional torts of its employees.

   c. Summer Camp Organization may be liable for Camp Counselor's conduct because Camp Counselor's conduct was foreseeable.

   d. Summer Camp Organization may be liable because Summer Camp Organization has a special relationship with children who participate in their programs and therefore owe children-participants a duty of protection.

3. Aero Airlines learned that a passenger infected with the highly contagious B1C2 virus traveled on its flight. Aero Airlines contracted with Spotless Cleaners, Inc. (SCI) to sanitize and clean the plane in which the infected passenger flew. SCI was indisputably negligent in its clean-up efforts causing Polly Passenger to further contract the virus on a subsequent flight. Polly sued Aero Airlines. Which of the following is the most likely outcome in this suit?

   a. Aero Airlines is not liable because it hired an independent contractor.

   b. Aero Airlines is not liable because of corporate immunity.

   c. Aero Airlines is liable because the independent contractor was negligent.

   d. Aero Airlines is liable because of the non-delegable duty doctrine.

PART TWELVE. JOINT TORTFEASORS

Review Exercises

1.

   a. Piper may choose to sue only the jaywalking pedestrian and obtain a full recovery of damages. Piper would be made whole; however, depending on the jurisdiction, the jaywalking pedestrian may be able to recover from the driving friend separately joining the driving friend as a third party in the case brought by Piper. Piper could also settle with the jaywalking pedestrian for damages proportional to their responsibility then release them from liability. Piper would not be made whole, but the jaywalking pedestrian would no longer be able to recover from the driving friend. R.3d Apportionment of Liability §§ 10, 23.

b. In a several liability jurisdiction, Piper may only sue the jaywalking pedestrian for damages proportional to their responsibility. Piper cannot be made whole without suing the driving friend, unless a court finds the jaywalking pedestrian was 100% at fault. R.3d Apportionment of Liability §§ 10, 23.

PART THIRTEEN. DEFENSES TO LIABILITY—GENERAL

1. Carl would not have been able to sue Donnie under the common law rule by which parents were immune from suit by their children. Today Donnie is still unlikely to be sued by Carl for this type of claim. If the state has abolished parental immunity, there is a possibility. However, even states that have abolished parental immunity are still reluctant to find liability for negligent supervision, such as that described here.

2. Mattias is a minor. The statute of limitations on Mattias's claim will not begin to run until he is of age. Thus, Mattias will likely not be time-barred from suing for a birth injury.

3.

   a. Parker can argue that the statute of limitations is tolled by their repressed memories of sexual abuse. There may also be a statutory extension to the statute of limitations. Phillip has a strong argument.

   b. Parker can bring a claim against the parish itself for negligent supervision if the facts suggest that the parish knew or should have known about the abuse and failed to take adequate steps.

4. A United States military doctor committed negligence in an emergency appendectomy procedure at Ft. Knox performed on a soldier. Which of the following statements is the most accurate?

   a. Since the government waived sovereign immunity, the patient can proceed with a lawsuit for negligence.

   b. The longstanding doctrine of sovereign immunity prohibits suit here.

   c. The patient's sole remedy arises under the Workers' Compensation statutes because it happened in the course of employment.

   d. The patient is barred from suing the federal government for malpractice under the *Feres* doctrine exception.

5. The National Highway Traffic Safety Commission (NHTSC), a federal government agency, has authority to mandate manufacturer recalls of products that it concludes pose an unreasonable risk of harm to consumers. The NHTSC received reports of 13 deaths relating to the deaths of drivers due to an ignition switch malfunction in Lamar Motors vehicles, but it took no action. The families of victims have filed a lawsuit against the NHTSC. What is the NHTSC's strongest defense to this suit?

a. That the claim is expressly preempted by state law.

b. That the claim is impliedly preempted by state law.

c. That the agency is immune because it is a federal government agency.

d. That the agency is immune under the discretionary function exception.

Appendix B

Practice Examination and Analysis

QUESTIONS

Here are two practice examination questions that author Ted Kionka has used on torts examinations in the past. Complete each question in the suggested time, including reading, outlining, and writing your answer. This section also includes analysis of the issues and rules you should have spotted and analyzed.

GENERAL INSTRUCTION

Assume that the following events (in both questions) take place in the mythical State of Calinois, which generally follows the prevailing common law of torts and the Restatement (Second) of Torts. Specifically, you may assume that Calinois has adopted the pure form of comparative negligence.

QUESTION ONE

(Suggested Time: One Hour)

Dudley Dunham owns a computer store in Chicago, Calinois. He has been the victim of a number of burglaries and burglary attempts. Finally, he decided, enough is enough. He installed a metal screen door, to which he connected several automobile batteries. According to his research, which is accurate, the batteries as wired together provide enough electricity to cause a severe shock to one touching the door, but not enough to cause serious or permanent bodily harm or death in ordinary human beings. On October 15, Dudley began electrifying his door with this device each evening between 11:00 p.m. and 6:00 a.m. He posted a sign on the door saying, "WARNING! THESE PREMISES PROTECTED BY AN ELECTRICAL ANTI-THEFT SYSTEM."

On November 1, Jonathan Apple purchased a computer system from Dudley's store. The computer turned out to be hopelessly defective. Despite numerous attempts, Apple was unable to get Dudley to repair or replace his unit. Apple finally reached the limit of his frustration. On the evening of November 1, Apple became intoxicated and went to Dudley's store. He arrived at 11:30 p.m., but he thought it was much earlier and that the store was open. Too drunk to read the sign, he grabbed the door, and received a severe jolt of electricity. The electrical jolt aggravated his already inebriated state. In a stupor, he staggered into the street and collapsed, unconscious. Seconds later, he was run over and severely injured by an automobile being driven by one Garner, who was driving *non-negligently.*

Analyze and discuss the liability of Dudley Dunham to Jonathan Apple.

QUESTION TWO

(Suggested Time: Two Hours)

Luke Skyman is a student pilot taking flying lessons at USI airport from Ace Flying School and Service, a commercial profit-making enterprise. Luke has had 20 hours of the required 40 hours of in-plane instruction. Under Federal Aviation Administration regulations, he is permitted to act as pilot of a single-engine airplane, and he can fly solo for learning purposes. However, under FAA rules, student pilots are permitted to take passengers only if a currently licensed flight instructor is sitting in the co-pilot's seat.

On December 1, Luke decided to go for a spin in an airplane. He went to the USI airport and rented an airplane from Ace. His friend, Fast Eddy Strickland, went with him. Fast Eddy used to be a flight instructor, but his flight instructor license is no longer current. Luke's girlfriend, Lois Lane, also went with him. She knew he was only a student pilot, and knew that student pilots cannot take passengers unless a licensed flight instructor is along, but she thought that Fast Eddy was still licensed.

When he signed up for the flight course, Luke was required as a condition of the course to sign a release which says, in part:

"I, Luke Skyman, hereby release Ace Flying School and Service and its officers and employees from all liability for damages for any injuries I may sustain as a pilot, passenger, or otherwise, as long as I am a student in this course."

Luke, Lois, and Fast Eddy got into the airplane. Luke sat in the pilot's seat and flew the plane; Fast Eddy sat in the co-pilot's seat; and Lois sat in one of the two back seats. The flight went without incident for about 20 minutes, when the plane's engine suddenly quit. Luke attempted to make an emergency landing in a nearby field located on Fred Farmer's farm, but the plane overshot the field and struck Fred's house, causing extensive damages. Fast Eddy was not hurt, but Luke and Lois were seriously injured.

It was later determined that the plane's engine quit because the plane ran out of fuel. Lois will testify that Luke failed to visually check the fuel tanks prior to take-off, as he was required to do by FAA regulations. However, Luke denies this; he will testify that he told Fast Eddy to check the fuel, and he relied on Fast Eddy to make this check. Fast Eddy denies any such request. Luke maintains that he was further misled by the fact that the fuel gauges on the airplane were broken and were stuck in the "full" position, a fact which is undisputed.

Analyze and discuss the rights and liabilities of Luke, Lois, Fred Farmer, and Ace Flying School and Service. Be sure to discuss how damages will be apportioned. Do not discuss any product liability theories.

ANALYSIS OF PRACTICE EXAMINATION ESSAYS

Analysis of Practice Examination Essays (from Author Ted Kionka)

QUESTION ONE

I. BATTERY

A. **Cause of Action.** Dunham is guilty of a battery. Battery is an intentional and unprivileged harmful or offensive contact with the plaintiff's person, caused by defendant.

As used in the intentional torts, "intent" means to have a purpose to cause the harm or the knowledge that the harm is substantially certain to occur. Here, Dunham's purpose was to cause at least an offensive contact with unprivileged entrants on his premises. While he did not do so directly, he set in motion the force that was intended to accomplish this harm indirectly. That is sufficient. Although Dunham apparently did not intend to harm *lawful* entrants—and Apple may have been a lawful entrant—he must have known that both lawful and unlawful entrants were substantially certain to be shocked. In the alternative, his intent to harm unlawful entrants will transfer to lawful entrants such as Apple. Therefore, the elements of a battery are present.

The question of Apple's status (trespasser, licensee, or invitee) is irrelevant for purposes of the basic cause of action, since a landowner is liable to even a trespasser for intentional or reckless torts.

B. **Defenses**

1. Defense of Property. The possessor of land or chattels has a privilege to use minimal force to prevent a trespass. Therefore, assuming for the sake of argument that Apple was a trespasser (a doubtful assumption), Dunham would have such a privilege.

   However, this privilege is subject to strict limitations. Ordinarily, the potential trespasser must first be asked to cease or leave. Only when he refuses is force allowed, and only then such minimal force as may be required to prevent the trespass. Moreover, the occupier assumes the risk of a mistake as to the status of the entrant. Thus, if Apple was not a trespasser (see part II.A., below), no privilege exists.

   Here, Dunham was not present; he used a mechanical device to prevent trespasses. The law is clear (as in the spring gun and other "trap" cases) that such a device can do no more than Dunham could do in person. Normally, such devices require a posted warning. It is doubtful that the warning here was adequate, as it did not apprise the visitor of the nature of the "electrical anti-theft system" he would encounter. Thus, the required warning was arguably missing. Moreover, although the force used was not calculated to cause serious bodily harm, it was probably excessive for this purpose. Thus, even if the privilege could be applicable, its scope was exceeded.

2. Consent. Dunham may argue that Apple consented to the harm (or assumed its risk) by proceeding in the face of his warning sign. However, consent is a subjective concept. Even assuming the text of the warning was adequate

(which it probably wasn't), Apple did not in fact see the warning because of his condition. While voluntarily intoxicated persons are often deemed sober for purposes of certain *objective* criteria in tort law, that may not be the case if a *subjective* test such as consent is applicable. This defense is not available.

3. Contributory fault. As a general rule, contributory fault is not a defense or a damage-reducing factor in intentional tort cases. If this is one of those jurisdictions where it is, then whether Apple was contributorily negligent will be discussed below.

II. NEGLIGENCE

A. Cause of Action. If, for some reason, the battery action fails, or if the plaintiff seeks to proceed on a non-intentional tort theory (e.g., to preserve defendant's liability insurance coverage), plaintiff could proceed in the alternative on a negligence theory.

The first issue in a negligence action is duty. Here, Apple's status on the premises would be important, since a general duty of ordinary care is owed to invitees (or, in some instances, to licensees). An invitee is one who enters the premises (a) held open to the public or (b) with the occupier's express or implied permission for a purpose involving business with the occupier. In the case of a store, the premises are usually held open to the public, and entrants come to do business with the occupier. Thus, both tests are applicable here.

The facts do not indicate whether Apple was standing on a public sidewalk or had crossed Dunham's property line when he touched the door. However, even assuming that he had entered the property, the evidence will support a jury finding that he was an invitee. While the scope of an invitation can be limited in time and space, custom suggests that past, present and future customers of a store have an implied invitation to enter the premises so far as they are able, to "window shop" or read the signs or look inside, at almost any time. Thus, in the absence of a clear warning to the contrary, Apple will probably be deemed an invitee.

Dunham may argue that an invitation may be limited in time and space, and that the public was not invited to enter the store after-hours. However, merely grabbing the door to determine if it was unlocked and if the store was open should not be deemed outside the scope of invitee status.

In the alternative, many jurisdictions have now combined the invitee and licensee status, and have extended the landowner's duty of ordinary care to licensees and to persons lawfully passing by on public sidewalks. Under any theory, it is likely that Dunham owed Apple a duty of ordinary care.

Once having found a duty of ordinary care, a breach of that duty is easy to find. A jury could determine that there was no adequate warning (see I.B.1., above), and that the device itself was unreasonably unsafe. If there was negligence, that negligence was clearly the cause in fact of plaintiff's harm. The proximate cause issue is discussed below.

B. Defenses. Dunham will argue that Apple was contributorily negligent in grabbing the door without reading his warning sign. He will argue that Dunham's failure to read the sign was due to his voluntary intoxication, which is no defense. For this purpose, a drunk is treated as if he was sober. However, the jury could find that the warning was inadequate to convey the true nature of the harm. Whether, and to what extent, Apple was contributorily negligent would be for the jury. In Calinois, a pure comparative negligence jurisdiction, Apple's negligence (if any) will merely reduce his damages. It does not bar recovery. For similar reasons, Apple will likely be found not to have assumed the risk. First, the warning is probably not sufficient to apprise Apple of the full nature and extent of the risk, an essential element of this defense. Moreover, unlike contributory negligence, assumption of risk is a subjective concept. Therefore, Apple's failure to read the sign does prevent this defense from operating. We do not reach the issue, whether it is a complete defense or only a damage-reducing factor.

C. **Proximate Cause.** From the foregoing, we see that Dunham may be liable in either battery or negligence for the injury caused by the electrical shock. But what about his injury from being run over by Garner's car? Dunham will undoubtedly argue that the foreseeable risk of injury that he created was, at most, the mild electrical shock and perhaps an injury from falling down as a result of that shock. He would agree that if plaintiff was unusually susceptible to side effects from the shock or fall, he would be liable for those side effects as well. But Apple was not such a person. Thus, under *Palsgraf* and *Wagon Mound* and their progeny, which represent the majority view, he is not liable for the unforeseeable event that occurred—Apple wandering all the way into the street, collapsing, and being run over. His duty, he says, is limited to the scope of the foreseeable risk, which did not include being run over by Garner.

Apple will counter that the risk that, because of the shock, he would stagger into the street was *not* unforeseeable. He will say that he was unusually susceptible by reason of his intoxication, and that under the "eggshell" plaintiff rule, which Dunham concedes, the aggravating effects of the intoxication cannot be disregarded. In any event, the foreseeable risk that Dunham created was the risk of some bodily harm to Apple, either from the shock itself or perhaps from a fall as a result of that shock. The rule is that if the same type of harm occurs as that which made defendant's conduct tortious, defendant cannot escape liability because the actual harm was greater than could have been foreseen, or because the exact way the injury occurred was not foreseeable.

For similar reasons, Garner cannot be a superseding cause. Although the intervening cause itself may not have been foreseeable, the injury that occurred was of the same type as that which made defendant's conduct tortious. In such a case, the intervening cause is not a superseding cause.

The foregoing analysis applies primarily to Dunham's negligence liability. In the case of intentional torts, broader proximate cause rules are applied. Therefore, in the battery action, there is little chance of a successful proximate cause argument. Defendant is liable even for unforeseeable consequences.

QUESTION TWO

I. LOIS v. LUKE

The elements of a common law negligence action are (a) duty, (b) breach of duty (negligent conduct), (c) causation, and (d) damages.

As to Lois, a passenger in Luke's plane, the duty question turns on whether Calinois has an applicable guest statute. Some jurisdictions have had airplane guest statutes, like automobile guest statutes which limit the liability of the driver or owner for injuries to a "guest" (i.e., nonpaying) passenger to injuries caused by the driver's reckless ("willful and wanton") misconduct. The trend is to repeal such statutes, and some have been held unconstitutional. While Lois is clearly a guest here, it is unlikely that such a statute exists. Even if it does, Luke's conduct may qualify as reckless.

Assuming the guest statute hurdle is overcome, there are several possible specifications of negligence. Luke may have been negligent in (a) taking a passenger (Lois) in violation of FAA regulations, since Fast Eddy did not meet the required qualifications (Regulation 1); (b) failing to personally make a visual check of the fuel tanks, also in violation of FAA regs (Regulation 2); and (c) making an inadequate landing.

In most jurisdictions, violation of a safety statute, ordinance, or administrative regulation is deemed negligence per se, provided (1) the safety purpose of the statute coincides with the negligence charged, and (2) the injured person is a member of the class for whose protection the legislation was adopted. Negligence per se means that the statutory violation alone proves negligence; the burden is then upon the violator to establish some legally recognized excuse for his violation. (In some jurisdictions, a statutory violation is merely evidence of negligence, like safety codes and custom and practice.)

Luke clearly violated Regulation 1, and its purpose is clearly broad enough to include injuries to passengers such as Lois. Indeed, passengers are the named beneficiaries. However, it is still necessary to show that the violation of the reg was a cause in fact of plaintiff's harm. Here, it seems doubtful. Fast Eddy was on board; his license had expired. While it could be argued that he was not as sharp or current as if his license had been renewed, it may be difficult to show that the lapse of his license alone had any effect on his ability to handle ordinary flying or even emergencies such as loss of an engine. This situation is analogous to the cases where courts have refused to accept evidence that a driver is unlicensed as proof of his negligence, unless he was unlicensed because of a failure to qualify for the license for substantive reasons.

Luke's violation of Regulation 2, however, is certainly negligence. The obvious purpose of requiring a visual fuel check is to prevent engine-out emergencies. The rule contemplates the possibility that fuel gauges may not be reliable. And the rule obviously is for the benefit of all on board.

Luke may seek to argue that his violation was excused because he delegated this task to Eddy, and reasonably assumed that it had been performed. However, this is not a recognized excuse, especially here where the duty will be deemed non-delegable because of the high risks involved. Moreover, Eddy had no duty to perform this task. At most, Eddy was guilty of nonfeasance of a gratuitous undertaking. Luke may also argue proximate cause, but to no avail. Such conduct can never be a superseding cause, where it was not intentional and was certainly foreseeable.

Luke may also have been negligent in performing his emergency landing. We first note that he will be held to the standard of the reasonably prudent pilot. No allowance will be made for his novice status, or for his youth even if he is a minor (the facts do not indicate). He may have failed to exercise the requisite skill in making the landing. Even though it was an emergency, he was required to exercise reasonable care under the circumstances (one of which was the emergency itself). His use of the emergency doctrine will be further curtailed because his own negligence created the emergency.

Another circumstance affecting the negligence issue is the dangerous nature of the activity. Although the aircraft is not a common carrier, Luke was required to exercise care commensurate with the danger involved in the activity.

Res ipsa loquitur cannot apply here, since res ipsa does not usually work against multiple tortfeasors (e.g., Luke and Ace).

Thus, it seems likely that Luke will be found liable to Lois in negligence. Does he have any defenses?

Lois could not have assumed the risk. Implied assumption of risk requires a full understanding and appreciation of a negligently created risk, followed by the plaintiff voluntarily encountering that risk. While Lois may have assumed the ordinary risks inherent in flying (primary sense), there is no indication that she was aware of any facts that would put her on notice of any pre-existing negligence or the likelihood of future negligence. In addition, in most jurisdictions, assumption of the risk no longer exists as a separate defense, having been merged into contributory fault.

It also appears doubtful that Lois could be found contributorily negligent. She did nothing that could be found to be lack of reasonable care for her own safety.

II. LOIS v. ACE

Ace owed Lois, a passenger in its plane, a duty of ordinary care. Even if there is a guest statute, Ace is not a party protected by such a statute.

Ace may have been negligent in failing to use reasonable care to (a) maintain the airplane (i.e., the fuel gauges), (b) ensure the fuel tanks were full when the plane was rented out, (c) warn Luke that the fuel gauges didn't work, and (d) make sure that Fast Eddy was a currently licensed flight instructor before renting the plane to Luke. Whether any of these was negligence is a question for the jury.

Lois may argue that the violation of the FAA regulation (Regulation 1) requiring a current flight instructor on board is negligence per se. (See discussion under I, above, as to the legal effect of a statutory violation.) There are two problems, however, with this argument. First, it is doubtful that this regulation was intended to apply to Ace; most likely, it creates a duty only on the part of Luke. Second, Ace can argue that its violation of the regulation was not the cause in fact or proximate cause of Lois's injury. See discussion in Part I, above.

Ace could also argue, as the allegations of negligence concerning the fuel, that Luke's failure to check the fuel visually was a superseding cause of Lois's injury, relieving Ace of liability. If an intervening cause is sufficiently significant, it can break the chain of causation between an actor's negligence and plaintiff's injury.

However, ordinary negligence is not deemed a superseding cause, especially when the intervening act was foreseeable and was part of what made the actor's conduct negligent in the first place. Such is the case here. Therefore, Luke's conduct is no defense to Ace.

III. LUKE v. ACE

Luke will argue that Ace was negligent in failing to use reasonable care to (a) maintain the airplane (i.e., the fuel gauges), (b) ensure the fuel tanks were full when the plane was rented out, and (c) warn Luke that the fuel gauges didn't work. Whether any of these was negligence is a question for the jury.

Here, Ace's major defense will be Luke's release. A release operates as an express assumption of risk, and is valid to relieve the actor of liability for his negligent conduct under certain conditions. In general, to be enforceable, the release must be clear on its face and the terms must be brought home to the plaintiff; its terms must clearly encompass defendant's negligence; and its enforcement must not be against public policy (e.g., where there is a great disparity in bargaining power between plaintiff and defendant and the activity is one in which there is a strong public interest or where plaintiff's choice of providers is restricted).

In this case, the terms of the release are clear and its enforcement does not appear to be against public policy. However, the terms of the release do not expressly refer to Ace's *negligence* liability. In such cases, the courts have usually declined to extend the effect of the release to defendant's negligence. Hence, it appears that the release would not bar an action by Luke based on Ace's negligence.

(Luke might also question whether the release should be construed as extending to activities outside the scope of the flying course. Here, Luke's relationship to Ace is the same as any other renter of aircraft. Since the release is ineffective for the reason stated above, however, we do not reach this issue.)

Ace's other defense will be contributory negligence. Calinois is a pure comparative negligence jurisdiction. This means that plaintiff's contributory negligence, if any, will be compared against the negligence of *all other persons* whose negligence contributed to plaintiff's injuries, and plaintiffs recovery will be reduced by the percentage of the total fault attributable to him. In this case, Luke was obviously negligent in failing to make a visual inspection of the fuel tanks before takeoff, and perhaps during the emergency landing. It will be up to the jury to decide if Luke was negligent, and if so the percentage of his fault. However, he can still recover part of his damages even if his fault is greater than 50%. Implied assumption of risk will not apply, because there is no evidence that Luke had actual knowledge of the risk and chose to encounter it.

IV. FARMER v. LUKE

The first issue is whether Luke is liable to Farmer for trespass to land. Trespass is an intentional entry upon the land of another without a privilege to do so. The question is, did Luke intend to enter Farmer's land? Although Luke apparently had no choice but to land the plane when it ran out of fuel, I will assume that Luke had a choice as to *where* he would land it. He could have chosen any of several fields. Therefore, it appears that his entry upon Farmer's land was intentional and therefore a trespass.

Luke's most likely defense is the privilege of private necessity. One is privileged to enter the land of another if it is (or reasonably appears to be) necessary to prevent serious harm to the actor. Luke probably chose to land in Farmer's field because it provided the safest choice available to him at the time. The privilege applies. But when the entry is for the benefit of the actor, the actor must pay damages for any harm done in the exercise of the privilege. Therefore, Luke will be liable for the damage to Farmer's land and buildings.

In the event that the trespass action should fail, or if the damages allowable to Farmer would be greater under a negligence theory (due to the necessity privilege), Farmer would undoubtedly have a cause of action in negligence based on Luke's negligent failure to check the fuel tanks, and possibly for making an inadequate landing.

V. FARMER v. ACE

As previously noted, Ace may have been negligent in failing to use reasonable care to (a) maintain the airplane (i.e., the fuel gauges), (b) ensure the fuel tanks were full when the plane was rented out, (c) warn Luke that the fuel gauges didn't work, and (d) make sure that Fast Eddy was a currently licensed flight instructor before renting the plane to Luke. Whether any of these omissions was negligence, and whether any of them was a cause in fact of the damage to Farmer's property, is a question for the jury.

VI. ACE v. LUKE

Ace may counterclaim against Luke for damage to the airplane, based on Luke's negligence in failing to make a visual check of the fuel tanks. In a pure comparative negligence jurisdiction, two parties who are both negligent and who each sustain damages in the same occurrence may both recover damages, reduced by the percentage of negligence attributable to each of them. Thus, Ace can maintain its counterclaim.

Ace would not have an action for conversion, because the use of the airplane was permissive and there was no intent to assert dominion or control inconsistent with Ace's ownership.

VII. ALLOCATION OF DAMAGES

Under the majority view, comparative negligence has no effect on the principle of joint and several liability. Therefore, all defendants who are found negligent are liable in accordance with Calinois' allocation of damages rules—each jointly and severally liable to each plaintiff whose injury was caused in part by that defendant's negligence for the full amount of that plaintiff's damages, reduced by that plaintiff's percentage of fault; severally liable; or liable under some hybrid joint liability scheme. Damages for trespass (an intentional tort) would probably not be reduced by comparative negligence, but Farmer could not possibly have been contributorily negligent.

In addition, assuming and to the extent defendants are jointly and severally liable, each such defendant can bring an action for contribution against the other. (If Calinois is a several liability state, there can be no contribution.) Under modern principles of comparative contribution, jointly and severally liable defendants who pay more than their proportionate share of plaintiff's damages may be entitled to recover from other such defendants who have paid less. In this phase of the case, the jury will assess each defendant's share of the total fault of all defendants. Thus, for example, assume the jury finds both Luke and Ace liable to Lois and Farmer, and Luke and Ace are jointly and severally liable. The jury might assess Luke's fault at 75% and Ace's fault at 25%. Plaintiffs Lois and Farmer could collect their judgments against either or both defendants, but Luke and Ace would then share the ultimate responsibility in a 75–25 ratio.

If Luke is found liable to Ace and Ace is found liable to Luke, each party to these claims can recover their damages from the other, reduced by the other's contributory negligence, without any offset.

Torts Midterm Examination Essay Problem

Prof. Porter
"The Concert"

Fannie was in line outside of Monroe Circle Garden Arena to attend DJ Tay's "Renaissance Eras" concert. Monroe Circle Garden (known as "MCG") is located in the city of New Amsterdam, in the state of New Amsterdam. The energy in the line of concertgoers was electric, and concertgoers were both excited and impatient about the concert, which didn't start for another two hours.

At this point, no concertgoers were allowed inside of MCG, and MCG staff were keeping guard around the line, which was cordoned off by crowd control barriers. Fannie, who was attending the concert with her friends, decided she would go and buy the group some snacks from the convenience store around the corner while they waited and held her place in the line.

Fannie went to the convenience store, purchased some snacks, and was walking back to the lengthy concert line when she noticed an exterior door to the arena was open! The open door displayed a sign that read, "MCG Staff Only." Fannie, curious, walked near the edge of the doorway, but not immediately in front of it. The door seemed to lead to a small hallway inside the arena. Just then, Fannie saw an MCG Security Guard inside walk past the doorway. The MCG Security Guard held a phone to his ear and paced back and forth in the hallway. At one point, in the middle of his pacing and conversing, the MCG Security Guard glanced in her direction, smiled, and waved his hand in a "come here" manner, seemingly beckoning her to come inside. Fannie thought, "*Oh em gee! A kind soul helping out a big fan! I may get to explore and see DJ Tay!!*" The Security Guard then turned away, walked down the hallway, and continued talking on the phone about what sounded like MCG Security-related matters. Fannie walked through the door and stepped into the hallway, amazed. The MCG Security Guard seemed to have disappeared, so Fannie walked down the hall to see where it led.

In reality, the MCG Security Guard had not even really noticed Fannie and had written her off as merely another fan on their way to the concert line. The MCG Security Guard had, in fact, smiled at an MCG Staff Member who was walking outside not far behind Fannie. That MCG Staff Member had been using a dolly to wheel boxes into the arena, and MCG Security Guard had waved for MCG Staff Member to come into the open door. Once MCG Security Guard had done so, he had turned away to resume an important security discussion with his boss; he had not even noticed Fannie walking through the door or down the hallway.

But now Fannie was inside the arena, having the time of her life! Not long after walking down the hallway, she had noticed a passageway marked "Backstage." "*Oh wow,*" Fannie thought. "*DJ Tay, here I come!*"

Fannie wandered down the passageway and soon found herself in the wings of the stage! And none other than DJ Tay was onstage rehearsing! Fannie was enraptured by DJ Tay's presence. She could not believe she was witnessing this living legend practice her craft—and she was getting an exclusive peek before all of her friends!

Suddenly, Fannie developed an intense desire for DJ Tay to know who Fannie was and to know that Fannie was her absolute biggest fan. Fannie wanted DJ Tay to know that DJ Tay's voice was angelic and that that angelic voice had changed Fannie's life. "I need to get her attention," Fannie whispered as she paced around the left wing of the stage, searching for something she could throw in DJ Tay's direction. Fannie then noticed a walkie talkie sitting on the floor nearby, which was labeled with a sticker that read "Property of MCG." Fannie immediately grabbed the walkie talkie, deciding she would throw it out onstage. Fannie did not want to scare DJ Tay or hit her with the walkie talkie. She just wanted DJ Tay to be alerted to the presence of her biggest fan. Fannie reared her arm back and threw the walkie talkie.

As the walkie talkie was airborne, DJ Tay was in the middle of a dance spin, and she noticed the walkie talkie careening towards her. DJ Tay happened to be extensively trained in dodgeball, a useful skill given how frequently fans hurled projectiles onstage during her career. Seeing the walkie talkie, DJ Tay was not scared at all. In fact, she enjoyed the sight of it, because it represented a dance challenge that she knew she could overcome. With finesse, DJ Tay transitioned from the spin into a somersault, completely dodged the walkie talkie, and continued in her dance routine. The walkie talkie crashed into the stage floor.

DJ Tay's entourage, watching from the audience floor, cheered and cried out, "Yes, Tay!" because they were so delighted by DJ Tay's improvisation and dance skill. But one person was not entertained by this series of events, and that was Federal Agent Elliot Porter, who was watching from stage right. Agent Porter was guarding DJ Tay during her concerts as part of an FBI investigation into a clandestine group of DJ Tay anti-fans—known as DisTayste—who often showed up at DJ Tay concerts and whose goal was to sow chaos and confusion by causing random disturbances that put the singer and the public in danger.

Agent Porter had seen Fannie throw the walkie talkie. Immediately, he sprang into action and dove onstage to try and catch the walkie talkie. Thankfully, DJ Tay had dance-dodged the projectile, and it had crashed onto the floor. Agent Porter retrieved the walkie talkie and looked up to ascertain Fannie's location. Seeing Agent Porter look at her, Fannie realized she might be in trouble and began running away. Agent Porter turned on the walkie talkie and dialed it to his partner, Agent Benson who was outside the arena. "I think I've located a member of DisTayste!" he told Agent Benson. "Finally!" Agent Benson responded on the other end, "Let me know when you've apprehended them."

And so began a cat-and-mouse pursuit through the halls of MCG arena, with Agent Porter chasing Fannie around the arena for about five minutes. At this point, Fannie's endurance ran out, and Agent Porter finally caught up to her in the hallway near the concession stands. Panicked, Fannie found herself running into a custodial closet to hide. But Agent Porter saw her go in.

Agent Porter, genuinely believing that Fannie was likely a member of DisTayste and therefore a continuing threat against DJ Tay, barricaded the door of the custodial closet with a chair from a nearby kiosk so that the door could not open. Agent Porter then realized that he no longer had the handcuffs that were usually attached to his belt. "*Shoot,*" he thought, "*I think my cuffs fell off as we were running.*" He knocked on the door and yelled to Fannie, "Ma'am, you're under arrest. Do not try to escape. I'll be back in a few minutes with my partner to read you your rights and take you into custody."

Agent Porter held up the walkie talkie to his mouth to call Agent Benson and ask her to meet him inside the arena so that they could conduct the arrest. However, just as he was pressing the button to make the call, he heard DJ Tay begin rehearsing his *absolute favorite* song, "Cuff it." Agent Porter, overcome with emotion, shouted out with glee and ran from the hallway into the arena space to watch the rehearsal.

The healing power of DJ Tay's rehearsal performance made Agent Porter forget all about the problems of the world, including the incident with Fannie. Hours rolled by, the concertgoers were let into the arena, and the concert began. For the duration of the entire concert, Fannie was inside the custodial closet. At a point, she began to yell and bang on the door. Because the music and audience cheers were so loud, however, no one heard her cries to be let out of the custodial closet. After an hour of banging the door and yelling, Fannie hopelessly gave up and accepted her fate. "I live here now," she whispered in utter dismay.

It was not until the concert was long over and maintenance staff were clearing the arena that they noticed the chair barricading the custodial closet. When they opened the door, they saw Fannie looking disoriented and afraid. Fannie was immediately taken to a hospital, where she was diagnosed with PTSD.

You are an associate at Nelson LLP, a prestigious firm founded by Mr. Nelson, the "Prince of Torts." On your way into work today, you notice that Fannie, DJ Tay, Agent Porter, and in-house counsel for Monroe Circle Garden (MCG) are all seated in the waiting area in the firm's lobby.

Mr. Nelson calls you into a conference room and explains that all of the people in the lobby are the firm's new clients, and each of them would like to sue based on the incidents described above. Mr. Nelson has asked for your help evaluating each plaintiff's prospects. He wants your written opinion as to whether he can establish causes of action for any torts on behalf of each of these new clients, plaintiffs **Fannie, DJ Tay, Porter, and MCG** against various defendants.

Mr. Nelson wants to know (1) whether each of these plaintiffs can potentially assert a prima facie case for any torts you can think of; and (2) whether the defendants to those claims can assert any defenses, and if those defenses are likely to succeed. He of course wants to know, ultimately, if the plaintiffs would likely prevail or fail in their respective cases.

After Mr. Nelson explains this, he hands you a research memo that the case team has compiled. The memo sets out the following: "The state of New Amsterdam has no prohibitions related to conflicts of interest (i.e., law firms are allowed to represent clients who may be opposing parties in a lawsuit)."

Please prepare your written opinion on the issues posed by Mr. Nelson.

Appendix C contains a model rubric from Professor Porter analyzing student responses to this question.

Appendix C

Assessment Rubrics for Examination Questions

Torts I Final Exam

Professor Abrams
Assessment Criteria for Essay Responses

This grading sheet identifies the criteria that I will use in grading your essay exams. Part A is a critical component because it confirms your subject-matter mastery in this course particularly. Part B is a critical lawyering component to develop across all subject matters. Part C is critical to preparing practice-ready students ready to advise real clients with limited resources and only lay understanding of the law.

A. Issue-Spotting Claims and Defenses Using Precise Rules to Reach Accurate Conclusions

• Spots relevant legal issues triggered by the facts presented, including claims and defenses. • Avoids discussing claims that are not presented by the facts. • States accurate legal rules governing each cause of action and each element using precise terminology. • Reaches a clear legal conclusion on all elements and claims. • Articulates counter arguments, as appropriate. • Explains jurisdictional splits, as relevant.	

B. Legal Analysis

• Analyzes the legal rules by applying the law to the facts provided in the fact pattern accurately and explicitly. Shows the reasoning that leads to the stated conclusion fully and completely.	

C. Client-Centered Framing

• Organizes analysis clearly and thoughtfully to maximize client understanding. • Explains in a client-centered manner why the rule is what it is, particularly when the outcome is adverse to the client's expectations or needs. • Explains *who* specifically will raise each claim and counter claim. • Grounds legal analysis of each legal claim in appropriate level of coverage given the viability of the claim consistent with client resources. • Clearly advises client of why particular claims may be advantageous or disadvantageous, particularly where multiple claims are analyzed. • Appropriately explains the result to the client in procedural, evidentiary, and litigation-based context. Not just "who will win," but "when" and "how" this might occur in the process.	

Professor Jamie R. Abrams
General Grading Criteria

The descriptions below will give you some idea of the reasons behind each grade.[1]

An 'A' exam would make a supervising attorney (client) (the intended audience) feel confident about relying on your work with little or no corrections or interventions. A client would be pleased that you prepared her for all possible counter arguments and legal obstacles that the case would likely encounter. The reader would understand "what" the law is, "how" it applies to her case, and (where appropriate) "why" the law is what it is or why it is as uncertain as it is.

<u>An 'A' exam will</u>:

(a) be easy to read due to strong large-scale organization, clarity, and focus;

(b) have missed no major causes of action or misstated any major rules of law;

(c) have further analyzed the minor or more subtle legal issues in the fact pattern;

(d) connect fact and law seamlessly to reason to legal conclusions;

(e) be based on a close, accurate, and thorough reading of the facts;

(f) ground legal advice in a sophisticated understanding of how a Torts case proceeds through the legal process

A 'B' exam would make a favorable impression on the intended audience. It would communicate that you know the law and legal analysis well. A supervising attorney would enjoy watching your growth and would feel confident that, with guidance, you will be a very good attorney. The work product might require some "gap filling" to thoroughly address all issues, to refine the precise terminology, or to tighten the analytical structure. The intended audience would generally understand the law, the conclusions, and the legal advice with strong clarity.

<u>A 'B' exam will</u>:

(a) be similar to, but lack the thoroughness, power, or polish of an 'A' paper;

(b) have generally hit "the big issues" and stated the law accurately, but missed some of the minor nuances and complexities;

(c) be generally well-organized, but may require the reader to reread certain sentences or paragraphs before fully grasping the author's point or may use excessive space to make minor points;

(d) state defensible legal conclusions, but further clarity may be necessary to understand the reasoning in all its contours;

(e) explain the "what" and "how" of the law, but may leave the client with further follow-up questions regarding why the result is as you suggest it is or why the other side might prevail

A 'C' exam would leave the intended audience uneasy about relying unguardedly on your work or unclear on how you produced the work. Your intended audience might pick up some interesting points of law from the work, but would feel compelled to rethink the legal reasoning and/or closely research your legal rules. However, a supervising attorney would

---

[1] Adapted from a model provided by the University of North Carolina Center for Teaching and Learning and by Professor Ruth McKinney of the University of North Carolina School of Law and from Mary Beth Beazley at Ohio State Law School.

likely see sufficient promise in your work to motivate him or her to invest time and energy in supervising your future assignments more closely.

A 'C' exam may:

(a) present some good thoughts, but contain little organizational structure;

(b) fail to identify all relevant issues fairly raised by the facts;

(c) mis-state or omit important facts;

(d) mis-state some propositions of law relevant to the facts;

(e) rely upon legal doctrine whose relevance is not immediately apparent, or which is not relevant to the facts provided

(f) fail to accurately or appropriately explain the meaning of the law discussed;

(g) present legal analyses which do not follow the logic of the legal doctrines learned in the course; or which are not internally coherent from beginning to end;

A 'D' exam would not be acceptable to a supervising attorney or to the client. It may provide a few cases or ideas from which they could begin on their own but would be wholly undependable standing alone. A supervising attorney would need to rework the document or assign it to a different associate. Both a judge and a supervising attorney might question the reliability of future work.

A 'D' exam may:

(a) significantly misstate the facts, legal doctrine, or major issues;

(b) significantly fail to use the facts from the exam hypothetical or legal authorities within the argument, present significant conclusions with little or no support, or fail to include significant arguments or major legal issues;

(c) contain so many organizational or analytical errors as to inhibit the reader from following the writer's thoughts;

An 'F' exam will show a fundamental lack of grasp of the legal doctrines studied in the course, and a failure to adequately apply those doctrines to the facts presented. An "F" represents the judgment of the professor that this student should re-take the course in order to show sufficient mastery of the subject to be allowed to continue to upper-division courses in the same area, or to sit for the bar exam.

In addition to the deficiencies of a "D" exam, an "F" exam may:

(a) demonstrate consistent lack of knowledge of or misapplication of legal doctrine;

(b) demonstrate a failure to closely read or understand the legal relevance of the facts;

(c) exhibit poor organization, inconsistent legal analysis, and conclusions which do not follow from the premises of the argument;

(d) spend significant time discussing issues not fairly raised by the facts

Prof. Porter
RUBRIC | Torts Midterm Examination Essay Problem

Self-assessment Note: The language in the rubric is meant to be an ideal example of how to write elements of each IRAC. Your answer does not need to match the language exactly. You should be checking your language to ensure all of the key components are present.

TOTAL SCORE___________________

(187 points are available; top scorer establishes 100%)

OVERALL ORGANIZATION AND WRITING STYLE

(0–10 points)_____/10

Logical organization of claims, use of headings, cohesive writing (e.g., use of transitions), correct party names, spelling, grammar. (10)

MCG v. Fannie (TRESPASS TO LAND)

(0–36 points)____/36

Issue: The issue is whether MCG has a prima facie case for trespass to land. (1)

Rule: Trespass to land is intentional entry onto land in the possession of another. (2)

Application(intent):

Statement of intent issue: whether Fannie intended to enter MCG arena. (1)

Statement of intent rules: Intent is purpose to cause a result or knowledge that a result is substantially certain to occur. (2)

Application [about purpose to enter] [knowledge is acceptable but less on point] (3)

Conclusion: There was intent. (1)

Application (entry):

[include some sort of statement about how Fannie did, in fact, enter the arena] Here, there was entry because Fannie walked through the door. (2)[1]

Analysis (land):

Issue: Was Fannie's entry onto "land"? (1)

Rule: Land includes generally everything reasonably above the land, including fixtures like buildings. (1)

Application: Here, Fannie entered land because she walked into MCG arena, which is a building affixed to the land. (2)

Conclusion: Therefore, actual cause is likely met. (1)

Application (in the possession of another):

Issue: We must determine if the land in question was in the possession of another. (1)

Rule: Some other human other than defendant must have a possessory interest in the land. (2)

---

[1] Some elements will not award as many points, given the rule might be so straightforward that it doesn't warrant a full IRAC. Use your judgment to decide which elements warrant a shorter analysis.

Application: Here, the element "in the possession of another is satisfied" because the evidence suggests that the arena is owned by MCG or some company/person other than Fannie. (3)

Conclusion: Therefore, the final element is met (1)

Conclusion (prima facie case: Because all of the elements are met, MCG likely has a prima facie case for trespass to land. (1)

Issue (defenses—consent): This issue now is whether Fannie can raise any viable defenses to the prima facie case. One defense that fits is the defense of consent; Fannie can argue that MCG consented to her entry because the security guard waved her into the building. (2)

Rule: Consent is willingness for conduct to occur. Consent may be actual or apparent. Actual consent is the subjective consent a defendant actually has in their mind. Apparent consent is words (express) or conduct (implied) reasonably understood by another to be consent. (4)

Application: Here, there was no actual consent on the part of MCG staff because Security Guard did not even notice Fannie and was waving to Staff Member. Therefore, there was no subjective consent on Security Guard's part. However, there is apparent consent here because Security Guard used conduct—waving and smiling—that is reasonably understood to show a willingness for a person to enter a space. [or strong argument to the contrary that it was not reasonably understood to be consent] (4)

Conclusion: The consent defense applies/does not apply. (1)

Overall Conclusion: Accordingly, MCG's claim for trespass will likely fail/succeed. (1)

<u>DJ Tay v. Fannie (ASSAULT):</u>

<u>(0–28 points): /28</u>

Issue: The issue is whether DJ Tay has a prima facie case against Fannie for assault. (1)

Rule: Assault is the intentional placement of another in reasonable apprehension of an imminent harmful or offensive contact. (2)

Application (intent):

Issue: Was there intentional placement? (1)

Rule: Intent is purpose to cause a result or knowledge to substantial certainty that a result will occur. (2)

Application: Here, Fannie satisfies the purpose type of intent: she had the purpose to cause DJ Tay to see the walkie talkie onstage, as is evidenced by the fact that she wanted to get DJ Tay's attention. Perhaps Fannie did not want to make DJ Tay believe that the walkie talkie would contact her, but Fannie at least has knowledge to a substantial certainty that throwing a walkie talkie near DJ Tay would result in DJ Tay thinking the walkie talkie might make contact with her person. (4)

Conclusion: Therefore, intent is met. (1)

Application (another)

Issue: We need to establish the element of another. (1)

Rule: Another is a human being other than Fannie. (1)

Application/Conclusion: DJ Tay is a person other than Fannie, so the element is met. (1)

Application (reasonable apprehension):

Issue: To be an assault, a person must be placed in reasonable apprehension. (1)

Rule: Apprehension is not fear; it is awareness. (1)

Application: There was apprehension here because DJ Tay noticed the walkie talkie careening towards her. Her lack of fear is irrelevant. (2)

Conclusion: There was reasonable apprehension. (1)

Application (imminent):

Issue: We must establish whether the potential contact at issue was imminent. (1)

Rule: Imminent means immediate, that it is about to happen. (1)

Application: The imminent requirement was met here, as the walkie talkie was flying in the air towards DJ Tay, as the result of a throw, and was therefore, within seconds, about to hit DJ Tay. (1)

Conclusion: The imminent requirement is met. (1)

Application (harmful or offensive contact):

Issue: Assault requires there to be a potential harmful or offensive contact. (1)

Rule: A harmful or offensive contact is some sort of indirect or direct touching that can hurt someone or offend them [you have to improve with this rule, based on what you know from battery] (1)

Application: Here, there was a potential harmful contact because the walkie talkie being hurled through the air was a hard object that, as the result of a throw, could have hit DJ Tay and hurt her. (1)

Conclusion: Therefore, the element of harmful contact was met. (1)

Conclusion: Because all elements were met, there is a prima facie case for assault. There do not seem to be any viable defenses. Therefore, DJ Tay is likely to succeed in her assault claim and Fannie would be liable. (3)

MCG v. Fannie (TRESPASS TO CHATTELS):

(0–32 points):______/32

Issue: Can MCG sue Fannie for trespass to chattels? (1)

Rule: Trespass to chattels is the intentional interference with or dispossession of a chattel in the possession of another. For trespass to chattels, some harm is required. (3)

Application (intent):

Issue: Did Fannie have intent? (1)

Rule: Intent is purpose to cause a result or knowledge to substantial certainty that a result will occur. (2)

Application: Here, Fannie satisfies the element of intent because she had the purpose of interfering with the chattel by throwing it. This is shown by the fact that she had a plan to use the chattel to distract DJ Tay and get her attention. The facts also tell us that Fannie "decided she would throw" the walkie talkie, indicating her purpose to interfere with it by throwing it. (3)

Conclusion: Therefore, the element of intent is met. (1)

Application (interference):

Issue: Fannie interfered with the walkie talkie. (1)

Rule: Interference is some sort of interaction with the chattel [Improvise this rule]. (1)

Application: Here, Fannie interfered with the walkie talkie because it was sitting on the floor and she grabbed and threw it, changing its position. (1)

Conclusion: Therefore, there was interference. (1)

Application (chattel):

Issue: Trespass to chattels must involve a chattel of some sort. (1)

Rule: A chattel is a piece of moveable property (as opposed to land/fixed property). (1)

Analysis: Here, there was a chattel because the property at issue was a walkie talkie, which is moveable, as is evidenced by the fact that Fannie threw it. (1)

Conclusion: Therefore, the chattel element is satisfied. (1)

Application (in the possession of another):

Issue: Was the chattel in the possession of another? (1)

Rule: Another person other than Fannie has to have had possession of the chattel for this element to be satisfied. (1)

Application: Here, the element is satisfied because the walkie talkie was in the possession of MCG—another entity, not Fannie—as was evidenced by the sticker on the walkie talkie stated "Property of MCG." (2)

Conclusion: Therefore, this element is satisfied. (1)

Application (Harm):

Issue: While the basic elements are established, Trespass to Chattels requires that some harm occurred. (1)

Rule: There has to be some legally cognizable harm to the chattel (or to the plaintiff). (1)

Application: Here, [this element is questionable] [I will accept harm, as evidenced by the fact that the walkie talkie crashed on the floor and since it is an electronic device, it probably suffered some sort of harm] [I will accept no harm, as evidenced by Agent Porter using the walkie talkie to call Agent Benson right after—i.e., it seemed operational] [thoughtful answers that consider both get full points] (3)

Conclusion: Therefore, there was/was not harm. (1)

Overall Conclusion (alternates):

Because all elements were met, there is a prima facie case for trespass to chattels. There do not seem to be any defenses. Therefore, MCG is likely to succeed in its claim against Fannie.

(OR)

There is no prima facie case for trespass to chattels. Therefore, MCG is not likely to succeed in their claim, and Fannie is not liable. (2)

Fannie v. Agent Porter (False Imprisonment/False Arrest)

(0–54 points):____/54

Issue: The issue is whether Fannie can sue Agent Porter for False Imprisonment. [You could call this "False Arrest" given a law enforcement officer was the defendant; that's as far as we really got into "false arrest"; equal points for either name of the cause of action] (1)

Rule: False Imprisonment is the intentional confinement of another, and the plaintiff is aware of or harmed by the confinement. (2)

Application (intent):

Issue: Did Agent Porter have intent? (1)

Rule: Intent is purpose to cause a result or knowledge to substantial certainty that a result will occur. (2)

Application: Here, the evidence suggests that Agent Porter had purpose to confine Fannie because he barricaded the closet with a chair and his goal was to prevent Fannie from escaping or moving freely. This is further indicated by his statement, "You're under arrest. Don't try to escape." This deliberate words and actions indicated his purpose to cause the result of her confinement. (4)

Conclusion: Therefore, the element of intent is met. (1)

Application (confinement):

Issue: Was there confinement? (1)

Rule: Confinement can be achieved through barriers and claim of lawful authority, among other things. Confinement can also be satisfied if plaintiff is confined for any appreciable amount of time. (3)

Application: Here, there was confinement because Fannie's movement was restricted by barriers: the walls and door of the supply closet and the chair barricading the door. Agent Porter also claimed to be using his lawful authority to detain Fannie when he said she was "under arrest." (3)

Conclusion: Accordingly, there was confinement. (1)

Application (another):

Issue: The next element is "of another." (1)

Rule: This element is satisfied by a human being other than defendant being impacted. (1)

Application/Conclusion: Here, the element is met because Fannie is another human being who is not defendant Agent Porter. (1)

Application (awareness/harm):

Issue: The next element is awareness or harm. (1)

Rule: Plaintiff must be aware of the confinement or harmed by it. (1)

Application: Here, Fannie was acutely aware of the confinement because she was yelling and banging on the door for a full hour. The facts also indicate that she was dismayed after an hour of being trapped. [And/or explanation about harm: Ultimately, Fannie was harmed by the confinement because she suffered from PTSD, which is an emotional harm]. (4)

Conclusion: The awareness or harm element is satisfied. (1)

Overall Conclusion (p/f case): Because all of the elements are established, Fannie has a prima facie case for false imprisonment against Agent Porter. (1)

Issue (defenses): Are there any potential defenses Agent Porter can raise? (1)

Application (defense of others):

Issue: One defense might be "defense of others." (1)

Rule: To raise defense of others, a defendant must establish that they reasonably believed that another person was faced with use of force or imminent use of force. If so, defendant may use reasonable force to defend another person. (3)

Application (reasonable belief in imminent force):

Issue: Did Agent Porter reasonably believe someone was facing use of force or imminent use of force? (1)

Rule: [Some sort of articulation about what you are looking for here, for example: Reasonableness is an objective standard, what most people think is normal. And imminence means it is about to happen.] (1)

Application: [I'll accept good arguments either way as to whether Agent Porter's "genuine" belief that Fannie was a member of DisTayste and therefore a continuing threat against DJ Tay was reasonable. That analysis should include some thinking about whether the force potentially threatened by Fannie was imminent.] (4)

Conclusion: (1) [either result]

Application (reasonable force):[2]

Issue: [Even if there were a reasonable belief in imminent use of force,] Agent Porter didn't use reasonable force.[3] (1)

Rule: The force someone uses in defense of others must be reasonable. Force can be bodily harm, offensive contact, or confinement. Reasonable means proportional (enough to avoid or minimize harm; not excessive; not retaliatory). (2)

Analysis: Here, the force used by Agent Porter was confinement, as he locked Fannie in the supply closet for what turned out to be hours. This was not reasonable; it was excessive because it went way beyond was a required to stop Fannie from potentially harming DJ Tay. Initially, Agent Porter meant to confine Fannie for a short time, but he forgot to do that, resulting in hours-long confinement, which is not reasonable. [Note: we don't have to analyze intent here or extended liability principle because we are not analyzing an intentional tort—rather, we are analyzing the defense according to its elements]. Perhaps the defense of others defense could be used to excuse the initial phase of the confinement, but it would not cover the excessive period of confinement. (4)

Conclusion: Therefore, the privilege of defense of others fails. (1)

Conclusion (liability): Because the privilege fails, Fannie would likely succeed in her claim of false imprisonment. (1)

---

[2] You should probably continue to analyze the rest of the defense because "reasonableness" is arguable here. Cover your bases by making an "even if" argument and continuing to analyze other aspects of the defense.

[3] I accept conclusion statements as the "issue" in the IRAC as well. Sometimes that just makes sense with the flow of the narrative. Bottom line: there must be some topic sentence that communicates the issue and element you are about to describe and analyze.

Mention of Section 1983: points if you saw the potential issue of Section 1983, (1) set forth its elements, (1) and dismissed it for lack of a "person acting under color of state law"—since Agent Porter is a federal agent, not a state agent (1)

Fannie v. Agent Porter (IIED)

(0–24 points): ______ /24

Issue: Was there intentional infliction of emotional distress? (1)

Rule: IIED requires intent to cause severe emotional distress; extreme and outrageous conduct; and severe emotional distress must result. Additionally, there must be a causal nexus between the conduct and the emotional distress. (3)

Application (intent):

Issue: The issue is whether there was intent. (1)

Rule: Intent is purpose to cause a result or knowledge to substantial certainty that a result will occur. (2)

Application: Here, Agent Porter did not have purpose to cause Fannie severe emotional distress because he did not mean to leave her in the supply closet for so long. His purpose, instead, was to arrest Fannie and have her taken into custody. Was there knowledge? [I will take good arguments either way, keeping in mind: knowledge is not about whether Agent Porter knew severe emotional distress *could* result; or whether he *should have known* it would result; he would have to *actually* know to a substantial certainty that it *would* result. There is a strong argument that he did not know that when he planned to confine her for a short time, but you could make the argument that he did. However, there is also a strong argument that he did not "know" that the confinement would cause emotional distress because he totally forgot about the confinement.] (5)

Conclusion: Therefore, there was/was no intent. (1)

Application (extreme and outrageous):

Issue: Was Agent Porter's conduct sufficiently extreme and outrageous? (1)

Rule: There is a high bar for what counts as Extreme and Outrageous conduct. It has to be something uncommon and something that would cause a spectator to exclaim "Outrageous!" [I'll take whatever correct rule you articulate here, including listing the factors of a power dynamic, exploiting a known vulnerability, repeated conduct]. (2)

Application: [Not sufficiently extreme and outrageous because that is a high bar] (2) (2 points for probably not extreme and outrageous; 1 point for a strong argument that this was extreme %0Ethis is not as compelling a conclusion, given the caselaw we covered).

Conclusion: [state conclusion, whichever you arrived to] (1)

Application (severe emotional distress):

Issue: Finally, was there severe emotional distress caused by the conduct? (1)

Rule: Severe emotional distress must be shown, and it must be caused by Defendant's conduct.

Application: There was severe emotional distress here, as Fannie experienced PTSD, a serious mental health condition. Based on the fact that Fannie banged on the door for an hour, then resigned herself to utter dismay, and given she was diagnosed with PTSD right after being found in the supply closet, it seems there was a causal nexus between the conduct and her severe emotional distress. (1)

Conclusion: Therefore, there was severe emotional distress caused by the conduct. (1)

Conclusion (p/f case): [appropriate conclusion for your findings] (1)

Ultimate conclusion: [It's likely this claim failed, so no need to analyze defenses; no ultimate liability]. (1)

Extra points for creative additional claims

(0–3 points): ________ /3

Up to 3 additional points may be awarded for additional claims that I did not see, if it is within reason

NOTES/QUESTIONS:

Appendix D

Glossary

A

abnormally dangerous activity An activity for which strict liability is imposed that (1) is not of common usage, and (2) creates a foreseeable and highly significant risk of physical harm even when reasonable care is exercised by all actors. R.2d § 519; R.3d Liability for Physical & Emotional Harm § 20.

appropriation Cause of action under invasion of privacy, in which defendant appropriates plaintiff's name or likeness for commercial gain. R.2d § 652C.

assault An intentional tort in which defendant causes plaintiff to reasonably apprehend an imminent battery. R.2d § 21.

assumption of risk An affirmative defense to negligence and other tort actions which bars or reduces plaintiff's recovery based on plaintiff's knowingly and voluntarily subjecting themselves to a risk of harm. The two main forms are express and implied. R.2d §§ 496A–496G. Implied assumption of the risk is usually no longer a separate defense, having been merged into a contributory fault defense.

attractive nuisance A popular name for the "child trespasser" doctrine (R.2d § 339) which subjects a possessor of land to a duty of ordinary care to a child whose trespass is foreseeable. See R.3d Liability for Physical & Emotional Harm § 51.

authority of law A privilege (defense to an intentional tort) which excuses conduct which would otherwise be tortious because the conduct is authorized by law.

B

battery An intentional tort in which defendant causes a harmful or offensive contact with plaintiff's person. R.2d §§ 13, 18.

bodily harm See **harm.**

burden of proof Rules of law determine which party has the burden of persuading the trier of fact that a fact is or is not true. In a civil (tort) case, the party having the burden of proof on a claim or defense must ordinarily prove it by a preponderance of the evidence. See R.2d § 328A.

bystander One against whom tortious conduct was not directed, or who was not the user or consumer of a product, but nevertheless sustained an injury as a result of defendant's actionable conduct. (1) In product liability cases, foreseeable bystanders are usually eligible to recover. (2) In actions for negligent infliction of emotional distress, most jurisdictions allow recovery by bystanders who witness an injury to a close family member. See R.3d Liability for Physical & Emotional Harm § 48.

C

case The form of action, under the common law writ system, in which the pleader could tailor their complaint to the facts of their particular case. This became the proper form of action for the tort of negligence. The forms of action are no longer in use.

cause in fact Any cause which is one of the factual causes of plaintiff's injury. R.3d Liability for Physical & Emotional Harm § 26.

collateral source rule The doctrine which prohibits defendant from receiving credit (against compensatory damages) for items for which plaintiff was reimbursed from a collateral source. R.2d § 902A(2). Examples: Medical expenses paid by medical insurance; lost wages reimbursed by Social Security or other wage-continuation insurance.

common law (1) English law promulgated by judges in the royal courts which was therefore "common" to the realm. (2) Any judge-made law, as distinguished from law created by statute or other legislation.

comparative fault The doctrine by which the negligence or other fault of plaintiff is compared to that of defendant and plaintiff's damages are reduced proportionately. It also includes comparing fault among tortfeasors for purposes such as contribution or several liability. Also called comparative responsibility. See R.3d Liability for Physical & Emotional Harm § 25.

compensatory damages Damages awarded to compensate plaintiff for a tortiously caused injury. R.2d § 903. The measure of compensatory damages is specific to each cause of action.

concert of action Conduct by persons pursuant to a common plan such that the tort of one is imputed to all. R.2d § 876; R.3d Apportionment of Liability § 15.

concurrent or consecutive tortfeasors Concurrent tortfeasors are those whose tortious conduct operates at the same time. Consecutive tortfeasors are those whose tortious conduct occurs at different times. In either case, if their conduct results in a single, indivisible harm to plaintiff, they are deemed joint tortfeasors. R.2d § 879; R.3d Liability for Physical & Emotional Harm § 26.

conduct In tort law, "conduct" includes both acts and omissions to act, and liability can usually be based on either. However, in certain situations no duty arises from mere inaction. See **misfeasance vs. nonfeasance.**

consent A privilege that negates an intentional tort.

consequential damages Damages sustained as a result of an injury to another—e.g., a husband's loss of consortium resulting from a tortious injury to their spouse; a parent's loss of a child's services resulting from an injury to the child. See, e.g., R.2d §§ 693, 703.

constitutional tort Some constitutional violations can be redressed directly by an action for damages, e.g., under 42 U.S.C. § 1983. Such causes of action are sometimes called "constitutional torts." See R.2d § 874A.

constructive knowledge Constructive knowledge is knowledge that one had a legal duty to acquire, and therefore the law will treat the person as if they had that knowledge, regardless of whether they did or not. In such cases, if defendant didn't know it, defendant should have known it. See **knowledge: should have known.**

contributory negligence A plaintiff's failure to exercise ordinary care for their own safety. R.2d § 463.

contribution A doctrine whereby one of two or more joint tortfeasors against whom plaintiff has obtained a common judgment, who has been required to satisfy that judgment in excess of their proportionate share, can recover that excess from any other joint tortfeasor who paid less than their share. R.2d § 886A; R.3d Apportionment of Liability § 23. Contribution is only available with respect to defendants who are jointly and severally liable.

conversion An intentional tort in which defendant has so seriously harmed or interfered with plaintiff's chattel that defendant can be required to pay plaintiff its full value. R.2d § 222A.

covenant not to sue A contract to settle a claim in which plaintiff does not release their cause of action but merely promises not to file or pursue a suit against defendant, or dismiss a suit already filed. See R.2d § 885; R.3d Apportionment of Liability § 24; **release; loan receipt agreement.**

D

defamation A communication which tends to harm plaintiff's reputation by lowering them in the estimation of the community or deterring others from associating or dealing with them. R.2d § 559.

discipline A privilege (defense to an intentional tort) based upon defendant's right to impose discipline upon plaintiff. Example: Defendant's right as plaintiff's parent or military superior. R.2d §§ 146, 147.

dram shop liability (1) A statutory cause of action to recover limited damages from a commercial vendor of alcoholic beverages for injuries to plaintiff resulting from a customer's intoxication; (2) any common law cause of action recognized against such a commercial venture.

duty A rule of tort law recognizing an obligation running from defendant to plaintiff, the violation of which gives rise to a tort cause of action.

E

eggshell plaintiff rule A rule providing that defendant is liable for the full consequences of plaintiff's injury or damages, even though greater in degree than would normally be a foreseeable result of the occurrence in question, due to the fact that plaintiff was unusually susceptible to the injury (or, indeed, for any other reason), provided injury of the same general type could have been foreseen. Sometimes stated as the "thin-skulled plaintiff" rule, or "you take your plaintiff as you find them." R.2d §§ 435, 461; R.3d Liability for Physical & Emotional Harm § 31.

F

false imprisonment An intentional tort resulting when defendant confines plaintiff within boundaries set by defendant. R.2d § 35.

false light in the public eye One of the subdivisions of the cause of action for invasion of privacy, in which defendant causes publicity which places plaintiff before the public in a highly offensive false light. R.2d § 652E.

fault Most tort causes of action include an element of fault—intent, recklessness, negligence, and even strict products liability in which the fault is placing a defective product in the stream of commerce.

foreseeability Foreseeability is not a separate element of any tort, but it can be a factor in determining issues such as duty, breach of duty, and proximate cause.

G

general damages Damages which at common law were presumed to flow from a tort and therefore did not have to be pleaded specially, such as pain and suffering. R.2d § 904. See **special damages**. Today, this category is often called "non-economic loss" or "pecuniary loss."

H

Hand formula A balancing test for determining whether conduct creates an unreasonable risk of harm and is therefore negligent. Proposed by Judge Learned Hand in *United States v. Carroll Towing Co.* The actor compares the **burden** (B) and utility of the conduct in question compared to alternative, safer conduct with the **probability** (P) that harm will result from the proposed conduct multiplied by the **gravity** of the harm that will probably result (L, or "loss") if the risk is realized. See **negligence; ordinary care.**

harm, physical harm, bodily harm As used in tort law, the term "harm" encompasses any loss or detriment. R.2d § 7(2). "Physical harm" means any physical impairment of the human body, land, or chattels. R.2d § 7(3); R.3d Liability for Physical & Emotional Harm § 4. "Bodily harm" includes physical impairment in the condition of plaintiff's body, or physical pain or illness. R.2d § 15.

I

immunity A doctrine that provides defendant a complete defense to conduct that otherwise would be an actionable tort, such as the family immunities, charitable immunity, and sovereign immunity. Unlike a privilege, an immunity does not negate the tort and must be raised as an affirmative defense, or it is waived. R.2d §§ 895A–895J.

impact rule The traditional common law rule that negligently inflicted emotional distress is not actionable unless defendant's negligent conduct resulted in an "impact" with plaintiff's person, however slight, so that the damages for emotional distress would be parasitic to the action for negligently inflicted bodily harm. R.2d §§ 436A, 456. See **harm**; R.3d Liability for Physical & Emotional Harm § 47.

imputed negligence Doctrines by which the negligence of A is treated as if it were also the negligence of B. A typical example is the vicarious liability of an employer for their employee's negligence (This is also known as "respondeat superior").

indemnity The right of defendant, against whom plaintiff has obtained a judgment, to shift the entire judgment to another tortfeasor. The right to indemnity may arise from an express agreement, operation of law, or a major disparity between defendant's fault and that of the other tortfeasor. R.2d § 886B; R.3d Apportionment of Liability § 22.

injury In tort law, the term "injury" includes the invasion of any interest which is protected by tort law. R.2d § 7(1). It is broader than terms such as "harm" and "physical harm," since it includes torts against relational and other intangible interests. See R.3d Liability for Physical & Emotional Harm § 4.

intent A term of art in tort law, meaning that the actor had either (1) the purpose to cause a particular result, or (2) knowledge that the result is substantially certain to occur. R.2d § 8A; R.3d Liability for Physical & Emotional Harm § 1. Intent is a necessary element of various torts.

intervening cause A cause of plaintiff's injury which comes into operation after the cause for which defendant is responsible and operates with or upon defendant's cause to produce the injury. R.2d § 441; R.3d Liability for Physical & Emotional Harm § 34. See **superseding cause.**

intrusion One of the subdivisions of the cause of action for invasion of privacy, in which defendant intrudes upon plaintiff's solitude, seclusion, or private life in a highly offensive manner. R.2d § 652B.

invitee In premises liability, an entrant upon defendant's land who is either (1) a business visitor or (2) a public invitee. R.2d § 332. An invitee is owed a duty of ordinary care. See R.3d Liability for Physical & Emotional Harm § 51.

J

joint tortfeasor One whose tortious conduct contributed with one or more other tortfeasors to cause a single, indivisible injury to plaintiff. See R.2d § 875 (called "contributing tortfeasors").

K

knowledge: had reason to know "Had reason to know" means that defendant had information from which a person of reasonable intelligence would infer that the fact in question exists, or that such a person would govern defendant's conduct on the assumption that the fact exists. R.2d § 12(1).

knowledge: should have known "Should have known" means that a person of reasonable intelligence and of reasonable prudence would have ascertained the fact, or had a duty to ascertain the fact, or would govern their conduct on the assumption that the fact exists. R.2d § 12(2).

L

last clear chance A disappearing doctrine used to avoid the defense of contributory negligence. If plaintiff is negligently in a zone of danger from which they cannot escape in time, and defendant has the last opportunity to exercise care to prevent the harm but negligently fails to do so, defendant cannot use plaintiff's prior contributory negligence as a defense. R.2d §§ 479, 480.

legal cause Another term for proximate cause. See R.2d § 431.

libel The publication of defamatory matter by (1) written or printed words or (2) another comparably permanent or equally harmful form. See R.2d § 568.

licensee In premises liability, an entrant upon defendant's land who is privileged to enter or remain but who is not an invitee. Example: a social guest. R.2d § 330. See R.3d Liability for Physical & Emotional Harm § 51.

loan receipt agreement A form of settlement in which defendant loans money to plaintiff interest-free, and which need not be repaid except from the proceeds of any amounts recovered from other tortfeasors responsible for the same injury. plaintiff agrees to pursue their claim against the remaining tortfeasors. R.3d Apportionment of Liability § 24

M

malice The term "malice" is used in various contexts in tort law but has no fixed meaning. As applied to the intentional torts, it usually means an intent to cause harm; in that context, the rule is that malice is not required for liability, although it may be relevant as to punitive damages. In defamation law, "actual malice" means the same as constitutional malice—knowledge that the statement is false or a reckless disregard for its truth. R.2d § 580A.

malpractice A term used to designate professional negligence—e.g., medical malpractice.

misfeasance vs. nonfeasance These terms are usually used when discussing the existence of a duty. If the only relationship between plaintiff and defendant is contractual, and defendant merely fails to perform their contract (i.e., nonfeasance), there is often no tort liability. But if defendant commences performance and is thereafter negligent (misfeasance), they may be liable because the commencement of performance is enough to activate a duty of ordinary care to plaintiff. See R.2d § 323; R.3d Liability for Physical & Emotional Harm § 37.

misrepresentation A misstatement of fact. At one time, only intentional misrepresentations were actionable; the name of the tort was "deceit." Today, the category is "misrepresentation" because some negligent (and even innocent) misrepresentations are actionable. R.2d §§ 525, 552, 552C.

mistake An element in some privileges, where defendant is mistaken about a fact or facts that give rise to the privilege. Mistake itself is not a defense, but it is sometimes relevant in determining whether a privilege exists.

misuse In product liability cases, using the product in some way that the manufacturer did not intend. If plaintiff's misuse was foreseeable, it is ignored, or it may constitute contributory fault. If plaintiff's misuse was unforeseeable, then defendant is not liable for an injury caused by that misuse. See R.3d Products Liability § 17, § 2 cmt. p.

mitigation of damages A doctrine that requires plaintiff, subsequent to an injury, to exercise ordinary care to try to alleviate its effects. If plaintiff fails to do so, they cannot recover damages for that part of the injury that could have been corrected. Sometimes referred to as the doctrine of "avoidable consequences." R.2d § 918.

motive The reason for one's act. It is usually said that in tort law, motive is irrelevant; only intent counts. But motive may be relevant on the damages issue in certain torts.

N

necessity A privilege (defense to an intentional tort) based upon defendant's right to trespass upon, convert, damage, or destroy plaintiff's property—typically used in an emergency to prevent greater harm. Under the doctrine of private necessity, defendant must compensate plaintiff for the damage. Under public necessity, no compensation is due, unless otherwise provided by statute or the due process clause. R.2d §§ 196, 197, 262, 263.

negligence The failure to exercise ordinary care for another's safety; the failure to act as a reasonably prudent person would act under the same or similar circumstances. R.2d § 283. The creation of an unreasonable risk of harm. R.2d § 282; R.3d Liability for Physical & Emotional Harm § 3. The reasonably prudent person determines the reasonableness of the risk by use of a balancing test such as the **Hand formula**.

nominal damages An insignificant sum (e.g., $1.00) awarded to plaintiff who has established liability but cannot prove the existence or amount of their actual damages. R.2d § 907. Not available as to some torts—e.g., negligence.

nuisance, private A thing or activity which substantially and unreasonably interferes with plaintiff's use and enjoyment of their land. R.2d § 821D.

nuisance, public An unreasonable interference with a right common to the general public. R.2d § 821B.

O

offensive contact In battery, an unprivileged contact is actionable, even if not harmful, if it is offensive—i.e., offends a reasonable sense of personal dignity. R.2d § 19.

ordinary care Care exercised by a reasonable person in the same or similar circumstances to avoid or minimize risk of harm to others. Also called "ordinary prudence" or "reasonable care."

P

per quod In defamation law, the type of defamation which is not actionable without proof of special damages.

per se By itself; taken alone. The concept is a general one with various uses. For example, violation of a statute is sometimes deemed negligence per se. In defamation, statements that are defamatory per se are actionable without proof of special damages.

physical harm See **harm.**

premises liability The special tort liability rules applicable to owners and occupiers of land, characterized by a group of duty limitations that provide restrictions on the negligence liability of possessors of land with respect to conditions or activities on the premises. See R.2d §§ 328E–387; R.3d Liability for Physical & Emotional Harm ch. 9.

prima facie case Evidence sufficient to make a submissible case (i.e., sufficient to support a jury's finding) on each element of a cause of action or defense. R.2d § 328B.

privacy A tort action based on (1) appropriation of plaintiff's name or likeness, (2) intrusion on plaintiff's seclusion, (3) public disclosure of private facts about plaintiff, or (4) placing plaintiff in a false light in the public eye. R.2d § 652A.

privilege A type of defense to tort liability which negates the tort on the ground that defendant had a legal right to act as they did. R.2d § 10. See **immunity.** Typically, privileges are found in the intentional torts, defamation, and privacy.

products liability A general term encompassing theories of tort liability of manufacturers or other suppliers of defective products, including (1) negligence, (2) breach of express or implied warranty, and (3) strict products liability. Special liability rules are applicable to such actions. See R.3d Products Liability.

proximate cause A concept that includes (1) rules of legal causation that limit the scope of defendant's liability for certain unforeseeable, remote, or indirect consequences; (2) superseding causes, which limit the scope of defendant's liability due to some intervening event that is the immediate cause of plaintiff's harm. R.2d §§ 430–61.

public disclosure of private facts One of the subdivisions of the cause of action for invasion of privacy, in which defendant publicizes plaintiff's private life in a highly offensive manner. R.2d § 652D.

public figure In defamation, one who has achieved a degree of fame or notoriety, either generally or as to a particular public issue or controversy. Different and more restrictive liability rules apply to defamation actions by public figures and public officials as compared to defamation actions by private persons.

publication In defamation, an intentional (or perhaps negligent), unprivileged communication of the defamatory statement to a third person. R.2d § 577.

punitive damages Damages awarded in addition to plaintiff's compensatory damages to punish defendant and to deter defendant and others from committing similar torts. Also called "exemplary" or "vindictive" damages. Available, if at all, only when defendant's tort was intentional or reckless, or when authorized by statute. R.2d § 908.

R

reasonable care See **ordinary care.**

reasonable person (reasonably prudent person) The imaginary person who serves as the standard of care in a negligence action. See **ordinary care; negligence; Hand formula.**

reckless conduct Tortious conduct involving a conscious disregard of risk of physical harm to plaintiff which is (a) known to defendant, (b) unreasonable, and (c) substantially greater than that which is necessary to make their conduct negligent. R.2d § 500; R.3d Liability for Physical & Emotional Harm § 2. Also called "willful and wanton conduct."

release A document by which plaintiff gives up their cause of action against defendant. See R.2d § 885; R.3d Allocation of Liability § 24; see **covenant not to sue; loan receipt agreement.**

res ipsa loquitur Latin for "the thing speaks for itself." A codified rule of circumstantial evidence in which plaintiff can make out a prima facie case of defendant's negligence by proving that (1) the instrumentality causing plaintiff's injury was under defendant's control at the relevant time, and (2) the occurrence was such that it would not have happened in the absence of defendant's negligence. See R.2d § 328D; R.3d Liability for Physical & Emotional Harm § 17.

risk A set of circumstances giving rise to the possibility or probability of an injury. See **negligence; Hand formula.**

S

scienter The term is an element of intentional misrepresentation (also known as "fraud" or "deceit"); it refers to defendant's knowledge of the falsity of their statement. In that context, it also includes unqualified statements of fact where defendant does not know if the statement is true or not.

scope of liability See **proximate cause.**

self-defense A privilege (defense to an intentional tort) based upon defendant's right to use reasonable force to prevent an unprivileged tort against their person. Similar privileges may be used to defend one's property and other persons. R.2d §§ 63–87.

slander The publication of defamatory matter by spoken words, transitory gestures, or other form of communication not amounting to a libel. R.2d § 568(2).

special damages Damages which at common law were not presumed to flow from a tort and therefore had to pleaded specially, such as medical bills and lost wages. R.2d § 904. See **general damages**. Today, this category is often called "economic loss" or "pecuniary loss."

statute of limitations A statutory time period during which plaintiff must commence their lawsuit. Ordinarily the statute begins to run when the cause of action accrues. The expiration of the statutory period gives defendant an affirmative defense to bar plaintiff's action. R.2d § 899.

statute of repose A statutory time period governing a particular activity (e.g., medical malpractice) which commences and expires at a fixed time, independent of the statute of limitations, so as to bar causes of action X years after defendant's tortious conduct occurred.

strict liability Liability without fault, i.e., liability which is imposed upon defendant for injury caused by defendant's activity (or for which defendant is similarly responsible) irrespective of whether defendant has exercised reasonable care. Sometimes called "absolute liability." See R.3d Liability for Physical & Emotional Harm §§ 20–25.

subject to liability Refers to the situation where the actor has engaged in conduct which is (or may be found to be) tortious, without regard to whether the other conditions to a finding of liability are present. R.2d § 5.

superseding cause A superseding cause is an intervening cause that the law deems sufficient to override the cause for which defendant is responsible and exonerates defendant from liability for defendant's tortious conduct. R.2d § 440; R.3d Liability for Physical & Emotional Harm § 34. See **intervening cause**.

survival statute A statute that overturns the common law rule that tort (and other) causes of action not reduced to judgment did not survive the death of either the victim or the tortfeasor. A "survival action" is a tort action brought on behalf of a decedent's estate for decedent's damages accruing between the moment of the occurrence and the moment of their death.

T

tortious conduct Conduct, whether by act or omission, which subjects the actor to tort liability. R.2d § 6. See **subject to liability**.

transferred intent A rule of extended liability applicable to and among the five original trespass actions (assault, battery, false imprisonment, trespass to land, trespass to chattels). Defendant's intent to commit any of these supplies the intent necessary for any other. Defendant's intent also transfers from their intended victim to their actual (but unintended) victim. R.3d Liability for Physical & Emotional Harm § 33

trespass (1) A tort cause of action for defendant's intentional (a) entry upon plaintiff's land (trespass to land) or (b) interference with plaintiff's chattel (trespass to chattel). (2) One of the forms of action under the common law writ system, traditionally limited to actions for directly inflicted injuries. Forms of this writ included (a) trespass vi et armis, for bodily harm, and (b) trespass quare clausum fregit, for trespass to land.

trespasser A person who enters or remains on land without permission and without a privilege to be on the land. Under traditional common law rules, with minor exceptions, the possessor owes no duty to trespassers except to avoid injuring them by intentional or reckless conduct. R.2d §§ 333–338. See also **attractive nuisance** (trespassing children). Under R.3d Liability for Physical & Emotional Harm §§ 50–51, a possessor owes a duty of reasonable care to all persons on their premises except "flagrant" trespassers, who are owed only the same duty as was traditionally owed to common-law trespassers.

V

vicarious liability Tort liability imposed upon A for the tortious conduct of B, based upon the existence of some relationship between A and B. See **imputed negligence**; R.3d Liability for Physical & Emotional Harm §§ 57–65.

W

willful and wanton misconduct See **reckless conduct.**

worker's compensation A statutory system of compensation for an employee whose personal injury or death "arises out of" and occurs "in the course of" their employment. The employer is liable without fault. An employee whose employment is covered by such an act usually has no common law tort remedy against their employer for physical harm occurring on the job.

wrongful birth An action brought by the parents of an unwanted child born with a physical or mental disability based on defendant's negligence with respect to failed contraception methods or failure to properly diagnose or treat a parent before or during pregnancy. Contrast **wrongful life**.

wrongful death A tort action brought on behalf of a decedent's surviving next of kin for their damages resulting from a tortious injury that caused decedent's death. R.2d § 925.

wrongful life An action brought by a child born with a physical or mental disability based on defendant's negligence with respect to failed contraception methods or failure to properly diagnose or treat a parent before or during pregnancy. Contrast **wrongful birth**.

Z

zone of danger rule In actions for negligent infliction of emotional distress, most jurisdictions now allow recovery if plaintiff was in the zone of danger created by defendant's negligence and suffered fright as a result of the risk of harm to plaintiff. See R.2d § 436; R.3d Liability for Physical & Emotional Harm § 47.

Table of Cases

Index